Global Issues Series

General Editor: **Jim Whitman**

This exciting new series encompasses three principal themes: the interaction of human and natural systems; cooperation and conflict; and the enactment of values. The series as a whole places an emphasis on the examination of complex systems and causal relations in political decision-making; problems of knowledge; authority, control and accountability in issues of scale; and the reconciliation of conflicting values and competing claims. Throughout the series the concentration is on an integration of existing disciplines towards the clarification of political possibility as well as impending crises.

Titles include:

Roy Carr-Hill and John Lintott
CONSUMPTION, JOBS AND THE ENVIRONMENT
A Fourth Way?

John N. Clarke and Geoffrey R. Edwards (*editors*)
GLOBAL GOVERNANCE IN THE TWENTY-FIRST CENTURY

Malcolm Dando
PREVENTING BIOLOGICAL WARFARE
The Failure of American Leadership

Toni Erskine (*editor*)
CAN INSTITUTIONS HAVE RESPONSIBILITIES?
Collective Moral Agency and International Relations

Brendan Gleeson and Nicholas Low (*editors*)
GOVERNING FOR THE ENVIRONMENT
Global Problems, Ethics and Democracy

Roger Jeffery and Bhaskar Vira (*editors*)
CONFLICT AND COOPERATION IN PARTICIPATORY NATURAL RESOURCE MANAGEMENT

Ho-Won Jeong (*editor*)
GLOBAL ENVIRONMENTAL POLICIES
Institutions and Procedures
APPROACHES TO PEACEBUILDING

W. Andy Knight
A CHANGING UNITED NATIONS
Multilateral Evolution and the Quest for Global Governance

W. Andy Knight (*editor*)
ADAPTING THE UNITED NATIONS TO A POSTMODERN ERA
Lessons Learned

Kelley Lee
HEALTH IMPACTS OF GLOBALIZATION (*editor*)
Towards Global Governance
GLOBALIZATION AND HEALTH
An Introduction

Nicholas Low and Brendan Gleeson (*editors*)
MAKING URBAN TRANSPORT SUSTAINABLE

Graham S. Pearson
THE UNSCOM SAGA
Chemical and Biological Weapons Non-Proliferation

Andrew T. Price-Smith (*editor*)
REGENERATION OF WAR-TORN SOCIETIES

Bhaskar Vira and Roger Jeffery (*editors*)
ANALYTICAL ISSUES IN PARTICIPATORY NATURAL RESOURCE
MANAGEMENT

Simon M. Whitby
BIOLOGICAL WARFARE AGAINST CROPS

Global Issues Series
Series Standing Order ISBN 0–333–79483–4
(*outside North America only*)

You can receive future titles in this series as they are published by placing a standing order.
Please contact your bookseller or, in case of difficulty, write to us at the address below with
your name and address, the title of the series and the ISBN quoted above.

Customer Services Department, Macmillan Distribution Ltd, Houndmills, Basingstoke,
Hampshire RG21 6XS, England

Global Governance in the Twenty-first Century

Edited by

John N. Clarke
*Humanitarian Liaison Officer, United Nations, New York, USA
and Post-doctoral Fellow, Yale University*

and

Geoffrey R. Edwards
*Reader in European Studies, University of Cambridge,
UK*

First published 2004 by
PALGRAVE MACMILLAN
Houndmills, Basingstoke, Hampshire RG21 6XS and
175 Fifth Avenue, New York, N. Y. 10010
Companies and representatives throughout the world

PALGRAVE MACMILLAN is the global academic imprint of the Palgrave Macmillan division of St. Martin's Press, LLC and of Palgrave Macmillan Ltd. Macmillan® is a registered trademark in the United States, United Kingdom and other countries. Palgrave is a registered trademark in the European Union and other countries.

ISBN 0–333–80256–X

This book is printed on paper suitable for recycling and made from fully managed and sustained forest sources.

A catalogue record for this book is available from the British Library.

Library of Congress Cataloging-in-Publication Data
Global governance in the twenty-first century / edited by John N. Clarke and Geoffrey R. Edwards.
  p. cm.
Includes bibliographical references and index.
ISBN 0–333–80256–X (cloth)
  1. International organisation. 2. International relations.
I. Clarke, John N., 1972– II. Edwards, Geoffrey, 1945–

JZ5566.4.G56 2004
341.2–dc22   2004046497

10   9   8   7   6   5   4   3   2   1
13 12 11 10 09 08 07 06 05 04

Printed and bound in Great Britain by
Antony Rowe Ltd, Chippenham and Eastbourne

Contents

Notes on the Contributors

John Agnew is Professor of Geography at UCLA, Los Angeles CA, USA. He is the author or co-author of a number of books on international political economy and geopolitics including *Geopolitics: Re-Visioning World Politics*; *Mastering Space: Hegemony, Territory and International Political Economy* (with Stuart Corbridge) and *The Geography of the World Economy* (with Paul Knox and Linda McCarthy).

John N. Clarke is Humanitarian Liaison Officer in the Bureau for Crisis Prevention and Recovery (United Nations Development Programme, New York) and Post-Doctoral Fellow, Yale University. He has previously served as an Advisor in the Early Warning and Contingency Planning Unit of the Office for the Coordination of Humanitarian Affairs (OCHA) at United Nations Headquarters, New York. From 1999–2000, he served as a Policy Advisor to Canada's then Minister of Foreign Affairs, the Hon. Lloyd Axworthy. He completed a PhD in International Relations at Peterhouse, Cambridge University.

Michael W. Doyle is Harold Brown Professor of United States Foreign and Security Policy, Professor of Law, and Professor of International and Public Affairs at Columbia University prior to which he was Edwards S. Sanford Professor of Politics and International Affairs, Princeton University (1987–2003). He has served as Assistant Secretary-General and Special Advisor to United Nations Secretary-General Kofi Annan, (2001–2003) and is a Fellow of the American Academy of Arts and Sciences.

Geoffrey R. Edwards is Reader in European Studies and Jean Monnet 'Chair' in Political Science in the Centre of International Studies, University of Cambridge, and a Fellow of Pembroke College, Cambridge. He formerly worked for a number of think tanks, including the RIIA (Royal Institute of International Affairs), Chatham House, having begun his career after taking his doctorate at the London School of Economics, in the Foreign & Commonwealth Office. He has written extensively on the European Union, its institutions and its external policies.

Mervyn Frost is Chair of International Relations at the University of Kent at Canterbury. His major publications are: *Towards a Normative Theory of International Relations, Ethics in International Relation* and *Constituting Human Rights: Global Civil Society and the Society of Democratic States.*

Fen Osler Hampson is Director of the Norman Paterson School of International Affairs, Carleton University, Ottawa, Canada and Professor of International Affairs. Since 1994 he has been a senior consultant to the United States Institute of Peace, Washington, DC. He is co-editor (with David Malone) of a new volume entitled: *From Reaction to Conflict Prevention: Opportunities for the UN in the New Millennium* and author (with Jean Daudelin, John B. Hay, Todd Martin and Holly Reid), *Madness in the Multitude – Human Security and World Disorder.*

Ronnie D. Lipschutz is Professor of Politics and Associate Director of the Center for Global, International, and Regional Studies at the University of California, Santa Cruz. His most recent books are *After Authority – War, Peace and Global Politics in the 21st Century* and *Cold War Fantasies: Film, Fiction and Foreign Policy.* He is also the author of *Global Environmental Politics: Power, Perspectives, and Practice*, a critical text on global environmental politics.

Robert A. Pastor is Vice President of International Affairs, Professor, and Director of the Center for Democracy and Elections Management at American University in Washington, DC. From 1985–98, he was Fellow and Founding director of several programs at The Carter Center and is the author or editor of 15 books, including *A Century's Journey: How the Great Powers Shape the World*, and *Toward a North American Community: Lessons from the Old War for the New.*

David Schneiderman is Associate Professor of Law at the Faculty of Law, University of Toronto. He has edited several books, including *The Quebec Decision; Charting the Consequences: The Impact of the Charter of Rights on Canadian Law and Politics* (with Kate Sutherland) and *Social Justice and the Constitution: Perspectives on a Social Union for Canada* (with Joel Bakan). He is founding editor of the quarterly *Constitutional Forum Constitutionnel* and founding editor-in-chief of the journal *Review of Constitutional Studies.* He is completing a book manuscript entitled *Investing Authority: The Constitutional Order of Economic Globalization.*

Geoffrey R. D. Underhill is Chair of International Governance at the Universiteit van Amsterdam. His research has focused on the political economy of trade and industrial adjustment across a range of developed economies as well as patterns of international co-operation for the regulation and supervision of global financial markets, and the impact of regulatory change in financial markets on the global monetary system and the wider economic development process. His most recent publication is an edited collection (with Xiaoke Zhang) *International Financial Governance under Stress: Global Structures versus National Imperatives.*

Graham Ward is Professor of Theology, University of Manchester and for the last six years has served as the senior executive editor of the Oxford University Press journal *Literature and Theology.* His book, *Cities of God* treats the postmodern situation and the inadequacy of certain older forms of theological discourse on the character and significance of the city with respect to that situation. It then attempts to construct a new way of doing theology from within the postmodern context that challenges some of the key assumptions and trajectories of postmodernity, but without either standing counter-culturally against it or being irrelevant to it.

Acknowledgements

For substantive comments, criticisms and in some cases lengthy discussions, we are grateful to Tanni Mukhopadhyay, Sanjay Ruparelia and Chandra Sriram. Justin L. Robertson also graciously read and re-read the introduction and conclusion of the volume – both of which improved substantially as a result of his efforts. Aubrey Charette, Matthew R. Baker and Matthew A. Hoover undertook research and helped prepare the final manuscript for publication.

Palgrave's 'Global Issues Series' Editor, Jim Whitman generously provided advice throughout the conceptualisation and production of the volume, while Shirley Tan helped ensure a smooth process of publication. Thanks to Cambridge University Press, which granted permission to reprint the following article as Chapter 9 of this volume: Michael Doyle, 'A more perfect union? The Liberal Peace and the Challenge of Globalisation' *Review of International Studies* 26 (5): 81–94, 2000.

Finally thanks to Shawna J. Christianson, John Clarke Sr. and Vilma N. Clarke for their comments, criticisms and support throughout the process of completing this volume.

List of Abbreviations

APEC	Asia Pacific Economic Cooperation
ASEAN	Association of Southeast Asian Nations
ATM	automatic teller
BIT	bilateral investment treaty
EU	European Union
FDI	Foreign Direct Investment
GATT	General Agreement on Tariffs and Trade
GDP	gross domestic product
HRW	Human Rights Watch
ICBL	International Campaign to Ban Landmines
ICC	International Criminal Court
ICSID	International Centre for the Settlement of Investment Disputes
IMF	International Monetary Fund
IPE	International Political Economy
MMT	Methyl Cyclopentadienyl Manganese Tricarbonyl
MTBE	Methyl Tertiary Butyl Ether
MNE	multinational enterprise
NAFTA	The North American Free Trade Agreement
NATO	The North Atlantic Treaty Organisation
NGOs	Nongovernmental Organisations
OAU	Organisation of African Unity
OAS	Organisation of American States
OECD	Organisation for Economic Co-operation and Development
OPEC	Organisation of the Petroleum Exporting Countries
UN	United Nations
UNDP	United Nations Development Programme
UNMIK	United Nations Interim Administration Mission in Kosovo
UNTAET	United Nations Transitional Administration for East Timor
USFAA	United States Federal Aviation Administration
WTO	World Trade Organisation

Introduction

John N. Clarke[1] and Geoffrey R. Edwards

Introduction

State sovereignty, the fundamental ordering principle of international relations since the seventeenth century, is under challenge. In particular, since the end of the Second World War, states have voluntarily limited their sovereignty through international treaties that in some regional instances have become putative constitutional orders. They have subjected themselves to global and regional economic regimes, which allow markets greater influence than ever before. Technological factors, not least the internet, have allowed for an unprecedented flow of information and ideas that have frequently tested the traditional state role of 'gatekeeper'. Other forces such as nation, tribe or ethnic groupings, sub-national actors, and others, have challenged existing orders from within states. These challenges are having profound political consequences. Since the 1970s, different analysts have proclaimed the emergence of a post-capitalist society, a 'coming anarchy', a 'clash of civilisations' an 'end of history' or, simply though perhaps less dramatically, a post-Cold War order.[2] While each of these analyses have contributed to the debate, rarefied frameworks inevitably oversimplify the real world. It is, however, clear that a fundamental shift has occurred in recent years, particularly in the pace, areas and oscillation between globalisation and fragmentation.[3] The attempt to shape and regulate the international system has a long history, in recent years captured in the phrase 'global governance' – a concept prominent in much of the contemporary study and practice of international relations.

The twentieth century, to use Eric Hobsbawm's phrase, was an age of extremes.[4] From total war and the defeat of Nazi Germany, to the use of the atom bomb on Hiroshima and Nagasaki, to the creation and increasing influence of the United Nations and the widening scope of human rights treaties, the twentieth century alternated between periods of striking violence and comparative peace in the shadow of possible nuclear conflict. The question now, in a post-Cold War world marked by the intensification of globalising and fragmentary pressures, is how to meet future policy challenges, ensure stability and develop the mechanisms and institutions necessary to provide effective global governance. Perhaps most importantly, can the existing state system deal effectively with new pressures, or will it struggle to keep pace with events essentially outside of its control? Will the growing influence of non-state actors, transnational and other forces, require a reconfiguration of the role of the State and ultimately, will the State represent anything more than one of several administrative units?

In the second half of the twentieth century, the notion that 'the strong do what they can and the weak suffer what they must'[5] was recast in the structural realism of Kenneth Waltz. Structural realism suggested that the international system was to be explained chiefly by reference to the power relationships among states.[6] The superpower rivalry of the Cold War elevated a profound insight to the level of orthodox dogma, resulting in an all but exclusive focus on the balance of power in the system.[7] While state power remains a critical variable, to adequately explain and understand a changing system requires a broader approach both empirically and in addressing normative questions as to what the international community 'ought' to aim for. A growing number of scholars have recognised that the domestic and international are, as never before, mutually constitutive in shaping each other.[8] In this increasingly complex environment, where the system shapes states and states in turn shape the system, both the policy-making process and the actual policy prescriptions themselves are ever more complex, requiring a balanced approach to domestic and international demands.

Today, the world is arguably more complex and more inter-related than ever before.[9] The increasing scope of international law has changed attitudes towards the responsibility of states, governments and, indeed, individuals. States have increasingly chosen to restrict their sovereignty by voluntarily acceding to treaties and agreements, whether in the areas of human rights, trade or criminal law. Democracy, in turn, has taken hold in many areas where it was formerly denied, whether fostered in order to promote international stability or because it is viewed as a 'good' in and of itself. Such trends have not always been seen as mutually reinforcing, the German Constitutional Court, for example, pointing to an incipient democratic deficit within an integrated European Union (EU) in the aftermath of the Maastricht Treaty on EU in 1993.[10] The acceptability and legitimacy of governance beyond the state continues to cast a long shadow over the European construct[11] and more widely, not least in the United States under the Administration of George W. Bush.[12]

Even before the end of the Cold War, identity issues were coming to play an increasingly important role – a trend which has increased substantially since 1989. This means that 'nation-states, sub-national groups, and transnational special interests and communities are all vying for the support and loyalty of individuals ... .'[13] At the same time, an emerging global culture and an increasingly cosmopolitan conception of the world have arguably both challenged and sometimes reinforced local identities, even while paradoxically, allowing for an identification with the peoples of other countries. This has been made possible by the increasingly globalised media, the influence of which can be seen in several recent civil wars, where it is often argued that Western policy was influenced by media pressure.[14] Indeed, communications technology has accelerated the policy-making process and shrunk geographic space, bringing the distant 'other' into the living rooms and onto the policy agendas of states capable of intervention.

Although power, especially military power, and sovereign states remain central to the international system, they now operate in an environment shaped by varying admixtures of politics, state and non-state actors, markets and technology.[15] Global governance therefore hinges on three inter-related elements, the changing nature of the **actors** and their relationship to each other, the increasingly complex **context** within which they operate and the nature of the often interdependent **trends** that taken together represent globalisation.[16]

In terms of actors, the EU may not be typical in the extent of its regional institutionalisation but it is not necessarily *sui generis*. Non Governmental Organisations (hereafter NGOs), work hand in hand with states, sometimes even lobbying for the use of force and the deployment of weapons to resistance movements in third states.[17] NGOs frequently work independently of governments and states, but have also been prominent in both forging creative partnerships – for example, in the landmines campaign, where they worked with states and particularly the Canadian government, to achieve the Ottawa Convention.[18] They also worked to disrupt negotiations which are perceived as proceeding behind closed doors among political elites. The round of 'anti-globalisation' political protests, in Seattle, Genoa and elsewhere, have increasingly commanded governments' political attention though their political impact remains limited.[19] Paradoxically, the spread of communications technology which has accompanied 'globalisation' has helped empower these groups. Some states have responded by involving NGOs in the political process, a change which helps both political elites and NGOs understand the concerns of the other.[20] Similarly, the need for partnership between the private and public sectors is at the core of the UN Secretary-General's initiative to create a 'Global Compact' and a range of other initiatives designed to foster collaborative policy-making processes, including governments, states and corporations. Though still dominated by states, the international system increasingly reflects the decisions, aspirations and actions of non-state actors. In short, the world is increasingly complicated by a proliferating number of phenomena and actors entering into ever more complex, interdependent relationships.

The inter-relationship of states is also changing. Western states have, in recent years, increasingly become partners in more traditional security areas. For example, the enlargement of the North Atlantic Treaty Organisation (NATO), the nascent development not simply of a Common Foreign and Security Policy but also a European Security and Defence Policy within the EU,[21] and the increasing joint production of arms where international collaboration can be seen in Europe, are all examples.[22]

This political mêlée can perhaps be best described as dialectical in two senses. Firstly, in the sense of a Hegelian ideational dialectic capable of motivating individuals and groups into action[23] and secondly, in the Marxist sense of a material dialectic in which material forces play a primary role in shaping the world or in a more recent formulation, where 'material advantages both sustain and explain intellectual advantages.'[24] Today, despite contestation between rationalists and social constructivists at a metatheoretical level, ideas not only motivate individuals to action, but are also the basis for establishing more formal institutions and regimes.[25] Nowhere can this be seen more clearly than in the post 1945 explosion in human rights instruments, including the signing of the Rome statute to create an International Criminal Court (ICC) in 1998 (and which came into force in July 2002 despite its rejection by the United States).[26] The resulting structure then defines the parameters within which state and non-state agents evaluate possible courses of action. The international system, in short, is a product of the reflexive interplay of ideas and material circumstances. Ideas shape the world – and the world shapes ideas. Seemingly random events may therefore conceal an existing or emerging order: not necessarily a 'new world disorder', with all of its pejorative connotations, but simply order at a different level.

The nature of global governance

In the absence of a sovereign, how does governance come about? Does it follow rules that we can know, understand and shape? Indeed, is it possible for leaders to effect change in the nature of the international system, or are they increasingly powerless in the face of developments with which they struggle to keep pace? Governance is, of course, a contested concept, condemned by some as little more than a liberal vacuity but employed by others as governmental-type activity which functions effectively because of general acceptance even if it is not endowed with the formal authority of government.[27]

The international system may still be based very largely on the principle of state sovereignty, but it is a principle that has been fundamentally transformed by a variety of international treaties in a diverse array of areas including human rights and international trade. Assessments as to key trends and their impact do, however, differ. In some regions, particularly, but not exclusively in Europe, the extent of co-operation and integration has created supranational bodies based on what is increasingly accepted as a constitutional order. For some, such as Kenichi Ohmae, the result as far as the global economy is concerned is a borderless world.[28] To others, particularly in a European context, it is more a phenomenon of multi-level governance and the regulation of intra, trans and supranational relationships.[29]

Global governance is manifest in many areas: economic integration and trade, attempts to control environmental degradation, ethical and legal principles that operate in the international system, socio-cultural challenges, the evolution in communications technology, security threats and in particular, the growth of sometimes competing regimes that increasingly regulate state behaviour. Some, are sceptical of its existence at all,[30] while others such as Hedley Bull foresaw the possible emergence of a 'neo-medieval form of universal political order' of shared authority among different entities.[31] Others envisage a normative project of humane governance which seeks to create 'a set of social, political, economic and cultural arrangements that is committed to rapid progress... .'[32] Ultimately, neither globalisation nor global governance are amorphous phenomena, but rather, have many constituent elements and trends which transcend rigid categorisation.

In some ways, it is easier to define global governance in terms of what it is not. First, the anarchic properties, and relative weakness of enforcement mechanisms in the international system mean that it cannot refer to any form of government similar to that which exists within states. The system is, however, regulated through, for example, the set of norms epitomised in the growing body of treaty law and regional political arrangements such as the EU. Though the normative and political elements are neither universally adhered to nor universally binding, they nonetheless curb and restrict the behaviour of states. In short, the term *governance* refers to the processes of regulation that take place across the system. In turn, the term *global* indicates a move beyond the scope of solely international (or inter-state) relations, thereby incorporating the plurality of actors now capable of influencing the system. *Global governance* therefore refers to the set of normative, social, legal, institutional and other processes and norms, which shape, and in some cases even regulate and control the dialectical interplay of globalisation and fragmentation. This relationship too, is reflexive: globalising and fragmenting trends shape global governance and vice versa.

Why does the system not collapse under the pressure of states ruthlessly pursuing their own interests? A partial answer is found in the concept of 'governance without government' or 'regulatory mechanisms in a sphere of activity that functions effectively even though they are not endowed with formal authority.'[33] This system of rules 'works only if it is accepted by the majority (or, at least, by the most powerful of those it affects), whereas governments can function even in the face of widespread opposition to their policies.'[34] For Rosenau, it is along this frontier between domestic and international politics that the international system takes shape.[35] As the boundaries between international relations and a broader world politics become more porous, it is difficult to draw fixed frames of reference, particularly from within any one discipline or approach; an interdisciplinary approach is therefore a necessity. States increasingly occupy a middle ground in this 'tension' between globalisation/fragmentation and governance. They must increasingly adapt to changes in the international system and in recognising their inability to solve global problems (with local impacts) alone, must, of necessity, cede authority 'up' to multinational regimes and organisations. Global governance is therefore not only an empirical reality, but the changing global environment and the demands of new policy challenges make it a necessity.

The need for global governance

Contemporary policy challenges commonly require co-operative international approaches to transnational policy challenges that have a direct impact on individual states, requiring both the strengthening of global governance mechanisms and also its continuous extension to address new policy challenges. Globalisation, brings with it both new opportunities and many challenges. Pollution does not respect international boundaries while terrorism, drugs, the proliferation of small arms, and other transnational problems not only dominate the political agendas of individual states, but require international co-operation if they are to be dealt with effectively. For example, the successful coca eradication and alternative development programs in the Chapare region in Bolivia has created a need for new foreign markets for the cash crops that are produced.[36] Similarly, combating terrorist fundraising requires inter-agency and inter-governmental co-operation. These examples are representative of a growing category of policy challenges faced by the international community.

These shared policy problems and others demand multi-lateral approaches – states must learn to co-operate more often and more effectively, both with each other and with an increasingly diverse group of non-state actors. These new global policy challenges share several common features:

1. They are often transnational and have direct domestic impacts.
2. No one state can successfully control them.
3. Solutions therefore require a multilateral approach which accounts for, and where possible incorporates the interests and inputs of key stakeholders.
4. Decisions have a 'knock-on' effect and as such, it is impossible to isolate policy options and outcomes from each other.
5. Policy development must therefore be holistic to the maximum extent possible.
6. Multilateral institutions must adapt to accommodate these changing/emerging challenges. States must, therefore, work to strengthen and, where necessary, create the processes and institutions needed for effective global governance.

The individual processes which, in aggregate, represent globalisation can to a certain extent be regulated and shaped, albeit imperfectly. Successful regulation of these trends requires multilateral co-operation and international and domestic institutions capable of managing international governance in the absence of government.

Given the complexity of global governance, it is helpful to think in terms of increasingly interdependent 'levels of governance' outlined in rather simplistic fashion in Figure 1. Decisions at the international level have direct impacts on both states and their citizens; conversely individuals, acting through a variety of channels are increasingly able to affect the international system, whether mobilised in favour of policy by an NGO or other group or by appealing directly to multinational legal bodies instead of domestic legal systems. Often, the private sector, NGOs and others permeate the system, though for the purposes of Figure 1, they are incorporated in the box for 'civil society', though they infuse all levels of it.

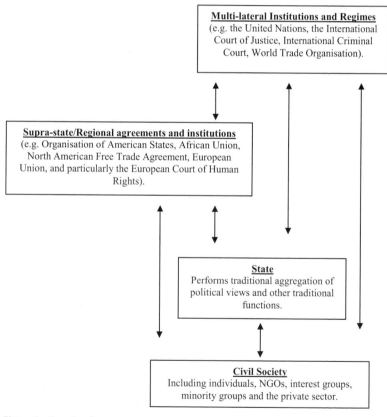

Figure 1 Levels of governance

Policy challenges cut across these different levels of jurisdiction as transnational trends have local effects and therefore, the governance challenge is for institutions at all levels – civil society, the State, regional and international organisations – to co-operate more regularly and effectively than before. States must balance the sovereignty they are required to sacrifice in order to achieve the benefits that will accrue from participating in any global governance arrangement.

This interdependent system draws the domestic and the international spheres closer together than ever before, providing individuals with a startling array of choices as to where their primary loyalty lies: is it 'above' the State in transnational and multinational institutions or multinational corporations; is it to the State; or is one's primary loyalty to 'below' the State, based in ethnicity, religion, race, class or some other grouping. These alternatives are, of course, not mutually exclusive, but rather, shape each other in complex ways. Identity, for example, does not work exclusively from the 'bottom up', but some argue in a 'top down' manner as well. More concretely, some have suggested that the structures of the EU altered the ideational and practical framework within which a Peace agreement in Northern Ireland became possible by providing a competing conception of identity to those which had previously fuelled unrest in Northern Ireland.[37] Others, given the disarray in which the EU Member States found themselves over intervention in Iraq in 2003, demur that the Union has had quite such an impact on states' self-perceptions. But, other multinational institutions may have a tangible though less immediate effect on the daily lives of citizens in states throughout the world. In short, Figure 1 illustrates the fact that *supra* and sub-state phenomena are inter-linked. These competing allegiances are particularly striking, given that citizens now possess greater education and previously unparalleled access to information and events occurring around the world.[38]

Governance, the State and power

Does governance result from the aggregation of micro-concerns and decisions, or is there a higher order of logic at work in these decisions? Certainly, attempts to order relations have been made, for example, in the regulation of markets, and the monitoring of human rights abuses among other activities. Recent trends such as the establishment of the World Trade Organization (WTO), the growth of treaty law, human rights declarations and other similar institutions and organisations seem to suggest increasing order, while among other phenomena, the breakdown in nuclear testing and the increase in international terrorism suggest at least some level of entropy.

The State retains a central role in the oscillation between globalisation and fragmentation. Does it remain the case, however, that it 'is best understood as the complex interplay between attempts to construct international regulatory mechanisms (often supported by the most powerful states) and the domestic needs of the states, and state representatives, which are to be constrained by them?'[39] States may remain primary brokers between international, transnational and domestic pressures in establishing new regulatory regimes but they are far from being the only actors. The State still plays a central role both in aggregating domestic political inputs from actors who are more and more influential, as the primary participant in multilateral processes and as the primary unit for aggregating the political views of its citizens. The sovereign functions of the State have therefore been transformed and not simply 'eroded' as has so often been argued.[40]

While power in world politics clearly still matters, new realities have changed the nature of power necessary to affect policy as well as the forums in which that power is exercised. Some continue to argue that power remains the key and the search for security, the inescapable purpose of international relations. And yet, even within the International Relations literature there has been some meeting of minds between neorealists and neoliberals on the importance of regimes. Basic assumptions might differ and there may be little consensus on the consequences of regimes, but there seems to be a more constructive exchange – though one that to others simply signifies the paucity of the 'neo-neo' debate, between those holding divergent views on the nature of the inter-State system and the likelihood of international co-operation in circumstances of anarchy or interdependence.[41] There are now so many regulatory regimes within the global system, especially within the global economy, that it is perhaps not surprising that political economists have been particularly preoccupied with questions of governance. The interplay between the global economy and the environment has become particularly complex, not least in raising fundamental questions about the continued capabilities and the prerogatives of the State in the system. The changing nature of the system and the growing importance of economic power, too, has led some to argue for the existence of 'soft power', which, may have a growing salience. It is a concept that can be illustrated by a number of cases, including that which led to the development of the Ottawa Convention.[42] This example illustrates both the continued centrality of states, but also, their increasing ability to work constructively with non-state actors. The nature and exercise of power has, in short, changed. States exercise power not only when they *influence* a decision, but perhaps more importantly when they shape the context, framework and rules/norms by and within which any decisions are arrived at.

Overview

The concepts of globalisation and global governance have often been appropriated by particular disciplines or approaches, only to be taken up – or back – by another, its reformulations sometimes ignored, sometimes implicitly absorbed. Rarely has there been an attempt to pursue an interdisciplinary approach which gathers together experts from different disciplines in an attempt to explore the variable elements of globalisation and global governance. This book therefore attempts to remedy this shortcoming by expanding the horizons of debate through an interdisciplinary approach. While each author takes into account the current debate in their particular discipline, the aim of this volume is to look ahead to the implications of recent trends for global governance.

Global governance is a 'macro' concept which encompasses the micro regimes that exist in specific issue areas. Many analysts have employed a 'top-down' analysis, explaining micro-changes through a grand narrative of macro trends. For all its advantages, however, this approach sometimes underestimates the relationship and impact of micro-changes on macro events. Today, the magnitude of information and the expertise required for the analysis of any issue or event underscores the value of interdisciplinary analysis. The need for specialised understandings of very specific issues means that it is difficult, if not impossible for any one analyst to master the wide range of issues required for a full and detailed understanding of the system. The most effective method for establishing broad international trends, then, is to address these changes by examining and synthesising the analyses of experts from different disciplines. This rationale underpins the structure of this book, which has a number of basic aims:

1. to move away from the traditional theoretical debates – whether the neo-neo debates of the 1980s and 1990s or the social constructivist 'turn' of the last decade and to use both theoretical and empirical analyses to gain a fuller understanding of the processes of global governance.

2. to avoid the myopia of addressing change through the lens of only one discipline and to develop a better balance between disciplines and approaches.

To ensure clarity in the debate, authors were first asked to describe the state of the debate about globalisation and to provide their perspective on the study of global governance; second, to assess the key elements both encouraging change and constraining the processes of globalisation and global governance and finally, to comment upon how global governance must evolve to address the changing pressures of globalisation. As previously stated, the relationship between globalisation and global governance is reflexive – that is globalisation shapes global governance and global governance shapes globalisation.

The first three chapters examine several normative and legal elements of global governance. In his essay, 'Christianity and Globalism', Graham Ward explores the logic of Judeo-Christian values as the basis for secular ethics which, in turn, constitute the fundamental basis for the establishment of states economic interaction. Throughout, he emphasises the centrality of technology in the dissemination of intellectual systems – in this case, Christianity. In this transformation from Christianity to ethical normativity, a moral legacy can be seen in a variety of contemporary debates, including the 'agency' of markets, issues of scarcity and distributional justice. For Ward Christianity's central position in the process of economic and cultural globalism, makes it uniquely positioned to provide a critique of globalism's practices.

Recognising the varied definitions of global governance, Mervyn Frost argues that the structures of global governance can be conceived of as a response to globalisation. As he points out, differing schools of thought have varied in their interpretations of how governance is delivered. The critical question he asks is how, if at all, do ethical issues arise for those actors participating in globalisation and in shaping global governance. For Frost, ethical issues are both empirically and normatively significant. Ethical matters are central to our understanding of the existing structures of global governance and in addressing the directions in which these structures could develop in the future.

The focus then shifts to the impact of international economic law on states. David Schneiderman examines the ways in which the regime of rules regulating foreign direct investment bind state actors. The first portion of his chapter examines the nature of this transnational regime and its constitution like feature, while the second section illustrates the impact of the regime through a case study of Bolivia. His case study suggests that international legal regimes are binding states in a new and increasingly intrusive manner.

The volume then shifts to focus on several policy-making processes and contexts. The geographer, John Agnew, examines the changing nature of space in relation to globalisation and global governance. He suggests that in geographical perspective there is an overwhelming imbalance in contemporary social science between the emphasis on the territories of states as the primary form of spatial organisation of politics and the increasingly geographically varied world that existing territorial government is ill-suited to manage and represent. The chapter identifies some of the ways in which contemporary human geography is attempting to understand the 'changing nature of space' in relation to the difficulties of global governance.

In his chapter entitled 'Global Governance and Political Economy: Public, Private and Political Authority in the 21st Century', Geoffrey Underhill aims to clarify our thinking about governance and the domain of the global political economy, and how we might make sense of the state-market relationship in the absence of global political authority. The chapter argues that to understand global governance processes in relation to the domain of political economy, we must move beyond concepts which either implicitly or explicitly conceptualise the state-market relationship in terms of separation and antagonism. The chapter outlines the emergence of the discipline of international political economy and its shared assumptions in the late twentieth century, its core questions and research agenda, and its remaining lacunae. It then elaborates the state-market condominium concept and how it might resolve some of the conceptual dilemmas concerning political economy and global governance. Finally, the model is applied and some of its practical and policy implications are examined.

For Robert Pastor, states and more specifically, Great Powers retain a central role in the development of global governance. However, the goals and means by which they pursue them are, today, fundamentally different from those which they pursued in the twentieth century, a reflection of the changing world in which they operate. He argues that though they still shape the world, they do so in much more subtle and indirect ways than was previously the case. Interestingly, Pastor notes that the seven major powers of the twenty-first century are the same as those of the twentieth century, though clearly the United States remains the most powerful of this group. As he points out: 'the enduring power of the United States derives as much from the institutions it established as from its wealth or weapons.'

Finally, the third section of the volume investigates several specific policy challenges, including human security, the environment and democratisation. Fen Osler Hampson argues that recent years have been characterised by a normative change in international relations, as embodied in the growing body of human rights conventions, in several recent single issue campaigns, such as the land mines campaign, the creation of an ICC and the growing desire to protect civilians in armed conflict, as embodied, for example, in Security Council Resolution 1296.[43] Each of these, are underpinned by a desire to promote human rights and provide 'human security' and as such, he explores three central themes: First, what does human security mean; second, what is the relationship between human security and globalisation and finally, what are the implications of human security for global governance.

Ronnie Lipschutz argues that societies are organised primarily in response to material conditions and secondarily by their social conditions. In particular, he examines the geological, biological and physical impacts arising from human activity over the past couple of centuries. Second he discusses the effects of the reorganisation of production on the environment over the last 50 years as a result of globalisation. Third, the impact of cultural globalisation on the environment is examined and finally, he examines the changes in the context of global governance and the ways in which people and institutions respond to these changes by regulating the practices that contribute to those changes.

Michael Doyle investigates the relationship between global governance and global democratisation. He begins with the broad ethical question of how the world could and should be organised at a political level. After outlining the principles which of 'the leading organisational political framework today', he then outlines its limitations exposed by increasing levels of globalisation. Finally he outlines possible responses to the challenges of globalisation, outlining the need for more democratically derived global norms.

Taken together, these chapters suggest that global governance is a dynamic process with normative, technical and institutional dimensions that combine in different ways to shape the international system. Our hope in assembling this interdisciplinary, multi-level collection of papers is to open a number of new areas for further analysis, and in particular, to begin a process of cross-fertilisation between different disciplines examining issues related to global governance. In doing so, we hope to have contributed to the development of a wider interdisciplinary lens through which the processes of global governance must increasingly be viewed.

Notes

1. Comments and opinions expressed in this chapter are those of the authors and not the United Nations.
2. See respectively: P. Drucker, *Post-capitalist Society* (New York: Harper-Business, 1994); R. Kaplan, 'The Coming Anarchy', *The Atlantic Monthly*, Volume 273, No. 2 (February 1994) 44–76; S. P. Huntington, 'The Clash of Civilizations?', *Foreign Affairs*, Volume 72, No. 3 (Summer 1993) 22–49 and 'If not Civilizations, What', *Foreign Affairs*, Volume 72, No. 5 (November/ December 1993) 186–194; For a lengthier treatment of this argument see Huntington's book on the same subject, *The Clash of Civilisations and the Remaking of World Order* (New York: Simon and Schuster, 1996); F. Fukuyama, *The End of History and the Last Man* (London: Hamish Hamilton, 1992); see also the articles on which this book was based: F. Fukuyama, 'The End of History?', *The National Interest*, No. 16 (Summer 1989) 3–18; and also, 'A Reply to My Critics', *The National Interest*, No. 18 (Winter 1989) 21–28.
3. This phrase is borrowed from Ian Clark's book, *Globalisation and Fragmentation* (Oxford: Oxford University Press, 1997), p. 201.
4. E. Hobsbawm, *The Age of Extremes* (London: Penguin Group, 1994).
5. Thucydides (trans. R. Crawley), *The Peloponnesian Wars* (London: Everyman Library J. M. Dent and Sons, 1948), p. 300. The diplomat was offering an explanation to the Melians as to why they should capitulate to Athenian demands.
6. For a recent critique of Waltz's approach, see I. Clark, 'Beyond the Great Divide: globalisation and the theory of international relations', *Review of International Studies*, 24 (1998) 479–498.
7. K. N. Waltz, 'Globalization and American Power', *The National Interest*, Vol. 59 (Spring 2000) 46–56.
8. This is part of an increasing number of social theories of international relations. See in particular A. Wendt, *Social Theory of International Politics* (Cambridge: Cambridge University Press, 1999). For alternative expositions of this argument, see: I. Clark, *Globalisation and International Relations Theory* (Oxford: OUP, 1999); J. Rosenau, *Along the Domestic-Foreign Frontier: Exploring Governance in a Turbulent World* (Cambridge: CUP, 1997); E-O. Czempiel and J. Rosenau (eds), *Governance without Government: Order and Change in World Politics* (Cambridge: CUP, 1992).
9. See R. O. Keohane and J. S. Nye, *Power and Interdependence* (Glenview, Illinois: Scott, Foresman and Co., 1989) and their more recent re-examination of this question in the article R. O. Keohane and J. S. Nye, 'Globalisation: What's New? What's Not? (And So What?)', *Foreign Policy*, No. 118 (Spring 2000) 104–119. See also: P. B. Evans, H. K. Jacobson and R. D. Putnam, *Double-Edged Diplomacy: International Bargaining and Domestic Politics* (Berkeley, California: University of California Press, 1993).
10. See, for example, J. H. H. Weiler, *The Constitution of Europe* (Cambridge: CUP, 1999); T. Banchoff and M. P. Smith (eds), *Legitimacy and the European*

Union (London: Routledge, 1999); D. Beetham and C. Lord, *Legitimacy and the European Union* (London: Addison Wesley Longman, 1998).

11. The EU faces a further Intergovernmental Conference to meet the demands of enlargement to include ten states of Central and Eastern Europe together with Cyprus and Malta with negotiations on a constitutional treaty drawn up not by governmental officials, but by a Convention made up largely of national and European parliamentarians.

12. Seen for example in the rejection of the International Criminal Court.

13. S. Brown, *New Forces, Old Forces, and the Future of World Politics* (Glenview, IL: Scott Foresman, 1988), p. 245. As cited in Rosenau and Czempiel, *Governance without Government* (Cambridge: CUP, 1995), p. 285. Brown described this phenomenon as 'polyarchy'.

14. See for example, L. Minear, C. Scott and T. G. Weiss, *The News Media Civil War and Humanitarian Action* (London: Lynne Rienner, 1996). See also W. P. Strobel, *Late Breaking Foreign Policy* (Washington: United States Institute of Peace, 1997).

15. Now more than ever, the State sits at the juncture between the domestic and the international. See for example, J. N. Rosenau, *Along the Domestic-Foreign Frontier: Exploring Governance in a Turbulent World* (Cambridge: CUP, 1997).

16. Globalisation might be thought of in the terms used by David Held *et al.* as 'a process (or set of processes) which embodies a transformation in the spatial organisation of social relations and transactions – assessed in terms of their extensity, intensity, velocity and impact – generating transcontinental or interregional flows and networks of activity, interaction, and the exercise of power'. D. Held *et al.*, *Global Transformations* (Cambridge: Polity Press, 1999), p. 16. For an overview of the globalisation literature, see: I. Clark, *Globalisation and International Relations Theory* (Oxford: OUP, 1999). See especially, Chapter 2, 'Globalisation', pp. 33–51.

17. For example in the case of Afghanistan: 'MSF even pressured the U.S. Congress to vote for the delivery of Stinger missiles to the resistance fighters.' R. Brauman, 'The Médecins sans Frontiéres Experience' in K. M. Cahill (ed.), *A Framework for Survival* (New York: Basic Books/Council on Foreign Relations, 1993), p. 217.

18. L. Axworthy and S. Taylor, 'A Ban for All Seasons', *International Journal*, 53, 2 (1998) 189–204.

19. The failure of the World Trade Organisation negotiations in Seattle, for example, had less to do with the protests outside, than the failure of governments to reach an agreement inside.

20. Former US Under-Secretary of State for Political Affairs, Thomas Pickering, has suggested that: 'Many years ago the State Department developed an arm of its bureaucracy to deal with the Congress; maybe now we need an NGO arm.' Interview, 'Mr. Diplomat', *Foreign Policy* (July/August 2001) 38.

21. This despite the very public divisions among the European Member States over the intervention in Iraq in 2003 and with the prospect of enlargement towards Central and Eastern Europe where governments are still very much influenced by considerations of territorial defence. The EU's continuing integration has frequently been cited as a test case of rival theories of international relations. See D. A. Baldwin (ed.), *Neorealism and Neoliberalism: the*

Contemporary Debate (New York: Columbia University Press, 1993), especially the chapters by R. O. Keohane and J. M. Grieco.

22. One author writes that through the 1980s, 'it became crystal clear that no single European nation could continue to develop and produce a full range of advanced technology weapons. To reach minimum efficient economies of scale, international collaboration in production became commonplace...' W. K. Keller, *Arm in Arm* (USA: Basic Books, 1995), p. 159. In addition, leading U.S. defence firms now concentrate on design, leaving the actual production of weapons to other, foreign firms. R. Vernon, *In the Hurricane's Eye: The Troubled Prospects of Multinational Enterprises* (Cambridge, Massachusetts: Harvard University Press, 1998), pp. 48–49.

23. For a more recent manifestation of this idea, see: F. Fukuyama, 'The End of History?', *The National Interest*, No. 16 (Summer 1989) 3–18. See also: F. Fukuyama, 'A Reply to My Critics', *The National Interest*, No. 18 (Winter 1989) 21–28.

24. F. Braudel, *A History of Civilisations* (London: Penguin, 1995), p. 74.

25. See, for example, P. J. Katzenstein, R. O. Keohane and S. D. Krasner (eds), *Exploration and Contestation in the Study of World Politics* (Cambridge, Massachusetts: MIT Press, 1999); J. Goldstein and R. O. Keohane (eds), *Ideas and Foreign Policy* (Ithaca: Cornell University Press, 1993); or J. G. Ruggie, *Constructing the World Polity* (New York: Routledge, 1998).

26. For an interesting argument as to why states accede to human rights instruments, see: A. Moravcsik, 'The Origins of Human Rights Regimes: Democratic Delegation in Postwar Europe', *International Organisation*, 54, 2 (Spring 2000) 217–252.

27. See, for example, J. N. Rosenau and E-O. Czempiel (eds), *Governance without government: order and change in world politics* (Cambridge: CUP, 1992), pp. 1–8. The Commission on Global Governance states: 'Governance is the sum of the many ways individuals and institutions, public and private, manage their common affairs. It is a continuing process through which conflicting or diverse interests may be accommodated and co-operative action may be taken. It includes formal institutions and regimes empowered to enforce compliance, as well as informal arrangements that people and institutions either have agreed to or perceive to be in their interest.' Commission on Global Governance, *Our Global Neighbourhood: the Report of the Commission on Global Governance* (New York: Oxford University Press, 1995), p. 2. For Nye and Donahue, governance is 'the processes and institutions both formal and informal, that guide and restrain the collective activities of a group.' J. S. Nye and J. D. Donahue (eds), *Governance in a Globalizing World* (Washington: Brookings Institutions Press, 2000), p. 12.

28. K. Ohmae, *The Borderless World* (London: Collins, 1990).

29. B. Jones and M. Keating (eds), *The EU and the Regions* (Oxford: Clarendon Press, 1995).

30. Strange suggested that instead, we have a 'ramshackle assembly of conflicting sources of authority.' S. Strange, *The Retreat of the State* (Cambridge: CUP, 1997), p. 199.

31. H. Bull, *The Anarchical Society* (London: Macmillan, 1977), p. 25.

32. R. Falk, *On Humane Governance: Toward a New Global Politics* (Cambridge: Polity Press, 1995), p. 2. For a discussion of the evolution of the traditional

theoretical debates, including the neo-neo debates, please see I. B. Neumann and O. Waever (eds), *The Future of International Relations* (London: Routledge, 1997).

33. Rosenau and Czempiel (eds), *Governance without Government: Order and Change in World Politics*, p. 5.
34. Rosenau and Czempiel (eds), *Governance without Government: Order and Change in World Politics*, p. 4.
35. See: J. Rosenau, *Along the Domestic-Foreign Frontier, Exploring Governance in a Turbulent World* (Cambridge: CUP, 1997).
36. For further information on the drugs eradication program, see UNDCP's newsletter, in this instance: 'The Bolivian Success Story', available at: http://www.undcp.org/newsletter_2000-06-26_1_page005.html. For information on the UNDCP agro-forestry project, see: http://www.undcp.org/bolivia/bolivia_project_agroforestry.html. Similar challenges are likely in post-Taliban Afghanistan. See, Transnational Institute, *Merging Wars: Afghanistan, Drugs and Terrorism*, TNI Briefing Series No. 2001/2 , Drugs and Conflict Debate Papers No. 3, (December 2001). Available at: http://www.tni.org/reports/drugs/debate3.pdf.
37. J. Stevenson, 'Peace in Northern Ireland: Why Now?', *Foreign Policy*, No. 112 (Fall 1998) 41–54.
38. Rosenau, 'Citizenship in a Changing...' in Rosenau and Czempiel (eds), *Governance without Government* (1995), Ch. 10.
39. I. Clark, *Globalisation and Fragmentation*, p. 201.
40. See also the conclusions of D. Held *et al.*, *Global Transformations* (Cambridge: Polity Press, 1999).
41. What came to be labelled the 'neo-neo' debate arose from the critique of Kenneth Waltz's 'structural realism' – otherwise known as neo-realism – by Robert Keohane and others who were often termed liberal institutionalists or neoliberals. See R. O. Keohane (ed.), *Neo-Realism and its Critics* (New York: Columbia University Press, 1986); D. A. Baldwin (ed.), *Neo-realism and Neoliberalism: The Contemporary Debate* (New York: Columbia University Press, 1993); and P. J. Katzenstein, *The Culture of National Security: Norms and Identity in World Politics* (New York: Columbia University Press, 1996).
42. Two individuals directly involved in the process, comment: 'The Ottawa Process was a fast-track process led by Canada to develop and conclude in the space of fourteen months a global ban on anti-personnel mines (APMs). There were only 424 days between Canadian Foreign Minister Axworthy's dramatic 5 October 1996 call for an international convention banning antipersonnel mines and the 3 December 1997 signature of that instrument. Only fifteen months later, the Ottawa Convention entered into force, becoming the most rapidly implemented multilateral convention of its kind in history. What enabled the process to achieve its objectives so quickly? The answer lies in the dynamic mix of public conscience, new actors, new partnerships, new negotiating methods, and a new approach to building security – making the safety of people a central focus of international attention and action.' M. Gwozdecky and J. Sinclair, 'Case Study: Landmines and Human Security' in R. McRae and D. Hubert (eds), *Human Security and the New Diplomacy: Protecting People, Promoting Peace* (Kingston: McGill-Queen's

University Press, 2001), p. 29. See also: L. Axworthy and S. Taylor, 'A Ban for All Seasons', *International Journal*, 53, 2 (1998) 189–204.
43. Security Council Resolution 1296, 19 April 2000, S/RES/1296 (2000). Security Council Resolutions are available online at: http://www.un.org/documents/scres.htm.

References

Baldwin, D. A. (ed.), *Neorealism and Neoliberalism: The Contemporary Debate* (New York: Columbia University Press, 1993).
Banchoff, T. and M. P. Smith (eds), *Legitimacy and the European Union* (London: Routledge, 1999).
Braudel, F. *A History of Civilisations* (London: Penguin, 1995).
Brown, S. *New Forces, Old Forces, and the Future of World Politics* (Glenview, IL: Scott Foresman, 1988).
Bull, H. *The Anarchical Society* (London: Macmillan, 1977).
Clark, I. *Globalisation and Fragmentation* (Oxford: Oxford University Press, 1997).
—— *Globalisation and International Relations Theory* (Oxford: Oxford University Press, 1999).
Commission on Global Governance, *Our Global Neighbourhood: the Report of the Commission on Global Governance* (New York: Oxford University Press, 1995).
Czempiel, E-O. and J. Rosenau (eds), *Governance without Government: Order and Change in World Politics* (Cambridge: Cambridge University Press, 1992).
Falk, R. *On Humane Governance: Toward a New Global Politics* (Cambridge: Polity Press, 1995).
Fukuyama, F. *The End of History and the Last Man* (London: Hamish Hamilton, 1992).
Held, D. *et al.*, *Global Transformations* (Cambridge: Polity Press, 1999).
Hobsbawm, E. *The Age of Extremes* (London: Penguin Group, 1994).
Huntington, S. P. *The Clash of Civilisations and the Remaking of World Order* (New York: Simon and Schuster, 1996).
Katzenstein, P. J., R. O. Keohane and S. D. Krasner (eds), *Exploration and Contestation in the Study of World Politics* (Cambridge, Massachusetts: MIT Press, 1999).
Keohane, R. O. (ed.), *Neo-Realism and its Critics* (New York: Columbia University Press, 1986).
—— and J. S. Nye, *Power and Interdependence* (Glenview, Illinois: Scott, Foresman and Co., 1989).
—— and J. S. Nye, 'Globalisation: What's New? What's Not? (And So What?)', *Foreign Policy*, No. 118 (Spring 2000) 104–119.
McRae, R. and D. Hubert (eds), *Human Security and the New Diplomacy: Protecting People, Promoting Peace* (Kingston: McGill-Queen's University Press, 2001).
Moravcsik, A. 'The Origins of Human Rights Regimes: Democratic Delegation in Postwar Europe', *International Organisation*, 54, 2 (Spring 2000) 217–252.
Nye, J. S. and J. D. Donahue (eds), *Governance in a Globalizing World* (Washington: Brookings Institution Press, 2000).
Ohmae, K. *The Borderless World* (London: Collins, 1990).

Rosenau, J. N. and E-O. Czempiel (eds), *Governance without government: order and change in world politics* (Cambridge: Cambridge University Press, 1992).

Simai, M. *The Future of Global Governance: Managing Risk and Change in the International System* (Washington, DC: USIP, 1994).

Wendt, A. *Social Theory of International Politics* (Cambridge: Cambridge University Press, 1999).

Part I

Normative and Legal Perspectives

1
Christianity and Globalism

Graham Ward

Let me begin by stating that this is a theological study. By that what I mean is that this essay is not a survey of Christian responses to the cultural phenomenon labelled 'globalism'. While recognising that the practices of faith communities, Christian or otherwise, constitute sociological subsystems that play out various anti- and prosystemic functions with respect to globalism, this essay is not a survey of such responses from a sociological perspective. Beyer (1994) and Castells (1997) have examined the effects of globalism in terms of the New Christian Right in America, suggesting Christian fundamentalism as one key response to global economics and polity.[1] Beyer also gives an account of liberation theology's response to global culture and explores other 'fundamentalisms' (Jewish and Islamic). What interests me more, working from within the tradition-based thinking of Christianity, working as a Christian theologian, is the relays and exchanges, correspondences and differences between what is going on in contemporary globalism and the universalist logics of the Christian faith. In a sense what I am asking in this essay is a question about different forms of participation in a cosmic system (or, at least, a system with a cosmic vision). This is how I am interpreting globalisation, as the production of an international matrix of exchange – electronic, economic and political – that embraces and effects all peoples and all commodities. Globalism is the ideology that issues from such globalisation; an ideology freighted with utopian dreams for the universal system. It is these universalist dreams that globalism shares with Christianity. Let me offer two illustrations, each demonstrating a certain parallelism which this essay is concerned to explicate more fully.

Tales of Two Economies I

At the end of Matthew's Gospel the risen Jesus makes the following proclamation: 'All authority in heaven and on earth has been given to me. Therefore go and make disciples of all nations, baptising them in the name of the Father and of the Son and of the Holy Spirit'.[2] It is one of the foundational texts for Christian missiology. The ending of the two other synoptic Gospels – Mark and Luke – contain similar, but not as elaborate statements (though scholars recognise that the last nine verses of Mark's Gospel are not found in earlier and more reliable manuscripts). What Matthew's statement makes plain is a major theological transposition affected by the coming of the Christ: the transposition from the ethnic specificities of Judaism to the universalism of the Christ through the liturgical practice of baptism in the name of the trinitarian God. In Matthew's day there were more Jewish people living in the Diaspora than Palestine itself, but nevertheless the picture of the cosmic Christ possessing all authority in heaven and on earth and the strong, imperative to go into all nations implies (as the Apostle Paul himself inferred) that the community of the faithful would be made up not just of those drawn directly from the Jewish genetic pool. Now, the Gentiles were included in the new covenant, the new dispensation of God's grace. The Jewish Messiah pointed Judaism towards its global horizons. The writer of Luke's Gospel dramatises this theological cataclysm and the *dissemination* it effected: 'repentance and forgiveness of sins will be preached in his name to all nations, beginning at Jerusalem'.[3] Jerusalem, which had gathered together Jewish people from all over the known world for the Passover (when the Christ was crucified), would be the epicentre for the new cosmic reorganisation. The writer of Luke's Gospel, in his Acts of the Apostles, narrates how the falling of Christ's Spirit upon the disciples – the anointing which authorised and empowered them out to preach the Gospel – came during the Feast of Tabernacles when 'Parthians, Medes and Elamites; residents of Mesopotamia, Judea and Cappadocia, Potnus and Asia, Phrygia and Pamphylia, Egypt and the parts of Libya near Cyrene; visitors from Rome (both Jews and converts to Judaism); Cretans and Arabs'[4] were all assembled in Jerusalem once more. Peter preached and 'three thousand were added to their number that day'.[5] The global mission in the name of a universalist salvation had begun.

As Wallerstein observes with respect to the establishment of the early world-trading-system in the late fifteenth and early sixteenth centuries, the rate of globalisation is governed by overcoming territorial particularity by technological means.[6] We will continually be revisiting the centrality of technology. The early church flourished in its own way but became increasingly fragmented under persecution. The degree to which Jerusalem remained its first mother church, followed later by Rome, is still uncertain. But there is little doubt that a major upturn in the expansion of Christianity came with the conversion of Constantine in 312 and the Edict of Milan issued in 313. The Edict, while granting religious freedom throughout the Roman Empire, was the first step in constituting Christianity as the religion of the Empire. It explicitly sought and associated divine favour with the Imperial common weal. Constantine himself wrote that 'My design then was, first, to bring diverse judgements formed by all nations respecting the Deity to a condition, as it were, of settled uniformity; and, second, to restore the health tone to the system of the world'.[7] His sentiments express here a new political theology being composed at the time by Eusebius of Caeserea in his *Ecclesiastical History*: that Constantine was a second Augustus and, like Augustus (who had created the conditions of world wide unity and peace for the coming of the Christ), the vehicle for the Providence of the Christian God. Eusebius forged a rhetorical link between the Christian church and the Roman Empire. He wove together, in his propagandising texts, two distinct economies – the theological and the political. Christian cosmology was now inseparable from its teaching on the salvation of the world and imperial ambitions. Constantine himself turned rhetoric into activity, by a) forging the systemic links which lay the foundations for Christendom and b) fighting Donatists and Arians, and so establishing the ideological parameters of the *corpus Christianorum*. The Imperial administrative and military networks provided Christianity with the technological means for expansion; the means of developing a logic at the heart of its monotheistic *credo*: 'After the victory of the Milian Bridge [312CE], Christianity was never again to lack an imperial patron'.[8]

With the fragmentation and decline of the Empire itself, Christianity was enabled, even required, to expand and establish (with Latin as the *lingua universalis*) the integrating infrastructures upon which Western European civilisation emerged from the Dark Ages into the glories of the various forms of Renaissance from the twelfth century onwards.

Tale of Two Economies II

When Christendom itself dissolved – as fledgling nation states grew stronger and schism racked the body of the Church – Christianity underwent a second major transformation which adapted it for the new forms of expansionism and imperialism that arose in the late fifteenth and early sixteenth centuries with respect to another economy: capitalism. Following the forced entrenchment of the Holy Roman Empire by the advancing Ottoman Turks – where territories of an earlier expansion by the crusades were brought under Arab dominion – Christianity's imperial ambitions were now channelled by both a new colonialism and a universalisation of its own identity in terms of 'religion'. That is, the several voyages first of exploration and then of colonisation (which were undertaken as much on theological as economic and political grounds) paralleled the rise of the generic category of 'religion'. 'Religion' is what Constantine dreamed of when he sought to 'bring diverse judgements formed by all nations respecting the Deity to a condition, as it were, of settled uniformity'. Still, in fifteenth century England, to speak of 'religions' was to speak about the various monastic orders. This followed a line of usage found in the thirteenth century with Aquinas: 'religion' was a practice or discipline of Christian believing. But by the late fifteenth century the word was coming to be employed to describe the universal grammar binding various forms of Christian practice by two leading Renaissance thinkers: Nicholas of Cusa and Marsilo Ficino. Gradually, as new lands and new peoples were being encountered, and the journals, letters and narratives of those encounters were laying the basis for the new science of ethnography, so 'religion' became a rhetorical tool for a new universalism. The need, following the warring factions of the Reformation, for a political and theological *detente*, gave 'religion' not just academic respectability but social and political force. Nevertheless, and this remains significant, 'religion's' universalism is issued in and through Christianity.

'Religion' became a category that eventually led to the study of religions forged by Christian thinkers. The word concentrated and bound together several cultural trends: an anthropological attention to the general condition of being human, a move towards viewing ethics as the common denominator for this human condition, and the development of the concept Nature. Through thinkers like the mid-seventeenth century Cambridge Platonists, Christianity became conceived in terms of a natural and therefore universal theology. So Peter Sterry could advise in 1675 in his *Discourse of the Freedom of the Will*:

> Look upon every person through this *two-fold Glass, the Blood, and Beauties of Christ. Christ hath died for all. The natural being of every*

person hath his *Rest* in the *Grave of Christ*, and is watered with his blood. *Christ lives in all.* His *Resurrection* is the *life* of the *whole Creation.* He is the *Wisdom*, the *Power*, the *Righteousness* of God in every work of *Nature* as well as of *Grace*. He is the *Root* out of which every *natural*, as well as *spiritual* Plant springs, which brings forth himself through every natural existence, and brings forth himself out of it, as the *flower*, the *brightest of the Glory of God.*[9]

Hence people everywhere came under the influence of Christ. The Christ-as-Logos Christologies of Alexandrian theology of the third century enters a new stage of development, coupled now with territorial expansion.

The technological possibilities of preaching the Gospel to all nations goes hand in hand in the development of a theology which makes conversion to Christ a matter of recognising the truth of the human situation and the created order. A new egalitarianism, a brotherhood of mankind, is announced in which God's justice is rendered evident in that the particularities of redemption in Christ is now globally available. Natural knowledge revealed broad *a priori* moral truths, truths 'concurrent with the sense of heathens and strangers, who do agree with us in all instances of morality' Benjamin Whichcote wrote. Thomas More concurred: 'And therefore we cannot say that every Idolatrous Heathen must perish eternally.'

There were various strands of Calvinism, Platonism and Arminianism that gave subtle shades to these emerging theologies of religion – on the whole Roman Catholics and Muslims were still beyond redemption. Furthermore, the development of the generic and globalising category of religion owed much to the political need for peace in many Western European countries following years of civil warfare conducted on the basis of conflicting Christian creeds. Natural theology, like the appeal to discover a universal language, an *Ursprach*, by the seventeenth century Bishop Wilkins, was a response to a set of contingent political circumstances. Nevertheless, what is evident is also a further unfolding of a logic at the heart of the Christian understanding of the redemption of the world.

Wallerstein in his monumental history of world trade and the development of a capitalist world-system views economics as the dynamic for modernisation and globalisation. He gives hardly any place to theological dynamics which, in fact, governed (even regulated) economic policy throughout the Mediaeval and Renaissance periods.[10] This is an oversight, for territorial expansion and the development of the world-system was, throughout the fifteenth and sixteenth centuries, a matter for intense theological discussion particularly by the Jesuits who were profoundly involved with missionary ventures. When we return the developments of Western Christianity into the picture we can perhaps understand globalism as issuing from a certain cultural, rather than simply, economic programme. Wallerstein raises an interesting question as to why Europe rather than China entered the theatre of world-trading, exploration and colonisation in the late fifteenth century. Agreeing with and quoting the work of William Willetts, he answers that 'this has something to do with the *Weltanschauung* of the Chinese. They lacked, it is argued, a sort of colonising mission because, in their arrogance, they were already the whole of the world'.[11] I would argue that the colonising mission felt by several European nations – but first and foremost Catholic Spain and Portugal – is endemic to the Spirit of Christianity which forever saw the other nations beyond itself who lacked the gospel. So that Christian missiology plays a part alongside embryonic mercantile covetousness and territorial ambitions in the development of the capitalist world-system. After all, these expeditions and explorations were profoundly speculative; they ran risks that required vision and drew on imaginations fired by more than simple acquisitiveness or opportunity costing. As sociologists and historians like Max Weber and R. H. Tawney point out, Western capitalism (and the material exchanges prior to formal monetary systems) is implicated in mindsets, habits, desires and household disciplines established by Christian practices of the faith. As several economists have also pointed out (Hayek and Hirsch, most prominently) the practise and the theory of economics issues from and proceeds upon a moral legacy of truth and promise, fiduciary and redemptive acts, construals of freedom. It was a legacy first forged in Christendom and later rendered universal when 'religion' devolved theological particularity into ethical normativity. A residual Christianity, in terms of its reduction to moral values, still makes possible the persuasive power of economic policy and informs the arguments engendered by any such policy. Economists like Hayek, Novak and Schumpeter are steeped in liberal ethics. The debates over whether markets have agency, or have outcomes that can be foreseen (and prevented), and the debates concerning scarcity, opportunity costs and distributional justice are all still dependent upon a moral legacy bequeathed by Christianity.[12] A more recent theological voice has drawn attention to the cultural currents that bring together Christian theology and economics in terms I will develop below. In a chapter entitled 'Christianity and the Capitalism of the Spirit', Mark C. Taylor writes:

> The Spirit of God represented in the eucharistic wafer is the currency of exchange, which establishes the identity of differences within the godhead and mediates the opposition between divinity and humanity throughout the history of salvation... Hegel's speculative philosophy actually anticipates the aestheticisation of money, which characterizes post-industrial capitalism. In the late twentieth century, something approximating the Hegelian Absolute appears in global networks of exchange where money is virtually immaterial. When read through Hegel's logical analysis of Spirit, it becomes clear that money is God in more than a trivial sense.[13]

Global flows: economies of signs

Where Latin American liberation theologians lament the disparity between the monetary and the divine economies, Taylor conflates the two. From the perspective of a Christian world-view economics cannot function as an autonomous force (that would concede the autonomy of the secular, which, in turn, would constitute a Gnostic heresy). On the other hand, the tradition-based reasoning of the Christian theologians has to read economic discourse, in so far as it is possible, in terms of its own tradition. For following Adam Smith the discipline of economics has accepted the secular world-view, and developed as a discourse concerned only with the logic of immanent activities. What Christianity seeks, then, with respect to its examination of economics, is threefold: first, the nature of the desire economics represents and the relationship of that desire to the wider cultural and political ethos; second, an understanding of its own history and teachings with respect to the development and effects of that desire; third, a critical judgement concerning that secular desire and its effects. The judgement is necessarily provisional, since all our judgements await the final unveiling of the truth in the eschaton. The judgement is the end of the examination, but the beginning of a process of amelioration. For the call would be to a new disciplining of that desire with respect to being faithful to the call of Christ. So, for example, for Christianity, global capitalism can only be a figure, a substitute, a surrogate for a misplaced desire for God. Capitalism cannot be a ground-base; a natural and empirically verifiable dynamic upon which a master-narrative of explanation for cultural change is founded. Substitution and surrogacy are fundamental to the exchange mechanisms described in economics, so it is what capitalism is figuring, what it is a substitute for, that Christian-based thinking investigates. Taylor, for example, like Hayek, figures capitalism as freedom; freedom defined as unfettered desire. The glamour of globalism, the seductive appeal of its internationalism, figures, I suggest, infinite desire – which, at times, is expressed the other way round: a desire for the infinite.

The second part of the examination of globalism, by Christianity, requires returning to one of the fundamental orientating principles of Christian thinking and faithful practice. That is, the importance of being caught between a memory of an inaugural past, a certain present realisation and the anticipation for what is not yet. Christian believers participate in a time-displacement, when viewed theologically. This is a participation in a eschatological mind-set rooted in a divine economy, as I shall explain. It is the nature of this participation which we need to explore further, because it is here that we can best understand contemporary conceptions of globalism as revisiting (kindly put), parodying (more harshly put), or peddling secular kitsch versions (most critically put), of Christian conceptions. In other words, continuing from the last section of the universalism of the category 'religion' – globalism can be understood as one more dissemination of a Christian *logos*. Hence, the importance of showing why the generic term 'religion' issues from Christianity and still effects a Christianisation in the 'study of religions' even when those other 'religions' are far from being practices of the Christian faith. Put in this way, it could be that Christianity, then, is able to facilitate the most far-reaching critique of globalism (understood both economically and culturally) by exposing its transcendental dreams and concealed aspirations. Globalism is an historical production with a profound Christian pedigree.

The divine economy in the Christian faith is conceived in terms of the nature of the triune God and the operation of the divine in the creation, maintenance and salvation world. The triune God differs entirely from a theistic conception of a frozen point outside and beyond the creaturely realm. Rather God as source of all is incarnate in the Son, Jesus Christ, by and through whom all things were created, and the Spirit forever negotiates the reciprocity of the love between the Father and the Son. Technically, these are termed the trinitarian processions – each being called forth by, and returning to, the other. The early Greek Fathers described the dynamic of the trinity as perichoretic – a circling dance. Creation issues from the heart of a profound giveness or emptying of one towards the other in the trinity, as such 'processions' become 'missions' or 'sendings out'. All that is, is then, held to be so because of the operation of the divine economy within creation. Things have no value of themselves. In fact, things do not exist in and of themselves. All things only have value with respect to the fact that they are gifted, given from and maintained by the presence of God. It is as if all things, when held up to the light of God, reveal the watermark of Christ within them. Things cannot be things, that is reified (in the Latin understanding of the term) or commodified (in the Marxist understanding of the term), unless prised from their participation in the divine economy and, hence, alienated from the ongoing work of the Creator.

The founding exchange mechanisms of economics can only come about, therefore, through such a reification and alienation in which the Good is calculated and calibrated accord to 'goods'. This reification and alienation is much more profound than the capitalist's tearing asunder of the labourer from the products of his or her labour. Marx only uncovered the secular logic of 'things' (ironically couching that logic in a rich religious vocabulary). What makes possible his thinking is a certain opacification of the natural which took place much earlier than industrialism. In this opacification of the natural the sacramental world is mechanised and understood in terms of positivist facts and calculable empiricisms. Put briefly, the difference between the sacramental and the secular world-views is a question concerning the nature of the economy in which one is participating: the divine economy or secular economics. And just as Nietzsche was correct in recognising that when man killed God man then replaced Him, so secular economics reinscribes divine economy within their immanent logics. As such the discourses on contemporary globalism, which speak in heady, ecstatic terms of the collapse of geographical space into flows, the erasure of national and continental boundaries, the electronic currents of capital investment, and the cultural polysemy of drinking Chilean wines, in (now affordable) Italian clothes, from glasses made in China, whilst sitting on Shaker-design chairs produced from Swedish pine and illuminated by candles refined from North Sea Oil – make manifest, materially, the attributes of God: omnipotence, omniscience and omnipresence. The vast homogenising, synthesising and integrating dynamics of globalism will perfect the realisation of Spinoza's monism: God is the one substance of which all else are modifications. Put more briefly, globalism becomes not a policy or the ideology of an international operation, but an environment, an atmosphere. It implicitly possesses and promotes a cosmology. It is, then, the final step in the cultural logic of secularism and, from a Christian perspective, idolatry: the world becomes God.

We find the same logic at work in the development and deepening of cyberspace. Without virtual reality globalism would not be possible. Digitalisation and simulacra, optic fibres and electronic mailing are the driving force behind the realisation of the global project. But, again, beneath the hype of cybernauts immersed in metaphors of light, who cruise weightlessly and anonymously along highways of information that dissolve time, location, cultural context, and identity lies Christian accounts of heaven, life beyond bodily imperfections and limitations, angels and angelic knowledge. Manuel Castells has called real virtuality the final turn of secularism.[14] Globalisation and the expansion of the virtually real are not creating parallel universes – the one imaginary and the other real – they are collapsing the distinction between the imaginary and the real. Hence Castells' 'real virtuality'. The world is now recreated again, only more perfectly, as simulacra. This is the realisation of the ancient dreams for the effect of *poeisis* – in Aristotle and Renaissance Platonists like Sir Philip Sidney: redeeming the world through creating it again, imaginatively. But inseparable from virtual perfections is an explicit costing: digitalisation is the final step in commodification. For what was once reified through the opacification of nature is now reproduced virtually in megabytes.

Globalism, then, as the construction of a world-system (of not just economic but cultural interdependence) is one more attempt by human beings to become divine. It is the continuation of the Prometheanism that goes back to the famous *Oration of the Dignity of Man* by Pico della Mirandola at the end of the fifteenth century. And desire behind the drive is infinite freedom. Freedom, defined as the infinite possibilities for choice; frictionless freedom proscribed by no bounds, either physical, cultural or historical. This is what sells it and persuades us of its value. But what is this infinite freedom? It must be that which lies beyond choice; since the expression of choice, since choosing itself, implies limitation. To be able to have all things simultaneously, to possess the fullness of the presence as present – only this can fulfil the dreams of infinite choice. Hence one of the key elements of global culture, as Paul Virilo recognised, is speed; perfection must be *instantaneous*. Perhaps then the desire behind the drive is actually one for oblivion, or what Michel de Certeau calls 'white ecstasy'. Certeau describes this ultimate *jouissance* in a language culled for various world-faiths. In a conversation constructed between two men meeting on a mountain Simeon the monk speaks of the 'final bedazzlement' in which there is 'an absorption of objects and subjects in the act of seeing. No violence, only the unfolding presence. Neither fold nor hole. Nothing hidden and thus nothing visible. A light without limits, without difference; neuter, in a sense, and continuous'.[15] This 'silent ecstasy', this transcendence which comes from recognising all particularities are infinitely reproducible and reducible to a digital coding and a pixel imaging; this transcendence which comes from seizing the presence of things in the present and understanding all locations as infinitely transferable; this transcendence which comes from the radical realisation of immanence – has other names: Heidegger's and Derrida's 'end of metaphysics'; Fukuyama's 'end of history', Jaron Lanier's (the man who coined the term 'virtual reality') 'experience of infinity';[16] Deleuze and Guattari's 'deterritorialisation; Lyotard's body without organs'; Baudrillard's 'hyperreality'; Arthur Danto's 'the end of art'; consumer satisfaction; the apotheosis of free-trade; and the call for the complete transparency of institutional operations by government agencies. The espousal of radical immanence is, ultimately, the abandonment of oneself to an impersonal and capricious logic locked into a desire for death; death as oblivion. It is a contemporary turn in Nietzsche's *amor fati*. Globalism is the ultimate synthesis of the Freudian psyche: the libidinal economy *becomes* the death drive. Enforced universal democratisation is the Freudian *stasis*, the zero degree dressed in the neoliberal language of freedom. Thomas Friedman, who has written one of the most popular books on globalisation observes that he is frequently asked 'Is God in cyberspace?' His answer is indicative of one of the axioms of globalisation: 'There is no place in today's world where you encounter the freedom to choose that God gave man than in cyberspace'.[17] Freedom of choice is harnessed to movement here albeit in an illusory manner – illusory because to choose is not to move, and where one moves to (whether, in fact, we can even talk of 'movement' at all) when space has collapsed under a rule of homogenisation is a real, not simply a semantic, question. Like creatures released from the pressures of gravity we float, we surf, we ride, we free-fall, we transcend a variety of human finitudes to become divine. To be global is to be divine: the most globalised figures (Hollywood film stars, sports and royal personalities, entrepreneurs like Soros, Gates and Branson) are the stars in the new global galaxies which inspire cult following, the saints of a new form of veneration.

This is the very point at which Christianity can intervene, recalling globalism to one of its origins and pointing up the differences between parent and progeny. It can partly do this because, in the move from universalism (a hallmark of Christianity as 'religion' and a hallmark of modernity in so many different guises) to globalism, Christianity as a practice is shaking off its affiliations with 'religiousness' and reclaiming its tradition-based modes of reasoning. The implosion of liberalism under the pressure of pluralism has brought about the demise of theological liberalism, Christian liberalism in this case. And the response to this implosion is not necessarily fundamentalism or biblicalism, but new appeals to reclaiming insights of the past, new analyses of orthodoxies, of subject-forming practices in confessional communities. The new right thinking among evangelical Christians, as the move towards conservative Roman Catholicism, *are* responses to the globalisation; purely counter-cultural responses (which nevertheless often employ the latest in telecommunication skills). Because in Christian teaching, the Kingdom of God has not yet fully come – because, as I said earlier, Christian thinking is caught between memory, participation and anticipation – there is always an element that remains counter-cultural. But it is an element, not a policy; an element which gives rise to Christianity as *Kulturkritik*. This will be important for what I wish to argue. In the wake of the collapse of socialism (whose demise, like liberalism's, came because its operational logic demanded a dialectic between itself and that which was other – capitalism, in this case – a dialectic globalism imploded); in the wake of the collapse of socialism, theological reasoning is, perhaps, the only form of effective *Kulturkritik* with respect to globalism. But effective cultural criticism cannot be done from a faith which polices its narratives and practices in order to create barricading walls against secular incursions. The rejection of theological liberalism in favour of tradition-based reasoning (which requires an academic investigation into the nature of the tradition and the nature of its orthodoxies) need not be simply counter-cultural. There is much within the tradition-based reasoning of Christianity which recognises that it is part of the world; not at war with it. Christianity cannot separate itself from the world. Its thinking epitomises the tensions that Roland Robertson has termed 'glocalisation' – the way in which the local and particular is commodified for the global and endlessly reproducible. Only, in Christian thinking the local community is given a density of significance in relation to the global Body of Christ. From this new standing upon the grammar of the faith Christianity can point to similarities and differences, to degrees of participation. For freedom is not defined in terms of an individual's range of choices in Christian thinking. Freedom is not customised and viewed in terms of the accumulation of commodities. My freedom to choose affects other peoples' livelihoods, and maybe their freedom to choose. The Italian clothes I can now afford are made affordable by cheap, possibly sweatshop labour somewhere in the world, hidden so that I might not see it – might not see the consequences of my choosing. Globalism renders all communities and societies virtual realities. Marx prophecies this when he examined how commodity exchange causes the social to disappear. Globalism turns individualism into a cosmic principle – hence the spirituality of globalism is inextricable from New Age self-enlightenment technologies and self-designed lifestyles. Christian thinking counters such a rampant atomism with its own accounts of participation. This does not mean, it cannot mean, that those who practice the Christian faith are not also involved in secular global operations. Part of globalism's cosmology is that none of us are exempt – even the poor and destitute become necessary aspects of global economics. But it does mean that Christian living and believing can act as an explicit critique of globalism's aspirations to transcend finitudes. It can do this in several ways, but what is important about these ways is that they are made possible on theological grounds, not moral grounds. This is crucial.

There has been a tradition since 1848, when facing some of the human consequences of industrialism, of a Christian social ethics. These ethics have pointed to the human suffering and degradation which results from various economic enterprises and government policies and prophetically called for justice and a fair distribution of the world's finite goods. As such Christian social ethics formed alliances with a number of liberal humanitarian pressure-groups, dissolving its distinctive theological narratives and accepting a moral common ground. As we saw above the universalisation of Christianity through forming the generic 'religion' functions to augment economic globalisation. As Stephen Long has put it: 'non-confessional theology has the same shape as the formal but contentless character of global capitalism. It recognises "value", but not substantive and particular goods'.[18] This not simply Christianity colluding, this is Christianity co-opted – erasing difference in terms of fellow feeling and co-operation. In the wake of economic globalism and the pluralist culture, that liberal humanism, departicularised Christianity and moral common ground becomes difficult to maintain. It has lost its credibility. Concurrently, those concerns with scarcity, the calculation of opportunity costs and redistributive justice are rendered infinitely more complex. For scarcity is about objects and their optimal use. It is associated with a concrete world of finite things. For its operations to be defined it is assumed that both the exchange of these finite things and the world in which they can be exchanged can be represented transparently and objectively. That world no longer is there; that mode of representational innocence is no longer there – if, even with modernity, it was ever there. The goods that globalism trades in are more informational and electronic than material – new forms of poverty, wealth and scarcity emerge. When scarcity is named we now have to ask where and what is being named, who is doing the naming, how the calculations for optimal use are being made, what is being left out of the equation (since something always is) and for what reason. 'Scarcities' are produced, they are disseminated, they are ideologically freighted. They are not seen and identified from no where. They are shifting and shifted throughout global transactions. They are not fixed, nor can they be controlled or even comprehensively surveyed. So how can they be redistributed? The old concept of scarcity belongs to an identity politics that cannot operate in a virtual world. In fact, the virtual world – manned (quite literally) in the majority by cosmopolitan elites – knows no such concept. Its operational logic is excess and abundance: everything is available, at any time.[19] And therefore, as a corollary, what does distributional justice mean in a network society where distribution belongs to flows of space, flows of information, flows of signs, flows of persuasion? What does social mean as distinct from cultural?[20] What does public policy mean when the public is no longer an identifiable and discrete group of people, and when the power for policy-making, when power as such, is radically decentralised?

The critique of participation in a global culture can no longer be adequately based on liberal ethics, which was quickly assumed into Christian social ethics. The critique on the basis of the tradition-based reasoning is, then, a theological critique which calls into question several issues:

1.   The language of transcendence with respect to globalism, which lends globalism a certain spiritual colouring, involves a category mistake. For one cannot be the author of one's own transcendence. There can be certain alterations made to personal consciousness – by alcohol and other chemical substances, by lack of sleep, by the low flickering of florescent lighting in supermarkets and shopping malls, by sexual engagement, by speeding or participating in a fast, roller-coaster ride, by perspectives which warp spatial dimensions vertiginously. But these experiences do not transcend the human condition; they alter

the consciousness of what still remains, quite adamantly, a human subject. Globalism may infinitely extend the range of experiences open to an individual; it may constitute that individual by various means into being a consumer of polyglot experiences – but its processes and operations are all immanent, all planetary, all concerned with a circle of exchange that is never broken and means, economically, that there is no free lunch. Transcendence, as grace, is gifted, the recognition of giftedness; it cannot be an object of one's choosing. It cannot be commodified at all. This leads us into the next critique of global participation, Christian thinking facilitates.

2. Transcendence is not, for Christianity, the obliteration of the finite. Its central appreciation of incarnation, of the divine made human, offers a positive account of finitude. The finite is completed, redeemed, by the divine – finds its proper direction, employment and significance. The finite is not a world of things to be overcome. Finitude, rather, marks the limitations of human longing and ambition; it sets them in its place and, in so doing, safeguards the human from the hubristic. The act of hubris is always an act of self-deification. The Christian logos first critiques, then, not the effects or the operations of globalisation, but its Promethean drive. It is a drive related to free-market capitalism, but rather than offer some outdated socialist critique of capitalism *as such*, what Christian thinking provides is a certain theological pathology of the drive itself. Novak has consistently reiterated what Pico della Mirandola first proclaimed: 'you decide who you are; you create yourself'.[21] Globalism runs with that gospel. But it is not a Christian gospel. By critiquing the very drive of globalism Christianity can then examine its effects and operations. This leads directly to its function as culture-critique.

3. Christianity, because it shares so much in common with globalism, can point to the absence which haunts and produces global culture. For Christianity understands the virtual nature of the real. Its eschatological account of creation and its history establishes a tension between what was, what is and what will be. Nothing can be accepted merely at face-value. Nothing can literally be what it seems to be. There is always a seeming, an appearing as. Put another way, the Christian world-view is fundamentally a semiotic one. Faith is a participation in the reading, production and unfolding of signs – signs of the Kingdom, signs of the incarnation, signs of the Gospel, signs which receive their true significance only in the coming again of Christ. The global world-view is also, to follow Baudrillard (and exemplified most clearly in the digitalisation of information), constituted in and through

an economy of signs. But these signs are divorced from signifieds. They flow endlessly into other signs, referring only to other signs: signs which are simulacra, signs which like fashions, come and go in a hyperventilating ephemerality. Their *telos* is the open desert, the infinite stretches of barely imaginable freedom which drives desire forever onwards and bears eternally the pain of having to choose one thing over and against another. The economy of globalism's signs expresses and perpetuates the empty nihilism of globalism's transcendental dream of liberation.

Conclusion

And hence to judgement: while Christian living in Christ seeks to extend *communitas*; globalism customises; while the Christian worldview 'in Christ' proclaims a participation which renders us members of another, interdependent; globalism interconnects for its own functional purposes atomised Video display units; while the practice of the Christian credo seeks that each may become all that God intend they become; globalism effects a policy of divide-and-rule (only no one is ruling now and the tyranny lies with the field of global operations themselves); while the ethics of the Good life 'in Christ' preaches one thing; globalism's ethos of death, lack, and anaemic infinite extols another. All this said, let me emphasise again, there is no pure Christian theology and no innocent Christian practice. Christianity and globalism intersect at many and at complex points. But that does not effect the critical role Christianity can and will perform with respect to economic and cultural globalism. And as I also have already said, it has this role because of its own historical involvement in the development of globalism; and because so many of globalism's aspirations are parodies of Christian hopes. Its figuration of unappeased, and unappeasable yearning, will, I suggest, lead to a return to the theological. The theological will, again, guarantee (will be the only means of guaranteeing) communal belonging in the collapse of the social into the cultural. For it will guarantee the identification of differences within the increasing indifferentiation which is produced by the immanent cultural logics of globalism. That could be worrying. Theologians need to be on guard. The next global wars may not be inter-national, or inter-racial, they could be inter-faith.

Notes

1. P. Beyer, *Religion and Globalisation* (London: Sage, 1994); and M. Castells, *The Power of Identity* (Oxford: Blackwell, 1997).

2. Matthew 28: 18–19.
3. Luke 24: 47.
4. Acts of the Apostles 2: 9–11.
5. Acts of the Apostles 2: 41.
6. I. Wallerstein, *The Modern World-System: Capitalist Agriculture and the Origins of the European World-Economy in the Sixteenth Century* (London: Academic Press, 1974), pp. 15–16.
7. W. H. C. Frend, *The Rise of Christianity* (London: Darton, Longman and Todd, 1984), p. 487.
8. W. H. C. Frend 482–3.
9. Peter Sterry could advise in P. Sterry, *Discourse of the Freedom of the Will* (London: 1675), p. 127. See also my *True Religion* (Oxford: Blackwell, 2000) for a more developed understanding of this new phase in the development of 'religion'.
10. Keynes had taken some account of Mediaeval economics in J. M. Keynes, *General Theory of Employment, Interest and Money* (San Diego, CA: Harcourt Brace, 1964). He drew his distinction between savings and investment on the basis of his investigations. But his interpretation of the usury has been challenged by B. Dempsey, *Interest and Usury* (Washington, DC: American Council on Public Affairs, 1943) and, more recently, S. Long, *Divine Economy: Theology and the Market* (London: Routledge, 2000).
11. I. Wallerstein, *The Modern World-System: Capitalist Agriculture and the Origins of the European World-Economy in the Sixteenth Century* (London: Academic Press, 1974), p. 55.
12. The move away from the gold standard in the mid 1970s suggests a major shift in monetary economies from that moral legacy in which 'promissory notes' ought to be redeemed, in which there are certain deontological duties which underpin economic exchange mechanisms.
13. M. C. Taylor, *About Religion: Economies of Faith in Virtual Culture* (Chicago: Chicago University Press, 1999), pp. 154–8.
14. M. Castells, *The Rise of the Network Society* (Oxford: Blackwell, 1996).
15. M. de Certeau, 'White Ecstasy', translated by F. C. Bauerschmidt and C. Hanley, in G. Ward (ed.), *The Postmodern God* (Oxford: Blackwell, 1997), p. 157.
16. J. Lanier and F. Biocca, 'An Insider's View of the Future of Virtual Reality', *Journal of Communication*, XLII, 4 (1992) 156.
17. T. Friedman, *The Lexus and the Olive Tree: Understanding Globalisation* (USA: Anchor Books, 2000), p. 469.
18. S. Long, *Divine Economy: Theology and the Market* (London: Routledge, 2000), p. 55.
19. S. Cooper, 'Plenitude and Alienation: The Subject of Virtual Reality', in D. Holmes (ed.), *Virtual Politics: Identity and Community in Cyberspace* (London: Sage, 1997), pp. 93–106.
20. One of the central thinkers on globalism, Immanuel Wallerstein, has recently observed: 'Where can we find "societies" other than in the minds of the analysts, or of the orators? Social science would, in my view, make a great leap forward if it dispensed entirely with the term' (I. Wallerstein, *The Politics of the World Economy* (Cambridge: Cambridge University Press, 1984), p. 2. Like 'community' it trails a moral legacy that can mask its

absence. I suggest what Christians need to consider now is not a social ethics but a cultural ethics.
21. M. Novak, *A Theology for Radical Politics* (New York: Herder & Herder, 1969), p. 36.

References

Beyer, P. *Religion and Globalisation* (London: Sage, 1994).

Castells, M. *The Rise of the Network Society* (Oxford: Blackwell, 1996).

——, *The Power of Identity* (Oxford: Blackwell, 1997).

de Certeau, M. 'White Ecstasy', translated by F. C. Bauerschmidt and C. Hanley, in G. Ward (ed.), *The Postmodern God* (Oxford: Blackwell, 1997), pp. 155–58.

Cooper, S. 'Plenitude and Alienation: The Subject of Virtual Reality', in D. Holmes (ed.), *Virtual Politics: Identity and Community in Cyberspace* (London: Sage, 1997), pp. 93–106.

Dempsey, B. *Interest and Usury* (Washington, DC: American Council on Public Affairs, 1943).

Frend, W. H. C. *The Rise of Christianity* (London: Darton, Longman and Todd, 1984).

Keynes, J. M. *General Theory of Employment, Interest and Money* (San Diego, CA: Harcourt Brace, 1964).

Lanier, J. and F. Biocca, 'An Insider's View of the Future of Virtual Reality', *Journal of Communication*, XLII, 4 (1992) 150–72.

Long, D. S. *Divine Economy: Theology and the Market* (London: Routledge, 2000).

Novak, M. *A Theology for Radical Politics* (New York: Herder & Herder, 1969).

Taylor, M. C. *About Religion: Economies of Faith in Virtual Culture* (Chicago: Chicago University Press, 1999).

Wallerstein, I. *The Modern World-System: Capitalist Agriculture and the Origins of the European World-Economy in the Sixteenth Century* (London: Academic Press, 1974).

——, *The Politics of the World Economy* (Cambridge: Cambridge University Press, 1984).

2
Ethics and Global Governance: The Primacy of Constitutional Ethics

Mervyn Frost

Global governance is a vague phrase generally taken to refer to the means by which, as one author puts it, a 'nobody-in-charge world' is managed.[1] *Governance*, roughly speaking, is an activity that falls short of *government* (the latter presupposes the existence of a determinate authority with a clear cut jurisdiction, which the former does not) and is often understood as 'the guidance and harmonisation of certain activities' in the global arena.[2] Structures of global governance emerge as a response to globalisation. As globalisation gathers pace the need for new forms of guidance and harmonisation will grow and we can expect that new forms of global governance will be created.

Just how we ought to understand globalisation and the emergence of global governance is a matter for ongoing scholarly debate. Neorealists have one view of the processes involved, whereas neoliberal institutionalists have another. This chapter does not offer a contribution to the debate about how best to understand and explain the mechanisms of globalisation and the emergence of structures of governance. Instead, it seeks to answer the following question: 'How, if at all, do ethical issues arise for those of us who are participants in processes of globalisation and global governance?'

Although there is now amongst IR scholars widespread acknowledgement that in some broad way ethics matters, the main schools of thought in the discipline do not accord a central place to ethics. These include the realist (including the neorealist), liberal institutionalist, and Marxian structural schools of thought, which are at one in portraying the international domain as one in which a set of core actors are severely constrained in the amount of ethical content they can include in their decision-making processes. These schools differ with regard to what actors are to be taken as the crucial ones in international relations, and, with regard to what social mechanisms are to be understood as regulating the relationships between them. However, what is common to many main stream approaches to International Relations is that they understand the operative constraints to have the effect of severely limiting the salience of ethics for the key actors in world politics. Roughly speaking they stress that the power relations in world politics rule out, in large measure, the possibility of taking ethics seriously. Ironically much the same can be said of much of the writing in what has come to be known as 'critical theory' in international relations. It is ironical because although authors in these schools overtly stress the importance of ethics, yet many instances of critical, post structural and post modern theory are preoccupied with the ways in which power determines, not only the behaviour of actors, but the ideas which they hold, including their ideas about ethics.[3] The focus remains, as always, on power rather than ethics.

The ongoing debate about the extent to which governments are following (or are failing to follow) ethical foreign policies reveals precisely the dominant ways of thinking about the role of ethics in international relations. Such debates continue for example in Britain, the United States and South Africa, to mention but three of many. In these it is supposed that governments have the option of whether to consider ethical considerations or not. The public debate ranges around the question 'Should governments take ethical considerations into account when they are devising their foreign policies?' The background assumption behind such a question is that it is possible for governments not to do this.

I have argued over a number of years now that this way of understanding what might be called 'The ethics question in IR' is wrong.[4] A concern with ethics is not of marginal concern to individuals or collective actors in the day to day practice of international affairs. It is also not marginal to those engaged in the practice of studying this field of human activity. In what follows I shall attempt to defend these claims. A proper understanding of just where when and how ethical matters become pertinent in international relations is crucial for our understanding of the existing structures of global governance and for our thinking about the directions in which these might be developed in future.

Let me start then by distinguishing between several different ways in which we, as individuals or as corporate actors, engage with ethical matters. Understanding these distinctions is important for a clear comprehension of the links between ethics and global governance. I shall distinguish between what is involved in:

- Encountering states of affairs requiring explicit ethical decision
- Engaging with ethics in interpreting and explaining international conduct
- Coming to grips with the ethical dimension involved in all human conduct

In making these distinctions I am, of course, speaking from within a particular discourse which allows these distinctions to be made. The language which I am using is not an a-temporal language valid for all time, but is the product of a long history. No doubt there have been and are other discourses which do not create the possibility of making precisely the distinctions I am about to discuss.

Encountering ethical decisions about global governance

We often *confront* ethical questions in an explicit way. From time to time in our lives we find ourselves confronting choices with an international dimension which we clearly recognise as having an ethical component. By way of demonstration let me mention some choices of this nature which have confronted me in my lifetime: Ought I to accede to military service knowing that this might well take me into action in a war that I considered unjust? Should I conceal in my home a person seeking to evade the police where they were pursuing him for the 'political crime' of establishing a connection with an international liberation movement? Should I support or seek to undermine a sanctions campaign in a foreign state where the campaign was directed at advancing a liberation struggle, of which I approved, but where the liberation movement included in its project the use of terrorist methods of which I disapproved? Should I accept favours from a foreign government seeking to influence me to teach, write and speak in favour of its diplomatic recognition?

Increasingly we come to face just such explicit ethical decisions with regards to matters of global governance. We all face such ethical choices independently of whether or not we hold high office. British citizens have to take decisions about proposed Europe-wide forms of governance pertaining to the control of migrants and asylum seekers. These involve difficult issues concerning the rights of migrants to freedom of movement versus the rights of citizens to protect their own interests. Israeli citizens face questions with an explicit ethical content about appropriate structures of governance for Palestinians in the region. We are all called upon to take some stance about appropriate forms of intervention (short and long term) in such places as the Great Lakes region of Africa.

In each of these cases we are aware, from the outset, that whatever decision we make will be based on both ethical and political considerations. Sometimes the decisions are relatively easy to make, but at other times they are difficult. The difficult ones arise when we as individuals find that we hold a number of ethical commitments which seem to conflict. For example, it often happens that *liberty* seems to call for one course of conduct, whereas *equality* seems to call for an opposed response, respect for national autonomy seems to pull against a concern with human rights, respect for religious freedom seems to contradict a concern for women's' rights, and so on. In such cases we seek to find a balance between these commitments. We struggle to find some way of bringing them into some coherent form. Many of us would profess a commitment to a range of values which include: liberty, equality, democracy, human rights, the rule of law, some notion of distributive justice, human welfare, and so on. In the face of a particular ethical puzzle the difficulty for us is to work out which decision would best demonstrate a coherent commitment to all of these values. Seeking coherence in these cases is the very stuff of ethical debate amongst ordinary people and scholars alike.

When we confront an ethical dilemma in the way in which I have outlined it above, we know ourselves to be engaged in confronting an ethical problem. We are able to distinguish such cases from the other kinds of choices we confront in our daily lives, such as those about how to maximise our pleasure, increase our income, solve a technical problem, make a political decision and so on.

Governments often confront ethical puzzles which have just the features which I have outlined. For example, the British government had to confront an ethical choice presented to it by Zimbabwe which sought to buy spare parts for the Hawk jet aircraft which it had bought from Britain. The ethical difficulty arose because the British government knew that these jet aircraft were being used for a war in the Peoples' Republic of Congo – a war to which the British government and a majority in the international community of states were vigorously opposed. Governments regularly have to decide whether or not to carry out 'business as usual' with states within which human rights abuses are taking place and within which democracy is under threat. Most dramatically states often have to decide what to do about human rights abuses in foreign places. To intervene is to flout a basic rule of international law concerning non-intervention in the domestic affairs of sovereign states, whereas not to intervene is to fail to uphold human rights values which are integral to any number of international legal instruments. In these cases, and in many others, governments stand before what are patently ethical choices.

When governments confront such choices there is often a heated public debate, both during the decision-making process and afterwards about what would constitute an appropriate ethical decision. Newspapers, pressure groups and pundits all set out well known arguments for and against given ethical positions on the question in hand. The debate is often carried out by caricaturing the opposing side as either 'idealist' or 'realist' where both labels are used in a pejorative sense.

Let me mention some more ethical issues to do with global governance which confront us in just this way. For example, at present we are all being confronted with ethical questions surrounding the next round of negotiations with regard to the World Trade Organization (WTO). Do we believe that it would be ethical to promote further trade liberalisation or not? Depending on the way we answer this, there are different courses of action open to us. Of course, how we answer this question will depend, *inter alia*, on what theories we use to explain how the global capitalist economy works. Those who explain it in Marxist terms will give a different answer to the one given by those who explain it in terms of monetarist economic theory. The answer we give to this question will determine what pressure groups, political parties, and positions we defend in the public domain. There are a number of other ethical issues which confront us when thinking about the future of global governance. Many of them are inter-linked. Governance issues with an explicit ethical dimension include:

- the reform of the United Nations (UN),
- questions about how much and to whom international aid should be distributed and by whom the distribution should be controlled,
- ethical questions about the control and conduct of humanitarian intervention,
- ethical questions about the structures to be set in place to contain the international crime syndicates,
- ethical questions to do with international regimes to be established to deal with all manner of environmental problems,
- ethical questions to do with regimes to control the activities of international hedge funds,

- ethical questions to do with the governance of labour relations in the global domain,
- questions about governance pertaining to the exploration and exploitation of the Antarctic, the sea, and outer space.

When we confront ethical issues like these, it is the case that from the outset we accept as the given, first, that we have a choice to make, second, that the choice to be made is (at least in part) an ethical choice (as opposed to an emotional, technical or political one), third, we accept as given some or other description of the situation about which the choice has to be made, and, fourth, we accept as given a specific set of ethical values which will inform us in our decision-making.

I wish to suggest (it is for the reader to test this assertion against the evidence) that for the most part, when people discuss the role of ethics as it pertains to questions of international governance, they have in mind the kind of circumstance which I have outlined above. They have in mind those cases where actors knowingly confront ethical choices about appropriate forms of global governance and where they know what kind of reasoning they will have to engage in to reach their decisions. In such cases the decision-makers (whether they be holders of high office or ordinary citizens) are like judges who hear cases before courts of law. Judges know that they are required to make a decision in law, and, they know what law to call upon in seeking to reach their decision. The nature of the choice and the parameters within which it is to be made are given in a strict way.

I have indicated one way in which we encounter ethical dilemma's pertaining to issues of global governance. If we use this mode of encounter with ethics as our point of departure we would expect an article dealing with the issue of ethics and global governance to evaluate different ways of tackling such ethical dilemmas. We would expect it to evaluate the merits of, for example, utilitarian, deontological, rights based, and care based ethical theories. The argument would be aimed at reaching a conclusion of the following form: 'When faced with an ethical problem pertaining to some issue of global governance here are some strong reasons for favouring a solution based on, for example, rule-utilitarian thinking.'

Ethics in the interpretation and explanation of international relations

Confronting ethical decisions as outlined above is but one of the ways in which a concern with ethics is important for those who are active in world affairs (and it must be remembered that most of us are active in this domain in one way or another). *Although the way of encountering ethics discussed above is important, it itself depends on a prior more fundamental level of ethical engagement.* The states of affairs pictured above where actors confront international governance questions which have an explicit ethical component, all presuppose that the actors in question already have made some or other interpretation of the circumstances within which they find themselves. In other words the actors in question have some view of what is happening and why. I shall argue below that we have already engaged in ethics when we come to hold a view about what is happening in a given situation.

All of us, whether we be professional social scientists or not, have to engage in the activity of attempting to understand the society (or societies) within which we find ourselves. The very process of getting on with our lives requires this of us. We all have some understanding of both our own society and those of others. In order to acquire this understanding we have to study (informally or formally) any number of social formations – these range from micro formations such as families, through to the macro formations such as empires. Our interest is sometimes focussed on contemporary formations and sometimes on historical ones. Thus many of us have some ideas about how the modern system of nation states emerged from earlier form feudal social formations. Those who are reading the present text are presumably interested in the social formation we know as 'the globalised world' which seems to be distinctively different form previous social formations based on feudal or mercantilist economic practices. This new order seems to call for the creation of distinctively different forms of global governance and gives rise to the production of books such as this one. One particularly important aspect of our globalised world seems to be what is known as global civil society, another is the system of sovereign states.

When we are engaged in the activity of interpreting a social formation we cannot but involve ourselves in the activity of interpreting the ethical frameworks embedded in them. For example, when we are trying to understand the international politics of the feudal era we shall inevitably find ourselves spelling out the role which those who were participants in it accorded to Christian religious and ethical beliefs. In like vein, when seeking to throw light on the international politics of the British Empire we shall have to take account of the ways in which actors during that period were guided by an ethic committed to civilising the natives, a belief that they were bringing Christianity to the heathens, and a belief in the ethical worth of a free market economy. Needless to say, many commentators on such historical forms give rival interpretations of the underlying ethical commitments which informed the actors during those periods. Some understand the actors to have been genuinely motivated by such ethical considerations, while others give an account which shows their ethical professions to be mere window dressing to cover baser motives for action. It is not my purpose here to evaluate these rival accounts. *Here I simply want to point out that a consideration of the ethics embedded in social formations is a crucial (and unavoidable) component of any and all attempts to understand such orders, – our own or others', past or present.* It simply would not be possible to offer any plausible interpretation whatsoever, of, for example, the recent international behaviour of Islamic states without some understanding of the set of Islamic religious and ethical ideas which are embedded in the practices within which they are acting. In like vein we could not offer a plausible interpretation of the behaviour of the United States in the international domain without some clear ideas about the pro democracy, pro free market and pro human rights ethical commitments which are embedded in the practices constitutive of both the leadership and citizens of the United States.

A key feature to note here is that when we engage in the interpretation of social formations, although we necessarily have to take account of the ethical beliefs embedded in the practices under investigation, *we often do this without being overtly conscious of the fact that we are engaged in an inquiry about ethics at all.* Thus were I to set myself the task of writing a scholarly article about the causes of the Boer War in South Africa, or about how the processes of globalisation are currently affecting the people in the poorest states of Africa, it may well turn out that in the texts which I produced on these topics I make no mention of the word 'ethics' at all. In the account of the Boer War I might confine myself to explaining it in terms of the 'national interests' of the states in question. With regard to globalisation in Africa, my text might refer to the mechanisms at work in the process, without any reference to the ethics of the actors involved. Nevertheless, it is easy to show that in order to interpret the events of that war I would have had to pay attention to the ethical frameworks which informed the practices within which the war took place. In like manner my account of globalisation would have to make assumptions about an ethical framework embedded in that institution which we know as the global market.

In order to demonstrate this let us consider the case of the Boer War (1898–1901) more closely. Were I to write of the political twists and turns which took place between the parties before the war broke out, it may well be that I would refer to the 'national interest' of the Boer Republics and the 'imperial interest' of the British. But in doing this I assume that both I and my readers know what constitutes a republic and what an empire. This requires of us that we know that a republic is a social form (a political institution in this case) within which people have set up ways of relating to one another which embody certain fundamental ethical commitments, about self-determination, citizenship, democracy, republicanism and so on. The same point may be made about the notion of empire. Using this notion presupposes that we who use it know that an empire, such as the British one, was an arrangement within which people set up structures of governance designed to embody certain ethical principles – principles to do with Christianity, the spread of civilisation, releasing people from the tyranny of primitive tradition and so on. It is hard to imagine that one could have any proper grasp of the notion of 'republic' or 'empire' without some grasp of the underlying ethical programmes or frameworks which are embedded in them.[5]

In this section my concern has been to highlight how, whether we are consciously aware of it or not, we engage with ethical matters whenever we engage in social interpretation. It would be difficult to downplay the importance of this, for, of course, we engage in social interpretation all the time. In all that we do in our day to day lives, our actions are guided by the interpretations we put on any number of social formations. For example, each day we put some or other interpretation on the international news which reaches us. When we read of international crime, or of nuclear tests in foreign countries, or of the hijacking of aircraft in international airspace, or of the plight of economic migrants, or of *coups d'etats* in foreign states – in each of these cases we engage in the business of social interpretation. Layers of interpretation are involved here. We read the interpretation which the newspaper journalists put on these matters, we compare these with what the broadcast journalists say, and, where possible, we take into account other sources (testimony from friends, acquaintances, learned colleagues, and the like) and, finally, in the light of all these, we then make our own interpretation of what transpired in the given case. In each and every case we make judgements about the ethical components of the practices within which the actions took place. This engagement with ethics, whether tacit or explicit, cannot be avoided.

When we are engaged in the business of social interpretation, it is important that we get our interpretations right. Thus, for example, when interpreting the behaviour of Islamic social formations, it is crucial that we get a correct hold on the set of ethical and religious ideas which underpin Islamic practices. Any misinterpretation of the Islamic views on what constitutes a proper ethical relationship between a believer and his/her God, and the proper relationship between believers, their priests and their governments, will result in a misunderstanding of what is going on in the case in question. Such misunderstandings might well lead to a failure to predict what the key actors will do in a given set of circumstances. In like manner it is imperative for any Islamic analyst who seeks to understand the behaviour of a democratic state in the international domain, that he/she understand what democrats take to be the proper ethical relationship between citizens and government. Thus, for example, it is only in the light of a correct understanding of a very specific set of ethical commitments that such an analyst would be able to make sense of the way in which President Clinton's power (internally and externally) shifted during the Monica Lewinsky scandal. His conduct during that period is only explicable once the interpreter has understood some quite complex ethical commitments embedded in the US polity. Key amongst these are ideas about what constitutes proper conduct (and what improper conduct) between a President and those who work for him. These ideas are ethical ideas.

When it comes to interpreting social affairs, getting the ethical dimension of the matter right is easier said than done. It is not simply a matter of observing the practice and describing its ethical foundations. For it is common knowledge that within many complex social formations whether they be religious, political or economic, there are often ongoing debates amongst the participants themselves about the ethical underpinnings of their social formations. Thus within Islam (as within Christianity, Judaism, Hinduism and Buddhism) there are fiercely fought disputes about the proper interpretation to be placed on the Koran and the teachings of the Mullahs down the ages. In seeking to interpret current practice within Islam an external interpreter will have to come to grips with current disputes about religion and ethics which rage within that practice. An interpreter will, for example, have to pay great attention to the disputes which continue between the Shia and Sunni traditions within the Islamic world.

Let me now bring this discussion back to the matter in hand, global governance. Whenever anyone (like a reader of this book for example) confronts questions to do with global governance, these questions will always be considered against a background of social interpretation. A person can only pose questions about appropriate forms of global governance once he or she has some view about what is going on in the international domain at the time. This interpretation of the existing circumstances requires, as we have seen, that the analyst make a more or less accurate interpretation of the ethical codes embedded in the social formations under investigation. It thus follows (to repeat the central point here) that a concern with ethics does not only arise at the point at which actors (individual or corporate) have to make explicit ethical decisions about global governance, but they also arise at this prior level. The implications of this are profound.

In order to illustrate the importance of this point, let us consider one of the major issues confronting us all at the moment, the governance of the global economy. This calls for a consideration, amongst other things, of the role of existing global institutions such as the WTO, the International Monetary Fund (IMF) and the World Bank, and their relationship to both states, corporations and individuals. Before any decisions can be taken about how these institutions of governance might be reformed, we need some interpretation of the social formations over which reformed governance structures are to be instituted. We need an understanding of states, the system of states, the global market, and of the relevant international organisations such as the WTO, the IMF, and the World Bank. In order to understand each of these social institutions we need to grasp the ethical components which are embedded in them. Thus, for example, we need to know what participants in sovereign states take to be the values embedded in those states. Typically participants value states as organisations within which the values of citizenship are realised, sometimes, too, the state is taken as a vehicle through which the value of national self-determination is expressed and protected. Other values often associated with statehood have to do with the protection of human rights, the protection of regional interests, the constitution and protection of democratic values, the provision of security, education and welfare services, and so on.

In like manner before we can contemplate new governance structures for the global market we need to know what it is and what values are embedded in it. We who participate in this market normally take it to be a social formation within which forms of private property are established and protected. The market is also normally understood as an arrangement within which contract is embedded as a fundamental value. To this must be added the values of freedom of association, freedom of speech, and freedom of movement. A well constituted market is one within which these are protected. Where these are not protected no market can flourish. Once we have understood the market, it then becomes relatively easy to understand what corporations, banks, the IMF, the World Bank and so on are. In a longer exposition one would have to spell out the ethical underpinnings of each of these.

Understanding what the WTO is now (which is a precondition for understanding how it might be reformed as an institution of global governance in future) requires both an understanding of the practice of states, and also of the practice of the world market. Understanding the ethical underpinnings of a social institution such as the WTO becomes decidedly complex because it requires of us that we bring together both an understanding of the ethic embodied in the system of sovereign states and the ethic embedded in the market. What the ethical underpinnings of these are is disputed, even amongst liberals. To repeat the central point, any act of interpretation will necessarily require some engagement with this ethical complexity.

It is important, yet again, that I stress that we who participate in the system of sovereign states and the global market often have vigorous arguments about what ethical systems are embedded in them. Thus, for example, free marketers give a decidedly different account of the ethical dimensions of the global market to the one given by those who interpret it through a Marxist lens. For my present purposes this is of no account, for all I wish to stress at this point, is that prior to taking any decision about global governance (which decision might well require an explicit ethical choice) we (a category which includes any actor whatsoever) need to have some interpretation of the existing social arrangements and *this act of interpreting the status quo, this act of spelling out the circumstances which currently pertain, requires of us that we have some 'take' on the ethical features of the social formations under scrutiny.* The ethical dimensions of the practices under consideration may be settled amongst those who participate in them or they may be disputed. In order to interpret the practice we who are interpreting it need to know what is taken as ethically settled and/or what ethical matters are still taken to be in dispute amongst the participants.

Ethics as fundamental to human conduct

The first category of ethical engagement which I mentioned above concerned those circumstances in which we stand before decisions which explicitly call for an ethical choice such as 'Should we (as individuals or as members of states) support the establishment of an International Court of Criminal Justice?' In making such decisions we might, for example, have to weigh up ethical considerations pertaining to the protection of individual human rights against ethical considerations to do with the value of state sovereignty. On this view we sometimes encounter circumstances which call for an ethical involvement, while at other times we do not. Let us call this form of ethical engagement, category one ethical engagement. Important features about this form of ethical engagement are that we only encounter it from time to time, and that when we do encounter it we are conscious of having done so (as in 'Should I from an ethical point of view support the creation of structures of global governance which erode the free market?')

The second category of ethical engagement discussed above is one which precedes the moment of decision characterised in category one ethical engagement. All instances which call for ethical decision necessarily take place in circumstances where the decision-maker already has in mind some interpretation of how things stand in the society in question. I indicated that the interpretation of social practices requires an understanding of the ethical commitments which the participants take to be embedded in them (and knowledge about the disputes amongst the participants about what precisely these commitments are). Thus a category one type ethical decision about what it would be ethically appropriate to do with regard to setting up structures of governance to oversee the arms industry in Iraq presupposes a prior interpretation of what is happening in that social formation known as the Iraqi state situated in the wider society of states. This requires that the decision-maker understands the ethical and religious values embedded in the Iraqi polity and that the interpreter understands the disputes about these which are current in Iraq and elsewhere. On this view those who are concerned about structures of world governance need to take note of the ethical codes embedded in the practices which are to be subject to such governance. Here they are called upon to understand the ethical underpinnings of the practices – they are not called upon to make ethical decisions themselves.[6]

Category two ethics still presupposes that we accept the standing of the interpreter and his/her interpretations as broadly unproblematic from an ethical point of view. Category two ethics simply insists that when investigating international social arrangements the interpreter has to pay attention to the ethical underpinnings of these practices (and the disputes about these underpinnings) as understood by the participants. It is when we turn to consider what is involved in being an actor in a social context (including the international one) that a third category of ethical engagement surfaces. This category of ethical engagement, let us call it category three ethics, is particularly important when it comes to making decisions pertaining to global governance.

Ethics as fundamental to the constitution of humans as social actors

Actors who consider questions of global governance are not free floating entities, who may be conceived of as existing outside of and independent from all social arrangements. Instead they are better understood as having been constituted as the actors they are within a complex set of social practices. In each practice within the total set they are constituted as actors of a certain kind. Their being actors of this or that kind may be said to be an institutional fact.[7] As actors constituted within a given practice they know how to carry out a range of actions appropriate to that status. They also know what would count as unacceptable behaviour for actors like them. Here is a simple example, those who have been constituted as citizens within a given democratic state, know what being a good citizen requires of them and they also know what would count as treasonable action.

Let me be more explicit in what I mean when I say that actors are constituted as such within a range of diverse social practices, by considering myself as an actor who is contemplating problems of global governance. I, who am considering such questions, am constituted as who I am in a range of social practices which include (the following list is illustrative not exhaustive):

- The family within which I am constituted as a father. I know what is called for in this role and I know what would count as making a mistake. There are international dimensions to this role in that I am called upon to protect my family's interests which on occasion might require, for example, migration and/or the establishment of offshore savings accounts. As a father who is leading his family through a process of migration I might have to make decisions about governance – I might support moves to establish a more lenient migration regime in my area of the world.
- A religious community (albeit a fractious and complex one) within which I am constituted as a Christian. I know what is required of me as a Christian and what would count as infringing the Christian canon. There are international dimensions to being a Christian

which have to do with providing aid to the poor, help to the oppressed, comfort to the suffering and so on. This might lead me to take a stand on matters relating to the governance of global food distribution systems.

• The community of scholars within which I am constituted as a Professor of International Relations – as such I know what is required of me in my life as a scholar and what would constitute a major misdemeanour in terms of the constitutive rules of the practice of scholars. I am called upon to uphold the appropriate standards both at home and abroad. With regard to issues of governance I might act to uphold/establish an international order within which academic freedom is respected.

• Civil society within which I am constituted as a rights holder through a system of mutual recognition with other rights holders. As a rights holder in this civil society I am required to respect the basic rights of others wherever they may be. The claims and counter claims in this domain are often international in their reach. As a rights holder I might become intimately involved in campaigns to make the International Court of Criminal Justice a functioning reality.

• A democratic state within which I am constituted as a citizen – as such I understand the range of possible actions which are appropriate for a citizen like me and conversely I understand what actions would undermine my standing as citizen.[8] As a citizen I have to consider what foreign policies of my state I should support and which not – especially with regard to possible structures of governance.

Here once again (as with category two ethics) a crucial point to notice about this set of practices within which I am constituted as father, Christian, professor, rights holder and citizen, is that each of them has embedded in it a set of values. The constitutive rules of each practice must be understood as advancing and nurturing a specific ethic. Thus whenever I am doing what I take to be the appropriate thing for a father to do, I take myself to be upholding the ethic which is embedded in the family as a social institution. Whenever I am acting in ways which I take to be appropriate to my constitution as Christian, I am upholding the values internal to the practice of Christianity. The same point can be made about my actions as scholar, civilian and citizen. *The central point in all this is that to be an actor is to be constituted as such within a social practice and that social practices have built into them specific sets of values or ethical codes. Thus to be an actor is to be established as* an institutional fact of a certain kind in a social form with an ethical dimension.

On this view ethics is not something which actors confront from time to time (which is how it was portrayed in category one ethics, above), but is an integral component of being an actor of this or that kind and is a component of all action. From this perspective to take 'the ethical turn' is not an option, which actors have. Rather to be an actor at all is to be engaged in a practice with an ethical dimension. This way of analysing the relationship between actors, practices and ethics is what I have called 'constitutive theory.'[9]

The outline of constitutive theory I have offered reveals the importance of what we might call the question of constitutional ethics. By this I mean that it is always appropriate to ask of any actor and any action (past, present or proposed) whether the action upholds or undermines the values embedded in the practice within which the actor is constituted as an actor of this or that kind. This is not a question which is only appropriate when the actor in question is consciously grappling with an ethical problem, or when the actor is trying to interpret the social practices of other people or even his/her own social practice. Instead constitutive theory shows that the ethical question about the fit between an act and the practice within which it is located is always an appropriate one to ask.

What is being asked for here is not whether a given action coheres with some values which the actor has more or less arbitrarily and subjectively chosen as his/her ethical commitment, but whether the act coheres with the values embedded in the practice within which the actor is established as an actor in good standing. Let me refer to a simple example which I mentioned earlier. We could ask the question of constitutional ethics about citizen Monica Lewinsky's sexual acts with the President of the United States. Our question would be about whether the acts were ethically appropriate for a citizen to engage in with her President. We could ask a similar question about President Clinton's conduct in this case. In each case we would not be asking whether their behaviour accorded with some ethical code which they had personally chosen, but we would be asking whether *as citizen* or *as president* their behaviour cohered with what is required of them constituted as they are as citizen and president respectively. There are interesting arguments to be had here about the limits of private and public roles. I shall not go into these. The important point here is that these ethical questions are about actors constituted within a specified practice, their actions and the ethics embedded in the practice. Enquiries about whether the citizen named here (Monica Lewinsky) and the President named here (Bill Clinton) adhered to Christian, Islamic, utilitarian, rights based, Judaic (or whatever) ethical codes are quite beside the point. What is at stake in this kind of ethical enquiry is whether the conduct of the actors constituted as citizen and president respectively was appropriate to the ethic embedded in the political practice in question.

Questions of constitutional ethics may be made of actors across the whole range of social practices. We can ask them of the conduct of fathers within the practice of family life, of Christians within the practice of Christianity, of footballers within the practice of football, of chess players within the practice of chess playing, of academics within the practice of university life, of citizens within states, of judges within legal systems, of states within the interstate practice, of rights holders within civil society, and so on.

I have already indicated that within a single practice questions of ethical constitution can become hugely complicated. Current issues within medicine arising from new technologies of genetic engineering provide many examples of this kind of complexity. The situation becomes even more complicated when the actors of whom questions of constitutional ethics are being asked are simultaneously constituted as actors within a whole range of practices. This happens, for example, when an actor making a decision about global governance is at one and the same time a father, a Christian, a rights holder, a citizen and a minister in a government. Questions of constitutional ethics in such cases are no longer merely about the actor's standing within a single practice, his act, and the ethics embedded in that practice, but now include questions about the relationships which hold (or do not) between the different practices and their diverse ethics. The question becomes one about a whole edifice of actor-constituting practices.

Let me give an hypothetical example of the kind of complexity which can arise here. Let us imagine that we are once again in the mid-1980s. A South African academic attends and participates in an international conference examining the strategic importance of the Cape Sea Routes. He is knowledgeable about his government's thinking and policies. Suppose that we subject his act of participation to questions of constitutional ethics. We note that this actor is constituted as all of the following: as a citizen of South Africa, as a member of the Anti-Apartheid Movement, as liberal democrat (as opposed to a communist), as a Christian, and as a member of the international academic community. In any conversation about the coherence of this act with the ethics embedded in the practices within which he is constituted as the kind of actor(s) outlined above, the following issues might be raised: Does what it is appropriate for an academic to do (hold open and critical discussions with fellow academics) mesh with the conduct required of a citizen in a state threatened by a hostile communist state (the requirement not to divulge information which might be of use to the enemy), and how does this mesh with what is required of an Anti-Apartheid activist (which is to aid 'The Struggle' in whatever way possible) and how do all of the above mesh with what is required of a Christian (which is not to give support to any group whose conduct could be construed as falling short of loving one's neighbour)? It might well be argued that fulfilling the requirements of academic life would require of this person that he infringe the requirements of citizenship, or vice versa. There are many other conflicts we can envisage between these practices.

In many of the things we do, we act as actors who are simultaneously constituted as actors in a whole range of practices. Generally we are confident that what we do may be shown to cohere with the ethics embedded in the diverse practices within which we are constituted as who we are. Acknowledging a failure to achieve such coherence would be to acknowledge that with regard to one or more of the practices in question our participation in them is hypocritical.[10]

We seek ethical coherence in what we do. We normally assume that other actors are doing the same. Thus when the President of the World Bank makes a speech in favour of liberalising trade relations between the poorest states in the world and the members of the Organisation for Economic Co-operation and Development (OECD) nations we interpret him as acting in accordance with the free-trade principles which underlie the World Bank, yet in doing this we take it that his action also coheres with his standing as a family man, as a member of some religious order, and as a member of the society of rights holders, global civil society and as a citizen of a state. In like manner we take it that what Tony Blair does as a Christian coheres both the values of the Christian community, but also with the values implicit in the other practices within which he is constituted as participant, the Labour Party, the British state and the European Union.

In this section I have pointed to the important ethical questions which may be asked of all actors and their actions. These questions are about the coherence (or lack of coherence) between being constituted as an actor of a certain kind within a specified practice, a particular act or set of acts, and the ethics embedded in the practice looked at as a whole. Such questions become particularly complicated when an actor is simultaneously constituted as an actor in a whole range of different practices. In such cases the interesting questions are about the coherence (or lack of it) between the ethics underlying the different practices.

Ethics and global governance

I have discussed three different ways in which ethical considerations may become pertinent to those considering the future of global governance. In the first category are those cases where an explicit ethical matter arises for an actor confronting a global governance question. At this point the actor in question might call in the advice of someone with expertise in international ethics.

In the second category I pointed out that all actors considering governance issues have to make interpretations of the existing states of affairs. I showed how these involve the interpreter making assumptions about the ethical commitments of those whose actions are being interpreted. This engagement with ethical matters might occur without the interpreter being aware of his or her being engaged in ethical interpretation at all. Here analysts, like the present author, have a role to play in pointing out to the parties who are making such interpretations what ethical assumptions they are making about those whose behaviour is being explained and interpreted. Getting the ethics wrong at this point would result in the actors in question misunderstanding what is going on in these cases. Decisions about structures of governance taken on the basis of misinterpretations are not likely to succeed.

Finally I argued that to be an actor is always to be constituted as such within some or other social practice which has embedded in it a particular ethic. All of us are simultaneously constituted as actors within a whole range of practices. On this view all action may be viewed as a form of ethical interpretation even if the interpretation is only implicit.

I was asked by the editors of this volume on *Global Governance in the twenty-first Century* to write a chapter on 'Why Normative Principles Matter.' In terms of category three ethics as outlined above the answer must be that normative principles matter in that only insofar as we have a grasp of the underlying social constitution of the actors involved in discussions about global governance (including ourselves), can we determine whether what they (we) do is ethically appropriate to their (our) social constitution. Knowledge of these embedded principles enables us to determine the range of possible actions open to an actor constituted in a particular way. The principles being discussed here are not ethical principles which actors may consider taking up or not. These are principles which are constitutive of the actors in question. To be a rights holder, citizen, president, chief executive, secretary general, and so on, is to be one who adheres to the principles inherent in the practice in question. Adhering to these principles is a prerequisite for him/her maintaining his/her status as that kind of actor.

Who are the actors involved in contemplating (discussing, negotiating about, setting up conferences on, and so on) possible forms of global governance? What are the practices within which they are constituted as such actors? Here is a list of the more obvious candidates which spring to mind:

- Presidents, Prime Ministers, Foreign Ministers and other members of governments of sovereign states.
- Officials of international organisations such as the Secretary-General of the United Nations, the President of the WTO, the President of the World Bank, the President of the IMF. High officials from other international organisations such as the Organisation of the African Unity (OAU), Organisation of American States (OAS), Association of Southeast Asian Nations (ASEAN), Organisation of the Petroleum Exporting Countries (OPEC), and other regional organisations.
- Office holders and members in organisations such as churches.
- Leaders and members of single issue pressure groups with global reach such as Amnesty and Human Rights Watch (HRW).
- Chairmen and Chief executive officers and shareholders of large corporations.
- Academics from the community of scholars.
- Ordinary men and women as citizens of states which are to be subject to the emerging structures of governance.
- Ordinary men and women as rights holders in global civil society.
- Members of nationalist movements (such as the Afrikaaner *Volk*, the Scottish Nation, the Basque Nation, the Quebecois Nation, the Kurdish Nation, to mention but a few of many such groups).

Many of us who are concerned with global governance are simultaneously constituted as actors within several of the practices mentioned in the list. Bill Clinton was President, citizen, Christian, rights holder in civil society, to mention but three of the roles he occupied while he was President. Other actors are simultaneously citizens, rights holders, nationalists, members of the board of corporations, members of HRW, members of churches, participants in international organisations, and so on. Being constituted as an actor in such an array of organisations poses particular problems for such people as circumstances and technologies change. Thus, for example, we who are citizens of states have to consider what would be ethically appropriate for people like us constituted as we are, to do with regard to the new technologies which make virtual wars possible. These are those 'wars' a state or international organisations may make use of high tech military hardware to inflict great damage on a target with very little risk of loss of life to itself.[11] Here we have to explore whether the possibilities created by this technology, fit with the ethical structures embedded in the whole set of practices within which we as actors are constituted as citizens. This process of reflection might result in reinterpretations which change and develop our constituting practices. Change through reinterpretation of the relationships between the full set of constitutive practices may be forced on us by any number of different kinds of events including, technological innovation, natural disasters (floods, weather change, epidemics), population movements, population increases, and so on.

Having listed the key actors involved in discussions about global governance and the practices within which they are constituted as such our next task must be to spell out the ethical underpinnings of the constitutive practices. I cannot take on this huge task in the present article, but can only point in the direction of what is required. What needs to be spelled out is how the practice known as the democratic state (in which that actor we know as the president is constituted as such) is built upon ethical ideas of representative democracy, human rights, the rule of law, and so on; the international practice known as the UN is founded on ethical ideas to do with peace and security between states and the promotion of human rights internationally; religious practices are often based on religiously inspired ethical ideals such as the Christian one of brotherly love; single issue pressure groups like HRW are based on ethical ideals embodying codes of human rights; corporations operative in that practice known as the market which embodies ethical ideas about human rights and in particular the right to own private property; global civil society is a practice within which men and women world wide recognise one another as the holders of first generation rights; and, those social practices which we know as nations are built upon ethical ideals to do with the self-determination of peoples.

In terms of category three ethics our task must be to study the ethical architecture of the key actors involved in discussions about global governance in order to determine the scope of ethically permissible action open to them. Three key aspects of this huge task deserve mention here. First, interpreting the internal ethic may be undertaken by anyone. The interpretation put forward by any particular occupant of an actor-role (President Clinton, for example) carries no particular claim to being the best interpretation. Second, of particular interest will be the task of attempting to determine how the internal ethic accommodates or can be modified to accommodate new extraneous developments such as technological changes, natural disasters, demographic changes, human migration flows and the like. Third, the most difficult task will be to determine how the ethical underpinnings of the different practices within which a single actor is constituted can be brought into some form of coherence. This is required if the actor is to avoid alienation, hypocrisy or contradiction in what he/she does. If coherence cannot be achieved a case has to be made for modifying one of the practices or in the extreme case abandoning it altogether.[12]

It is with regard to this last feature that the most pressing ethical issues relating to global governance debates arise. It seems to me that the major actors contemplating global governance are all constituted as actors in the practice of democratic and democratising states, on the one hand, and in the practice of global civil society on the other. Key questions to ask are whether the ethics underpinning these two practices are compatible, and, if they are, what have the compatible ethical theories to say about a range of the new circumstances facing us in the world today, such as high speed global financial markets, the internet, global crime, pollution on a global scale, problems of mass migration, virtual war, and so on, to mention but a few.

Consider briefly global civil society. A very large number of people in the world today consider themselves to be participants in this practice within which they are recognised as holders of packets of rights which are not granted to them by the states in which they happen to live, but are accorded to them simply because they are human beings. Within this practice there are arguments about what rights the participants have. Some favour a short list of negative liberties, others claim a fuller list which includes second and third generation rights. All agree though that as a minimum, rights holders (let us call them civilians) have the negative liberties which include the rights of the person (the right not to be killed, assaulted, tortured, and so on), the right to freedom of movement, association, contract, conscience, academic freedom and the right to own property. A key feature of this practice is that the participants in it consider that the rights claims they make do not depend for their validity on them being able to show membership of some or other polity. Quite the contrary civilians often judge the merits of political organisations such as states, by the extent to which they uphold their pre-existing civil society rights.

In terms of category three ethics it makes sense for us to seek the ethical underpinnings of the practice we know as global civil society within which participants are constituted as civilians. What are the ethical values nurtured within this practice? The brief answer is that this practice creates and nurtures those values associated with the idea of individual autonomy. What people in this practice value is the way in which as rights holders they are able to achieve and express the value of human autonomy. What precisely is involved in being autonomous is a highly contentious topic which I cannot go into here. But the core idea is straightforward enough. Within the areas circumscribed by their rights individuals are free to construct their lives as they see fit. Some may opt for puritan lives, others for lives in pursuit of pleasure, some for the Christian way of life, others for a Judaic one, and so on. To be a civilian in civil society is to be participant in a practice premised on the value of individual autonomy. This severely constrains what kinds of actions civilians *qua* civilians can undertake.

But just as many of us who are concerned about global governance are constituted as actors (civilians) in civil society, so too, are we constituted as citizens within particular states within the practice of democratic and democratising states. The vast bulk of existing states belong to this practice. People in those states which are not functioning democracies profess to be moving in that direction. In this practice we are constituted as citizens who have a right to stand for office, to participate in elections of office bearers, to hold the elected officials to account once they have been elected and so on. I have no time to discuss the details of what is involved in a fully developed notion of citizenship.

What is the ethic embedded in the practice of democratic states? Here I shall have to rest content with the rather vague assertion that it is a democratic ethic, one which stresses that certain important values are realised and brought into existence when the relationship between citizens and their government is one constructed on democratic lines. *The fundamental value here is once again a notion of autonomy.* This is not merely the autonomy realised in exercising the rights of a civilian in civil society, but is that kind of autonomy realised in participating in the process of lawmaking for oneself and for one's fellow citizens. According to the democratic ethic people are most autonomous when they in some sense govern themselves. What is so important about being accorded the status of citizen, is that in being recognised as such, one is recognised as a human being with the right to participate in a form of self government at the highest level. To deny a person citizenship is to condemn that person to some or other form of government by others.

What is crucial to citizenship, though, is that by definition it is a status which is to be found within some or other state. This linking of citizenship to state is important because for the most part the highest level of lawmaking takes place at this level. So to participate in making the laws at this high level, which in turn governs rule making at subsidiary levels, is a particularly important form of autonomy.

It is important once again to stress that citizens in the system of democratic and democratising states are not all agreed on a single understanding of the ethic which undergirds their practice. There are ongoing debates about different democratic theories such as that between the advocates of theories of representative democracy and the supporters of theories of participatory democracy. These are best understood as skirmishes in a broadly conceived justificatory tradition.

For constitutive theory, a key question is whether the ethics embedded in these two practices are compatible or not? Are people who are trying to be both civilians and citizens living a contradiction? Elsewhere, I have made the case in detail that it is a precondition for our constitution a fully fledged citizens in democratic states that we be constituted as civilians in civil society.[13] There is not enough space here to repeat the whole argument. If it is correct though then this places severe limits on what actors who consider themselves to be both civilians in global civil society and citizens in the society of democratic states may do when it comes to setting up new structures of global governance. In particular what is ruled out as incompatible with such standings are any proposals to curtail the basic rights which people enjoy in global civil society (a society without borders).

In this chapter I have outlined three different ways in which those contemplating the future of global governance might take ethical questions under consideration. I have attempted to make the case that it is the last of these that is the most important. *This asserts the importance of inquiring into the ethical constitution of the key actors involved in discussions about global governance.* Progress in the structures of global governance are made through our attempts to bring into coherence the ethics which underpin the overall constitutional structure within which we are constituted as the actors we are and to use what coherence we are able to achieve to adapt our practices to take into account new technologies and changed circumstances.

Notes

1. H. Cleveland, *Managing a Nobody-In-Charge World: Governing a Pluralistic World* (New York: Aspen Institute for Humanistic Studies, 1981).
2. M. Simai, 'The Changing State System and the Future of Global Governance', *Global Society: Journal of Interdisciplinary International Relations*, XI, 2 (May 1997) 141.
3. M. Frost, 'A Turn Not Taken: Ethics in IR at the Millennium', *Review of International Studies*, XXIV, Special Issue (December 1998) 119–32.
4. Frost 1998; M. Frost, 'Common Practices in a Plural World: The Bases for a Theory of Justice', in M. Lensu and J-S. Fritz (eds), *Value Pluralism, Normative Theory and International Relations* (London: Macmillan in association with *Millennium: Journal of International Studies*, 2000), pp. 1–23; M. Frost, 'Putting the World to Rights: Britain's Ethical Foreign Policy', *Cambridge Review of International Affairs*, XII, 2 (Summer 1999) 80–90.
5. Once again I must stress that there might well be heated arguments between interpreters of these events about what precisely the ethical underpinnings of the social forms in question were. Conceding this in no way undermines my central argument which is that an engagement with such ethical matters is unavoidable for those involved in social interpretation.
6. They are not called upon to determine whether action x is more ethical than y. Rather they have to ascertain what ethical system infuses the social arrangements in question. This might be seen as a task for objective inquiry.
7. J. Searle, *The Construction of Social Reality* (Harmondsworth: Penguin, 1995).
8. I should mention here that being constituted as a member of a nation is not important to me, but I acknowledge that for many people it is. Nationalists are those who have learned the range of appropriate actions for people constituted as such.
9. M. Frost, *Ethics in International Relations: A Constitutive Theory* (Cambridge: Cambridge University Press, 1996) and *Constituting Human Rights: Global Civil Society and the Society of Democratic States* (London, Routledge, 2002).
10. We make claims of hypocrisy against, for example, those who claim both to be good Christians (Jews, Hindus, or Buddhists) and who systematically engage in a long term of torture against those whom they name as their enemies. Doing the latter might cohere with what is required of members of a specific police force, but it is difficult to square the ethic of this police force with the ethics of the religious communities mentioned above.
11. See M. Ignatieff, *Virtual War* (New York: Henry Holt, 2000).
12. When white South Africans found that continued membership of the *apartheid* state could not be brought into coherence with membership of the society of democratic and democratising states and with membership of global civil society, they were forced to abandon that practice known as the *apartheid* state.

13. M. Frost, *Ethics in International Relations: A Constitutive Theory* (Cambridge: Cambridge University Press, 1996).

References

Cleveland, H. *Managing a Nobody-In-Charge World: Governing a Pluralistic World* (New York: Aspen Institute for Humanistic Studies, 1981).

Frost, M. *Ethics in International Relations: A Constitutive Theory* (Cambridge: Cambridge University Press, 1996).

——, 'A Turn Not Taken: Ethics in IR at the Millennium', *Review of International Studies*, XXIV, Special Issue (December 1998) 119–32.

——, 'Putting the World to Rights: Britain's Ethical Foreign Policy', *Cambridge Review of International Affairs*, XII, 2 (Summer 1999) 80–90.

——, 'Common Practices in a Plural World: The Bases for a Theory of Justice', in M. Lensu and J.-S. Fritz (eds), *Value Pluralism, Normative Theory and International Relations* (London: Macmillan in association with *Millennium: Journal of International Studies*, 2000), pp. 1–23.

Ignatieff, M. *Virtual War* (New York: Henry Holt, 2000).

Searle, J. *The Construction of Social Reality* (Harmondsworth: Penguin, 1995).

Simai, M. 'The Changing State System and the Future of Global Governance', *Global Society: Journal of Interdisciplinary International Relations*, XI, 2 (May 1997) 141.

3
Globalisation, Governance, and Investment Rules

David Schneiderman[1]

Introduction

If work on globalisation emphasises the obsolescence of the state, a focus on 'governance' can help to bring the state back in, though in a diminished capacity. Global governance's research agenda underscores the state's increasing marginal authority, sharing with other entities the regulation of economic and social matters. Though work on 'governance' often includes government,[2] it emphasises the role of international regimes and networks in solving particular problems and the participation of non-state actors in these institutional arrangements.[3] State functions are described as moving upwards – to new international institutions – downwards – in partnership with private actors – and, presumably, to nowhere – the redistributivist function of the state, for instance, is diverted formally to no specific place.[4]

The regulation of foreign investment is one such realm where state power has been in retreat and authority moving elsewhere. Through a series of interlocking agreements at the transnational, regional, and bilateral levels, a legally binding regime for the protection and promotion of foreign investment has been constructed above national states to enable the free movement of capital. The investment rules regime aims to secure advantages for foreign investors over democratic rule by limiting, through constitution-like arrangements, the capacity of self-governing communities to intervene in the market.

Though this regime binds state actors to constitution-like disciplines, states are deeply implicated in both the construction and maintenance of the regime. These self-binding disciplines are drafted, negotiated, and enforced, but not exclusively, by state actors.

Once in force, the role played by non-state actors in the regime's enforcement mechanisms can be of greater significance than the role played by states. The investment rules regime entitles foreign investors to enforce legal commitments by taking advantage of the regime's dispute settlement mechanisms, though no similar economic rights may be available to investors at the national level. These mechanisms, once triggered, provide court-like venues for the resolution of investor claims. If a favourable ruling is secured, it is then lodged in the judicial system of the rogue state. In the past, foreign investment conflict has been mediated through the aegis of national states, so the direct availability of remedies to foreign investors (in the form of monetary damages, for instance) thus is extraordinary.

Not only is state capacity marginalised, so is the role of other civil society actors. The investment rules regime places little or no value on the public interest pursued by state policy that is not founded on the logic of economic rationality. Nor are civil society actors usually accorded any standing in these disputes – their concerns are ruled out of court. All of these claims are explored in a case study, discussed in Parts Two and Three of the chapter, concerning the privatisation of vital water resources in Cochabamba, Bolivia. As water rates doubled, the local populace rose up and forced the departure of the transnational water consortium led by International Water Ltd., a subsidiary of San Francisco-based Bechtel. The company now seeks compensation for lost profits from the government of Bolivia under a bilateral investment treaty (BIT). Before undertaking this discussion, in Part One the core elements of the investment rules regime are outlined and its likely impact on state capacity to intervene in markets evaluated. I suggest that investment rules generate entitlements that are constitution-like in both form and in substance.

The investment rules regime not only removes investor-state disputes from local apparatuses, it subjects state actors to non-local rules that discipline state action in much the same way as do constitutional rules. Gill similarly describes the binding legal disciplines of economic globalisation as the 'new constitutionalism'.[5] He refers to the quasi-legal restructuring and institutional reforms that sacrifice democratic decision-making within states to the logic of efficiency and market credibility. These 'binding constraints' insulate key aspects of the economy from the influence of politicians and the mass of citizens. A focus on the legal and juridical instantiations of economic globalisation are good indicators of the breadth and depth of what might be called the 'imperial constitution'.[6]

What the investment rules regime signals is the demise of the post-war compromise of 'embedded liberalism'.[7] Those institutions of the state that citizens reasonably will look to for shelter from the hardships of the market are disabled, under the constitution-like regime of investment rules, from taking measures for societal self-protection.[8] As Cerny notes, the state's steering functions – its capacity to promote economic competitiveness – is enhanced at the very same time as the state is less able to deliver on its social-welfare commitments.[9] If the state of Bolivia is encouraged to generate legal rules that promote the transfer of water resources into private hands, at the same time it is disabled from delivering on substantial social commitments regarding access to those same resources. In the course of this chapter, we will have identified the outlines of a regime which both contributes to global governance and that institutionalises constitution-like disciplines on state actors in regard to economic subjects – those contestable matters that traditionally are the business of state policy.

The transnational regime

The protection of foreign investment long was an issue of controversy between the countries of the North and South. For a stretch of time through the twentieth century, the less developed and developing world insisted on control over the admission and activity of foreign investment. The countries of the South now appear to have yielded their position, succumbing to the imperatives of contemporary economic life.

A transnational legal framework for the protection of foreign investment has come clearly into view. This interlocking network of rules for the protection and liberalisation of Foreign Direct Investment (FDI) can be found in bilateral investment treaties (BITs), regional trade agreements such as NAFTA and the European Energy Charter Treaty, and at the multilateral level in the Agreement on Trade-Related Investment Measures (TRIMs).[10] The World Bank has issued Guidelines on the Legal Treatment of Foreign Investment,[11] a similar set of non-binding investment principles has been agreed to in APEC, while the OECD attempted, unsuccessfully, to complete a Multilateral Agreement on Investment to which other states outside of the OECD would have been invited to accede.[12] It now is proposed that the Free Trade of the Americas Agreement expand the North American Free Trade Agreement (NAFTA's) reach to include the entire Western Hemisphere (though momentum towards an agreement has been stalled).

The pace of global BIT growth has been relentless. According to the UN Commission on Trade and Development, at year end 2001 more than 2,099 BITs had been completed involving over 175 countries.[13] At the regional level, NAFTA's investment chapter and its related provisions have codified a set of protections long sought after by developed countries in the international community.

In previous work I have argued that NAFTA and the investment rules regime of which it is a part have constitution-like features.[14] The rules and institutions comprise a strategy of precommitment[15] that binds future generations to certain, predetermined institutional forms that constrain the possibilities for political practice. Like constitutions, they are difficult to amend, include binding enforcement mechanisms together with judicial review, and oftentimes are drawn from the language of domestic constitutions. Tantamount to a bill-of-rights for investors, the regime entitles investors to sue state parties for damages before international trade tribunals for violations of investment protections.

Many of the obligations undertaken in the investment rules regime are organised around the idea of 'non-discrimination'.[16] States may not distinguish, for the purposes of legal regulation, between domestic and foreign investors. According to the national treatment rule, foreign investors are to be treated as if they were economic citizens within the host state. Most-favoured nation status mandates that foreign investors receive the best treatment accorded by the host state to investors from any other state. Also connected to the principle of non-discrimination are prohibitions on performance requirements, such as rules that call for the use of local labour, goods, and services.

Other rules mandate not just equality of treatment, but place substantive limits on state control. Among these are the 'minimum standard of treatment' rule and the takings rule. The former is an omnibus standard of 'civilised' justice that includes both procedural and substantive components, possibly including a prohibition on takings.[17] It was described earlier in the century as being 'nothing more nor less than the ideas which are conceived to be essential to a continuation of the existing social and economic order of European capitalistic civilisation'.[18] The takings rule – the prohibition on expropriation and nationalisation – has been described as the 'single most important goal' of the US bilateral investment treaty programme.[19] The intention, according to Vandevelde, has been to develop a body of state practice in international law establishing high standards in regard to expropriations.[20] It should be uncontroversial to suggest that the rule is informed by US

constitutional experience under the fifth and fourteenth amend-
ments.[21] Attempts at this kind of 'transference' of municipal property
rules on to the international plane are not uncommon.[22] Lauterpacht
acknowledged many years ago that municipal legal practice 'must to a
certain extent occupy the place of a source of law' for international
practice.[23]

The takings rule typically prohibits measures that 'directly or indirectly' expropriate or nationalise investment interests and measures
that are 'tantamount to' expropriation. The classic candidate caught by
this prohibition are outright takings of title to property by the state –
the nationalisation of the forces of production under socialism, for
instance. Outright expropriations of title, however, have greatly diminished in number and pose little threat to current investment.[24] One
study recorded 83 expropriations in 1975 alone and yet only 11
between the years 1981 and 1992.[25] No doubt, these numbers continue
to decline. Rather, what is of concern here are not express takings but
what are called 'creeping' expropriations (measures that cumulatively
amount to expropriation), 'regulatory' expropriations (measures that so
impact on an investment interest that they are equivalent to a taking),
and 'partial' expropriations (measures that take only part of an investment interest).[26] Regulatory changes that 'go too far' (in the words of
Justice Oliver Wendell Holmes) are intended to be caught by this
rule.[27]

The prohibition on takings amounts to an exceptional remedy
for foreign investors. Should an investment have been subjected to
measures equivalent to expropriation, these provisions entitle foreign
investors to sue before international trade tribunals. Arbitration panels
are constituted under the auspices of international facilities (such as the
International Centre for the Settlement of Investment Disputes (ICSID)
at the World Bank in Washington), at the behest of complaining states
or investors with a protected investment interest. Panel awards then are
enforceable within the domestic courts of the offending state party. As
mentioned, these prohibitions are unique in that most international
obligations require that the state party to an agreement, rather than a
private actor, initiate mechanisms for compliance.[28]

As regards the breadth of these disciplines, the experience under
NAFTA's takings rule is instructive. Given the wide range of measures
that can be caught by the takings rule, it should come as no surprise
that firms have invoked the prohibition (or its earlier incarnation in
the Canada-US Free Trade Agreement) to challenge market regulations
that impair a variety of different investment interests. There were

reports that Ontario's proposed public auto insurance plan, and the cancellation of contracts to transfer public property into private hands (Toronto's Pearson Airport), triggered threats of litigation. Major US tobacco companies threatened to challenge Canadian federal government proposals that would have mandated the plain packaging of all cigarettes sold in Canada.[29] Though each of these cases concerned merely the threatened use of NAFTA's investor-dispute process, one reasonably can conclude that these threats played a role in circumscribing the range of social policy choices available to these governments.

Arbitral proceedings also have been launched under NAFTA. The Ethyl Corporation's challenge of a Canadian ban on the import and export of the toxic gasoline additive Methyl Cyclopentadienyl Manganese Tricarbonyl (MMT) can be the most notorious. The classification of MMT as a 'dangerous toxin,' Ethyl claimed, amounted to an expropriation under NAFTA. The Canadian federal government settled the Ethyl claim for $13 (US) million subsequent to losing an interprovincial trade dispute under a Canadian intergovernmental agreement.[30] In another dispute, United Parcel Service (UPS) is claiming $230 million in lost profits as a result of Canada Post cross-subsidising courier services with profits generated from its publicly-funded regular delivery service.[31] Recently, US tobacco producer Philip Morris has threatened to sue Canada for banning the use of the words 'light' and 'mild' on cigarette packages sold in Canada.[32] Not all disputes emanate from US firms. In a reverse-Ethyl case, Vancouver-based Methanex is suing for losses suffered by the phasing out of the gasoline additive Methyl Tertiary Butyl Ether (MTBE) in the state of California.[33]

Only a handful of dispute panel decisions under NAFTA's Chapter 11 have been rendered to date. We have learned that non-discriminatory regulations (measures that do not target foreign investors but that are facially neutral) are caught by the expropriations rule.[34] Only those measures, however, that are 'substantial enough'[35] or are 'sufficiently restrictive'[36] will give rise to a claim of expropriation – not very instructive standards of review. We also have learned, in another case, that NAFTA's rule will catch not only instances of outright seizure of property (the easiest case) but also 'incidental interference' with an investment which has the effect of depriving owners of a 'significant part' of the 'use or reasonably-to-be-expected economic benefit of property'[37] – what is a 'reasonable' expectation of economic benefit will, of course, be highly contested between investors and states. We also have learned that compensable expropriations must amount to a 'lasting deprivation of the ability of an owner to make use of its economic rights,' though the deprivation may be 'partial or temporary'.[38]

By now, the characterisation of NAFTA as 'constitutional' should not be viewed as controversial. The decision of the NAFTA panel in the *S. D. Myers* case should lay to rest any further doubt in this regard. Professor Bryan Schwartz, in a separate opinion, describes trade agreements like NAFTA as having 'an enormous impact on public affairs in many countries'.[39] Schwartz goes so far as to liken these agreements to 'a country's constitution' for they 'restrict the ways in which governments can act and they are very hard to change.' While governments usually have the right to withdraw from these agreements with proper notice, Schwartz admits that this 'is often practically impossible to do.' 'Pulling out of a trade agreement may create too much risk of reverting to trade wars, and may upset the settled expectations of many participants in the economy.' Amendment is made no easier, he writes, 'just as it is usually very hard to change a provision of a domestic constitution'.[40] The decision in *S. D. Myers*, and in other recent NAFTA disputes, confirms that the investment-protection provisions of NAFTA have the effect of prohibiting state behaviour that is considered excessive by trade tribunals: those measures that substantially impair investment interests, even if unintentionally, indirectly, and only partially.

If, in the contemporary world, the outright taking of title by the state is less likely to occur, taking problems more likely will arise in a wide variety of perhaps unanticipated settings. Consider circumstances where a foreign investor establishes an investment at the invitation of the host state, perhaps entering into an arrangement to run a former state enterprise. What is the liability of the host state when the established investment gives rise to vociferous opposition from within the host country? What capacity is there for states to change course – to make what de Tocqueville called 'repairable mistakes'?[41] More specifically, what are the linkages between local rules governing the operation of a denationalised state enterprise and transnational rules for the protection of foreign investment? These, and other questions, are taken up in the next two parts.

Local resolve

The investment rules regime mostly is silent as regards the privatisation of public enterprise.[42] Typically, obligations do not arise until an investor establishes an investment within the host state. The exception to the rule – and the new emergent standard, perhaps – is the model

US BIT. The US standard mandates non-discrimination in regard to the admission and establishment of foreign investment, in which case, investors are entitled to national treatment even before they enter the geographical space of the host state.[43] Usually, though, investment rules attach only to those foreign investments already established.

Post-privatisation, the investment rules regime constrains state capacity in some significant ways. For those states having denationalised, the process of privatisation will be difficult to undo if bound to comply with investment treaty obligations. For once having privatised, foreign investors with an interest in the privatised enterprise typically are entitled to the 'minimum standard of treatment required by international law.' In addition, investments are safeguarded from measures which so impair investment interests that they amount to a taking. There usually are no carve-outs or reservations for takings – nor can they be justified with reference to the promotion of health of the protection of the environment – they simply are beyond the realm of acceptability. Hence, there are no countervailing considerations in the case of a taking, only those that favour the protected investment: takings may only be for a public purpose, be non-discriminatory, and be accompanied by the provision of just compensation without delay that is immediately realisable and fully transferable. When states take measures that impact negatively on protected investment interests, then, they may not seek to justify those measures with reference to any other considerations.

Water privatisation increasingly has become a tool for cash-starved countries to generate much needed revenue. Multilateral financial institutions like the World Bank have fuelled privatisation initiatives by making denationalisation a condition for receiving Bank support.[44] Bolivia was one such country where the Bank actively promoted the privatisation of water and sanitation services. According to the Bank's cost assumptions, water concessions awarded in three urban centres in Bolivia could 'liberate' public funds in the order of US$13–15 million.[45]

Bolivia already had undertaken to privatise a number of state-owned enterprises.[46] But under the reported pressure from the World Bank in 1998 (the Bank then would guarantee a US$25 million loan to refinance water services),[47] the Bolivian government introduced a 'Drinking Water and Sanitation Service Provision Law' which provided a 'regulatory umbrella' for the transfer of water and sanitation services to the private sector, including co-operative wells established and operated by local indigenous populations.[48] For cities with populations over 10,000, such as Cochabamba (Bolivia's third largest), concessions would be awarded and public subsidies terminated.[49] This the Bank characterised as 'progress' for it reduced 'public subsidies for operational expenditures'.[50] The Bank called upon Bolivia to halt public subsidies that kept water prices down.

About 40 percent of Cochabamba residents are not connected to a water supply. This extreme disparity in access to water could be improved, it was believed, if water draining down the Tunari mountains was diverted and accessed through a tunnel. To this end, Cochabamba's water system was leased in June 1999 to Aguas del Tunari, a consortium of two international companies, led by International Water Ltd., a subsidiary of San Francisco-based Bechtel Enterprises, and three Bolivian companies with close links to the national ruling coalition.[51] The consortium would contribute US$52 to $60 million of its own capital while the balance of US$129 million would be raised over the 40 year life of the concession. The public sector would contribute US$70 million in order to finance the Misicuni tunnel in order to bring water through the Tunari mountains – a public investment frowned on by the World Bank.[52] The concession would guarantee to Aguas del Tunari a reported annual minimum 15 percent return on its investment.[53]

A 1999 World Bank report acknowledged that a 'sharp increase of water tariffs of an average of 38 percent at the beginning of the project and another 20 percent once the project is fully operational, necessary to attain the negotiated 16 percent rate of return on equity, will not be easy to implement and political pressures will be exerted for the Government to provide public subsidies'[54] Yet that pressure would have to be resisted, the Bank insisted.[55] The Government agreed: there would be no further public subsidy beyond the cost of the tunnel. Users would be expected to 'pay in full' for services.

Water rates almost doubled. According to Schultz, in a city where the minimum wage is less than US$100 per month, many families saw their bills rise by US$20, others saw them quadruple.[56] A 35 percent rise in rates was typical[57] – some families had their water bills total one quarter of their monthly income.[58] All of this was occurring even before any appreciable improvement in services.[59] According to International Water Ltd. executive, Geoffrey Thorpe, if people failed to pay, water services would be terminated.[60]

The citizens of Cochabamba took to the streets in protest from mid-January and April 2000.[61] A general strike shut down the city for four straight days. The government of Bolivia agreed to a price roll back with local leaders but subsequently responded by sending in 1,000 police and military troops to occupy the city for two days in early February. Tear gas and rubber bullets held citizens at bay; local leadership were arrested. More than 175 protestors were injured, while two youths, it is reported, were blinded. Following the declaration of a national state of siege by President Hugo Banzer in April 2000, one 17 year-old youth, Victor Hugo Daza, was killed while walking home from a part-time job.[62]

Though the government of Bolivia actively had promoted the privatisation plan, it now had lost control of the situation. In the midst of this civil turmoil, Aguas del Tunari executives were advised by police that their safety could no longer be guaranteed, and so the company fled Cochabamba.[63] As the company had abandoned the concession, the government of Bolivia declared the contract revoked. To the delight of civil society forces mobilised in opposition to the privatisation scheme, the municipality retook control of the water utility. The company disputes that it abandoned the concession, rather, it argues that it was pushed out by civilian and government agitation.

International Water Ltd., a lead member of the consortium and a Bechtel subsidiary, originally was incorporated in the Cayman Islands. Shortly after the water concession in Bolivia was secured, International Water incorporated under the laws of the Netherlands.[64] A 1992 Netherlands-Bolivia BIT conveniently could protect the International Water's investment.[65] The company filed its dispute with the ICSID at the World Bank in February 2002.[66] Though these proceedings remain secret, the company reportedly is seeking compensation for the expropriation of its investment in the amount of US$25 million.[67] 'We expect to get our money,' advises Michael Curtin, IWL consultant and President of Aguas del Tunari.[68]

Local rules/transnational restraints

The consortium aims to supplant local law by seeking refuge under the investment rules regime for the protection of foreign investors. In this way, investment protections aim to supersede national rules and grant preferred status to foreign investors over most other considerations. In this part, I review the conflict between the local and the transnational not to resolve definitively this legal dispute but to identify the disciplinary effects of this regime for global governance on local rules.[69]

If the dispute were to be determined by local rules, the result under Bolivian constitutional law might very well be different than under the

BIT. The Bolivian constitution protects private property, to be sure, but this fundamental right is subject to the proviso that 'it fulfils a social function' (Art. 7). Private property is guaranteed, in other words, provided that its use 'is not prejudicial to the collective interest.' Expropriation of private property also is permitted under the constitution. Takings must be for 'reasons of public benefit or when property does not fulfil a social purpose' so long as it is 'authorised by law and [accompanied] with just compensation' (Art. 22).

The Bolivian constitutional provisions concerning property are patterned on the legal thought of late nineteenth and early twentieth century progressives. Latin American constitutional clauses of this sort – that declare the institution of property is to serve social functions – usually are traceable to the influence of French legal theorist Léon Duguit.[70] For Duguit, public authority was justified to the extent that the state served certain social needs. Similarly, private property was justifiable to the extent that it served a social mission – it could be limited to the extent that it did not.[71] The rights of private property, according to this account, no longer could be considered in isolation from the society out of which they are constituted. Limitations on property rights are to be expected, then, in order to further societal goals – particularly those goals expressed in foundational constitutional text.

Bolivian constitutional law not only declares that property serves social functions, it makes it the duty of the state to protect the 'national patrimony.' Natural resources, including lakes, rivers and thermal waters, are declared under the constitution to be the 'original domain of the State' (Art. 136). Private 'economic power' is declared to be subject to public authority (Art. 135) while the private concentration of economic power is not permitted if it 'endanger[s] the economic independence of the state' (Art. 134). Yet the constitution also permits the state to take measures for the 'concession and allotment to private individuals' of national property, in other words, for privatisation (Art. 136). Concessions for public services, however, are 'exceptionally made' and 'may not be granted for a period of more than 40 years' (the length of the Aguas del Tunari concession) (Art. 135).

In addition to maintaining the capacity of the state to meddle significantly with property rights, the state undertakes other constitutional obligations that fall under the rubric of social obligations. Labour is declared to be 'a duty and a right' which constitutes 'the basis of the economic and social order' (Art. 156). The state undertakes to create conditions 'which will guarantee employment, stability of work, and fair remuneration to all' (Art. 157). The Bolivian state also 'has the obligation to defend human capital by protecting the health of the population' and to 'strive for the improvement of the living conditions for the family as a group' (Art. 158).

This latter constitutional commitment complements well international obligations regarding access to vital resources such as water. The right to health in the International Covenant on Social and Cultural Rights (Art. 12) has been interpreted by the Committee on Social and Cultural Rights to extend not only to 'timely and appropriate health care but also to the underlying determinants of health, such as access to safe and potable water and adequate sanitation...'[72] Bolivia, together with other State signatories, are expected to refrain from taking measures which interfere with enjoyment of the right to water and to adopt the necessary measures directed towards the full realisation of that right.

Recall that the Bolivian constitution permits the state to take private property provided it is done according to law and with the provision of just compensation. Compensation usually is determined according to independent expert appraisal together with judicial oversight.[73] The Bolivian takings rule, however, should be read together with other constitutional obligations that condemn private monopolies, entrust natural public resources to the state, and commit the state to protecting the social health of the populace.

Does the cancellation of the Aguas del Tunari concession contract amount to a compensable taking under Bolivian constitutional law? It likely does not.[74] Even if this did amount to a constitutionally-proscribed taking, the fact that Aguas del Tunari held the investment for a short time and increased water rates so that this scarce commodity was available only to wealthy segments of society, that water and other thermal resources are considered part of the national patrimony, and that Bolivia (the poorest country in Latin America) has little ability to pay a large compensation award, could be taken into account in determining the amount of compensation due.[75]

Under the Netherlands-Bolivia bilateral investment treaty, however, a different result may ensue. The takings rule is expansive – it refers to deprivations rather than merely to expropriations and nationalisations.[76] Measures 'depriving, directly or indirectly' Dutch investors of their investment interests are not permissible under any circumstances unless non-discriminatory, in the public interest, done with due process of law and accompanied by the payment of just compensation, without delay, freely transferable and in Dutch currency (Art. 6).[77] No other criteria will influence a determination of whether a compensable taking has occurred and the amount of compensation owed. As noted in a recent dispute panel ruling established under ICSID auspices, 'no matter how laudable and beneficial to society as a whole [the measure may be] ... the state's obligation to pay compensation [for expropriatory measures] remains'.[78]

Does the premature cancellation of a concession contract, and the return of property to the national state, trigger this obligation to pay full compensation under the BIT? Friedman maintains that a breach of contractual obligation between a state and foreign investor generally does not give rise to an expropriation under international law.[79] Instead, some form of remedy is expected to be available under the national law of the host state, and so access to local courts is encouraged. White holds the opposite view, that a compensable taking occurs wherever there is premature cancellation of a contract by the nationalising state or where there is indirect termination such that the 'concessionaire's rights have been virtually destroyed through governmental interference'.[80] Similarly, both Brownlie[81] and Higgins[82] argue that cancellation of a contract triggers the compensation requirement. Recent arbitral rulings under NAFTA (discussed in Part I) confirm that any 'lasting deprivation of ... economic rights,'[83] gives rise to the requirement of compensation. Contemporary investment treaty practice is summarised neatly by Sacerdoti: '[a]ll rights and interests having an economic content come into play' under the investment rules regime.[84]

The definition of 'investment' in the Netherlands-Bolivia BIT mirrors contemporary investment treaty practice. Investments comprise 'every kind of asset' and, more particularly, 'rights granted under public law, including rights to prospect, explore, extract and exploit natural resources' (Art. 1.a).[85] This comprehensive definition typically covers concession contracts and similar kinds of interests.[86]

Aguas del Tunari likely will argue that Bolivia also is in breach of other provisions of the Netherlands-Bolivia BIT that give rise to the duty of compensation. These could include the claim that the company was denied 'fair and equitable treatment' and 'full security and protection' of its investment by Bolivia (Art. 3).[87] By failing to quell the local uprising and neglecting to guarantee the personal security of company management, Aguas del Tunari might argue, the value of its investment was lost. If successful in this argument, the investment rules regime would provide warrant for even more brutal responses to local resistance against the effects of economic globalisation.[88]

Should the Netherlands-Bolivia BIT give rise to a compensable event, the compensation provisions are stringent. Compensation is expected to be 'prompt, adequate and effective,' based on the genuine value of the investment payable from the date of the expropriation, without delay, 'effectively realisable and immediately transferable.' This is akin to the US BIT standard, long argued to be the standard mandated by international law. No other considerations may be factored in, only the financial loss to the investor.

The investment rules regime signals, then, that the strictest standards will apply in determining when compensation is due and the amount of compensation that is required to be paid. The logic of economic rationality framed in constitution-like terms limits political action in regard to economic subjects. Politics, in other words, are rendered subservient to the market, even in regard to such matters as access to water and the promotion of public health.

Recent ICSID jurisprudence suggests that transnational strictures can be bypassed, at least temporarily. By invoking appropriate treaty language, governments can limit remedies available under contract by having these disputes resolved in local courts even though a BIT may also be in place governing investor-state relations. In a case concerning the privatisation of water and sewer services in the Argentinean province of Tucumán, a French company sought damages of US$300 million under an Argentine-French BIT.[89] After the price for services rose dramatically (as they did in Cochabamba), citizens across the Argentinean province organised a payment boycott, forcing the operator to give up its concession.[90] The concession contract required that 'interpretation and application' of the contract be submitted to the 'exclusive jurisdiction of the Contentious Administrative Tribunals of Tucumán.' According to the ICSID panel convened to hear the claim, as the contract made no reference to the BIT signed three years earlier, the company was expected first to seek a remedy before Tucumán courts. Only if the company was 'denied access to the courts' or if 'the judgement of those courts were substantively unfair' or there otherwise was a denial of 'rights guaranteed to French investors under the BIT,' could the company then seek relief under the BIT.[91] A different result, however, was reached in an ICSID ruling issued two years earlier concerning a concession contract for the operation of port terminals in Buenos Aires. Though the contract required that, for all purposes, the parties submit themselves to the jurisdiction of the federal tribunals of Buenos Aires, the company also could seek a remedy under an Argentina-US BIT which entered into force five months after the date of the concession contract. The BIT amounted to a 'generic invitation to all the investors who are nationals of the other Contracting State to submit the settlement of their possible disputes to ICSID jurisdiction.'[92] This invitation superseded any earlier commitment to submit disputes only to local courts.

The Aguas del Tunari contract appears to resolve the jurisdictional question in favour of the company. Though the concessionaire recognises the laws and courts of Bolivia, Article 41 stipulates that the contract does not amount to a renunciation of mechanisms for the resolution of controversies established under international treaty and recognised by the law of Bolivia. Furthermore, the Parties expressly accept the jurisdiction of ICSID and other dispute resolution bodies.[93]

Reports are that the Republic of Bolivia intends to challenge the jurisdiction of the ICSID to hear Aguas del Tunari's claim on the basis that the company has no relationship to the Netherlands[94] and that when the Dutch company took control of Aguas del Tunari this was done in a manner contrary to the terms of the concession contract.[95] Bolivia also likely will rely on the 'unforeseen impossibility' (or *force majeure*) clause[96] in the concession contract which suspends obligations under contract in the event that it is impossible to carry out by reason of acts of God, natural disasters, or even public protests for social, political or environmental reasons.[97] The government is relieved of having to perform obligations (as long as events giving rise to impossibility of performance are not the fault of government) but only for so long as the reasons for suspension persist.[98] It is expected, then, that the company will resume operations once the conditions giving rise to impossibility are removed. The contract stipulates that 'under no circumstances' does an unforeseen event 'imply the release of the Parties from an obligation to pay the other party.'[99] Whether the formal requirements of the clause have been satisfied and whether these events provide grounds for termination of the contract will be matters of critical importance to the Bolivian side of the case.

It is difficult, however, to predict the outcome of the legal dispute between Aguas del Tunari and the Republic of Bolivia. After all, it concerns controverted facts, Bolivian constitutional law, the concession contract, and international economic law. Moreover, the proceedings remain confidential. Rather than resolving these legal claims, the point here has been to underscore the ways in which the regime of rules governing the treatment of foreign investment will have the effect of disciplining state actors in directions which may be at odds with national commitments expressly made in constitutional text. It is at this point that the governance of foreign investment, which entitles non-state actors to overtake state constitutional norms, cuts closest to the bone of national sovereignty and sacrifices all on the altar of economic liberalism.

Conclusion

The object of this chapter has been to explore the parameters of the new global regime for the governance of investment disputes. This regime, I argue, has constitution-like features and effects. As a precommitment strategy, it disables state actors from intervening in markets in order to make the world safe for foreign investment. Investors themselves have standing to enforce these commitments before international trade panels. The scope of investment protection treaties together with mechanisms for dispute settlement ensures that foreign investors are accorded the highest possible protections. All policy objectives, including constitutional ones, are rendered subservient to the goal of promoting and protecting foreign investment.

The dispute over a contract to privatise water delivery in Cochabamba, Bolivia helps to make material this regime of global governance. Though the legal controversy has yet to be resolved conclusively by an international dispute panel, the outlines of the conflict suggest that the aims and objectives of the investment rules regime is at odds with national commitments to ensure that property serves social functions, that vital natural resources are protected, and that the health and welfare of citizens is secured. The binding effect of the regime is to make it almost impossible for a contracting state to change its mind – denying the ability of democratic states to make reversible mistakes. Though the dispute concerns a consortium (with no tangible connection to the Netherlands), suing under a Bolivia-Netherlands investment treaty, the world-wide web of BITs ensures that the disciplinary strictures of the investment rules regime will have global effects. Citizens, however, are nowhere factored into the equation. Their role is limited to acquiescing to the spread of market rationality all over the world in the hope that they can rise to the level of the market's beneficiaries, in short, to be consumers in the new world order.

Notes

1. Faculty of Law, University of Toronto (david.schneiderman@utoronto.ca). Many thanks to Dr. Jorge Asbun who provided advice on constitutional matters in Bolivia, Melissa MacLean who shared her work on the water

wars, Moira Gracey who translated key texts from Spanish into English, and Kajal Kahana who provided last minute research assistance.

2. J. N. Rosenau, 'Governance, Order, and Change in World Politics', in J. N. Rosenau and E-O. Czempiel (eds), *Governance Without Government: Order and Change in World Politics* (Cambridge: Cambridge University Press, 1992) pp. 1–29.
3. O. R. Young, *Governance in World Affairs* (Ithaca and London: Cornell University Press, 1999).
4. S. Strange, *The Retreat of the State: The Diffusion of Power in the World Economy* (Cambridge: Cambridge University Press, 1996).
5. S. Gill, 'Globalisation, Market Civilisation, and Disciplinary Neoliberalism', *Millennium: Journal of International Studies*, XXIV (1995) 399–423.
6. M. Hardt and A. Negri, *Empire* (Cambridge, MA: Harvard University Press, 2000) p. 9.
7. J. G. Ruggie, *Constructing the World Polity: Essays on International Institutionalization* (London and New York: Routledge, 1998).
8. K. Polanyi, *The Great Transformation* (Boston: Beacon Press, 1957).
9. P. G. Cerny, 'Globalization and the Changing Logic of Collective Action' in C. Lipson and B. J. Cohen (eds), *Theory, Structure in International Political Economy* (Cambridge: The MIT Press, 1999) pp. 111–41 at 136.
10. A. A. Fatouros, 'Towards an International Agreement on Foreign Direct Investment?' in OECD Documents, *Towards Multilateral Investment Rules* (Paris: OECD, 1996) 47–67.
11. I. F. I. Shihata, *Legal Treatment of Foreign Investment: The World Bank Guidelines* (Dordrecht: Martinus Nijhoff Publishers, 1993).
12. D. Schneiderman, 'The Constitutional Strictures of the Multilateral Agreement on Investment', *The Good Society*, IX, 2 (1999) 90–95.
13. UN Conference on Trade and Development, *Bilateral Investment Treaties, 1959–1999* (New York and London: United Nations) pp. 1, 4. Germany leads the pack, having negotiated 124 BITs, Switzerland (95), France and the United Kingdom (92), China (94), Romania (90) and Egypt (84), follow closely behind. The United States falls in the top 30 countries, with 43 BITs concluded as of 1 January 2000 (UNCTAD (2000) 17).
14. D. Schneiderman, 'NAFTA's Takings Rule: American Constitutionalism Comes to Canada', *University of Toronto Law Journal*, XLVI (1996) 499; D. Schneiderman, 'The Constitutional Strictures of the Multilateral Agreement on Investment' (1999) 90–95; D. Schneiderman, 'Investment Rules and the New Constitutionalism', *Law and Social Inquiry*, XXV (2000) 757.
15. J. Elster, *Ulysses Unbound* (Cambridge: Cambridge University Press, 2000).
16. J. H. Jackson, *The World Trading System: Law and Policy of International Economic Relations*, 2nd edn (Cambridge: The MIT Press, 1997).
17. E. Borchard, 'The "Minimum Standard" of the Treatment of Aliens', *Proceedings of the American Society of International Law*, XXXIII (1939) 51–63; A. H. Roth, *The Minimum Standard of International Law Applied to Aliens* (Leiden: A. W. Sijthoff's Uitgeversmaatschappij, 1949).
18. F. S. Dunn, 'International Law and Private Property Rights', *Columbia Law Review*, XXVIII (1928) 175.
19. K. J. Vandevelde, 'The BIT Program: A Fifteen-Year Appraisal' (1–4 April 1992) 534; K. J. Vandevelde, 'The Political Economy of a Bilateral

Investment Treaty', *The American Journal of International Law*, XCII (1998) 621–641.

20. K. J. Vandevelde, 'The BIT Program: A Fifteen-Year Appraisal' (1–4 April 1992) 25.
21. P. Wild Jr., 'International Law and Mexican Oil', *Quarterly Journal of Inter-American Relations*, I, 9 (1939) 10; R. R. Wilson, 'Property-Protection Provisions in United States Commercial Treaties', *American Journal of International Law*, XLV (1951) 85.
22. M. Sornarajah, *The International Law on Foreign Investment* (Cambridge: Cambridge University Press, 1994) p. 294.
23. H. Lauterpacht, 'Decisions of Municipal Courts as a Source of International Law', *British Yearbook of International Law*, 10 (1929) 89.
24. L. F. Powers, 'New Forms of Protection for International Infrastructure Investors', in T. H. Moran (ed.), *Managing International Political Risk* (Oxford, UK: Blackwell, 1998) p. 128.
25. L. Wells Jr., 'God and Fair Competition: Does the Foreign Direct Investor Face Still Other Risks in Emerging Markets', in T. H. Moran (ed.), *Managing International Political Risk* (Oxford, UK: Blackwell, 1998), pp. 15–43.
26. K. J. Vandevelde, 'The BIT Program: A Fifteen-Year Appraisal' (1–4 April 1992) 121.
25. *Pennsylvania Coal* v. *Mahon*, 438 US 393 at 1569 (1922).
28. A. H. Roth, *The Minimum Standard of International Law Applied to Aliens* (Leiden: A. W. Sijthoff's Uitgeversmaatschappij, 1949), p. 62.
28. D. Schneiderman, 'NAFTA's Takings Rule: American Constitutionalism Comes to Canada' (1996) 499.
30. D. Schneiderman, 'MMT Promises: How the Ethyl Corporation Beat the Federal Ban', *Encompass Magazine*, III, 3 (February 1999) 12–13.
31. I. Jack, 'UPS Suing Ottawa for $230M', *The National Post* (22 April 1999). A NAFTA panel ruling has shrunk the scope of the UPS claim, however. See S. Chase, 'Tribunal Cuts Suit Against Canada' *The Globe and Mail* (23 November 2002) B3.
32. S. Chase, 'Tobacco Firm Warns "Mild" Cigarette Ban May Violate NAFTA', *The Globe and Mail* (16 March 2002).
33. H. Scoffield, 'Methanex Set to Sue Uncle Sam under NAFTA over Gas Additive', *The Globe and Mail* (3 November 1999).
34. *Pope and Talbot Inc. and Government of Canada* (2001) Interim Award (26 June 2000) World Trade and Arbitration Materials 13: 19–59, para. 96.
35. *Ibid.*
36. *Ibid.*, para. 102.
37. *Metalclad Corp.* v. *United Mexican States* (2001) 40 International Legal Materials 36, para. 103.
38. *S. D. Myers, Inc.* v. *Government of Canada*, (2001). International Legal Materials 40: 1408, para. 283.
39. *Ibid.*, para. 34.
40. *Ibid.*
41. A. de Tocqueville, *Democracy in America* (Chicago: Chicago University Press, 2000), p. 232 (translated by H. C. Mansfield and D. Winthrop).
42. D. Schneiderman, 'Constitutional Approaches to Privatisation: An Inquiry into the Magnitude of Neo-Liberal Constitutionalism', *Law and Contemporary Problems*, LXIII (2000) 83–109.

43. This is the standard in the US-Bolivia BIT of 1998 (Art. II).
44. See V. Shiva, *Water Wars: Privatization, Pollution and Profit* (Toronto: Between the Lines, 2002); M. Barlow and T. Clarke, *Blue Gold: The Battle Against Corporate Theft of the World's Water* (Toronto: Stoddart, 2002).
45. World Bank, *Bolivia: Public Expenditure Review*, Report No. 19232-BO (Geneva: World Bank, 14 June 1999), p. 156.
46. P. Guislain, *The Privatisation Challenge: A Strategic, Legal, and Institutional Analysis of the International Experience* (Washington: The World Bank, 1997), p. 125.
47. G. Yaron, *The Final Frontier: A Working Paper on the Big 10 Global Water Corporations and the Privatisation and Corporatisation of the World's Last Public Resource* (Ottawa: Polaris Institute and the Council of Canadians, 15 March 2000), p. 69, online: www.canadians.org/bluepl.pdf (accessed 9 April 2001).
48. W. Finnegan, 'Letter from Bolivia: Leasing the Rain', *The New Yorker* (8 April 2002) 45.
49. World Bank, *Bolivia: Public Expenditure Review* (14 June 1999), p. 141.
50. *Ibid.*, 146.
51. M. MacLean, 'Beyond the Limits of State-Led Political Reform: Neoliberal Democracy and the Conflict over Water Privatisation in Cochabamba, Bolivia', paper presented to the Canadian Political Science Association Conference (31 May 2002) 12, 16; E. Lobina, 'Cochabamba: Water War', Public Service International Research Unit (June 2000) 4 at www.psiru.org (accessed January 31, 2003).
52. World Bank, *Bolivia: Public Expenditure Review* (14 June 1999), p. 152.
53. W. Finnegan, 'Letter from Bolivia' (8 April 2002) 45.
54. World Bank, *Bolivia: Public Expenditure Review* (14 June 1999), p. 152. Troubled by the amount of public subsidy in this project, the Bank reports that an alternative project 'could have provided a less costly and fully private financed alternative'.
55. *Ibid.*
56. J. Schultz, 'In the Andes – Echoes of Seattle' (23 March 2000), online: www.democracyctr.org/onlinesnews/water.html (accessed 9 April 2001).
57. J. Schultz, 'Bolivian Protestors Win War Over Water' (7 April 2000), online: www.democracyctr.org/onlinesnews/water.html (accessed 9 April 2001).
58. W. Finnegan, 'Letter from Bolivia' (8 April 2002) 43–53.
59. M. MacLean, 'Beyond the Limits of State-Led Political Reform: Neoliberal Democracy and the Conflict over Water Privatisation in Cochabamba, Bolivia', paper presented to the Canadian Political Science Association Conference (31 May 2002) 13.
60. W. Finnegan, 'Letter from Bolivia' (8 April 2002) 47.
61. In addition to the sources mentioned above, the conflict is described in some detail in Entrevista de Ana Esther Ceceña con Gabriel Herbas, 'La Guerra del agua en Cochobamba', *Chiapas*, 14 (2002) 97–114.
62. W. Finnegan, 'Letter from Bolivia' (8 April 2002) 47.
63. W. Finnegan, 'Letter from Bolivia' (8 April 2002) 51.
64. L. Dolinsky, 'Notes From Here and There', *The San Francisco Chronicle* (11 February 2001), online: http://ptg.djnr.com/ccroot/asp/publib/story.asp (accessed 12 April 2001); Finnegan 2002, 52.
65. In International Centre for Settlement of Investment Disputes, *Investment Treaties*, Vol. 4 (Dobbs Ferry, NY: Oceana Publications, Inc., 1993).

66. *Aguas del Tunari S. A.* v. *Republic of Bolivia*, Case No. Arb/02/03 at www.world-bank.org/icsid/cases/pending.htm (last accessed 2 February 2003).
67. D. Zoll, 'Soaking the Poor', *San Francisco Bay Chronicle* (13 December 2000), online: www.sfbg.com/News/35/11/11becht.html (accessed 9 April 2001).
68. L. Dolinsky, 'Notes From Here and There', *The San Francisco Chronicle* (11 February 2001), online: http://ptg.djnr.com/ccroot/asp/publib/story.asp (accessed 12 April 2001).
69. I should emphasise that I do not purport to offer a legal opinion about Bolivian constitutional law or the likelihood of success of either party in the international trade dispute. As an expert in Canadian constitutional law, this would be a difficult thing to do. Rather, my intention is a more modest one: to outline the parameters of a conflict between local and transnational rules.
70. C. F. Trigo, *Derecho Constitucional Bolviano* (La Paz: Editorial Cruz del Sur, 1952) 414–15.
71. L. Duguit, *Manuel de droit constitutionnel*, 3e. edn (Paris: Ancienne Librarie Fontemoing and Cie, Éditeurs, 1918) 295.
72. General Comment No. 14. The Committee expanded on this reading of the right to health in its General Comment No. 15 to include not only the right to 'timely and appropriate health care but also to the underlying determinants of health, such as access to safe and potable water and adequate sanitation, an adequate supply of safe food, nutrition and housing, healthy occupational and environmental conditions, and access to health-related education and information.'
73. C. W. Urquidi, *A Statement of the Laws of Bolivia in Matters Affecting Business*, 4th edn (Washington: OAS, 1974), pp. 298–99.
74. This is the opinion of Dr. Jorge Asbun, a lawyer in Cochabamba, Bolivia, in a communication dated 29 July 2002.
75. Dr. Asbun advises, however, that Bolivian courts consider nothing else but the 'objective' value of the good expropriated, as if it were a 'forced sale' (*vendiera forzosamente*). Communication dated 29 July 2002.
76. See R. Dolzer and M. Stevens, *Bilateral Investment Treaties* (The Hague: Martinus Nijhoff Publishers, 1995), at 98.
77. Bolivia/Netherlands Bilateral Treaty (10 March 1992) in International Centre for Settlement of Investment Disputes, *Investment Treaties*, Vol. 4 (Dobbs Ferry, NY: Oceana Publications, Inc., 1993).
78. *Compania del Desarrollo de Santa Elena and the Republic of Costa Rica*, Final Award, ICSID Case No. ARB/96/1 (17 February 2000), para. 72.
79. S. Friedman, *Expropriation in International Law* (London: Stevens and Sons Ltd, 1953), p. 153–57.
80. G. White, *The Nationalisation of Foreign Property* (London: Stevens and Sons Limited, 1961), p. 166.
81. I. Brownlie, 'International Law at the Fiftieth Anniversary of the United Nations: General Course on Public International Law', *Recueil des cours*, CCLV (The Hague: Martinus Nijhoff, 1995) 143.
82. R. Higgins, 'The Taking of Property by the State: Recent Developments in International Law', *Recueil des Cours*, CLXXI (1982) 340.
83. *S. D. Myers, Inc.* v. *Government of Canada*, International Legal Materials 40 (2001), 1408, para. 283.

84. G. Sacerdoti, 'Bilateral Treaties and Multilateral Instruments on Investment Protection', *Recueil des Cours*, Vol. 269 (1997) 251–460 at 381.
85. Bolivia/Netherlands Bilateral Treaty (10 March 1992) in International Centre for Settlement of Investment Disputes, *Investment Treaties*, Vol. 4 (Dobbs Ferry, NY: Oceana Publications, Inc., 1993).
86. R. Dolzer and M. Stevens, *Bilateral Investment Treaties* (The Hague: Martinus Nijhoff Publishers, 1995), at 30.
87. Bolivia/Netherlands Bilateral Treaty (10 March 1992) in International Centre for Settlement of Investment Disputes, *Investment Treaties*, Vol. 4 (Dobbs Ferry, NY: Oceana Publications, Inc., 1993).
88. Which already is the case elsewhere in the world. See A. Roy, 'The Greater Common Good' in *The Cost of Living* (New York: The Modern Library, 1999), p. 1 at 9.
89. *Compañía de Aguas del Aconquija* v. *Argentina*, 40 International Legal Materials 426 (2001).
90. Reports are that price of services rose by 104 percent once the Argentinean affiliate took over operations. See N. Giarracca, 'The Social Protest for Water in Tucuman, Argentina', at www.nadir.org/nadir/initiative/agp/free/imf/argentina/txt/tucuman/social_protest.htm (accessed January 31, 2003).
91. *Ibid.* at 443.
92. *Lanco International* v. *Argentina* 40 International Legal Materials 456 (2001), at 471.
93. 'Las estipulaciones del presente Contrato no podrán interpretarse como renuncia por parte de los Accionistas, los Assionistas Fundadores, incluyendo los Accionistas Ultimos, a mecanismos de Resolución de controversias establecidos en tratados internacionales reconocidos por la República de Bolivia' (Art. 41.3); 'Las Partes reconocen que dichos Accionistas y Accionistas Ultimos del Concessionario incluyendo los Accionistas Fundadores son libres para ampararse en aquellos métodos de resolución de disputas que puedan serles legalemente disponibles de acuerdo a la Ley Boliviana (como por ejemplo arbitraje bajo las reglas de CCI, ICSID, o UNCITRAL y otros organismos internacionales similares). Las Partes acuerdan cooperar en el proceso arriba mencionado, en la medida que les sea permitido por Ley' (Art. 41.5).
94. See www.aguabolivia.org/prensaX/Prensa/2002/Diciembre... (11 December 2002) (accessed 2 February 2003).
95. The argument is detailed in R. Bustamante, 'Apuntes Juridicos Sobre El Cal "Agua Del Tunrai"' at http://cgiac.org/analisisX/CONFLICTOS/Aguatunari.htm (accessed 19 June 2002). Bustamante argues that the transaction by which share control was handed over to the Netherlands company was contrary to the concession contract. The contract called for prior approval of the Superintendent – the transaction only was approved afterwords.
96. J. Langman, 'Bechtel Battles Against Dirt-Poor Bolivia', *San Francisco Chronicle* (2 February 2002) available at www.sfgate.com/cgi-bin/article.cgi?file=/chronicle/archive/2002/02/02/MN14536.D (accessed 31 January 2003). On force majeure, see A. Mouri, *The International Law of Expropriation as Reflected in the Work of the Iran-US Claims Tribunal* (Dordrecht: Martinus Nijhoff Publshers, 1994), 229 ff.
97. 'Se entiende Imposibilidad Sobreviniente, un evento de caso fortuito o de fuerza mayor, una acción de las fuerzas de la naturaleza quedando

comprendidas tambien les roturas y/o fallas gràves imprevisibles e ìntempestivas de instalaciones y equipos pertenecientes al Concesionario, cualquier problema en el Túnel Principal que impida la continuidad en su funcionamiento o cualquier otro evento, acciòn o inacciòn de un tereeo, incluyendo protestas públicas por razones ambiéntales, sociales o politicas' (Art. 42.3) [The term Unforeseen Impossibility means an accidental event or one of great force, and action of natural forces understood also to include unforeseeable and untimely breaking and/or grave faults in the plants and equipment belonging to the Concessionaire, any problem in the Principal Tunnel that prevents continuation of its functioning or any other event, action, or inaction of third parties, including public protests for social, political or environmental reasons.]

98. En caso de acaecer hechos de Imposibilidad Sobreveniente, los derechos y las obligaciones que surjan del contrato y que sean afectados por dichos hechos, seran suspendidos mientras duren dichas causales de conformidad con law clausula 42.6 y 42.7. El Concesionario debera notificar con law mayor brevedad possible, las causales de Imposibilidad Sobreveniente al la Superintendencia de Aguas una vez qduiera conciomiento del hecho e informar por escrito el hecho, seqalando los plazos y las medidas que se tomaran para superado, en la medida de lo possible (Art. 42.1). [In the case of events of unforeseen impossiblity, the rights and obligations that arise out of this contract and which are affected by said events, will be suspended as long as such reasons persist in accordance with clause 42.6 and 42.7. The Concessionaire must notify the Water Superintendency as soon as possible after becoming aware of the reasons, and provide written information of the event, indicating the timelines and measures that will be taken to overcome it, insofar as is possible.] 'Mientras dure el hecho catalogado de Imposibilidad Sobreveniente en la Clausula 42.3, las Partes estan exentas de cualquier responsbilidad por la demora o incumplimiento de sus obligaciones' (42.6). [While the fact categorised as an Unforeseen Impossibility under Clause 42.3 lasts, the Parties will be exempt from any and all responsibility for delay or failure to perform their obligations.]

99. 'Un evento de Imposibilidad Sobreviniente bajo ninguna circunstancia, implicará la liberación de las Partes de una obligación de pago a la otra parte' (Art. 42.8). [An event of Unforeseen Impossibility under no circumstances will imply the release of the Parties from an obligation to pay the other party.]

References

Barlow, M. and T. Clarke, *Blue Gold: The Battle Against Corporate Theft of the World's Water* (Toronto: Stoddart, 2002).

Borchard, E. 'The 'Minimum Standard' of the Treatment of Aliens', *Proceedings of the American Society of International Law*, XXXIII (1939) 51–63.

Brownlie, I. 'International Law at the Fiftieth Anniversary of the United Nations: General Course on Public International Law', *Recueil des cours*, CCLV (The Hague: Martinus Nijhoff, 1995) 9–228.

Bustamante, R. 'Apuntes Juridicos Sobre El Cal "Agua Del Tunrai"' at http://cgiac.org/analisisX/CONFLICTOS/Aguatunari.htm (accessed 19 June 2002).

Cerny, P. G. 'Globalization and the Changing Logic of Collective Action' in C. Lipson and B.J. Cohen (eds), *Theory, Structure in International Political Economy* (Cambridge: The MIT Press, 1999) pp. 111–41.

Chase, S. 'Tobacco Firm Warns "Mild" Cigarette Ban May Violate NAFTA', *The Globe and Mail* (16 March 2002).

—— 'Tribunal Cuts Suit Against Canada', *The Globe and Mail* (23 November 2002) B3.

Compania del Desarrollo de Santa Elena and Costa Rica, Final Award, ICSID Case No. ARB/96/1 (17 February 2000).

Czempiel, E-O. 'Governance and Democratization ', in J. N. Rosenau and E-O. Czempiel (eds), *Governance Without Government: Order and Change in World Politics* (Cambridge: Cambridge University Press, 1992), pp. 250–271.

de Tocqueville, A. *Democracy in America* (Chicago: Chicago University Press, 2000), translated by H. C. Mansfield and D. Winthrop.

Dolinsky, L. 'Notes From Here and There', *The San Francisco Chronicle* (11 February 2001), online: http://ptg.djnr.com/ccroot/asp/publib/story.asp (accessed 12 April 2001).

Dolzer, R. and M. Stevens, *Bilateral Investment Treaties* (The Hague: Martinus Nijhoff Publishers, 1995).

Duguit, L. *Manuel de droit constitutionnel*, 3rd edn (Paris: Ancienne Librarie Fontemoing and Cie, Éditeurs, 1918).

Dunn, F. S. 'International Law and Private Property Rights', *Columbia Law Review*, XXVIII (1928) 166–180.

Elster, J. *Ulysses Unbound* (Cambridge: Cambridge University Press, 2000).

Entrevista de Ana Esther Ceceña con Gabriel Herbas. 'La Guerra del agua en Cochobamba', *Chiapas* 14 (2002) 97–114.

Fatouros, A.A. 'Towards an International Agreement on Foreign Direct Investment?' in OECD Documents, *Towards Multilateral Investment Rules* (Paris: OECD, 1996) 47–67.

Finnegan, W. 'Letter from Bolivia: Leasing the Rain', *The New Yorker* (8 April 2002) 43–53.

Friedman, S. *Expropriation in International Law* (London: Stevens and Sons Ltd, 1953).

Giarracca, N. 'The Social Protest for Water in Tucuman, Argentina' at www.nadir.org/nadir/initiative/agp/free/imf/argentina/txt/tucuman/social_protest.htm (accessed 31 January 2003).

Gill, S. 'Globalisation, Market Civilisation, and Disciplinary Neoliberalism', *Millennium: Journal of International Studies*, XXIV (1995) 399–423.

Guislain, P. *The Privatisation Challenge: A Strategic, Legal, and Institutional Analysis of the International Experience* (Washington: The World Bank, 1997).

Hardt, M. and A. Negri, *Empire* (Cambridge, MA: Harvard University Press, 2000).

Higgins, R. 'The Taking of Property by the State: Recent Developments in International Law', *Recueil des cours*, CLXXVI (1982) 259–391.

International Centre for Settlement of Investment Disputes, *Investment Treaties*, Vol. 4 (Dobbs Ferry, NY: Oceana Publications, Inc., 1993).

Jack, I. 'UPS Suing Ottawa for $230M', *The National Post* (22 April 1999).

Jackson, J. H. *The World Trading System: Law and Policy of International Economic Relations*, 2nd edn (Cambridge: The MIT Press, 1997).

Katzarov, K. *The Theory of Nationalisation* (The Hague: Martinus Nijhoff, 1964).

Lauterpacht, H. 'Decisions of Municipal Courts as a Source of International Law', *British Yearbook of International Law* 10 (1929) 65.

Langman, J. 'Bechtel Battles Against Dirt-Poor Bolivia', *San Francisco Chronicle* (2 February 2002) available at www.sfgate.com/cgi-bin/article.cgi?file=/chronicle/archive/2002/02/02/MN14536.D (accessed 31 January 2003).

Lipschutz, R. D. with J. Mayer, *Global Civil Society and Global Environmental Governance: The Politics of Nature from Place to Planet* (Albany: State University Press of New York, 1996).

MacLean, M. 'Beyond the Limits of State-Led Political Reform: Neoliberal Democracy and the Conflict over Water Privatisation in Cochabamba, Bolivia', presented to the Canadian Political Science Association Conference (31 May 2002).

Metalclad Corp. v. United Mexican States XXXX, *International Legal Materials*, XXXVI (2001).

Moran, T. H. (ed.), *Managing International Political Risk* (Oxford, UK: Blackwell, 1998).

Mouri, A. *The International Law of Expropriation as Reflected in the Work of the Iran-U.S. Claims Tribunal* (Dordrecht: Martinus Nijhoff Publishers, 1994).

Oppenheim, L. *International Law: A Treatise*, I, 8th edn, edited by H. Lauterpacht (London: Longman's Green, 1949).

Pennsylvania Coal v. *Mahon*, 438 US 393 at 1569 (1922).

Polanyi, K. *The Great Transformation* (Boston: Beacon Press, 1957).

Pope and Talbot Inc. and Government of Canada, Interim Award (26 June 2000), *World Trade and Arbitration Materials,* XIII (2001) 19–59.

Powers, L. F. 'New Forms of Protection for International Infrastructure Investors', in T. H. Moran (ed.), *Managing International Political Risk* (Oxford, UK: Blackwell, 1998), pp. 125–138.

Rosenau, J. N. 'Governance, Order, and Change in World Politics', in J. N. Rosenau and E-O. Czempiel (eds), *Governance Without Government: Order and Change in World Politics* (Cambridge: Cambridge University Press, 1992), pp. 1–29.

Rosenau, J. N. and E-O. Czempiel (eds), *Governance Without Government: Order and Change in World Politics* (Cambridge: Cambridge University Press, 1992).

Roth, A. H. *The Minimum Standard of International Law Applied to Aliens* (Leiden: A. W. Sijthoff's Uitgeversmaatschappij, 1949).

Roy, A. 'The Greater Common Good' in *The Cost of Living* (New York: The Modern Library, 1999).

Ruggie, J. G. *Constructing the World Polity: Essays on International Institutionalization* (London and New York: Routledge, 1998).

Sacerdoti, G. 'Bilateral Treaties and Multilateral Instruments on Investment Protection', *Recueil des Cours*, Vol. 269 (1997) 251–460.

Schneiderman, D. 'NAFTA's Takings Rule: American Constitutionalism Comes to Canada', *University of Toronto Law Journal*, XLVI (1996) 499.

——, 'MMT Promises: How the Ethyl Corporation Beat the Federal Ban', *Encompass Magazine*, III, 3 (February 1999) 12–13.

——, 'The Constitutional Strictures of the Multilateral Agreement on Investment', *The Good Society*, IX, 2 (1999) 90–95.

——, 'Investment Rules and the New Constitutionalism', *Law and Social Inquiry,* XXV (2000) 757.

——, 'Constitutional Approaches to Privatisation: An Inquiry into the Magnitude of Neo-Liberal Constitutionalism', *Law and Contemporary Problems,* LXIII (2000) 83–109.

Schultz, J. 'In the Andes – Echoes of Seattle', *The Democracy Center* (23 March 2000), online: www.democracyctr.org/onlinesnews/water.html (accessed 9 April 2001).

——, 'Bolivian Protestors Win War over Water' (7 April 2000), online: www.democracyctr.org/onlinesnews/water.html (accessed 9 April 2001).

Scoffield, H. 'Methanex Set to Sue Uncle Sam under NAFTA over Gas Additive', *The Globe and Mail* (3 November 1999).

Myers, S. D. Inc. v. Government of Canada, *International Legal Materials,* XL (2001) 1408.

Shihata, I. F. I. *Legal Treatment of Foreign Investment: The World Bank Guidelines* (Dordrecht: Martinus Nijhoff Publishers, 1993).

Shiva, V. *Water Wars: Privatization, Pollution and Profit* (Toronto: Between the Lines, 2002).

Sornarajah, M. *The International Law on Foreign Investment* (Cambridge: Cambridge University Press, 1994).

Strange, S. *The Retreat of the State: The Diffusion of Power in the World Economy* (Cambridge: Cambridge University Press, 1996).

Trigo, C. F. *Derecho Constitucional Bolviano* (La Paz: Editorial Cruz del Sur, 1952).

Urquidi, C. W. *A Statement of the Laws of Bolivia in Matters Affecting Business,* 4th edn (Washington: OAS, 1974).

Vandevelde, K. J. 'The BIT Program: A Fifteen-Year Appraisal', *Proceedings of the American Society of International Law* (Washington, DC., 1–4 April 1992) 534.

——, 'The Political Economy of a Bilateral Investment Treaty', *The American Journal of International Law,* XCII (1998) 621–641.

Wells Jr., L. 'God and Fair Competition: Does the Foreign Direct Investor Face Still Other Risks in Emerging Markets', in T. H. Moran (ed.), *Managing International Political Risk* (Oxford, UK: Blackwell, 1998), pp. 15–43.

White, G. *The Nationalisation of Foreign Property* (London: Stevens and Sons Limited, 1961).

Wild Jr., P. 'International Law and Mexican Oil', *Quarterly Journal of Inter-American Relations,* I (1939) 9.

Wilson, R. R. 'Property-Protection Provisions in United States Commercial Treaties', *American Journal of International Law,* XLV (1951) 83–107.

World Bank, *Bolivia: Public Expenditure Review,* Report No. 19232–BO (Geneva: World Bank, 1999).

Yaron, G. *The Final Frontier: A Working Paper on the Big 10 Global Water Corporations and the Privatisation and Corporatisation of the World's Last Public Resource* (Ottawa: Polaris Institute and the Council of Canadians, 2000), online: www.canadians.org/bluepl.pdf (accessed 9 April 2001).

Young, O. R. *Governance in World Affairs* (Ithaca and London: Cornell University Press, 1999).

Zoll, D. 'Soaking the Poor', *San Francisco Bay Chronicle* (13 December 2000), online: www.sfbg.com/News/35/11/11becht.html (accessed 9 April 2001).

Part II

Policy Making Processes and Context

4

The Changing Nature of Space

John Agnew

From one point of view, terrestrial space is inert. It is simply the geographical surface upon which physical, social, and economic practices and ideas exert their influence. But because the impact of practices and ideas is historically cumulative and geographically differentiating, space can be thought of as having long-term effects on the conduct of human life because of the very unevenness in the spatial distribution of physical resources and human capabilities. In this way, space is turned into place or 'lived space': the humanly constructed settings for social and political action. Contemporary Geography has abandoned the view once characteristic of many of its Anglo-American and German practitioners that physical geography is determining of other features of geographical difference across geographical scales from the local to the global. Rather, social and economic practices are now seen as primary in creating geographical differences of all kinds.

In the modern political realm lived space has been almost invariably associated with the idea of state-territoriality; politics is about modes of government within and patterns of conflict and co-operation between the territories or tightly bounded spaces of modern states. Plausibly, however, this rendition of the association between politics and place is both historically and geographically problematic. Not only is the state territory relationship a relatively recent one, it is one that has never completely vanquished other types of political geography (such as network-based kinship and city-state or core-periphery imperial political systems) around the world. Writing about 'failed' or 'quasi' states in locations as diverse as East Africa or Southern Europe, for example, often misses the fact that the absence of a working state bureaucracy throughout a given state's territory does not signify the absence of either politics or of alternative governance arrangements working non-territorially.

'Political space,' therefore, cannot be reduced to state-territoriality for two reasons. One is that states are always and everywhere challenged by forms of politics that do not conform to the boundaries of the state in question. For example, some localities have kinship or patronage politics, others have ethnic or irredentist politics oriented to either autonomy or secession, and others support political movements opposed to current constitutional arrangements including the distribution of governmental powers between different tiers of government within the state. The second is that state boundaries are permeable, and increasingly so, to a wide range of flows of ideas, investments, goods, and people that open up territories to influences that are beyond the geographical reach of current governmental powers.

Consequently, in geographical perspective there is an imbalance between the overwhelming emphasis in the contemporary social sciences on territorial states as the main vehicles of governance and the geographically variegated world that current territorial government is ill-suited in and of itself to manage and represent. A literature has begun to develop in Geography that addresses the sources of this political impasse and, to a degree, suggests possible solutions to it.

In this chapter I offer a critical survey of the various strands of the emerging literature. Firstly, two strands are distinguished that focus on the singularity of the present, suggesting that contemporary 'time-space compression' augurs a post modern world in which the fixed territorial spaces of modernity no longer match a new world of kaleidoscopic and jumbled spaces in which speed conquers established geopolitical representations. One of these strands, however, maintains a focus on the role of the agents of capital in creating this new world, the other tends to highlight the impact of new communication and representational technologies such as round-the-clock news reporting, the Internet, and new weapons systems. Two other strands see greater continuity between present and past in the configuration of space. One sees new local spaces interlinked with existing territorial ones producing a mosaic pattern to global development with local as much as global forces leading the process. A second sees powerful states, above all the United States, sponsoring a new global 'market access' regime that is producing a new geopolitics of power in which control over flows of goods, capital, and innovations increasingly substitutes for the fixed or static control over the resources of territories. Thus, states (and regions and localities within them) vie for access to the world's resources not through empire-building or territorial expansion but through command over world markets. These two last strands have produced the main alternative governance proposals, respectively, in terms of multi-tiered governance and discussion of the limitations of territorial models for a world of flows.

Time-space compression and the end of history

Early in the twentieth century Hegel seemed to have had it right. History seemed to have culminated with the advent of the European nation-state and the nation-state seemed to be the highest form of governance, accepted as representing the fundamental essence of Western civilisation. Now a new end of history has appeared. This time, however, it is one in which the globe substitutes for the state. The ease with which space is now overcome, militarily, economically, and culturally, is seen as creating a world in which 'all that is solid melts into air,' to borrow a phrase from Karl Marx. Capital now moves around the world at the press of a button, goods can be shipped over great distances at relatively low cost because of containerisation and other innovations, cultural icons represented by such products as blue jeans and Coke bottles are recognisable the world over, and Stealth technology undermines the ability of territorial military power to police its air space. A new post modern world is emerging in which old rules of spatial organisation based on linear distance-decay of transportation costs and territorial containing of external effects have broken down.

Under the new 'flexible accumulation' associated with globalisation the unique attributes of particular places in fact take on greater value for what they can offer to increasingly mobile capital, from specific types of labour market to fiscal incentives. The need for rapid access to information has privileged those 'world cities' that have good connectivity to other places. The local availability of entrepreneurship, venture capital, technical know-how, and design capabilities differentiate 'attractive' from 'unattractive' sites for investment. At the same time, tastes are increasingly volatile, subject to manipulation through advertising and the decline of status-markers other than those of consumption. Niche markets associated with different social groups increasingly cross national boundaries, giving rise to cross-national markets that can be served by factories located in any one of them or, for labour-intensive goods, produced wherever labour costs are lower.

To David Harvey, for example, one of the main advocates of this point of view, the 'condition of postmodernity' does not therefore signify the decreasing importance of space.[1] Rather, it represents the latest round in capitalism's long-term annihilation of space by time in which capitalists must now pay 'much closer attention to relative locational advantages, precisely because diminishing spatial barriers give [them] the power to exploit minute spatial differentiations to good effect. Small differences in what space contains in the way of labour supplies, resources, infrastructures, and the like become of increased significance'.[2] Politically, this gives local populations and elites the incentive to organise to represent themselves as best as possible in the struggle for mobile assets. They can be expected to turn 'homewards' and away from relying on national states to represent their interests. Political fragmentation, therefore, is a likely outcome of the increased place differentiation of the current era.

Yet, ultimately the expected world is one in which where you are will no longer matter, materially or culturally. Implicit in the perspective is an imminent decline in the significance of place as first technological conditions and then social relations produce an increasingly homogenised global space, within which local difference will be purely the result of human volition. Only in the here-and-now is there increased differentiation as new technologies conjoined to the unchanging imperative of capital accumulation work unevenly across the face of the post modern world. The historical record offers little comfort to this teleology. Wealth and power always seem to pool up in some places and not in others. Only this time around the pattern is a much more localised one than that associated with the era of national-industrial capitalism and its welfare states.

Drawing particularly on the philosopher Henri Lefebvre,[3] Edward Soja[4] argues that thinking about space has changed alongside the material impacts suggested by Harvey. In particular, Soja claims evidence for a 'spatial turn' in contemporary social science in which the previously dominant historicist approaches are increasingly challenged and displaced by ones in which 'lived space' is conjoined with 'perceived' and 'conceived' space to build a 'shared spatial consciousness ... to take control over the production of our lived spaces'.[5] In other words, a critical spatial imagination has been stimulated by recent transformations in the production of space giving rise to a new 'spatial politics' that fundamentally challenges hitherto dominant historical-social conceptions of political change. From this point of view, the end of history is thus as much intellectual and political as it is material.[6] As yet, however, the 'normal' social sciences show little or no evidence of the 'spatial turn,' notwithstanding the strong logical case that Soja makes for its arrival.[7] To them, to quote a famous phrase of the writer

William Faulkner about the American South, 'the past isn't dead, it isn't even past.'

A second strand in the literature on time-space compression emphasises more the role of speed in postmodernity than the enhanced importance of local places or lived space. Indeed, in this understanding, 'the power of pace is outstripping the power of place'.[8] Accepting the rhetoric of the gurus of the Internet world and the 'Third Wave,' this perspective sees the world as on a technological trajectory in which global space is being 're-mastered' by a totally new geopolitical imagination in which accelerating flows of information and identities undermine modernist territorial formations. Drawing on such writers as Paul Virilio,[9] 'Places are conceptualised in terms of their ability to accelerate or hinder the exchanges of global flowmations'.[10] Space is re-imagined not as 'fixed masses of territory, but rather as velocidromes, with high traffic speedways, big bandwidth connectivities, or dynamic web configurations in a worldwide network of massively parallel kineformations'.[11] The main danger here, as McKenzie Wark[12] notes, is that of mistaking a trend towards massively accelerated information flow with a deterritorialised world in which where you are no longer matters. It still matters immensely. Some places are well-connected, others are not; media and advertising companies work out of some locations and cultures and not out of others. The simulations of the media are still distinguishable (for some people) from the perils and dilemmas of everyday life. Pace is itself problematic when the images and information conveyed lead to information overload and fatigue more than accurate and real-time decision-making. The much hyped televisual world must still engage with an actual world in which most people still have very limited daily itineraries that root them to very particular places. To think that geopolitics is being replaced by chronopolitics is to project the desire for a boundaryless world characteristic of an older utopianism onto an actual world in which the old geopolitical imagination is still very much alive and well. History has not yet ended in instant electronic simulation. History is not the same as the History Channel.

Globalisation and the new geopolitics of power

The other strands of thinking are less apocalyptic about recent change in the nature of space. They see recent shifts from more to less territorialised modes of social and political organisation as growing out of previous features of global political-economic organisation. In particular, they emphasise that the spatial organisation or spatiality of development is increasingly 'constructed through interactions between flow economies and territorial economies'.[13] It is not a question of either/or but of how one relates to the other. Where the strands differ is in the relative roles they ascribe to economic-technological and geopolitical forces.[14]

In the first strand, a number of different territorial-organisational dynamics are distinguished so as to better monitor the trend towards globalisation and its challenge to established modes of regulation and governance. In this understanding, local sources of advantage maintain a role that cannot produce complete locational substitutability for businesses moving investments from place to place. Michael Storper,[15] for example, distinguishes four dynamics that work differentially across economic sectors and world regions:

> In some cases, the opening up of inter-territorial relations places previously existing locationally specific assets into a new position of global dominance. In a second set of cases, those assets are devalued via substitution by other products that now penetrate local markets; this is not a straightforward economic process, however; it is culturally intermediated. In a third set of cases, territorial integration permits the fabled attainment of massive economies of scale and organisation, devalues locationally specific assets and leads to deterritorialisation and widespread market penetration. In a fourth set of cases, territorial integration is met by differentiation and destandardisation of at least some crucial elements of the commodity chain, necessitating the reinvention of territory-specific relational assets.

Globalisation of trade, foreign direct investment, and production, therefore, is not just about an emerging geography of flows but how flows fit into and adapt to existing territorial or place-based patterns of economic development.

The point is that 'globalisation does not entrain some single, unidirectional, sociospatial logic'.[16] Rather, place-specific conditions still mediate many production and trade relationships. For example, most multinational businesses still betray strong national biases in investment activity and the intersection of various external economies and 'relational assets' (to use Storper's term) give different places different competitive advantages in expanding their economic base. Various modes of local regulation and governance evolve to handle the development process.

It is often not quite clear, however, what is new about all of this. The world's economic geography has long been a product of a mix of localising and globalising pressures, as world-systems theorists have long maintained.[17] A genuine scepticism about the empirical basis to globalisation as a pervasive process is also conjoined with a fairly economistic rendering of what is happening.[18] This is where the second strand comes in, not denying the complexity of the spatial impact of globalisation so much as offering a different account of its origins and novelty.

From this point of view, contemporary globalisation has its origins in the ideological geopolitics of the Cold War with US government attempts at both reviving Western Europe and challenging Soviet-style economic planning by stimulating a 'free-world economy' committed to lowering barriers to world trade and international capital flows.[19] Globalisation, therefore, did not just *happen*. It required considerable political stimulation without which technological and economic stimuli to increased international economic interdependence could not have taken place. From the American viewpoint, all states ideally would be internationalised; open to the free flow of investment and trade. This not only contrasted with the closed, autarkic character of the Soviet economy, it also had as a major stimulus the idea that the depression of the 1930s had been exacerbated by the closing down of international trade.

In the five decades after 1945 American dominion was at the centre of a remarkable explosion in 'interactional' capitalism.[20] Based initially on the expansion of mass consumption within the most industrialised countries, it later involved the systematic reorganisation of the world economy around massive increases in the volume of trade in manufactured goods and foreign direct investment. This was definitely not a recapitulation of the previous world economy that Lenin had labelled 'imperialist.' Abandoning territorial imperialism, 'Western capitalism ... resolved the old problem of overproduction, thus removing what Lenin believed was the major incentive for imperialism and war'.[21] The driving force now was not export of capital to colonies but the growth of mass consumption in North America, Western Europe, and Japan. If before the Second World War the prosperity of the industrialised countries had depended on favourable terms of trade with the underdeveloped world, now demand was stimulated mainly at home. The products of such industries as real estate, household and electrical goods, automobiles, food processing, and mass entertainment were all consumed within, and progressively between, the producing countries.

The welfare state helped to sustain demand through the redistribution of incomes and increased purchasing power for basic goods.

Beginning in the late 1960s this *international* system started to change in profound ways that augured the onset of globalisation. First came increased levels of international trade following the revolutionary effects of the Kennedy Round of the General Agreement on Tariffs and Trade (GATT) in the mid-1960s. This was followed in 1971 by the US abrogation of the Bretton Woods Agreement of 1944, liberating currencies from a fixed exchange rate to the US$ so as to improve the deteriorating trade position of the US economy. This set currencies free to float against one another and created the globalised financial system now in place around the world. Third came the globalisation of production associated with dramatic increases in the level of foreign direct investment. Initially led by large American firms, by the 1970s and 1980s European, Japanese, and other firms had also discovered the benefits of production in local markets to take advantage of macroeconomic conditions (exchange rates, interest rates, and so on), avoid tariff and other barriers to direct trade, and gain knowledge of local tastes and preferences.

With the collapse of the alternative Soviet system since 1989, largely because of its failure to deliver the promise of increased material affluence, the 'American' model has emerged into prominence at a world scale. An approach set in train in the 1940s to counter the perceived threat to the American model at home by exporting it overseas has given rise to a globalised world economy that is quite beyond what its architects could have foreseen at the outset of the Cold War. Yet, that is where its roots lie, not in recent technological changes or purely in the machinations of American big business. Globalisation has geopolitical more than technological or economic origins.

Globalisation has also had dramatic effects on global political geography, affecting the political autonomy of even the most powerful states.[22] One is the internationalisation of a range of hitherto domestic policies to conform to global norms of performance. Thus, not only trade policy but also industrial, product liability, environmental, and social-welfare policies are subject to definition and oversight in terms of their impacts on market access between countries. A second is the increased global trade in services, once produced and consumed largely within state boundaries. In part this reflects the fact that many manufactured goods now contain a large share of service inputs – from R&D to marketing and advertising. But it is also because the revolution in telecommunications since the 1980s means that many services, from banking to design and packaging, can now be provided to global markets. Finally, the spreading geographical reach of multinational firms and the growth of international corporate alliances have had profound influences on the nature of trade and investment, undermining the identity between national territories and economic processes. Symptomatic of the integration of trade and investment are concerns such as rules on unitary taxation, rules governing local content to assess where value was added in production, and rules governing unfair competition and monopoly trading practices.[23]

None of these policy areas is any longer within the singular control of individual sovereign states. They all must live in an increasingly common institutional environment; including the United States. Unfortunately, as demonstrations at the November 1999, World Trade Organization (formerly GATT) meeting in Seattle made clear, the global institutional environment is not one currently open to democratic demands. Indeed, the globalising world is marked by a crisis of governance as existing national-state scale institutions cannot offer the spatial reach needed to regulate increasingly worldwide and world-regional transactions but existing global-scale institutions are still creatures of the most powerful states and dominant interest-groups from them.

Governing a globalising world

In response to the perceived 'governance deficit' implicit in the gap between the spatial reach of existing national-state scale institutions and the changing geography of the world economy a number of studies have begun to examine the possible geographical options. One tendency, drawing largely on the sort of analysis provided by Michael Storper, involves the possibilities for multi-tier governance. In this understanding, because global-local relations are always mediated across a range of geographical scales different regulatory institutions should be located at different scales in a hierarchy from the local to the global.

A second tendency offers less a spatial logic for governance under globalisation than a historical analysis of the geopolitical conditions that now prevail and that thus direct current debate over the 'best' form that new strategies of governance might take. One approach is to examine the claim that existing territorial arrangements within the world's most powerful state, the United States, can serve as a model for future transnational governance. This argument takes as its starting point the idea that the United States government is the major sponsor of globalisation and sees the US domestic model as a suitable one for the future regulation and management of the world economy as a whole, combining an openness to expansion through accretion of new territory and a division of public powers that gives private capital a central role in governance. Whatever its strengths, however, this claim fails to take into account the non-territorial character of globalisation, reducing the viability of territorial designs such as the US federal model and suggesting the superiority of what Susan Roberts has called 'from-below' initiatives based on increasing the voice and political impact of diverse groups with distinctive stakes in the emerging global economy but without necessary connections to existing national-state institutions.[24]

New political spaces

A number of authors have distinguished a hierarchy of levels of governance at which different mixes of regulatory activities and political disputation can be lodged. Some might emphasise one level over others, such as the world-regional or regional trading bloc or[25] the global city-region.[26] But all are concerned to argue for a spatial logic of levels or tiers as an alternative to the current concentration of governance at the national-state level.

Allen Scott, for example, provides a fairly thorough discussion of the emergence of a set of new political spaces of which the world-regional, city-region, and global are the most novel.[27] The national-state and local tiers already have relatively long standing institutional histories and high levels of political legitimation. Although there are 'common and recurrent political questions (for example, about trade, workers' rights, gender issues, the environment, political representation)'[28] at all levels, many issues need addressing now both at levels 'below' and 'above' that of existing states. The global city-region is particularly important in Scott's formulation. Not only is it the level at which competitive economic advantage is increasingly decided, due to the external economies of industrial clustering, but it is also the level at which popular involvement in political regulation is most effectively concentrated, not least because this is a geographical scale most associated with the 'lived space' of everyday life.

The tier arrangement is not a mere fantasy to Scott and others. Rather, trends towards a mosaic of global city-regions and world-regional organisation (as with the European Union (EU) and North American Free Trade Agreement (NAFTA) are well under way. What remains more problematic is the possibility, and desirability, of increased governance at a truly global level. Here, though, the emerging market access regime of transnational liberalism may call forth from businesses themselves a demand for regulation, such as that recently coming from the financier George Soros, to enforce the rules of global business equally across all actors.[29] Global markets as presently constituted will never be able to do this. The danger is that governance at this level will be well beyond the range of popular democratic control. At the same time, however, local units may well begin to adopt policies that conflict with or even undermine the operations of higher-level ones, as with individual US states pursuing their own policies in relation to foreign states or the WTO.[30]

American federalism and global governance

Regional trading blocs and global city-regions are undoubtedly part of the emerging alternative to national-states as the primary units of global governance. Increasingly, however, calls for more effective governance beyond the national state are dominated by fairly formal schemes based on 'up-scaling' of established national models. The most important of these, given the contemporary global geopolitical situation, is that of the United States, which now informs debates over, for example, the 'deepening' of the EU through a federal model or proposals for revamping international institutions such as the UN system.

The American federal model has a number of attractive qualities, not the least of which is its 'pure territoriality,' or rigid hierarchy of territories with functions allocated to levels on the basis of the spatial scope of their externalities, and its separation of powers between different 'branches' of government to reduce the concentration of public power. American 'constitutionalism,' the continuing reference to a founding document, the Constitution, and unending debate over its meaning and applicability, appeals as an institutional logic because, like any future model of global governance must do, the US 'experiment' started from scratch. The emphasis on 'balance' between levels of government provides a means of sorting out multiple functions by tier in a way that other proposals for multi-level governance typically do not.

But it is the role of the US as a global geopolitical force that pushes the US model to the fore irrespective of its particular relevance. An important element in American emergence as a world power early in the twentieth century was projection of the American experience as an inherent aspect of US government foreign policy. This not only reflected a well-established American distaste for a foreign policy uninformed by the specific values the United States was supposed to 'represent,' going back to the founding of the country itself, it also served to present the United States as a relatively benign, even 'innocent' Great Power, committed to doing good in the world by intervening to vanquish evil and establishing institutions that would move the world beyond its territorial division into mutually antagonistic states. Woodrow Wilson, President of the United States from 1913 to 1921, was the leading figure in establishing an American commitment to global institutionalism, even though defeated in his own efforts by those either seeing the US as a traditional Great Power or doubtful about the benefits of any kind of active presence in world affairs. Wilson's idea of a 'new world order' that would reorganise the world benignly in America's image has been a persisting if contested theme of American foreign policy.[31]

Projection of the American federal model onto a world scale is problematic, however, for a number of reasons.[32] The first is the inflexibility of the division of powers and the difficulty of revising it within a rigid constitutionalism.[33] The system is only partially democratic because elite-based institutions such as the US Senate and the federal judiciary rely, respectively, on the equality of territorial units and review of new law through the lens of an eighteenth century document. Amending the Constitution is also extremely difficult without widespread and substantial nationwide support. It requires a two-thirds vote of both houses of Congress and three-quarters of the states by simple majority of their legislatures. The separation of powers itself reduces accountability and limits the possibility of coordinated policy-making absent an external threat that encourages consensus but then demonises domestic opposition as 'un-American.'

This raises the second problem: the difficulty of political opposition within the American system. One critical test of democratic or open governance, exactly what is lacking in current world-regional and global-level institutions, is the extent to which opposition is not only allowed but also nurtured. Yet, the American model rests, as Tocqueville was the first to notice, on widespread consensus about institutions and the policies that they produce.

The presumption of consensus relies on an ideological feature of American history that is not replicable elsewhere or at a global scale. This is the sense of providential mission that has inspired both American institutions and the territorial expansion of the United States into North America. The idea of 'American exceptionalism' has been a vital part of the American national experience, providing an ideological adhesive to paper over the vast number of class, racial, ethnic, regional, and other cleavages that have always rent the American population. American federalism is not readily disentangled from such particular origins or likely to work well without an appropriate heroic story to inform its everyday operations. It cannot be treated as a simple technical or instrumental 'solution' to the 'problem' of governance. Finally, in a globalising world the spatial pattern of externalities is no longer strictly territorial. Transnational forces create communities of interest and defence that are not well represented within a territorial conception of the public realm. In this setting the possibility of neatly allocating regulatory, distributory, and allocative functions to different territorial units is much reduced. As the span of control needed to govern various economic and cultural activities conforms increasingly to webs of interconnection between widely scattered regional nodes, the territorial structure of American federalism offers less purchase on the world to which it must adjust. The emergence of 'global city-regions' as centres of economic dynamism, for example, challenges more than the existing system of national states. It also calls into question the possibility of squeezing the new geography of economic activity into an eighteenth century spatial model of political organisation.

The proliferation of 'power sources' without a territorial form mandates that we look towards a proliferation of control mechanisms rather than to a single model of governance reproducing a single national experience at a global scale. By way of example, Susan Roberts points to an alternative framework based on the proliferation of groups such as the International Forum on Social Justice and other transnational alliances representing discourses of justice, democracy, and environment that run against the grain of both nationalism and the dream of a market-run world without any political regulation of economic activities.[34] Democratic governance in a globalising world, therefore, is a matter of process more than scale. Inquiry should thereby focus on 'how to harness transnational forces – be they economic, social or political – in the name of democracy'.[35]

Conclusion

In this chapter I have briefly surveyed contemporary thinking in Geography (and allied fields) about the changing nature of space and the consequences of this for ideas about governance in a globalising world. Notions of 'time-space compression' have been particularly influential in the field at large. But it is rather those writers focusing on past-present continuities in the emergence of a globalising world who have more to offer concerning the possibilities of governance beyond the national state. The literature is still evolving, however, and current analyses are limited and tentative. What does seem clear is that Geography is grappling with the linkage of globalisation and governance and, notwithstanding differences in terminology and approach, may have a contribution to make to the wider debate in the social sciences.

Notes

1. D. Harvey, *The Condition of Postmodernity* (Oxford: Blackwell, 1989).
2. Harvey 1989, p. 294.
3. H. Lefebvre, *The Production of Space* (Oxford: Blackwell, 1991).
4. E. W. Soja, *Postmodern Geographies: The Reassertion of Space in Critical Social Theory* (London: Verso, 1989); E. W. Soja, *Thirdspace: Journeys to Los Angeles and Other Real-and-Imagined Places* (Oxford: Blackwell, 1996); E. W. Soja, 'Thirdspace: Expanding the Scope of the Geographical Imagination', in D. Massey, J. Allen and P. Sarre (eds), *Human Geography Today* (Cambridge: Polity Press, 1999).
5. Soja 1999, p. 277.
6. R. A. Dodgshon, 'Human Geography at the End of Time? Some Thoughts on the Idea of Time-Space Compression', *Society and Space*, XVII, 5 (1999) 607–20.
7. See P. J. Taylor *et al.*, 'On the Nation-State, the Global, and Social Science', *Environment and Planning A*, XXVIII (1996) 1917–95.
8. T. W. Luke and G. Tuathail, 'Global Flowmations, Local Fundamentalisms, and Fast Geopolitics: "America" in an Accelerating World Order', in A. Herod, G. Tuathail and S. M. Roberts (eds), *An Unruly World? Globalization, Governance and Geography* (London: Routledge, 1998), p. 72.
9. P. Virilio, *Speed and Politics* (New York: Semiotext(e), 1986).
10. Luke and Tuathail 1998, p. 76.
11. Luke and Tuathail 1998, p. 76.
12. M. Wark, *Virtual Geography: Living with Global Media Events* (Bloomington: Indiana University Press, 1994), p. 93.
13. M. Storper, 'Territories, Flows and Hierarchies in the Global Economy', in K. R. Cox (ed.), *Spaces of Globalization: Reasserting the Power of the Local* (New York: Guilford, 1997), p. 31.
14. A. Leyshon, 'True Stories? Global Dreams, Global Nightmares, and Writing Globalization', in R. Lee and J. Wills (eds), *Geographies of Economies* (London: Arnold, 1997).
15. M. Storper, 'Territories, Flows and Hierarchies in the Global Economy', in K. R. Cox (ed.), *Spaces of Globalization: Reasserting the Power of the Local* (New York: Guilford, 1997), p. 35.
16. K. R. Cox, 'Introduction: Globalization and its Politics in Question', in K. R. Cox (ed.), *Spaces of Globalization: Reasserting the Power of the Local* (New York: Guilford, 1997), p. 16.
17. See, for example, G. Arrighi and B. Silver (eds), *Chaos and Governance in the Modern World System* (Minneapolis: University of Minnesota Press, 1999).

18. For example, K. R. Cox, 'Introduction: Globalization and its Politics in Question', in K. R. Cox (ed.), *Spaces of Globalization: Reasserting the Power of the Local* (New York: Guilford, 1997).
19. J. A. Agnew and S. Corbridge, *Mastering Space: Hegemony, Territory and International Political Economy* (London: Routledge, 1995).
20. J. A. Agnew, 'The United States and American Hegemony', in P. J. Taylor (ed.), *The Political Geography of the Twentieth Century* (London: Wiley, 1993).
21. D. P. Calleo, *Beyond American Hegemony: The Future of the Western Alliance* (New York: Basic Books, 1987), p. 147.
22. J. A. Agnew, 'The United States and the Wider World', in F. Boal and S. Royle (eds), *North America: A Geographical Mosaic* (London: Arnold, 1999).
23. P. Cowhey and J. Aronson, *Managing the World Economy* (New York: Council on Foreign Relations Press, 1993).
24. S. M. Roberts, 'Geo-governance in Trade and Finance and Political Geographies of Dissent', in A. Herod, S. M. Roberts and G. O. Tuathail (eds), *An Unruly World? Globalization, Governance and Geography* (London: Routledge, 1998).
25. J. H. Mittelman, 'Rethinking the New Regionalism in the Context of Globalization', *Global Governance*, II (1996) 189–213.
26. For example, A. J. Scott, *Regions and the World Economy: The Coming Shape of Global Production, Competition, and Political Order* (Oxford: Oxford University Press, 1998).
27. Scott 1998.
28. Scott 1998, p. 141.
29. G. Soros, 'Capitalism's last chance?' *Foreign Policy*, CXIII (1998/99) 55–66.
30. For example, B. P. Denning and J. H. McCall, 'States' Rights and Foreign Policy', *Foreign Affairs*, LXXIX, 1 (2000) 9–15; J. O'Connell, 'WTO, State Law on Collision Course', *Los Angeles Times* (23 January 2000) M6.
31. A. Perlmutter, *Making the World Safe for Democracy: A Century of Wilsonianism and its Totalitarian Challengers* (Chapel Hill: University of North Carolina Press, 1997).
32. See J. A. Agnew, 'The Limits of Federalism as a Model of Transnational Democracy', in J. Anderson (ed.), *Trans-national Democracy* (London: Routledge, 2002).
33. D. Lazare, *The Frozen Republic: How the Constitution is Paralyzing Democracy* (New York: Harcourt Brace, 1996).
34. S. M. Roberts, 'Geo-governance in Trade and Finance and Political Geographies of Dissent', in A. Herod, S. M. Roberts and G. O. Tuathail (eds), *An Unruly World? Globalization, Governance and Geography* (London: Routledge, 1998).
35. J. Goodman, 'The European Union: Reconstituting Democracy beyond the Nationstate', in A. McGrew (ed.), *The Transformation of Democracy?* (Cambridge: Polity Press, 1997), p. 182.

References

Agnew, J. A. 'The United States and American Hegemony', in P. J. Taylor (ed.), *The Political Geography of the Twentieth Century* (London: Wiley, 1993).
——, 'The United States and the Wider World', in F. Boal and S. Royle (eds), *North America: A Geographical Mosaic* (London: Arnold, 1999).

——, 'The Limits of Federalism as a Model of Transnational Democracy', in J. Anderson (ed.), *Trans-national Democracy* (London: Routledge, 2002).

Agnew, J. A. and S. Corbridge, *Mastering Space: Hegemony, Territory and International Political Economy* (London: Routledge, 1995).

Arrighi, G. and B. Silver (eds), *Chaos and Governance in the Modern World System* (Minneapolis: University of Minnesota Press, 1999).

Calleo, D. P. *Beyond American Hegemony: The Future of the Western Alliance* (New York: Basic Books, 1987).

Cowhey, P. and J. Aronson, *Managing the World Economy* (New York: Council on Foreign Relations Press, 1993).

Cox, K. R. 'Introduction: Globalization and its Politics in Question', in K. R. Cox (ed.), *Spaces of Globalization: Reasserting the Power of the Local* (New York: Guilford, 1997).

Denning, B. P. and J. H. McCall, 'States' Rights and Foreign Policy', *Foreign Affairs*, LXXIX, 1 (2000) 9–15.

Dodgshon, R. A. 'Human Geography at the End of Time? Some Thoughts on the Idea of Time-Space Compression', *Society and Space*, XVII, 5 (1999) 607–20.

Goodman, J. 'The European Union: Reconstituting Democracy beyond the Nation-state', in A. McGrew (ed.), *The Transformation of Democracy?* (Cambridge: Polity Press, 1997).

Harvey, D. *The Condition of Postmodernity* (Oxford: Blackwell, 1989).

Lazare, D. *The Frozen Republic: How the Constitution is Paralyzing Democracy* (New York: Harcourt Brace, 1996).

Lefebvre, H. *The Production of Space* (Oxford: Blackwell, 1991).

Leyshon, A. 'True Stories? Global Dreams, Global Nightmares, and Writing Globalization', in R. Lee and J. Wills (eds), *Geographies of Economies* (London: Arnold, 1997).

Luke, T. W. and G. Tuathail, 'Global Flowmations, Local Fundamentalisms, and Fast Geopolitics: "America" in an Accelerating World Order', in A. Herod, G. Tuathail and S. M. Roberts (eds), *An Unruly World? Globalization, Governance and Geography* (London: Routledge, 1998).

Mittelman, J. H. 'Rethinking the New Regionalism in the Context of Globalization', *Global Governance* II (1996) 189–213.

O'Connell, J. 'WTO, State Law on Collision Course', *Los Angeles Times* (23 January 2000) M6.

Perlmutter, A. *Making the World Safe for Democracy: A Century of Wilsonianism and its Totalitarian Challengers* (Chapel Hill: University of North Carolina Press, 1997).

Roberts, S. M. 'Geo-governance in Trade and Finance and Political Geographies of Dissent', in A. Herod, S. M. Roberts and G. O. Tuathail (eds), *An Unruly World? Globalization, Governance and Geography* (London: Routledge, 1998).

Scott, A. J. *Regions and the World Economy: The Coming Shape of Global Production, Competition, and Political Order* (Oxford: Oxford University Press, 1998).

Soja, E. W. *Postmodern Geographies: The Reassertion of Space in Critical Social Theory* (London: Verso, 1989).

——, *Thirdspace: Journeys to Los Angeles and Other Real-and-Imagined Places* (Oxford: Blackwell, 1996).

——, 'Thirdspace: Expanding the Scope of the Geographical Imagination', in D. Massey, J. Allen and P. Sarre (eds), *Human Geography Today* (Cambridge: Polity Press, 1999).

Soros, G. 'Capitalism's last chance?' *Foreign Policy* CXIII (1998/99) 55–66.

Storper, M. 'Territories, Flows and Hierarchies in the Global Economy', in K. R. Cox (ed.), *Spaces of Globalization: Reasserting the Power of the Local* (New York: Guilford, 1997).

Taylor, P. J. *et al.*, 'On the Nation-State, the Global, and Social Science', *Environment and Planning A* XXVIII (1996) 1917–95.

Virilio, P. *Speed and Politics* (New York: Semiotext(e), 1986).

Wark, M. *Virtual Geography: Living with Global Media Events* (Bloomington: Indiana University Press, 1994).

5
Global Governance and Political Economy: Public, Private and Political Authority in the Twenty-first Century

Geoffrey R. D. Underhill

This volume demonstrates that global governance is a contested concept. In view of the evidence presented, it is difficult to refute this assertion. Given the historical predominance of national and local decision-making procedures and the traditional difficulties of co-operation in the international domain, it is also not surprising that global governance should be so contested as a concept and as a process. This is particularly the case where there is a clash of democratic legitimacies, in the sense that what one democratically organised society might decide is in tension with the orientation of others, but many of the problems must still be resolved collectively. What is much less contested is that the domain of the economy is one in which the pressures and incentives for establishing global governance mechanisms are considerable, as are the problems of setting them up. Global governance processes (or the lack thereof) must wrestle continuously with the tensions created by the integration across borders of economic processes and corporate structures, wherein regulatory and other forms of jurisdiction in terms of governance remain more resolutely national. There are also few domains where the actors, the context, and the dynamics are more complex or difficult to manage.[1]

One might also argue that it is in the domain of economic issues and management that governance is most developed, either through state-to-state agreements and institutions such as the WTO or the IMF, through sub-state inter-agency regimes such as the Basle Committee on Banking Supervision, or through private sector co-operation such as the governance of the reinsurance market or the International Chamber of Commerce arbitration processes. This is the terrain of the state and the market in global context, which is the subject of political economy in general and of the emerging discipline of International Political Economy (IPE) since the 1970s. Global economic governance is certainly anarchic in the sense of lacking a central recognised authority, but it is surprisingly highly organised and institutionalised relative to other policy domains. Despite what many free-market economists might claim, this order is anything but spontaneous.

This chapter aims to clarify our thinking about governance and the domain of the global political economy, and how we might make sense of the state-market relationship in the absence of global political authority. The chapter will begin by outlining the emergence of the discipline of IPE and its core assumptions in the late twentieth century, its core questions and research agenda, and its remaining lacunae. It will then demonstrate that the core conceptual issue in IPE remains the nature of the state-market relationship, and that further conceptual work is required. To understand global governance processes in relation to the political economy, we must move beyond concepts which either implicitly or explicitly conceptualise the state-market relationship in terms of separation and antagonism. The way we view this relationship has a considerable impact on how one understands prospects for change in the structures – the normative and material underpinnings – of world order. Scholars need to take a final a decisive step in accepting that, in empirical and conceptual terms, the state and the market are part of the same, integrated system of governance: a state-market condominium. The chapter will then elaborate the state-market condominium concept and how it might resolve some of the conceptual dilemmas concerning political economy and global governance. It will then go on to apply the model and to develop some of its practical and policy implications.

International political economy as an emerging discipline: ecumenism and diversity[2]

Economists and political scientists of various hues have competed within their respective disciplines and with each other to present an understanding of global governance issues and the economic domain. While more collaborative efforts would have been constructive, the dynamics of research and publication strategies have mostly militated against co-operation. Nonetheless, the idea of working across disciplines or indeed integrating the insights of political science and economics, the better to understand global governance, is not entirely without precedent. The emergence of IPE as a field of enquiry, while mostly drawing on scholarship in international relations and political science, shows at least some serious attempts

If one may for a moment commit the error of anthropomorphising a scholarly discipline which is diverse and fragmented, IPE has often had trouble making up its mind whether it is a sub-field of International Relations, or whether it is something broader and more inclusive: sub-field *versus* inter-discipline? Should it focus on the special nature of the system of states, along the lines of more traditional international relations,[3] or should it develop its roots in the intellectual movements which emerged as classical/radical political economy, in turn developing branches across a broad range of social science traditions?

This schizoid nature of the discipline is not surprising. There is a simultaneous need: a) to establish theoretical and methodological orientation and, b) to define their relationship to related fields of economics, sociology, and political science. Over time, IPE scholars have hailed from a wide variety of backgrounds. While many have emerged as dissenters (to a greater or lesser degree) to traditional, state- and security-centric international relations,[4] this is not necessarily the dominant background of scholars in the field. Many who have contributed to the emergence of IPE have come from comparative politics or political economy, recognising that as the global system became more integrated and interdependence increasingly a feature of relations among states, national systems could not longer be considered on their own.[5] Still others hailed from economics, including the pioneering and much missed Susan Strange, recognising the need for insights from both international relations/political science and international economics to be brought together in a social science synthesis,[6] or from economic history, such as Charles Kindleberger.[7] Still others emerged from the world of international organisations, turning practical insight to innovative theoretical contributions.[8] In addition, IPE scholars have covered an extraordinary range of subjects in the global system, from regional or country focus to north-south issues, from particular policy issues/sectors to specific social groups.

What holds the field together amidst such diversity is a few shared conceptual assumptions: i) that the political and economic domains are interdependent; ii) political interaction is one of the principal means through which the economic structures of the market are established and in turn transformed; and iii) that there is an intimate connection between the domestic and international levels of analysis, and that the two cannot meaningfully be separated off from one another.[9]

This leaves room for considerable disciplinary ecumenism and an innovative willingness to draw insights from fields as diverse as the scholarly backgrounds of the IPE pioneers themselves.

This section will argue that this diversity of origin and of analytical approach militates strongly towards interpreting IPE not as an off-shoot of traditional International Relations, but as rooted in the broad tradition of political economy which emerged in the European enlightenment. The field has outgrown IR and should not feel constrained by the debates which have framed state- and security-centric IR scholarship in the post-war period. In time, IR will come to IPE as a more comprehensive approach to understanding world order, not the other way around, especially as IR itself is forced to come to terms with the world post-Cold War.[10] In this sense, it is also broader than contemporary economics because of its roots in the classical debates of the eighteenth century. IPE is thus a better starting point for considering the problems of global governance than either traditional IR or economics, precisely because of the nature of the underlying assumptions and the diversity of its scholars.

The beginning was in fact a revival. During the 1960s, a range of scholars in IR and foreign policy analysis (not to exclude other branches of political science) began to consider the observable fact of *interdependence* and what it meant for our understanding of the world around us. Increasingly, foreign affairs would not be understood on their own, but in relation to the tensions between domestic considerations and relations with other states and their own domestic dynamics. The otherwise rigid division between the international domain, international politics as politics among states, gave way to a blurring of the levels of analysis distinction in the work of a range of scholars. To this end, James Rosenau produced *Linkage Politics*, having examined in his earlier work the various domestic influences on the formulation of American foreign policy.[11]

This merged into a debate about 'transnational relations,' wherein *international* was placed in opposition to the more sophisticated concept of *trans-national* relationships. While international was taken to denote relations of state to state, transnational politics involved relationships which cut across the domestic-international divide but need not necessarily involve states, but would include their activities as well. Interdependence among states and their societies[12] was central to this debate, and transnational relations involved a wider range of actors than feature in traditional IR: both non-state and sub-state actors, including private actors and official institutions of more less formal nature.

The bag was open – such concepts represented a serious challenge to the traditional contention that world politics was about what states-as-units did, and greatly expanded the empirical terrain on which the nascent IPE would operate. One should note an important point, however. There was always division on how far one should go in this direction, especially as established disciplines did not always welcome scholars hailing the newness of IPE. Was 'transnational relations' primarily about what states did, with the influence of a few sub- and non-state (but nonetheless essentially official) actors like international organisations thrown in, or was it about a more radical conceptual departure from traditional IR scholarship, to include a wider range of issues and actors, including those not linked to formal government? The difference is well represented by two special issues of prominent journals on transnational relations: the 1971 issue of *International Organization* edited by Keohane and Nye, and the issue of *International Affairs* edited by Susan Strange in 1976.[13] These two special issues laid out an important division in the discipline which still remains. The dispute has yet to be settled: are we studying the ways in which economic and political factors in the international system affect each other in an ongoing fashion, or are we seeking to explain the ways in which underlying social structures and relationships, among a range of actors and institutions, generate the patterns of institutionalised and other aspects of political authority in a transnational world? As Strange might have put it, 'politics of international economic relations,' or 'transnational *political economy?*'

There were also disputes about basic assumptions of agency and method. One trend was the application of methodologically individualist rational choice to IPE.[14] These more formal and quantitative rational choice contributions under the 'positive political economy' label represent a growing direct overlap of neo-classical economics and IPE.[15] Meanwhile, the world economy was undergoing rapid change from the early 1960s, leaving room for other research methodologies. International trade was developing rapidly, and (in particular US) corporations were spreading throughout the world. The rise of the Euromarkets signalled a transformation of the financial system, and the 1970s proved to be a decade of economic turmoil, of oil politics, and of developing country challenges to the structures of the global political economy. This process of economic transformation had a clear international politics dimension to it – trade policies had always been highly charged politically, both *within* and *among* states in the system, and the emerging strains in the international monetary system likewise proved politically controversial. This proved fertile ground for a series of major and interdisciplinary research projects on the political economy of trade and monetary relationships among states and their societies.[16] This concern with a variety of policy issues in the global system also found its echo in the study of *international regimes*.[17] The study of international regimes became a veritable growth industry in the 1980s and 1990s, with studies ranging from environment to security regimes, and involving relatively state-centric approaches to those involving a wider range of actors and concepts of transnationalism.[18] Indeed, the concept was extended to cover a range of private actors and processes in the discipline.[19]

Further contributions to the debate on interdependence came from comparative political economists[20] as European and other regional integration projects accelerated.[21] It was increasingly difficult to remain a country specialist without absorbing the impact of structural changes in the global economy – the debates about corporatism and the role of organised interests were forced to 'go global.'[22] IPE and comparative political economy needed each other as much as ever, though this was not of course universally accepted.

So far I have entirely neglected the radical tradition in IPE, the better to deal with it now. The Marxist tradition of political economy has never undergone the bifurcation of 'orthodox' political science and economics. In other words, radical political economy has provided some of the most fruitful ground for advancing the cause of IPE. Indeed, over time the radical and the 'orthodox' have moved closer together – we are all 'marxian' (small 'm') in one way or another as we argue about the impact of economic structure and problems of inequality in this period of global economic integration.

Perhaps the most obvious of the long-standing radical contributions to IPE is the contribution of dependency theorists, in the sense that north-south relationships are by definition global in scope. Dependency theory was critical of Marxist work while drawing heavily upon it, emphasising the uneven development and inequalities of the capitalist system. Dependency theories were often genuinely systemic in their approach, lending themselves to international relations though seldom finding favour with the mainstream discipline. The insights of dependency theorists concerning uneven development and inequality have been difficult to ignore, and despite ongoing discomfort the mainstream has increasingly accepted some of the basic observations of dependency theorists.

Some radical political economists have found their way closer to the mainstream discipline. Fred Block's analysis of post-war international monetary relations remains as useful today as when originally written in the turbulent 1970s.[23] More recently, Robert Cox was the author of an important innovation with an approach which bridged international relations/IPE and the domestic level of analysis in important respects. His 'neo-Gramscian' approach,[24] resolutely post-structuralist in its theory, has been embraced in whole or in part by a sizable proportion of IPE specialists. It provides a flexible set of intellectual devices which help one grasp the relationship between economic structures and political interaction lying at the heart of the market-authority relationship to which Susan Strange constantly drew attention. Cox also served to remind one of the importance of linking IPE to its historical roots as he drew heavily on Marx, Gramsci and Karl Polanyi (as had others), and other disciplines, particularly history as represented by Fernand Braudel. While Cox (like dependency theorists) focused more on inequalities and class in the global system, his conceptual devices cross levels of analysis and admit the relevance of a wide range of public and private actors and, crucially, the relationships among them in a pattern of global governance. The emphasis on the trans-nationalisation of class and (related) corporate power was also developed by Kees van der Pijl and the 'Amsterdam School,'[25] as well as scholars such as Stephen Gill at York University in Canada.[26]

Similar to wider developments in the social sciences, 'new' issues have made their way onto the IPE agenda. Of particular note is the rise of feminist scholarship and work on the environment – heralding feminist and 'green' approaches to IPE.[27] As with many questions in IPE, the normative content of these debates is important, indeed central. Different perspectives and scholars emphasise different aspects of the normative agenda, and much of the underlying debate is ultimately about values, not simply analysis and research tools.[28]

To summarise the points so far, the more the state-market relationship was explored, the more the traditional analytical assumptions of orthodox economics and political science/international relations could be questioned. The empirical examination of social and economic interdependence across political boundaries threw into question the levels of analysis assumptions of comparative politics and international relations. What is the respective role of international versus domestic constraints, and how are they linked as the world becomes more transnational in nature? What role for structure versus agency in this process of transformation?

In other words, the emergence of IPE was a re-awakening and re-linking of the study of 'things international' with the broad tradition of social science scholarship from the French Physiocrats onwards, via Smith, Marx, Keynes, Polanyi, and the pioneers of the contemporary period. It came into its own as a diverse, open, and contentious subject field well-rooted in the broader concerns of social science and drawing on a considerable range of disciplines and conceptual devices/traditions. The ecumenism of IPE is welcome and will aid, rather than hinder, successful understanding of the complex world around us, as it has always done in pursuits of the human mind. Over time the field has become characterised by a concern with how the pieces of the global puzzle fit together: the social, the normative, the formal and institutionalised, the public and the private, the local and the global. This leaves considerable room for specialised research and investigation (one might say, *requires* it), but requires a broad understanding of the nature of political authority and governance in a variety of settings.

Something, however, is needed to give focus to the empirical and conceptual diversity. It was argued above that a core set of concerns *does* frame the debate and hold the enterprise more or less together, and that these grew out of the revival of IPE from the 1960s onwards. These core assumptions were: i) that the political and economic domains are interdependent; ii) political interaction is one of the principal means through which economic structures are established and in turn transformed; and iii) that there is an intimate connection between the domestic and international levels of analysis.

But what do these core assumptions imply in terms of questions to structure enquiry? Given my arguments about roots, we might look (unexpectedly for some) to Adam Smith for guidance.[29] He sought to explore the considerable tension between the pursuit of narrow self-interest and the public good. His core question was, how might this tension be resolved? One might not agree with his market prescription, but this central issue is useful for us concerning the contemporary global market: what ought to be the public good in terms of the wider process of governance? Whose interests do and should prevail in the various tiers of institutions and less formal arrangements which constitute global governance? What is the relationship between economic structures and political authority (loosely defined) in the process of global change?[30]

This question is central because it encapsulates what the field has come to be about in all its diversity. It brings together debates about actors, structure and agency, about the nature of the domestic-international relationship, and about which issues should be on the research and policy agendas. And the core institution of political authority remains the state, however embattled, embedded as it is in the fabric of the global and the local. What do we think a state is, what do we think a market is, and how, if at all, are they/should they be related? Even if one focuses on formal patterns of political authority, in particular the state, one should be drawn to investigate how it is situated in the wider (increasingly transnational) social context, how public and private interact, how the politics and markets interact. This leaves ample room for normative concerns such as who should get what and how, the appropriate nature of governance, and guidance as to how we might improve the global order.

If the relationship between political authority and markets is the core question, then the discipline must move beyond mere invocation in terms of dealing with it. For too long, scholars have either merely invoked the inter-relationship in terms of mutual effects, or assumed it. Either way, the relationship has not been adequately conceptualised. This is important, because the way we conceptualise political authority, the market, and their relationship affects how we respond to them, what we can do with them in terms of policy and broader patterns of governance both within and beyond the context of state decision-making. It affects how we can change global order, and for what purposes.

Models of state and market

The problem is as follows. If most IPE literature insists that political authority and markets are interdependent, the relationship is usually portrayed as one of interdependent antagonism. Political logic, particularly the logic of states, pulls in one direction. Economic logic, the logic of the markets, pulls in another. Political expediency or legitimacy may be invoked to override market forces, or market forces may defeat attempts at political definition of outcome, but either way, states and markets exist in antipathy to each other.

The state-market dichotomy

The distinction between the state and the market is commonplace in everyday discussion. The intelligent media reveals just how common it is. Newscasts and newspapers are divided into sections on politics, business (which really ought to be labelled 'economy'[31]), culture, media, sport, and so on. At the edges, these worlds meet: politics can interfere with the Olympics, which is 'sport', and governments might interfere in merger and takeover business decisions, something which they should or should not do, depending on one's standpoint. Yet the clear distinction between the state and the market is something in which we all, in contemporary society, partake and understand. The distinction goes so far as to anthropomorphise 'the market,' to treat markets as if they were agents who did things, and had intentions and consciousness like human beings or individual firms. One hears daily how 'the market reacted vigorously to the announcement by the European Central Bank,' or 'the market has succeeded in getting around government policy'. Policy-makers ask themselves how the market will react to a measure proposed to the legislature. The potential reaction of the market is often invoked as a reason why a particular solution would not work. In this way, we assign to markets the capacity to circumvent regulations, tax laws, or to be fruitful and multiply their kind. We all know that this is a sort of shorthand for the reactions, or lack thereof, of a range of different economic agents interacting in complex circumstances. Yet we live and breath this shorthand as if it were real, as if markets really did do these things. The concept of markets as 'things' goes very deep; our societies are organised in large part around market mechanisms for the production and exchange, so this is not surprising. Yet if the concept implicit in this discourse is inaccurate, as I claim it is, then we are prisoners of our own rhetoric to the extent that we act as if it were true.

Where does this clear distinction come from? I would argue that we can find its intellectual and ideological roots in the nineteenth century and the rise of both industrialisation and the emergence of democratic forms of governance. The arguments of Karl Polanyi (to whom we shall return later) are useful here.[32] In the first place, industrialisation could not have taken place without the process of 'commodification' of the vital factors of production, land, labour, and capital, beginning in Britain. By this, Polanyi literally meant creating new legal devices whereby these factors of production could be exchanged freely and privately on the market. Common land and ancient occupancy rights of ordinary rural dwellers were thus revoked through the 'acts of enclosure'. Some landlords opposed this, but others saw it as an opportunity to release themselves from a paternalistic burden and improve agricultural productivity, or even to sell up in order to repay debt borne of extravagance. Money as capital over time entirely replaced land as the store of value and became common throughout the economy as a medium of exchange for commodities, and money itself came to be bought and sold on financial markets. Finally, labour had to be 'set free' in the sense that without a certain mobility of labour, from the land to industrial employment, the industrial market economy was unlikely to function effectively. Correspondingly, 'Poor Laws' restricting the poor to their parish of origin and the common law rights of tenants to occupy their dwellings were superceded, sending the dispossessed in search of employment, usually in the new industrial cities. Industry could draw on the new mobility of labour, and agriculture emerged as a business employing new machinery, just like industry. This sort of story was repeated in different ways and circumstances across Europe.

Once the market began to function as the core element of industrial society, it was not long before individuals and social constituencies forgot that things had ever been different. A private realm of commodity and financial exchange, including labour, emerged to replace the world of mercantilism and the residue of the middle ages. The private business affairs of individuals interacting in the market were largely separate from the concerns of state, especially as states in the nineteenth century did relatively little in terms of contemporary expectations. At the risk of considerable simplification, states worried about other things, especially security and empire building (though the empire building largely involved using security policy to hand favours to the King and assorted cronies). The state-market distinction was borne and entered the collective consciousness as part of an inalienable reality, except to radicals (for example, Marx), who questioned the very basis and justice of the system itself, and continue to do so.

The public-private, state-market distinction is mirrored in scholarly debate. Alongside these historical developments emerged a science of economics which focused on explaining the pattern of market interactions, both in terms of how it worked and how it might work better. It was a science which was relatively unconcerned with how the transformation to the market had taken place, or whether it might be in turn superceded. Debates *within* economics were varied and complex enough, and remain so today, to maintain intellectual momentum.

Meanwhile, developments in what is more readily acknowledged as the realm of the public domain, government, helped to reinforce the state-market, public-private distinction. Democratic movements sought to wrest private power over government from the King and his cronies and to place it in the hands of elected representatives. Limiting the private, arbitrary power of the monarch meant creating a public sphere or domain of interest to everyone, the sphere of government in the public interest and for the public good. This movement was accompanied by ideas of individual rights, constitutionally and legally enforced, which would limit the capacity of government to intrude in the day-to-day affairs of citizens, as people came to be known. The roots of this democratic constitutionalism were deep in the Enlightenment which started in the late seventeenth century, ironically at the very moment that absolute monarchy was perfected by Louis the Sun King.

Not surprisingly, the liberal ideas behind this political movement had links to the ideas which had produced the private domain of property and the market – as a bulwark against the arbitrary exercise of power by authoritarian landlords and monarchs. Political philosophers such as Rousseau, Montesquieu, Locke, and Kant shared much with the classical political economists of the Scottish enlightenment: David Hume, Adam Smith, or David Ricardo. The public-private distinction became part and parcel of the cry which echoed across Europe and the Americas for rights and freedom in the context of representative government based on democratic practices. Not surprisingly, private 'economic' freedoms, the right of ordinary entrepreneurs and labourers to pursue legitimate economic activities free from the restrictions of the mercantilist oligopolies maintained by the monarch and his political allies, were included in the movement. The result was the eventual emergence first of the market mechanism as a powerful organising principle promoting industrialisation and commerce. This was followed, on the whole much later, by the emergence of limited and eventually largely-democratic forms of representative government. Democracy was in many cases as much a response to the misery of industrialism as it was to the arbitrariness of absolute monarchy.

So there came to be a realm of private, democratically and constitutionally guaranteed rights of individuals to participate in the very public business of selecting the government. At the same time there was a private domain of economic freedoms which constituted the market, from which some, as always, did better than others. It was a short step towards an intellectual system which not only justified and reinforced this state-market dichotomy, but also quite rightly recognised the historical interdependence of market and constitutional freedoms. It is worth noting that democratic practice never succeeded in penetrating the private domain of the market, and indeed it was often part of the argument that it should not.

In this regard we can now take a moment to observe how contemporary scholarly disciplines continue to reinforce the very strong popular perception of a state-market dichotomy. We can do this through a brief examination of what remain the two most prevalent strains of political and economic thought in western European societies, the liberal and realist schools. Liberal and realist scholars represent more or less polar opposites in the debate on the state-market relationship in the global economy, but each in its own way maintains a clear distinction between the two.

Liberal scholars, particularly in neo-classical economics, have strongly advocated the market as an organising principle for our developing world political economy. In a long tradition of liberal idealism, advocates of the global market view it as an escape from the disabilities of politics,[33] and a march towards the natural and spontaneous order of the Austrian school,[34] underpinned by the harmony of interests which Adam Smith was convinced could be allowed to flourish under certain carefully nurtured conditions.[35] While Smith himself was ultimately sceptical about the possibility of preventing the eventual corruption of a market economy into a series of rent-seeking arrangements sponsored by the market actors themselves, others have rushed in where Smith was very careful to tread.[36]

Despite the caution of Smith and others,[37] transnational integration dominated by market processes is often seen as an ideal state of affairs[38] in which there would be an end to the interference of the sectional interests which characterise most forms political interaction, and the states of the international system in particular. This view is of course underpinned by the usually implicit assumption that states and markets are antithetical organising principles: hierarchy, power, and coercion versus decentralisation, spontaneous interaction, and even liberty.

The other side of the debate most typically starts from realist principles in international relations, underpinned by a corresponding (but more often explicit) assumption that the economic and political domains are again separate entities. As Hans Morgenthau puts it in the sixth of his six principles of political realism: 'Intellectually the political realist maintains the autonomy of the political sphere, as the economist, the lawyer, and moralist maintain theirs.'[39] Here the argument is that politics will, in the nature of things, dominate economic processes, particularly in the international domain.[40] It is not surprising that a lively debate exists which pits the tradition of political realism against the 'globalisers' of liberal-idealist heritage. It is a continuation of the realist-idealist controversy which goes back to the interwar period and beyond.

In sum, the intellectual apparatus of scholarship provides considerable reinforcement to the commonly-held view that states and markets, private versus public domain, are distinct entities, and that indeed they *should* be so. However, political economists, comparative or international, will be apt to protest at this point that there are other ways of looking at the question which focus on the *relationship* between states and markets. This point provides an appropriate bridge to a critique of the state-market dichotomy and elaboration of the state-market condominium model.

The state-market condominium

Can one really claim a meaningful and empirically verifiable distinction between political authority and the market? If so, where does one place authoritative political decisions on environmental regulation, trade law, or competition law, all of which have huge implications for transaction costs in market-based economic competition, both within and across borders? Are these very political matters in the public domain of politics and states, or the private domain of the market (and one should note that these policies are heavily influenced by the interests they affect)? How would one answer such a question? It is argued that one cannot, if one attempts to maintain a distinction between states and markets for other than occasional analytical purposes.

If one were to go back in time, one would discover that the distinction between political and economic interaction was not perceived as clearly as it is today. Perhaps that is simply because we are so much more sophisticated in contemporary times, and one mark of sophistication is greater degrees of analytical specialisation. Yet the way in which the production and distribution of wealth was accomplished, the way in which society produced and distributed benefits (or lack thereof) across social constituencies, was historically tied in an intimate fashion to the way in which the powerful chose to organise it for the rest of us. A mediaeval landlord saw little difference between control of the land and food production on the one hand, and the broader pattern of governance of the world around him on the other. Peasants laboured to produce food and gave most as taxes in exchange for the use of common land and for security in a turbulent world. Peasants also represented expendable bodies for defence. The landlord and Church on whom the system rested used a mixture of accepted spiritual doctrine and naked power to ensure that this continued to be the case. In turn, Louis XIV of France, a rather successful ruler, saw little difference between his personal interests and fortunes as monarch and the centralised economic organisation of the realm which he initiated: 'l'Etat, c'est moi,' as he put it, and that included control over the production and trade of many key commodities in the economy. In both cases, the system of production was intimately linked to the broader socio-political order.

Political economy focuses precisely on the reciprocal relationship between political authority and the private pursuits of economic agents in the market. As argued above, Adam Smith put this question at the core of political economy in the first place. He lived in times of rapid change in eighteenth century Scotland and northern England, and was therefore strongly aware of history, and how the different ways in which societies provided for their sustenance and surpluses (and the distribution thereof) affected the patterns of social structure and authority over time. The changing ways in which who gets what, when, and how lends form and substance (sometimes rather unpleasant) to society and to its more formal institutions of governance, to the rules by which it lives, and shapes who has power over whom. In this Smith shared much with his eventual critic, Marx.

Critically, Smith observed that there was an ongoing tension between the private passions and interests of individuals, and the collective needs of the wider community – a tension between the pursuit of self-interest and the fulfilment of the public good. His core question was, how might this tension be resolved?[41] Are we permanently faced with iniquity and compulsion to order the affairs of humankind? Must the powerful always abscond with the lion's share of the benefits of human endeavour, making the world miserable for the rest? What forms of governance might help us to curb the exclusionary excesses of rulers and the rich, usually one and the same, and permit the innovative capacity of human beings to come to bear on the process of economic development?

He argued that, under certain conditions contrived and enforced by political authorities, competitive markets might help us to turn the pursuit of private gain toward achieving the important common aim of producing and distributing wealth in the most optimal fashion possible. One might, as said, disagree with his prescription, but the problem he posed remains central to political economy and governance, international or otherwise. Smith's core question can also be reformulated in more contemporary terms. We *have* the market, indeed an increasingly global one, but not always the carefully contrived conditions Smith recommended. The market has furthermore proved less stable, less equal, and less harmonious in operation than he and many of his successors thought would be the case, hence radical critique and many of the demands for alternate forms of governance. Power is clearly not the preserve of the formal institutions which pretend to monopolise it, particularly states – private market power is very much part of the pattern of governance we experience.

Seen in this light, Smith's core question can help us re-evaluate the state-market dichotomy and its relevance to our understanding of the contemporary global economy. He gets us back to the nature of the reciprocal relationship between political authority and private pursuits in the market: what ought to be the public good in terms of the wider process of governance? Whose interests do and should prevail in the various tiers of institutions and less formal arrangements which constitute global governance? What is the relationship between market structures and political authority (loosely defined) in the ongoing and accelerating process of global change?[42]

These questions, as stated earlier, encapsulate what the study of political economy and governance is about, despite all its diversity. What do we think a state or market is, and are they/how are they/should they be related? Furthermore, we need to be reminded that how we think about political authority, the market, and their relationship affects how we respond to them, what we believe we can do with them in terms of policy both within and beyond the context of state decision-making. It affects how we can change global order, and for what purposes. It is unsatisfactory that a discipline trying to get away from the state-market dichotomy characterises the interaction of states and markets as a sort of tug-of-war between market forces and state attempts to control or direct them.[43]

If we really do have a *political economy*, we must demonstrate, empirically and conceptually, how the whole is greater than the sum of its parts, *how* states and markets are integral to each other in the process of governance. If not, it is impossible to resolve the argument about whether states or markets are really in control, and to explain why both states and markets appear so different today relative to three decades ago. We need to take our Polanyi[44] and the notion of political economy seriously: he argues that the market makes no sense without the state, that indeed the market system was created and enforced by the state, as outlined earlier in this chapter. The idea of a separate economic domain without politics was to him a stark utopia which failed, resulting in surely the greatest human tragedy of the modern period: the depression, fascism, and the Second World War.

Somehow we need to conceptualise how states are embedded in wider, increasingly transnational social structures; how key socio-economic constituencies of non-state (usually business) actors are integrated into the institutional processes of states; how the agency of these actors, through state policy institutions, are central to the process of global economic transformation and to the terms of competition among market agents. The claim is, then, that the political economy is something greater than the sum of the state-market parts. This means that there is still one more and crucial conceptual step to take in order to move beyond the tug-of-war position of state-market dichotomy. The concept of states and markets as separate (if interacting) entities is an often useful abstraction, but we need to remind ourselves that states and markets are not separate *things* as such. They are never, in fact, found alone. Many of the most important political decisions a community can take concerns the way in which markets should and shall work. In this sense, states and markets are part of the same integrated ensemble of governance, a state-market *condominium*, and should be thought of as such. The regulatory and policy-making institutions of the state are one element of the market, one set of institutions, through which the overall process of governance operates. The structures of the market are constituted as much and simultaneously by the political processes of the state – and the political resources of the various interests involved in the policy process – as by the process of economic competition itself; likewise the political and regulatory process is as much part of the strategies of firms as the game of investment and marketing.[45] The preferences of market agents and other constituencies of market society are integrated into the institutions of the state through policy and regulatory processes at domestic and international levels of analysis, depending on their individual organisational capacities/coherence, and of course power. The incentives and constraints of state policy and regulation are in turn part of the landscape of decision-making by firms as they compete with each other. Policy and regulation, just like the competitive strategies of firms, confers advantages on some and costs on others. At the same time, some are more capable of affecting the policy outcome than others.

In creating a market as a mechanism of governance, then, we take a political decision to *delegate* to private individuals the very public responsibility of organising the creation and distribution of wealth. This is true whether at domestic or global level, and whether the decision is conscious or not. This implies a certain accountability of private economic agents to the public domain, especially in a democracy. We can argue about the terms of that accountability, but the idea that the private sector somehow exists in another world of 'free' enterprise is not sustainable in fact or in normative terms. Echoing Polanyi, there is nothing spontaneous or natural about a market as the primary organising principle for economic activity; it is an act of public policy. For good or ill, political economies have been different in the past (which includes Soviet-style central planning), and may well be so in the future. Furthermore, markets work in very different ways depending on the economic activity in question, the sector, and the historical and cultural setting across the global economy.

The state-market condominium model provides for a more sustainable explanation of states, markets, and governance. According to the model, the adjustment process and pattern of economic interaction is managed simultaneously through the process of economic competition among firms on the one hand, and the policy and regulatory processes of the state, on the other. Market agents enhance or protect their position and prosperity by making simultaneous calculations through their business strategies, deploying their competitive resources, and through the deployment of their political resources in the decision-making processes of the state. This is clearly visible in corporatist systems in western Europe, where even labour is integrated into both state policy processes and the strategic decision-making of firms, or in the close integration of private firms/associations into the system of bureaucratic management which characterises the economic development process in Japan and other parts of Asia. The point is less obvious to observers of Anglo-Saxon political economies where the independence of the private sector appears more marked than in other societies. But the considerable evidence of 'regulatory capture' of the agencies of governance in the US economy should indicate the need to avoid the stereotypes developed in particularly the economics literature. A market without institutions and governance, including some form of judicial authority or arbitration, is inconceivable.

Of course this conceptualisation of states and markets appears counter-intuitive in our era of global integration increasingly dominated by private sector market processes. Our contemporary experience of modern capitalism and the prevalence of economic modes of analysis engraves on our intellects the idea of the state-market dichotomy. Yet Adam Smith is again useful here – he pointed out that the very public responsibilities of generating and distributing wealth could be successfully accomplished by private agents. More worrisomely in Smith's opinion, the reverse is also true, as shall be seen below. This however does not render the economy any less political: one can delegate authority and decision-making power, but one cannot de-politicise the system as such. It remains an ensemble of governance.

There is also nothing surprising in the idea that a transnational state-market condominium may have multiple institutions of authority, some state, some international. In this sense, the phenomenon of multiple state sovereignties in the global economy does not detract from the model. Anyone who lives in a federal state or indeed the European Union (EU) should be comfortable with this assertion. Furthermore, as the pattern of material interests in national political economies has become more transnational, so the state has changed. The state has become far more a facilitator of global market processes than a protector of domestic market structures and interests over the past three decades. The pattern of political authority and governance becomes more transnational in symbiosis with the transformation of the market. The state has progressively delegated a number of tasks either to private bodies or to institutions of international co-operation, though it maintains its functions in terms of domestic political legitimacy and all the tensions that entails.

In this sense what we have seen is not so much a *retreat* of the state in the face of market forces, but a transformation of the state in symbiosis with the transformation of markets. We have changing forms of state emphasising different functions over others, not an emasculation as such. There may be a retreat of the state from particular activities and functions, but if one properly understands the dynamics of the state-market condominium, it should be clear that the form and functions of the state will continue to evolve as indeed they have in the past.

Practical and policy implications

This brings me to a relatively brief discussion of the practical and policy implications of the model in a situation of increasingly multilevel governance. Some of these have been alluded to above. Five interrelated points can be made in relation to problems of global governance.

i)   If we cease thinking about states and markets as opposing dynamics in permanent tug-of-war with each other, we might put an end to a particularly sterile debate. We would stop expecting, or indeed hoping, that one might triumph over the other, whatever one's preferred outcome. It is not going to happen, because the two go together. We cannot somehow wish politics out of markets or the other way around, and the behaviour of private market constituents is anyway inherently political, whether we choose to recognise it or not.

This both complicates and liberates the process of governance from the constraints of more orthodox approaches to states and markets. The model certainly implies that a variety of solutions are possible. There is no single alternative, but the choice is not thereby rendered easy. Although we may opt for more or less liberal solutions, we cannot simply rely on market forces to 'sort it out', and must devote more time to the question, 'what kind of market, to serve what kind of society?' The nature of the market is inherently contestable, and there is no single equilibrium point which can be rationally determined. In this sense the outcome and potential solutions to problems are genuinely open-ended and societies are free to choose. Multiple equilibrium models are much the order of the day, but the variables are political and institutional as well as 'economic' as such. This greatly complicates the task of decision making. We need to confront this world of bewildering choice and imperfection head on, remembering that perfection is itself nothing to do with the real world. It is an abstract concept with which we can help ourselves to aspire, but with which we can also get ourselves into trouble through the pursuit of utopia and misplaced idealism.

ii)   The model implies that *exclusive* reliance on concepts of perfect competition, optimality, and general equilibrium are likely to yield misleading policy prescriptions and even a misunderstanding of the problem at hand. By understanding that the market operates simultaneously through competitive processes and the policy process, now a policy process which extends across borders, we can much better come to terms with the rent-seeking behaviour of both private and public actors. If we do not expect firms or other market agents to behave according to models of perfect competition, we will more easily understand that rent-seeking behaviour is not the exception, but the rule. If we all admit that perfect competition is an abstraction from a messy, more prosaic reality of various forms of second best market-fixing, we can begin to see more clearly the reality of political economy: if the state does not rig the market, private interests will. It is better that we make clear and well-informed decisions about how and why we want it rigged in particular ways.

We can never therefore disconnect the world of policy choice from the rather dirty world of self-interest and particularistic advantage. We should be aware that governments sometimes constitute the most private interests of all, and a fulsome democratic process is there for a reason. We should *also* understand that there is nothing particularly noble about the interests of business or any other economic agent. Nobility of intent is bound to be in short supply. Business in a market system, particularly big business, carries huge responsibilities in terms of the realisation of public policy objectives. It does not exist in some purely private market domain where it can do nothing but good, or indeed ill to its detractors. None could be more clear on this point than Adam Smith, who advocated market solutions but remained guarded in important ways:

> The interest of the dealers...in any particular branch of trade or manufactures, is always in some respects different from, and even opposite to, that of the public. To widen the market and narrow the competition, is always in the interest of the dealers.... The proposal of any new law or regulation of commerce which comes from this order, ought always to be listened to with the greatest precaution....[46]

Democratic processes should be understood as much for keeping private interests accountable for the public interest functions they perform in our societies, as they are for keeping politicians accountable to the electorate. The rhetoric of the free market makes it all too easy to forget this point.

iii) If the state-market condominium model helps us to come to terms with the endemic nature of particularistic rent-seeking, we might stop expecting it to be a smooth, equilibrium process. The global integration process is not about the rational pursuit of optimality or spontaneous market development, but is driven by particularistic interests. As different constituencies compete to shape the process to their own advantage, the multiple equilibrium idea comes back to mind, and there are good and bad equilibria in various guises. Furthermore, as political and economic competition to control the terms of market integration proceeds, we become aware that we are not integrating like entities. Just as even the most 'rational' of corporate mergers often founder on tensions between contrasting corporate cultures, we should expect local and regional ways of doing things to come together in dynamic and sometimes difficult tension. Integration is not of like with like, but a linking together of diverse state-market condominiums. It will be a bumpy process and diversity is bound to persist. Strict convergence to single 'rational' standards is unlikely to be possible or healthy, and there is no single formula which can admit of universal application. Many models will work, each infused with different values. The democratic process must ensure that a choice of values and solutions is consistently available, even to the weak and economically deprived.

iv)   If global integration is an imperfect, bumpy process infused with rent-seeking activity and the pursuit of private gain, and a straightforward equilibrium outcome is unlikely, then we should expect and prepare for crisis, particularly financial crisis. The Asian crisis caught everyone napping, bar a few, and we should have been better prepared. But there is a further point: if equilibrium is problematic and crisis likely to occur, perhaps we should devote less time to casting aspersions on solutions which appear to 'interfere' with the rationality of the market, such as capital controls. Such policy devices can obviously be wrongly and inappropriately employed. But my model would indicate that the same can be said of free market solutions too. Private greed must not be allowed to plunge the political economy into troubled waters.

v)   Most importantly, the state-market condominium model allows us to understand how markets are integral to governance and the formal activities of government. The state *is* involved in the market and *should* be involved in the market, and the market cannot function as a system without the political and regulatory processes which the state represents. We should be very wary, echoing Smith, of those who argue that the state should leave market agents alone to get on with the job – there is nothing sacred about them and market agents are more than likely pursuing a narrow private agenda. State interference could well be ill-informed or simply wrong, but the same can be said of the functions performed in the public interest by market agents.

Thus the market is also closely tied to the issue of political legitimacy, particularly in a democratic context. If the functioning of the market does not satisfy enough of the people enough of the time, we have a problem. This might apply as much to 'no growth' or 'slow growth', as it does to *unequal* growth. In this sense, distributional outcomes matter: aggregate gains may not always be the crucial variable. If market pressures bring democratically unacceptable results, they must be rethought and redesigned, and they *can* be. If change induced by market forces comes at a politically unacceptable pace, the potential benefits of liberal solutions may be lost for lack of political realism. The bottom line is therefore not an economic one, but a political one, and the *outcome* must be perceived as legitimate.

Conclusion

In this chapter, it has been argued that a conceptual leap must be taken to rethink the way in which we understand the relationship between states and markets in the context of an increasingly integrated global economy. We should abandon models of state and market which see them as different, opposing dynamics in constant tension one with the other. A model of states and markets which conceptualises them as part of the same ensemble of governance is needed. This implies a reassessment of the distinction between the public and the private, and of the nature of the public good in global governance processes.

The state-market condominium model permits a more realistic assessment of the possibilities and constraints on governance in our global era. The approach is important because it focuses on agency, the capacity of human beings to make normatively informed policy choices concerning the nature and direction of change. We need to focus on who the political constituencies are which need to be challenged in order to correct the balance of costs and benefits of aspects of global economic integration, particularly the problem of inequality and poverty.

The state-market condominium model therefore renders operational policy relevant research in political economy and infuses our understanding of the global economic development process with agency. There *is* room for discretionary policy and action, even for the relatively vulnerable. We can, at least to a limited degree, affect the norms and values which underpin global order. As long as we see only a tug-of-war between the state and the market, then the benefits of one will be overshadowed by the costs of the other. The point is that we cannot have one without the other. They exist in symbiosis.

Political authority in global governance is therefore not just vested in the formal institutions of states and their offshoots of governance such as regimes, as legal and constitutional theory would have it. It is also present in the agents of the market as part of the state-market condominium. The market *is* governance, even as it appears to work in mysterious, private ways. Herein lies one of the most fundamental problems: our systems of democratic accountability are nationally based, whereas our systems of production and the market are so no longer, if indeed they ever were. The EU is wrestling with this problem, and the speed of institutional adaptation is frustratingly slow. The model suggests that if global capitalism is to remain stable and to produce benefits which outweigh the costs, then we must fully confront the 'Bretton Woods problem': whether liberalisation is good or bad, it will only work if it satisfies enough of the people enough of the time. The 'people' are still organised in political communities called states. If for example the shadow of financial crisis so darkens their horizons, the political communities we call states can and will react and withdraw, with ugly results for us all as they default on debt and renege on co-operatively negotiated obligations. This is not very likely in the advanced economies, which are relatively well placed to cope, but we all anxiously watch Argentina, Brazil, and Turkey in this regard. Other large and militarily powerful states with disastrously weak economies, like Russia, were recently on the brink. The fate of modernisation in China and India we do not yet know.

Whether we like it or not, we are in a situation of rapid change; we cannot go back. We must use what political agency we have in government and as citizens to shape the process in ways which tend towards stability, preserving vital aspects of local and national autonomy, and helping weaker societies to adapt, thus preventing the rise of political ugliness of the sort we saw in the 1930s and in the breakdown of Yugoslavia or the ongoing crisis in Indonesia. We know that markets often derail, and we should anticipate this. Europe, Canada, and other countries committed to multilateral forms of governance and a long-run commitment to social justice, have a vital role to play but have done relatively little to promote the mechanisms of governance which correspond to these values. There are many routes to global integration, we have choice, and we should exercise it.

Notes

1. See Introduction to this volume.
2. This section is adapted from G. R. D. Underhill, 'State, Market, and Global Political Economy: Genealogy of an (Inter-?) Discipline', *International Affairs*, Vol. 76/4 (October 2000), 805–24.
3. In the vein of H. Morgenthau, *Politics among Nations: the struggle for power and peace* (New York: Alfred A. Knopf, 1956), or K. Waltz, *Theory of International Relations* (Reading, Mass.: Addison-Wesley, 1979), or S. Krasner, 'International Political Economy: Abiding Discord', *Review of International Political Economy*, Vol. 1/1 (Spring 1994) 13–28.
4. Examples include Robert Keohane and Joseph Nye, or James Rosenau in his more 'IPE mode.'
5. Examples would include Peter J. Katzenstein and Peter Gourevitch, who have both long been associated with one of the most important journals in the field, *International Organisation*.
6. Her clarion call came in S. Strange, 'International Economics and International Relations: a case of mutual neglect', *International Affairs*, volume 46/2 (April 1970) 304–315.
7. Whom Susan Strange always regarded as the founder of contemporary IPE and whose hegemonic stability hypothesis (in *The World in Depression*

1929–39 (Berkeley: University of California Press, 1973)) had enormous influence on the discipline as it developed.

8. Robert Cox clearly fits this category – see discussion below.
9. G. R. D. Underhill, 'Conceptualizing the Changing Global Order', in R. Stubbs and G. Underhill (eds), *Political Economy and the Changing Global Order*, 2nd edition (Oxford: Oxford University Press, 2000), pp. 4–5.
10. See M. Cox, K. Booth and T. Dunne (eds), *The Interregnum: Controversies in World Politics 1989–1999*, special issue of *Review of International Studies*, Vol. 25 (December 1999).
11. J. N. Rosenau (ed.), *Linkage Politics: Essays on the Convergence of National and International Systems* (New York: Free Press, 1969); —— (ed.), *Domestic Sources of Foreign Policy* (New York: Free Press, 1967); ——, *Public Opinion and Foreign Policy: an operational framework* (New York: Random House, 1961).
12. R. O. Keohane and J. Nye, *Power and Interdependence: World Politics in Transition* (Boston: Little Brown, 1977), pp. 8–11.
13. R. O. Keohane and J. Nye (eds), *Transnational Relations and World Politics*, special issue of *International Organization*, Vol. XXV (summer 1971); S. Strange (ed.), 'Transnational Relations', special section of *International Affairs*, Vol. 52/3 (July 1976).
14. R. Axelrod, *The Evolution of Co-operation* (New York: Basic Books, 1984); R. O. Keohane, *After Hegemony: co-operation and discord in the world political economy* (Princeton, NJ: Princeton University Press, 1984); M. Olson, *The Rise and Decline of Nations* (New Haven: Yale University Press, 1982).
15. J. Alt and K. Schepsle, *Perspectives on Positive Political Economy* (Cambridge: Cambridge University Press, 1990).
16. See A. Shonfield, V. Curzon *et al.*, *Politics and Trade* (Vol. 1) and S. Strange, *International Monetary Relations* (Vol. 2) of *International Economic Relations of the Western World 1959–1971*, A. Shonfield (ed.) (Oxford: Oxford University Press, 1976).
17. The pioneering volume in question drew on Keohane and Nye's Power and Interdependence (*op. cit.*); see S. Krasner (ed.), *International Regimes* (Ithaca: Cornell University Press, 1983).
18. See T. Risse-Kappen (ed.), *Bringing Transnational Relations Back In: Non-state actors, Domestic Structures, and International Institutions* (Syracuse: Cambridge: Cambridge University Press, 1995).
19. See A. Claire Cutler, V. Haufler, and T. Porter (eds), *Private Authority in International Affairs* (Syracuse: State University of New York Press, 1999).
20. See respectively P. J. Katzenstein (ed.), *Between Power and Plenty: foreign economic policies of advanced industrial states* (Madison: University of Wisconsin Press, 1978); P. Gourevitch, 'The Second Image Reversed: the International Sources of Domestic Politics', *International Organization*, Vol. 32/4 (Autumn 1978), pp. 881–911; *Politics in Hard Times* (Ithaca: Cornell University Press, 1986), and J. Zysman, *Governments, Markets, and Growth* (Ithaca: Cornell University Press, 1983).
21. See H. Hveem, 'Explaining the Regional Phenomenon in an Era of Globalization', in Stubbs and Underhill (eds) (2000), *op. cit.* 70–81.
22. See J. Greenwood and H. Jacek (eds), *Organized Business and the New Global Order* (London: Routledge, 2000).

23. F. Block, *The Origins of International Economic Disorder* (Berkeley: University of California Press, 1977).
24. See R. W. Cox (with T. Sinclair), *Approaches to World Order* (Cambridge: Cambridge University Press, 1996); ——, *Production, Power, and World Order* (New York: Columbia University Press, 1987).
25. See the widely cited K. van der Pijl, *The Making of the Atlantic Ruling Class* (London: Verso, 1984), and more recently, *Transnational Classes and International Relations* (London: Routledge, 1998).
26. S. Gill (ed.), *Gramsci, Historical Materialism, and International Relations* (Cambridge: Cambridge University Press, 1993).
27. See S. Whitworth, 'Gender and International Political Economy', in R. Stubbs and G. Underhill (eds), *Political Economy and the Changing Global Order*, 1st edition (London: Macmillan, 1994), *op. cit.*, 116–129, and the same author's article 'Theory and Exclusion: gender, masculinity, and international political economy' in Stubbs and Underhill, *Political Economy*, 2nd edition, *op. cit.* (2000) 91–101. Other recent works in the veritable explosion of feminist writings on the global political economy include M. Marchand and J. Parpart, *Feminism/Postmodernism/Development* (London: Routledge, 1995); V. S. Peterson and A. S. Runyan, *Global Gender Issues*, 2nd edition (Boulder: Westview Press, 1999). On green approaches, see E. Helleiner, 'IPE and the Greens', *New Political Economy*, Vol. 1/1 (1996) 59–77.
28. See chapter one of S. Strange, *States and Markets* (Oxford: Blackwell, 1988).
29. On Smith's contribution to political economy, see: A. Skinner, '*Introduction*' to Adam Smith, *The Wealth of Nations* (London: Penguin, 1970); R. Heilbroner (ed.), *The Essential Adam Smith* (Oxford: Oxford University Press, 1986). The points under discussion here draw on an earlier article, G. R. D. Underhill, 'The Public Good versus Private Interests in the Global Monetary and Financial System', *International and Comparative Corporate Law Journal*, Vol. 2, No. 3 (2000) 335–359.
30. Once again, the point Susan Strange made so long ago in 'The Study of Transnational Relations', *op. cit.*, 1976.
31. The Anglo-Saxon press is particularly guilty of this, as if 'economy' were only about what business does, and not about labour, consumers, and regulators.
32. K. Polanyi, *The Great Transformation* (Boston: Beacon Press, 1944).
33. W. Wriston, in *The Twilight of Sovereignty* (New York: Scribner, 1992), argues that the global integration processes driven by the rapid growth of information technology spells, if not the end of the nation-state as such, a rapid and beneficial dilution of state power over space and peoples; see particularly Chapter 8, 'Borders are not Boundaries.' Kenichi Ohmae argues from a more conventional standpoint, arguing that contemporary business strategies and the rise of consumer choice has produced an increasingly interlinked economy bypassing traditional state functions, a process once again characterised as fundamentally liberating; see *The Borderless World* (London: Collins, 1990) and *The End of the Nation-State: the Rise of Regional Economies* (London: HarperCollins, 1995).
34. See F. A. Hayek, *The Constitution of Liberty* (London: Routledge and Kegan Paul, 1960); ——, *Individualism and Economic Order* (London: Routledge and Kegan Paul, 1949); K. R. Leube and A. H. Zlabinger (eds), *The Political Economy of Freedom: Essays in Honour of F. A. Hayek* (Vienna: Philosophia Verlag, 1985).

35. C. Napoleoni, *Smith, Ricardo, Marx* (Oxford: Basil Blackwell, 1975), p. 30. See also A. Smith (edited by E. Cannan), *An Inquiry into the Nature and Causes of the Wealth of Nations* (New York: The Modern Library, 1937), for example, p. 99 and pp. 118–143.
36. Smith was particularly wary of the role of vested interests in policy-making; see citation note 46.
37. Such as the renowned interwar realist E. H. Carr, *The Twenty Years Crisis 1919–1939: an Introduction to the Study of International Relations* (London: Macmillan, 1946), esp. Chapter 14 (Conclusion).
38. Cerny discusses globalisation as an ideal-typical discourse in P. G. Cerny, 'Globalisation and Other Stories: the Search for a New Paradigm for International Relations', in *International Journal*, Vol. LI/4 (Autumn 1996) 625.
39. H. J. Morgenthau, *Politics among Nations* (New York: Knopf: 1956), p. 10.
40. E. B. Kapstein, in *Governing the Global Economy: International Finance and the State* (Cambridge, MA: Harvard University Press, 1994), has argued that states are still very much in control of the process of global financial integration, working through the co-operative regulatory and supervisory processes of the Basle Committee on Banking Supervision, among others.
41. See Napoleoni, *op. cit.*
42. A point made by Susan Strange some time ago in 'The Study of Transnational Relations', in *International Affairs*, Vol. 52/3 (July 1976) pp. 333–345.
43. See for example R. Gilpin, *The Political Economy of International Relations* (Princeton, NJ: Princeton University Press, 1986); H. M. Schwarz, *States versus Markets: History, Geography, and the Development of the International Political Economy* (London: Macmillan, 1994), which is particularly useful for putting contemporary developments in historical perspective; and R. Boyer and D. Drache, *States against Markets: the Limits of Globalization* (London: Routledge, 1996). It is in fact a small step from some of the contributions in the Boyer and Drache volume to the position argued in this paper, particularly where they draw on the works of H. Innis and K. Polanyi.
44. Polanyi, *The Great Transformation, op. cit.*
45. See G. R. D. Underhill, *Industrial Crisis and the Open Economy: politics, global trade and the textile industry in the advanced economies* (Basingstoke: Macmillan, 1998): 18–25; passim.
46. A. Smith (edited by E. Canaan), *An Inquiry into the Nature and Causes of the Wealth of Nations* (New York: The Modern Library), p. 250.

Selected References

Boyer, R. and D. Drache, *States against Markets: the Limits of Globalization* (London: Routledge, 1996).
Cox, R. W. *Production, Power, and World Order* (New York: Columbia University Press, 1987).
Gilpin, R. *The Political Economy of International Relations* (Princeton, NJ: Princeton Univ. Press, 1986).
Keohane, R. O. and J. Nye, *Power and Interdependence*. (Boston: Little Brown, 1977).
Polanyi, K. The Great Transformation (Boston: Beacon Press, 1944).
Strange, S. States and Markets (Oxford: Blackwell, 1988).
Stubbs, R. and G. Underhill (eds), Political Economy and the Changing Global Order, 2nd edition (Oxford: Oxford University Press, 2000).

6
The Great Powers in an Age of Global Governance: Are They Still Great?

Robert A. Pastor

In the past century, as throughout history, mankind has witnessed the rise and fall of great powers and the dissolution of empires. The twenty-first century is the first without empires or colonies. The great powers negotiate rules, which constrain all of them, and they grope toward defining a new system of global governance. They don't seize each other's land. They pursue their interests with each other in international organisations rather than in gunboats. They have all signed treaties affirming a single set of human rights principles. They focus more on gaining access to markets than on securing resources. They spend more for social security than for weapons. They coax warring ethnic groups to make peace. The three European powers seek unity and harmony with each other rather than alliances and war against each other. All these changes arise from the fact that the great powers pursue different goals at the beginning of the twenty-first century than they did in the twentieth, and the new goals reflect a different world.

The very concept of 'great powers' seems to belong to the nineteenth century – a time when monarchs ruled empires, dispatched mercenary armies to control their dominion, and played the 'great game' of imperialism against each other. In 1901, when Great Britain buried its longest-reigning monarch, Queen Victoria, the world's royalty came to pay their respects. Most of them were related: Kaiser Wilhelm II of Germany and Tsar Nicholas II of Russia were the Queen's nephews. Yet just three years earlier, Wilhelm had decided that Germany would build a fleet to surpass England's, and seven years earlier, Nicholas had approved a secret alliance with France aimed at containing Germany. Each such decision by a single individual, without public debate, was a step toward the Great War.

Like the other monarchs of the day, Victoria was devoted to imperialism. But she was popular in England in large part because she understood that an emperor could no longer rule England's empire. She reduced her role to a symbolic one, and freely elected leaders governed. Thus in England the regal pageantry was more form than substance. But in Germany, Russia, China, Japan, Turkey, and Austria-Hungary, emperors ruled, and they defined their era by the colonies and territories they acquired.

Today, elected leaders, not monarchs, govern all of the great powers, although in China the elections are controlled by the leadership of the Communist Party. Still, the principle is almost universal that legitimate power derives from the consent of the governed – not from divine right nor naked threats. About one-third of the governments in the world do not practice this principle, but, of those, only a handful reject it.

None of the great powers rule the world. But of the 191 members of the United Nations (UN), seven countries are responsible for half of the world's trade, two-thirds of the world's output, and nearly three-quarters of the world's defence expenditures. The great powers are still defined in terms of their ability to influence or respond to events far beyond their borders. They still shape the world, but in much more subtle and indirect ways than they did at the beginning of the twentieth century. The principal goal of the great powers is to advance the economic and social interests of their people, and their leaders recognise that achieving that goal requires an international system that promotes trade and investment and contains and tries to resolve conflicts. The United States is the only superpower today. But where political and economic goals predominate, superpower status is less important than it was 100 years ago, when the great powers were carving up the world. Indeed, the enduring power of the United States derives as much from the institutions it established at the end of World War II as from its wealth or weapons.

As the goals of the great powers have changed, so too have the ways they pursue these goals. Military and economic power are so profoundly different from their 1900 equivalents that they have not simply altered the ways wars are fought or avoided. The very meaning of 'power' and the game of international politics have changed. Consider the following:

- One present-day nuclear submarine has more firepower than all the world's armies possessed in 1900. Yet both the United States and the

Soviet Union, which possessed 93 percent of the world's nuclear weapons, were defeated in costly local wars by poor developing countries.
- Of the world's 100 greatest economies, 51 are companies and 49 are countries. One of those companies – General Motors – produced nearly the same amount of goods and services in 1997 as did all of Europe in 1900.[1]
- One fibre optic cable can carry more information in a minute than all the world's telegraph and postal services could haul in the entire year 1900. Television brings every world crisis into the living rooms of billions of people, but most care more about the cost of living than the cost of dying half a world away.

Some of the ends and the means of foreign policy are new, but the seven major powers have not changed. At the dawn of the twentieth century, three countries – the United States, Japan, and Germany – emerged from isolation or internal division to challenge the great powers of the nineteenth century. Although Japan and Germany were vanquished in a war at the century's midpoint, all three were dominant again as the twenty-first century began. The United States, Japan, and Germany – in that order – had the strongest economies and the highest military expenditures at the beginning of the twenty-first century. France and England had declined from their imperial perches of 1900, but their economies, armed forces, and permanent seats on the UN Security Council still qualified them to be in the select group. Russia and China experienced the most extreme swings in power during the century, but both remain world powers because of their permanent seats on the Security Council and their impact on the world.

The thesis of this chapter is that states[2] are still the principal actors in the international system, but the way they define their goals and the world in which they seek to achieve them has *fundamentally* – though not completely – changed over the past 100 years. They continue to compete, but in a game that bears little resemblance to the contest for colonies in 1900. Today they pursue social and economic goals that require interstate co-operation and adherence to international rules. Traditional security concerns have diminished, but new fears of global terrorism have riveted the great powers. To understand the prospects for war or peace, prosperity or economic depression, global governance or anarchy in the twenty-first century, we need to understand how and why the great powers altered their goals and the system.

What accounts for these changes? The United States arrived on the world stage at the turn of the century with a set of revolutionary principles that rotated the old system almost on its head. If these principles had not been backed by US power, they could not have prevailed. If the United States had flexed its muscle without the principles, it might have replaced some of the old imperialists, but it would not have dismantled imperialism.

Albert Einstein mused at the dawn of the nuclear age that everything had changed except our ways of thinking. Similarly, our views of foreign policy have not adjusted to the century's journey. We continue to fear 'another Munich' or 'another Vietnam,' but the threats of the future bear little resemblance to the traumas of the past. Moreover, historical metaphors sometimes blind us to new opportunities. Let us examine some new ways of looking at global governance and the current political landscape, and let us describe these new perspectives as 'maps.'

Six maps of the post–Cold War world

The international political landscape was so confusing in the aftermath of the Cold War that some leaders pined nostalgically for the old bipolar world in which every event could be described as a success or failure by the United States or the Soviet Union. Without clear landmarks dividing the world into East and West or North and South, scholars and policymakers have had to find new ways to define the world. One school of thought, with many variations, contends that the era of the nation-state, like that of dinosaurs, has passed and that twenty-first century maps should discard it as a fossil. There are many other explanations. Let me summarise six of the most influential perspectives:

1. **Globalisation.** Advances in technology and communications coupled with the rising power of multinational enterprises (MNE) have globalised politics and economics and reduced the role of the state. Kenichi Ohmae asserts that this 'irreversible' process is leading 'to a genuinely borderless economy' and improved standards of living for all.[3]
2. **Clash of Civilisations.** The new international order is defined by struggle between civilisations rather than by global integration. Samuel P. Huntington identifies nine major civilisations: Western, Latin American, African, Islamic, Sinic, Hindu, Orthodox, Buddhist,

and Japanese. 'The rivalry of the superpowers,' he argued, 'is replaced by the clash of civilisations.' Economic integration will not homogenise these cultures; they will remain distinct and irreconcilable.[4]

3. **New World Order.** The end of superpower rivalry allowed the UN Security Council to play the role that its designers intended: to take 'collective measures for the prevention and removal of threats to the peace' and encourage respect for human rights. The UN coalition that drove Iraq from Kuwait marked the birth of a 'new world order.'[5] And the new world order appeared just in time, since globalisation reduced states' ability to manage effectively transnational activities. Only some form of global governance can deal with problems of proliferation of weapons of mass destruction, financial volatility, massive flows of refugees, trade disputes, or genocide.[6]

4. **The Democratic Peace.** World politics is a function of domestic politics, and peace depends on the spread of democratic values and regimes. Democracies do not fight one another, at least after they are consolidated, and so the principal threats to world peace occur among dictatorships or between dictatorships and democracies.[7]

5. **Pan-Regions.** technology has compressed distances, and since 1947 international agreements have dismantled most trade and investment barriers. The result, however, has been not one world but three: trade within each of three pan-regions – Europe, North America, and East Asia – has increased much more rapidly than trade between them. Each of these pan-regions is led by a dominant power: the European Union (EU) by a unified Germany; North America by a predominant United States; and East Asia by Japan, but increasingly contested by China. These three regions account for about 80 percent of the world's product and trade.[8]

6. **States.** The international system has changed in profound ways, but states remain its most important actors. As always, the great powers have a greater capacity to influence the character and to shape the rules of the international system, but all states have a voice and a vote in the international organisations that apply the rules over a wide domain of activities.

Each of these maps of the world emphasises certain landmarks and omits others. The *globalisation* thesis highlights the increasing integration of the world economy and the homogenisation of products, tastes, and even ideas. World trade has grown three times as fast as world output since World War II,[9] and the principal instrument of this growth has been the MNE, like Ford, Disney, or Shell, with operations in many countries. Only a few thousand MNEs now account for close to half of the world's industrial output and trade.[10] Globalisation is a natural starting point for thinking about the contemporary world. The rapid flows of goods, services, technology, and capital among states tie countries together and compel people, firms, and governments to adapt, compete, or fall behind.[11] Global competition has forced companies to specialise more, which has provided consumers with more choices and with higher-quality and/or cheaper products.

On the negative side, nations pay a price in increased vulnerability and dependence on foreign companies. A country that wants to supplement its domestic savings with foreign capital must keep its budget balanced and its currency stable. If it doesn't, foreign capital will flee as quickly as it arrived. Economies lifted by foreign capital can suddenly collapse when it departs, as Mexico discovered in December 1994 and East Asia discovered in July 1997. The discipline of the market has always been unforgiving; what is new is the magnitude of the flows and the speed of money's entrance and exit.

In 1971 Raymond Vernon, then a professor at the Harvard Business School, wrote that MNEs had contributed significantly to the welfare of the world but that they put 'sovereignty at bay' because they are 'not accountable to any public authority that matches it in geographical reach.'[12] Others have argued that globalisation has reduced the power of the state by compelling governments to compete against each other to use tax incentives and cheap labour to attract scarce foreign investment. The evidence, however, doesn't support the argument that the state is weak and endangered. In the industrialised countries the percentage of gross domestic product (GDP) going to government expenditures has nearly tripled since 1960, to roughly 50 percent. In developing countries the percentage nearly doubled during the same period, to about 28 percent. In other words, in relation to the size of its economy, the state in the richer countries is twice as large and growing faster than in the poorer countries. An increasing proportion of government expenditures involve financial transfers to the aging or the infirm. Globalisation might be shrinking the world, but governments are growing bigger, and they are responding to a wider array of popular needs.[13]

States have reduced trade barriers, and this has facilitated global integration. But this has not occurred because states are the passive agents of MNE interests. Quite the contrary, Raymond Vernon argued that in the 1990s the problem of the MNEs is not that they are jeopardising sovereignty but that states are over-regulating and constraining them and thereby diminishing global welfare.[14]

The trend towards global homogenisation often evokes a backlash in groups or states that feel alienated or disenfranchised and fear losing jobs or dignity. The road toward globalisation is not straight. Every trade barrier that is dismantled puts firms at risk, and sometimes generates pressures for protectionism. The spread of US popular culture through movies and CNN provokes reactions from fundamentalists, ethnic chauvinists, or ordinary people who fear a loss of autonomy.[15]

Samuel Huntington's argument – that the new divisions of the world are defined by a *struggle between distinct, irreconcilable civilisations* – deepens our understanding of the cultural roots of this reaction to globalism and to US power. His thesis is particularly cogent in explaining the Islamic worldview. Yet one cannot help but question the significance of culture clash in international politics when the worst conflicts in this century have occurred within rather than between civilisations. Two of the world's most barbaric twentieth-century wars occurred within the single civilisation Huntington refers to as 'Western.' As the Cold War was becoming less relevant, the worst conflict occurred within the Islamic world, between Iran and Iraq. In the first decade of the post–Cold War world, the worst case of genocide occurred within the African civilisation, in Rwanda and Burundi. Religion is a central element in defining 'civilisations,' and yet the Christian crusades against Islam pale in their intensity and in the number of deaths when compared to the wars between Catholics and Protestants and between Sunnis and Shiites.

The *new world order* has several different faces, some of them old. International economic institutions established in the aftermath of World War II – such as the World Bank, the General Agreement on Tariffs and Trade (GATT), and the International Monetary Fund (IMF) – have lifted dozens of countries out of poverty, expanded global trade, and prevented a global financial collapse and depression. Other intergovernmental organisations (IGOs) and non-governmental organisations (NGOs) have emerged to protect human rights, eradicate disease, promote development, mediate conflicts, and encourage disarmament. This is the essence of global governance.

Has the end of the Cold War freed the UN to be all that President Franklin Roosevelt wanted it to be? During the Cold War, each superpower wanted to prevent the other from using the UN for its purpose, and the result was the paralysis of the UN. There is no question that the end of superpower rivalry has permitted the UN Security Council to play an increasingly active role in many of the world's conflicts. Of the 55 peacekeeping operations launched by the UN Security Council since 1948, over three-quarters – were approved since the Cold War ended. The entire UN system has been rejuvenated, and the creation of new institutions like the International Criminal Court may improve the prospects for global governance.[16]

International institutions are important actors on the contemporary world stage, and the treaties they enforce obligate and constrain their members. The World Trade Organisation (WTO), which replaced GATT, sanctions governments that increase their trade barriers. The EU enforces the maze of agreements among its 15 members to permit the free flow of trade, capital, and labour. But preventing war and making peace, particularly within countries, have proven far more difficult for the UN and regional organisations to achieve than cutting tariffs by their sister organisations. Setbacks in Iraq, Angola, Bosnia, and Sierra Leone led one writer to conclude, 'In the last year of the century, the newer, saner world order confidently anticipated when Communism collapsed a decade ago is nowhere to be seen. International organisations from the UN and North Atlantic Treaty Organization (NATO) to an embattled West African peacekeeping organisation seemed powerless.'[17] These setbacks should remind us not to confuse the tool with the mechanic. International institutions can only address a crisis if the great powers choose to collaborate, as they did in the Gulf War. If the great powers cannot agree, then the door of the UN Security Council is closed.

The United States has always been ambivalent about whether it wanted to strengthen or limit the UN. Its position at any given time depended, not surprisingly, on whether it viewed a specific action as serving its interests. Even in the case of the Gulf War, President George Bush did not consult the UN in making his decision to drive Saddam Hussein from Kuwait; he decided first and then sought international legitimacy and support. President Bill Clinton's request in July 1994 for a UN Security Council resolution to restore constitutional government to Haiti was similarly motivated: It was intended not to strengthen the UN but to support a US initiative. In the case of Kosovo, NATO decided to begin the bombing of Serbia without UN authorisation because of the opposition of Russia and China. In brief, the new world order bears some similarities to the old one.

The *democratic peace* – the idea that democracies do not fight each other suggests that the critical division in the world is between democratic and non-democratic regimes. A burgeoning literature has tested and refined this thesis, developing variations including the proposition that new fragile democracies might be more bellicose than dictatorships[18] and that narrowly based democracies might fight with more broadly based ones.[19] Recent empirical research suggests that the prospects for peace are enhanced as democratic governments join international organisations and trade more with each other. From 1950 to 1985, when all three variables – democracy, IOs, and trade – were present, the probability of violent conflict was reduced by 72 percent.[20]

The spread of democracy in the world in the last few decades is significant for two other reasons besides inhibiting governments from fighting each other. Governments that are elected by their people in a free environment are more civil and responsive to their people than those that are not, and second, democratic governments are more likely to act collectively in defense of global norms of human rights and democracy.[21]

The *pan-region* perspective visualises the world in terms of three groups of states. With more than 40 years of experience in trying to harmonise trade, investment, and domestic policies, the EU is the most integrated of the three regions. It has created a new currency (the Euro) and aspires to coordinate its foreign and defense policies. The North American Free Trade Agreement (NAFTA), which took effect in January 1994, doubled trade and dramatically expanded investment among Canada, Mexico, and the United States in five years. East Asia does not have a regional grouping comparable to the EU or NAFTA, but the Association of Southeast Asian Nations (ASEAN) was established in 1967 to promote economic co-operation, and it now includes 10 southeast Asian countries. The cool relationship between the region's two main powers – Japan and China – makes it difficult to negotiate, a free-trade area. In the meantime, Japanese foreign direct investment has begun to connect the region.

Despite concerns that each pan-region could become an exclusive trading bloc, the major country within each pan-region is too dependent on world trade to permit this to happen. The two issues of most concern to the pan-regions are to deepen integration by harmonising policies and to enlarge the regions by including countries on their peripheries. The EU plans on a significant expansion toward Eastern and Southern Europe by 2004. In December 1994 the United States joined 33 other countries in the Western Hemisphere in a pledge to begin negotiations toward a free-trade area by the year 2005. Finally, Asia Pacific Economic Cooperation (APEC), a group of 21 countries, agreed to establish a free-trade area on both sides of the Pacific by

2020. These deadlines are optimistic, but they indicate that the countries within each region believe that their growth depends on trade and that is growing faster within each pan-region than between them.

These five worldviews seem to suggest that the era of the nation-state is passing because of the rapid erosion of sovereignty by cultural disintegration, global integration, supra-national regulation, or inter-state combination. But a closer analysis permits one to see the central role played by states in each of these views, as many of their proponents would acknowledge. For example, though he asserts that cultural variables are the most important for explaining state behaviour, Huntington also recognises that 'states remain the principal actors in world affairs,' and the conflict scenarios he develops at the conclusion of his book involve struggles between states, not civilisations.[22] Thomas Friedman writes that superpowers are being replaced by supermarkets, but he argues that because of globalisation and open borders, states matter more, not less, in making the rules and enforcing them. 'The hidden hand of the market will never work without a hidden fist...And the hidden fist that keeps the world safe for Silicon Valley's technologies is called the US Army, Air Force, Navy, and Marine Corps.'[23]

The *democratic peace* rests on the foundation of states. The pan-regional map is also composed of states, with one state in each region predominating. The United States accounts for nearly 90 percent of the gross product and 73 percent of the trade in North America. Japan accounts for 70 percent of the gross product and one-third of the trade among the 10 nations of East Asia. And Germany accounts for 23 percent of the gross product and 28 percent of the fifteen-nation EU.[24]

In the nineteenth century, nationalism seemed a far weaker political idea than liberalism or socialism, but *all three found expression principally within states*. Nationalism infused states with energy and direction, sometimes positively, sometimes destructively. Similarly, by the end of the twentieth century, the interests and preferences of states are being redefined by globalisation, identity, and democracy, and by new actors (NGOs, MNEs, IGOs) promoting these interests and ideas.[25]

Although IGOs, such as the European Commission or the WTO, are increasingly important in a widening band of issues, their power stems from agreements between states. States must weigh carefully the costs of violating an agreement, but they always retain the right of self-defense. States join regional organisations because their leaders calculate that the benefits exceed the costs. 'States,' Robert O. Keohane and Joseph S. Nye Jr. remind us, 'continue to command the loyalties of the vast majority of the world's people.'[26] But in a world in which growth is sustained by trade, investment, and new technology, integration is a better defense than autarchy.

These six maps are not mutually exclusive. Indeed, if they were translucent and placed on top of one other, they would provide a thicker description of a multidimensional world. For example, they would help us understand the inter-relationship of economic integration and cultural reaction. To explain the spreading impact of the Asian financial crisis, one might borrow insights from globalisation or contrast the effect of the crisis within and among the pan-regions. To evaluate the successes or failures of the UN in the crises in Rwanda or Bosnia, one could refer to the new world order thesis.

States are still the pivotal actors in the international system, but each of the other perspectives adds to our understanding of the terrain on which states maneuver to defend themselves or to advance their interests. Which states are the most important? To answer this question, we need to define power and then identify the countries that have it.

Power and its champions

'Power' is an elusive term. In his attempt to define it, Joseph Nye Jr. first compared power to the weather – easier to talk about than to understand – and then to love – 'easier to experience than to define or measure.'[27] If power is defined in traditional military terms as the capacity to crush an enemy, then nuclear weapons are the main indicators, and the United States and Russia are still the world's two most powerful countries. If power is defined as a country's capacity to produce goods and services, then GDP is a better indicator, and the world is led by a triad of the United States, Japan, and Germany.

The concept of power has changed over time. In the seventeenth and eighteenth centuries it was widely believed that the governments that could enlist and feed the most soldiers and tax the largest population would win the wars, so power was often equated with the size of a state's population and the amount of land it had under cultivation. In the nineteenth century, industry and railroads were more important sources of power than agriculture or the size of territory. Russia had a larger population than Germany but was weaker because it lacked the latter's modern railroads and industrial structure.

From the first industrial revolution through the chemical, nuclear, and information revolutions, the country that first developed a key technology or possessed the resources on which it depended found itself ahead of the power curve. Britain's invention of the steam engine and its abundance of coal gave it a head start in the industrial revolution. Moreover, certain kinds of states were better able to exploit particular stages of industrialisation. The Soviet Union, for example, was able to harness the power of central planning to develop massive steel, chemical, and capital equipment industries, but its command economy proved to be a liability in the computer era. Japan learned the hard way that using an army to secure oil and coal, as it did in the 1930s, was far more costly and less effective than relying on the market and technology, as it did five decades later.

Current conventional wisdom holds that state power derives from economic growth and technological innovation.[28] Technologies become a source of power if they can compress time, distance, or space. The Internet is the most powerful new technology because it transmits knowledge and information to more people, faster, cheaper, and more easily than any existing means of communication. From 1988 to 1998, the decade in which the Internet grew to widespread use, it stimulated an entire industry and, by 1998, accounted for about one-third of US economic growth.[29]

The Internet and information power expand the capacity of individuals and NGOs to influence foreign policy and international politics. There is no better example of this than Jody Williams, a young woman working from a modest home in Vermont. In just six years, through the Internet, Williams organised a coalition of 1,300 NGOs in 60 countries that drafted an international convention to ban the production, storage, and use of land mines worldwide. Despite the opposition of the United States, Russia, and China, the NGOs mounted such a successful lobbying campaign that representatives of 122 countries signed the convention in Ottawa in December 1997. Williams won the Nobel Peace Prize for her role in organising it. The great powers then found themselves having to adapt to a new international obligation that constrained their freedom of action. A public entrepreneur used a new technology to further an international norm: This is a new kind of power in a new age.

How one defines power influences one's perception of the shape of the world, and vice versa. In a world of autarchy and protectionism, land is a source of power. Land is less important in a world of free-trade, and a small state like Singapore or an island nation like Japan can be wealthy and powerful. As Richard Rosecrance has noted, our understanding of the meaning of power has changed as the world has moved from the 'territorial state' to the 'trading state' to the 'virtual state,' where information and virtually all factors of production are mobile.[30]

State power is generally visualised in terms of 'hard power' – military forces, population, economy (GDP, trade), territory, and natural resources.[31] The beauty of 'hard power' variables is that they can be measured, and they are universally recognised as indicators of power. But we need to pause and consider a number of questions before leaping to the conclusion that a country with plenty of hard power can automatically get its way. First, are variables comparable, one to another? China's army is 10 times as large as Japan's, but its economy is one-sixth as large. Which country is more powerful? Second, can variables be weighted and combined to come up with a single index of power? Adding population to military expenditures is like mixing apples with ball bearings. And third, what is the 'conversion ratio' for determining the amount of hard power necessary to change an adversary's position? Robert Dahl's oft-cited definition of power as the ability to get others to do what they otherwise would not do[32] does not answer this question. Without knowing an adversary's initial preferences or motives for changing, there is no way to tell whether the use of power is decisive.

And it is very difficult to discern motives, even of oneself, let alone of one's adversary. Hans Morgenthau, who spent some time trying to discern motives, ultimately dismissed the exercise as 'futile and deceptive.'[33] In computing a 'conversion ratio' of changing power to result, where do we fit such intangible factors as nationalism? As the Vietnamese and the Afghanis proved, intangible factors can be strong enough to defeat the most awesome military machines.

Nye improves on Dahl's definition conceptually by distinguishing between hard power and 'soft power,' which he defines as 'indirect or cooptive ... getting others to want what you want.'[34] Soft power derives from persuasion or attraction. The Germans did not force Chile in the nineteenth century and China in the early twentieth to accept their military advisers; Germany was invited to send advisers because Chilean and Chinese leaders thought the German army was an effective model.

While soft power improves our understanding of power, there are two problems with the concept. First, it is intangible and impossible to measure. There are, however, surrogate indicators of a country's attractiveness. Japan's soft power stems from its reputation as a technological leader, which developed gradually over two decades, beginning in the late 1950s. US soft power is evident in the one million immigrants and

500,000 foreign students who are attracted to the United States each year. They are signs that people want to live in and learn from the United States. The popularity of US movies and of CNN reflect US cultural influence.

In contemplating whether to come to the aid of the French in their war against the Vietnamese Communists in 1954, President Dwight Eisenhower recognised that 'an asset of incalculable value' to the United States was its standing 'as the most powerful of the anti-colonial powers.' This 'moral position of the United States,' he concluded, 'was more to be guarded than the Tonkin Delta, indeed than all of Indochina'[35] – a wise assessment of one dimension of US soft power.

The second problem in assessing 'soft power' is that it is obviously related to hard power. It is not a coincidence that the countries that have hard power or have been most successful at certain moments in history are also the most 'attractive.'

In the late 1950s, the Soviet Union's apparent success in transforming itself from a poor Third World country into the second-greatest power influenced Third World leaders searching for alternative models to that of the West. Fidel Castro acknowledged that Soviet success in space with *Sputnik* and the apparent 'missile gap' in their favour attracted his interest, thus changing the course of Cuban history.[36] The relationship between hard and soft power has not been explored adequately, but it seems that a country's success makes it more attractive as a model, which in turn reinforces its image as a great power.

Over the course of the century, such universal norms as self-determination have become forces constraining states. The development of an international regime on human rights has compelled states to defend their actions at annual meetings of the United Nations Human Rights Commission (UNHRC) in Geneva and in other fora. The power to define norms may be as important in the next century as the power to draw the boundaries of colonies was in the last.

The more we have tried to understand 'power' the harder it has been to grasp. But we can make some useful distinctions. First, we can identify military and economic indicators of hard power, even if we can't easily compare or aggregate them. Second, nationalism and international norms have made the use of physical force more costly, and soft power has grown in importance. Finally, there are no simple answers to the questions of what kinds of power are most likely to be effective in compelling or persuading an adversary, even in war, but especially in peacetime or in negotiations.

What constitutes a great power?

By almost any of the indicators of hard and soft power, it is not hard to identify the seven great powers. The three traditional categories of power are size (population and territory), economy, and military power. As the century closed, the United States was the preeminent power in virtually all categories, but it shared its lead in the economy and military spending with Japan and Germany, and in military personnel and weaponry with Russia and China. Great Britain and France were members of the nuclear club and ranked from fourth to seventh in most of the economic and military areas. A united EU surpassed the United States in all economic indicators and came in second or third in the military areas.[37]

To what extent does this picture of power in the 1990s reflect longer trends? A ranking by similar indicators in the mid-1980s would have shown the Soviet Union first or second in all the military and most of the economic categories. Soviet power, which seemed so formidable, collapsed in a few short years. Power was redistributed after the Cold War just as it had been after both world wars.

Let us examine the long-term trends in several indicators of power. Beginning with population, the three European powers – Germany, Britain, and France – ranked fourth, seventh, and eighth in 1900 and eleventh, sixteenth, and eighteenth in 1995. The EU as a whole, however, ranked third in 1995, just below China and India, which together accounted for about 38 percent of the world's population. Until its dissolution, the Soviet Union ranked third, a place now filled by the United States, the only major industrialised country whose population continues to expand at a moderate rate. (About half of US population growth is due to immigration.)[38]

China's and Russia's armed forces have been larger than other nations' for most of the century because of their large population and territory and because of internal and external threats. On the eve of both world wars, the US armed forces were small, ranking eleventh, below even Romania and Spain. After World War I (in 1920) the US Army ranked fifth, and in 1950 it ranked third in size. Unlike the United States, which caught up after entering the wars, Japan and Germany built their militaries beforehand. Germany had the second largest armed force in 1914 and 1940; Japan was eighth in 1914 and seventh in 1940. Great Britain and France fell between the two. After World War II the three European governments and Japan reduced their armed forces, so they ranked from fourteenth to twenty-fifth.

Economic indicators show the resilience of the Japanese and German economies. Within 15 years of their defeat in World War II, Germany and Japan had recovered to become the fourth and sixth largest economies, respectively. By 1980 Japan had leaped over Germany and both had surpassed France and England, and by 1990, with the decline of the Soviet Union, they were second and third.[39] The trends in world trade reveal much about the distribution and variation of world power in the twentieth century. Great Britain dominated world trade from the middle of the nineteenth century to the eve of World War II, when it was overtaken by the United States. Germany and Japan became powerhouses in trade before World War II, but they did not recover their prewar strength until 1980, when they moved into second and third places. With Germany in the pivotal trading role, EU exports and imports were more than twice those of North America.

The triad of the United States, Japan, and Germany also dominates the world of research and development – an indicator of future technological prowess – with the United States spending $168.5 billion in 1997; Japan, $75.1 billion; and Germany, $37.4 billion. Japan, however, leads the field in the numbers of patent applications.[40]

At the beginning of the twenty-first century, these three powers – the United States, Japan, and Germany – have global interests, but an increasing share of their wealth comes from the regions they lead. The two most important trading partners for the United States are its neighbours in North America. An expansion of NAFTA to the entire hemisphere would create a region with twice the population of the EU and with a comparable market. Germany is the EU pivot. Japan and China are still competing within an inchoate but increasingly connected East Asian region.

Another important source of power, particularly in the post–Cold War era, are the five permanent seats on the UN Security Council, whose holders have the right to propose or prevent UN peace-keeping operations. Each of the great powers except Germany and Japan holds a permanent seat. These seats are another example of how the meaning of power has changed over time. During the Cold War, the United States and the Soviet Union were viewed as the two most powerful states for many reasons, but their UN veto was not one of them. The United Nations was not a consequential actor on security issues. As the UN Security Council has become a critical instrument for legitimising interventions, the votes of all five permanent members have become more valuable. Any great power that wants the UN to act must secure the votes or acquiescence of the permanent members. As their votes gained in value, countries began to trade them like legislators swapping votes.

But like any other institution, the UN is more than a reflection of its members' current interests; it is also a prisoner of the moment it was established. In 1945, Japan and Germany were defeated and excluded from the UN. Today, when economies carry more weight than armies, the countries with the 2nd and 3rd largest economies – Japan and Germany – still lack permanent seats in the Security Council.

What conclusions can one draw from the indicators of power? Until World War II, world power was concentrated in Europe. Germany was the ascending power that catalysed a coalition against it. Although Great Britain could no longer rule the seas, British diplomats skillfully used their declining assets to continue to play a balancing role. The Soviet Union recovered slowly from its revolution and World War I, but it was able to mobilise its population in war and subsequently in peace to lift the country to the second rank of power before collapsing in the century's last decade. The United States had the economic power to rank first since the beginning of the century, but its military potential was tapped only after it was drawn into the two world wars. The United States did not retreat from power after World War II or after the Cold War, but despite its preeminent position it displayed considerable ambivalence about global leadership.

In Asia, Japan followed a trajectory similar to Germany's. After World War II it devoted its energies to economic growth and technological development and raced ahead of the Soviet Union to become the second economic superpower. Whereas Russia rose and then declined, China followed the opposite trajectory. The twentieth century was not kind to China: the turmoil of foreign intervention, revolution, civil war, and the Cultural Revolution made it more a victim of global politics than an actor. But in the last 20 years of the twentieth century China's spectacular growth gave the country a new sense of confidence, perhaps even an aggressive urge to reshape parts of Asia.

Even a cursory analysis of the indicators of power would identify these seven states as the world's major powers. India, with the world's second-largest population and as a democracy, could be considered an eighth great power; indeed, India decided to test nuclear weapons partly in order to be considered a great power, but as a colony for half the century, and a country that suffered economic stagnation, civil war and multiple border conflicts for much of the rest, India has not had a global impact. Other states might join or supplant the great powers in the twenty-first century. The most obvious candidates are now considered regional powers; their influence in their own regions is considerable, possibly exceeding that of the major powers. In Latin America, Brazil, Argentina, and Mexico are regional powers; in Africa, Nigeria and South Africa; in the Middle East, Iraq, Iran, and Egypt; and in Asia, India, Indonesia, and Pakistan have influence beyond their borders.

Global governance in the liberal epoch

The great artist Georges Braque once explained that he created the space in his paintings before he drew the actors. That is a good way to think about the world. Since the seventeenth century, states have defined the world's space. The great powers drew their own figures, and until recently they also drew most of the other figures on the global canvas. But by the mid-point of twentieth century, international institutions and values, established by the leadership of the United States, began to define the world's space.

In 1900 Great Britain and France held sway over immense empires, and Germany and Japan felt that their time had come. Collisions between the great powers were unavoidable. China, on its knees, was an object of Japan's ambitions; France and Russia, of Germany's. The United States was divided about whether to board the imperialist train. Not long after it annexed the Philippines, the United States recognised that it had made a mistake – colonialism was wrong not only for the colonies but also for the colonisers and the international system.

Woodrow Wilson developed this idea into a vision of a world order very different from anything in history. Wilson believed that acceptance by the international community of the principle of self determination was not only the best alternative to colonialism; it was the answer to the primordial question of how to prevent wars between states. If all countries respected the rights of others to determine their future 'under Republican forms of government,' then this principle would eliminate the causes (that is, the spoils) of war while raising the costs by ennobling nationalism.

From this simple idea flowed many others: self-determination meant governments should be independent and accountable to their people; democracy within nations would increase the prospect of peaceful relations between them; countries, like people, should be juridically equal, not divided or dominated by the great powers into spheres of influence; security should be defended collectively by international organisations, not by a balance of power; markets should be open to all, not parceled out to each power; international relations should be defined by rules freely negotiated by states; and barriers to trade and investment should be dismantled.

In brief, the new world – the Liberal Epoch – would not be defined from above by emperors or dictators but from below, by citizens and consumers. Citizens would choose their leaders in a free political market within their state, and consumers would choose their products in a free economic market that would expand as technology shrank the world. In the old world, leaders ruled by divine right. In the new epoch, leaders would be compelled to respond to popular preferences or lose elections. Citizens would be shareholders in the state, just as they might own stock in a business. To stay in business, firms would need to respond to their shareholders' demand for profits and to the changing preferences of their consumers. The world of empires and monopolies would be replaced by one of democratic governments and private markets.

The US vision was enunciated during World War I, institutionalised during World War II, and crowned after the Cold War. The key to the century's riddle and the US vision, however, is not in the wars but in the peace that followed. The wars altered the distribution of power, but the peace sketched the space within which states and other actors worked.

The peace of 1919 was resented, and it sowed the seeds of the next war. The peace of 1945 was decisive in one sense, divisive in another, and visionary in a third. It was decisive in its success in remaking the three defeated countries – Germany, Japan, and Italy – into solid, pacific democracies. It was divisive in its failure to forge a durable consensus among the Big Three, making it impossible during the Cold War for the UN Security Council to fulfill its role. It was visionary in the establishment of international economic institutions that permitted the most rapid and widespread growth in world history and a fifteen-fold expansion of world trade.

The peace after the Cold War was ambiguous, but its challenge was similar to that of the others: to integrate the losers into the winner's system, in this case, a market-oriented international system composed of mostly democratic states. The victory was not unconditional, and so the victor's ability to influence the losers was limited and varied considerably. The Eastern European governments broke from the Soviet Union and sought new economic ties with the EU and security within NATO. The Soviet Union disappeared and was replaced by

15 independent republics. All suffered difficult transitions, but virtually all sought a path toward democratic modernity. China is moving toward its vision of these two goals in its own way – first expediting the economic reforms it had begun in 1978, then experimenting with local elections as the Berlin Wall fell, and finally, as the century closed, quietly and reluctantly debating wider political reforms. Vietnam pursued limited economic reforms. Cuba and North Korea, like satellites orbiting a planet that had disappeared, could not break their circular paths, condemning their regimes to irrelevance or roguishness and their people, to poverty.

The two distinguishing characteristics of the post-Cold War peace are implicit in the awkward transitions of the former Communist governments. First, all claimed to accept the goals of democracy and free markets, and virtually all began to move towards those goals, albeit with varying speeds and degrees of commitment. Second, the great powers have all sought good relations with each other; none has viewed another as irredeemably hostile. This may be the first time in history that the major powers – both winners and losers – accepted the same goals and desired good relations. These two features establish the foundation on which the Liberal Epoch rests.

To return to Braque's canvas, the Liberal Epoch allows the actors to define the size and shape of their place. That is the vision's real power and durability: New challengers can overtake established powers by what they produce or invent; they do not have to go to war or seize their colonies to displace them. All states have a voice and a vote in the international institutions. Any of the regional powers that can sustain a high rate of economic growth over an extended period of time will accumulate the influence that will permit it to join the great powers. Whereas the funeral of Queen Victoria, with its attending royalty, symbolised the ruling cabal at the beginning of the twentieth century, Group of Seven summit meetings and the inauguration of newly elected presidents are symbols of governance at the beginning of the twenty-first century. Any state with free elections can join the democratic club, and the criterion for membership to the Group of Seven is not divine right but GDP. The incentive system embedded in the Liberal Epoch encourages states to grow and be democratic, and, more importantly, it permits the powerful states to ascend the ladder of influence without making war.

The test of a democratic system is whether it permits people to change leaders or policies peacefully. The test of the international system is how it reacts to ascending powers. Most historians agree that the greatest danger to world peace occurs when a rising power believes the established powers are preventing it from achieving its destiny. At that point the established powers feel threatened and compelled to take a stand, resulting in a conflict in which all the powers use force for defensive reasons. One indication of the relative effectiveness of the Liberal Epoch is the way in which two of the three ascending powers in the twentieth century – Germany and Japan – responded to the Westphalian system and to the Liberal Epoch. Both forcefully challenged the old system several times in the century. Today, Josef Joffe writes that 'the rules of the international game *favour* Germany,' and Kenneth Pyle concludes that 'more than any other country, Japan was the beneficiary of the post-war international order.'[41] Although many believe that the existing system favours the United States, the second- and third-wealthiest powers, according to these two authorities, think the system favours them. This is the operational definition of a stable system: one in which principal challengers have more at stake in preserving the system than toppling it.

The Liberal Epoch has a private market and a public arena and laws for each. In the early part of the twentieth century, countries defined their economic goals in terms of acquiring gold, minerals, and natural resources; that is why colonies were so vital. Today the economic goals that are most important are jobs, markets, capital, and technology. As Joffe notes, 'It is welfare, not warfare, exports rather than expansion that animate most European states.'[42] To achieve these economic goals, states must pursue very different policies than they did when they sought to defeat their rivals. Instead of threatening their neighbours, they need to reassure them. Instead of dictating the terms of trade, they need to negotiate rules of access to markets that apply to everyone. Instead of hoarding gold, they need to encourage investments by assuring stability and rule of law. Instead of freezing capital, they need to avoid frightening investors. If they fail, capital flees, the budget is out of balance, unemployment grows, and leaders are reminded of the first law of economics: people or countries that live beyond their means will have to pay for their excesses by reducing their consumption and their independence. This is what is meant by the discipline of the market.

A simple law also governs the public arena: leaders who lose touch with the needs and aspirations of their people will be replaced. Perhaps the biggest difference between the dawn and the dusk of the twentieth century is the degree to which the goals of states are now defined by these two interlocking public and private markets and their dual systems of accountability.

The Liberal Epoch replicates several characteristics of a pluralist democracy at an international level. A pluralistic system of global governance puts a premium on process as distinguished from goals, which are shared and therefore not debated. Everyone wants prosperity and peace; the hard questions are 'how' questions: how to achieve these shared goals? There are no magic answers to the 'how' questions, and there are many views. In a pluralistic system, decisions are made both within states and among them on the basis of elections and democratic debate. The outcome is usually a compromise among contending interests and perspectives. The process is often messy, but by trying to respond to the various interests and perspectives, it instills civility in a body politic. This is evident, however, only when one compares it to a system in which rulers are selected by divine right or by force. The latter regimes appear the most stable, particularly at moments when authority is unquestioned, but they are the most brittle when new actors demand seats at the table. That is the strength of the Liberal Epoch because its canvas allows new actors to emerge in both the private sector and civil society and to channel their influence at each level of governance – local, national, and international. It has permitted the flourishing of a transnational society in which MNEs in the private market and NGOs in the public arena of one nation can connect with their counterparts in other countries and can thus challenge states to alter their policies or make good on their promises.

NGOs are often entrepreneurs in the public arena. Like MNEs in the private sector, NGOs seek niche issues that have been neglected (for example, the banning of landmines) or a value that is not being advanced (for example, the rights of indigenous peoples) and they mobilise groups and other NGOs to lobby governments to address the problem (for example, to approve a convention on biodiversity or protecting children's rights). NGOs have spread beyond their activities in economic development and human rights to work in such areas as democratisation and disarmament, areas that were long believed to be the sole prerogative of states. NGOs hold their governments accountable.

There are those who believe that state power and sovereignty have diminished as a result of the spread of these NGOs, the increasing authority of IGOs, and the pressing nature of globalisation. Jessica Mathews saw a 'power shift': 'The steady concentration of power in the hands of states that began in 1648 with the Peace of Westphalia is over.'[43] Susan Strange argued that globalisation has fundamentally changed the nature of production and the source of finance and has begun to change beliefs, perceptions, ideas, and tastes. These forces and the international institutions established to manage them have eroded the traditional attributes of sovereignty and accountability and have allowed a shift in power from states to firms.[44]

These trends toward greater influence by the market and trans-national groups are real, but their effect on the states' role as the principal actors in the international system is debatable and exaggerated. 'After all,' as Daniel Yergin and Joseph Stanislaw remind us in their book on the battle between government and the marketplace in the twentieth century, 'there is no market without government to define the rules and the context. The state creates and maintains the parameters within which the market operates.'[45]

States are increasingly influenced by NGOs and constrained by international regimes, but states decide the rules that IGOs enforce, and the great powers retain a veto on the most important decisions related to the use of force. Beyond security issues, IGOs serve multiple purposes, from regulating the world economy and environment to deflecting criticism. When the IMF compels a government to tighten its fiscal belt, the US secretary of the treasury breathes a sigh of relief that it is the IMF managing director who is the target of discontent (although not all foreign governments are impressed by the distance between the two institutions).

The great powers do not exercise the same kind of control over the international system today as they did 100 years ago, when monarchs, for the most part, ruled centralised empires. Forty-six nations signed the UN Treaty in July 1945; the organisation today includes 191 countries. Power is not as concentrated as it was then, but it is also not as diffuse as one might expect from a quadrupling in the number of states. In 1946 the top four powers in the world accounted for roughly three-quarters of the world's domestic product; 50 years later the top seven accounted for 65 percent. In 1950 the top five powers accounted for 82 percent of the world's military spending; in 1993, seven accounted for nearly 70 percent.[46]

The influence that the great powers can wield depends on the particular institution and decision. Weighted voting in most economic institutions gives the great powers more influence than other states, but not enough to direct the institutions. The Group of Seven summit meetings offer the great powers (except China and only sometimes including Russia) an opportunity to negotiate common responses to current problems. In the WTO, the United States and the European powers exert disproportionate influence in setting the agenda and the parameters of the agreement, but the dispute-settlement mechanism is autonomous and frequently makes judgements against one or more of the great powers. In the UN Security Council, each of the permanent five members has the power to veto decisions.

Whether the great powers have more or less power today than they did in 1900 is not easy to determine because power is more difficult to measure. But there is no question that the great powers continue to exert substantial influence over the full range of issues on the contemporary agenda, and sometimes their influence is greatest when it is least recognised. For example, since 1986 the total amount of capital sloshing around the financial markets of the world increased eightfold, to $1.5 trillion a day. Many writers attributed this surge in globalisation to market forces. This confuses cause and effect. The dramatic increase in foreign investment is the result of concerted efforts by US and other Western governments to persuade developing and former Communist governments to liberalise their financial markets. When the state barriers were dismantled, so much capital began to flow that states felt rich or became poor almost overnight.[47]

The twenty-first century: trajectories, threats, and opportunities

One way to think about the distinctiveness of the US-designed Liberal Epoch is to contrast it with the painting of the world that would have been drawn by Nazi Germany or Soviet Russia. Each power had a global vision based on one of the three big ideas of the twentieth century – Nazi Germany on fascism and monopoly capitalism, Soviet Russia on communism and state capitalism, and the United States on democracy and private enterprise.[48] Each idea has weight and explains part of the reason for the influence of each of the three states. But the state's power explains the global success of the idea rather than the other way around. If Germany had prevailed in World War II or the Soviet Union in the Cold War, the world today would be nasty and brutish. That was George Orwell's nightmare. Instead, the United States prevailed, and the world awoke to Woodrow Wilson's dream.

Before trying to peer into the future we should recall the unpredictability of recent history. In the late 1980s the conventional wisdom held that the two superpowers would continue their struggle into the next century. Then, overburdened by excessive defence spending, the two superpowers would be overtaken by Japan. Some even thought the scenario had already occurred. 'The Cold War is over,' proclaimed the Asian scholar Chalmers Johnson, 'and Japan won.'[49] But suddenly the Japanese 'bullet train' stalled, and it continues to have trouble restarting. The Soviet Union imploded, and Russia sank so low that by 1996 its economy was overtaken by those of Brazil and India. Two years later Japan's stock market suffered a one-day drop in which it lost more value than the Russian economy produced that year. Although many believed that a country's economic growth was harmed when it spent too much on defence, US military spending was roughly equal to the total spent by the other six powers in the mid-1990s, and yet its economy outdistanced those of its competitors.[50] So much for the conventional wisdom. The only safe prediction is that when the economy of a great power grows faster than the others, people will look to it as a model. The three great capitalistic economies offer different prototypes for those searching for the holy grail of development. The United States' model is the most laissez-faire; Japan's, the most collusive between government and business; and Germany's, the most concerned about social welfare.

The contemporary world is closer to Wilson's vision than it is to the world that he tried to convert, but we should be under no illusion that his dream is today's reality. There are still wars, tyrants, and protectionism, and some countries still covet their neighbours' lands. Moreover, Wilson's core idea of self-determination, like many worthy goals, has been tarnished by its evil twin, 'ethnic cleansing,' the assertion of one group's identity by denying another's. Nonetheless, Wilson redefined the goals of states and the international system, and this has changed world politics more fundamentally than anything. A century ago, states used force to acquire territory and resources; today that's the exception. And wars have changed as well. In the first five years after the Cold War ended in 1989, two scholars identified 96 conflicts, but only five were between two internationally recognised states. The rest were within states.[51] Each state maintains an army to defend its security, but it pursues economic goals as much and, in some ways and cases, more than before.

Whether the Liberal Epoch will endure, deepen, and expand will depend in part on the direction of US leadership and the nature of tomorrow's challenges and opportunities.

If the United States closed its military bases in Japan, South Korea, and Europe, the habits learned during the past 50 years might survive the immediate tectonic shift, but the US withdrawal would eventually be profoundly destabilising. In Europe, the relationship between France and Germany could become strained, and Eastern Europe would feel more vulnerable from both the east and the west. If the United States were to withdraw its troops from Japan and South Korea, the Japanese would probably rearm, leading to an arms race with China. In brief, what seems to be a stable new world of economic interdependence might look very different if one element – a security guarantee – were withdrawn, and no other confidence-building, compensatory structure replaced it. It is hard to envision a post-NATO security arrangement in Europe at this time, but it would have to include a combination of disarmament and a new structure that would credibly assure the independence of central Europe. In Asia, the powers would have to overcome a mountain of suspicion before considering a quadrilateral security guarantee involving the United States, Japan, China, and a united Korea.

The two countries whose future trajectories are hardest to predict are China and Russia. President Bill Clinton posed the problem diplomatically: 'How Russia and China define their own greatness will have a lot to do with how the twenty-first century comes out.'[52] The central questions facing both countries are whether they will remain united, and whether and how long it will take them to complete their transitions to democratic market economies.

What will the United States do? In the short and medium terms, the United States is committed to keeping its armed forces in both the European and Asian theatres and in playing a leadership role in the world, with some caveats and reservations. If the United States were asked to withdraw its armed forces, which is unlikely but not impossible, it would do so, but until the transitions in Russia and China are clearer, a departure of US forces would create more problems than it would resolve.

What does history suggest for the US trajectory? It will be erratic: often unilateral, niggardly, and small-minded in its support for its international institutional offspring; occasionally organising its allies in an effective approach to a problem but mostly focusing on its own social and economic concerns and the external dimension of these concerns. The foreign policy agenda pursued by the United States after the Cold War was closely tied to such domestic issues as drugs, immigration, corruption, crime, trade, and jobs, and it is driven by domestic groups, either ethnic (Cuban, Jewish, Eastern European) or issue-based (abortion, religious persecution, human rights). Divided government – with presidents and Congresses of different parties – reinforced the incoherence of the policy, particularly as the two political parties moved further apart in their constituent bases and their philosophies.

Despite these centrifugal pressures and, indeed, perhaps because of the way they interact, US foreign policy will continue to pursue these goals, and while unilateral actions will likely remain an important component of US policy, public opinion increasingly is demanding partnerships.[53]

The trauma of September 11th dramatically affected these priorities, giving heightened attention to security concerns. The United States effectively marshaled global support to overthrow the Taliban regime in Afghanistan and to pursue a comprehensive strategy against global terrorism. But as the United States focused on its next target – in Iraq – the global coalition fragmented.

An activist America will inevitably encounter problems. The sheer power of the United States carries within it the seeds of its own opposition, not just from adversaries, but also from friendly governments, who will disagree with particular policies, will resent unilateral US 'police' actions, or will want to carve out some space for their own leadership. France, in particular, wants the EU to serve as a balance to US power. That is one reason that Samuel Huntington has argued that the world is moving toward a 'uni-multipolar' world, that is, one in which the United States needs to approach problems with 'some combination of other major states.' The United States retains veto power on some actions, but if it acts unilaterally, it risks stimulating new alliances against it.[54] The Liberal Epoch not only provides space for criticising authority, it encourages it. This is the strength of the system because by encouraging criticism, it defuses destructiveness, provided that the great powers, especially the United States, respond in an appropriate fashion. Some criticism of the superpower is inevitable. Lord Carrington once advised the United States that the burdens of power need to be borne: 'You're always in a hiding to nowhere if you're the big boy in town. You simply can't in that position hope for your reward on earth. The British had a lot of practice at that.'[55]

Since the Cold War's end, the great powers have collaborated more than at any other time in the century, but this trend toward co-operation was impeded by NATO's enlargement, suffered a setback in Kosovo, and was severely tested by differing views of how to approach Iraq.

Challenges and opportunities

A new world has not emerged, but the outlines of one, a Liberal Epoch, are becoming visible. Many architects and builders are constructing it piece by piece without a master plan. They are guided by both human-itarian and realistic instincts, shards of a collective memory, and the need to respond to awful events. Sometimes, there is a feeling of dis-order or even chaos, but what is more remarkable is that the project has any coherence at all, and that is partly because the new epoch rests on the firm foundation of international norms. These have been articu-lated in the UN Charter, the Universal Declaration of Human Rights, and the International Covenants. They define universal values.

Four pillars, still unfinished, will hold up the Liberal Epoch. The first pillar is international law – treaties, conventions, and rules that embody the universal norms. The body of international law is expanding rapidly in international commerce, finance, and intellectual property rights, but also in human rights (of gender, minorities, children, labour, refugees), environmental rights, democratisation, and disarmament. The second pillar is composed of international courts, tribunals, or panels that try to judge violations of the laws or settle disputes. The strongest panels are at the WTO, but the world is experimenting with new venues for trying international crimes, whether torture by a former Chilean dictator or genocide by a sitting Yugoslavian president.

The third pillar relies on monitoring and incentives to encourage compliance, and the fourth pillar is punishment for violating the rules. These two pillars of enforcement are essential for maintaining a Liberal Epoch, but they remain weak. The debate on Iraq in the UN Security Council and in the world was the first real attempt to come to grips with the challenge of enforcing a UN-imposed Treaty (in the form of Security Council resolutions) on Iraq.

NGOs have worked with small and middle powers, like Canada and Norway, as rule-makers and monitors. They have provided expertise and popular support to transform norms into treaties and to construct new institutions to judge behaviour or settle disputes. They monitor state actions and helped victims petition the courts and international organisations for redress or to correct an injustice.

Effective and legitimate enforcement requires a decision by the UN Security Council and thus the approval or acquiescence of the great powers. The weakness of the last two pillars stems from the absence of political will and a unifying vision among the great powers. Most of the contemporary challenges to the international system emerge from within failed states or by the actions of 'rogue' states. Either because they lack the capacity or are democracies, the great powers are reluct-ant to risk their people's lives in conflicts where their direct security interests are not threatened. That explains why the international community has not found a successful formula for coping with such problems. In the case of Iraq, the United States government was readier to use force in large part because of the trauma of September 11th – but France, Germany, Russia, and China, having not experienced that trauma, and being worried about the implications of US force in the Middle East, were reluctant to accept the US view.

Nonetheless, the great powers are the gatekeepers to the UN Security Council. When power is exercised in ways that the system and the major states view as legitimate, such as in the Persian Gulf War, then existing institutions – notably the United Nations – become stronger. When the great powers use force for self-interested purposes that other states do not consider legitimate, international institutions are diminished and the fragile collective security system, such as it exists, is eroded. Kofi Annan, the secretary-general of the UN, put this point most sharply when he wrote that the UN 'will have the potential to advance the interests of all the states only so long as it does not appear to serve the narrow interests of any one state or group of states.'[56] The UN will be tested periodically by the tyrants of pariah regimes. The more credible its threat the less likely that force will be needed to compel compliance with UN resolutions, but assembling a coalition time and again to meet the threats of incorrigible tyrants is taxing, in all senses of that word.

These are all reasons why the United States must pursue a new and different kind of leadership if the Liberal Epoch is to succeed. Unilateral US imposition of sanctions combined with its unwillingness to contribute or fulfill its obligations to international organisations weakens the very system it has established. Washington must lead by example and take action with multilateral authority. Beyond the steps necessary to establish, manage, and sustain a liberal system, our picture of the future depends on how a number of challenges are addressed.

The most important and dangerous set of problems arises among the great powers. World war can only occur if one or more of these powers fight another. Whether this is likely depends, to a great degree, on whether the transitions in China and Russia toward market democracies succeed and whether the other great powers can forge partnerships with these two governments. There is no challenge more important than this one! The industrialised democracies must open space on the international landscape for Russia and China to play important roles; if either feels excluded or cornered, the authoritarians in both states will be strengthened and the prospect for successful transitions would be diminished. World war is not inevitable if the transitions fail and one or two countries revert to an authoritarian mode, but co-operation and an effective UN collective security system is unlikely. World peace is not assured if the transitions succeed, but the prospects for co-operation on dealing with global security problems are much improved. Assuming that Russia and China become successful market-oriented democracies, and the great powers devise a new system of collaboration, then they will face a host of pressing security issues, including proliferation of weapons of mass destruction; instability in the Caspian area (the 'Eurasian Balkans' of Central Asia, as Zbigniew Brzezinski called them in a provocative analysis)[57]; revolutionary fundamentalism in the Middle East; rivalries between India and Pakistan, China and India, Iran and Iraq; North Korea; ethnic conflicts; and rogue and failed states. 'Regional powers' may have more influence in their areas than do the great powers. Such powers include India, Nigeria, South Africa, Indonesia, Brazil, and Iran do not have the reach of the great powers. Constructive roles need to be found for these countries, and they should be encouraged to build 'security communities,'[58] where states are assured that their differences will be settled peacefully.

A second challenge concerns the growing gap between rich and poor countries. The World Bank and regional development banks have been the principal instruments for promoting development and narrowing the widening gap between rich and poor, and these institutions should continue to focus on the poorest countries. While an increasing proportion of the world's population is born in the poorest countries, an increasing share of the world's wealth is produced and consumed in the EU, Japan, and the three NAFTA countries. The question is whether these three pan-regions can be enlarged in a manner that integrates poorer countries. Only the EU has had a concerted 'regional' strategy for raising the living standards of the poorer countries and regions in its community. The transfer of resources to the four poorest countries ranges from roughly 2–4 percent of the GDP of the countries – a not insignificant sum – and there is evidence that the policies have narrowed the disparities in income. North America lacks such a policy, but should adapt from Europe's experience a plan for lifting Mexico to the first world economically.[59] Each pan-region should not be an exclusive fortress. Rather each should be a laboratory, experimenting with ideas and rules that can subsequently be applied globally. But a critical problem is to prevent marginalisation of those countries, especially in Africa, that are outside each region. The third challenge – after the transitions in Russia and China and the enlargement of the three pan-regions – is to develop more effective means for global governance. The

UN Security Council needs to be expanded to include Japan, Germany, and several regional powers. At the same time, the voting process needs to be changed; if each of these countries has a veto, the Security Council will return to an earlier era of paralysis. Single-country vetoes should expire (except in a few cases in which a permanent member is directly engaged); each of the permanent members should find partners if they want to stop UN actions. The EU faced a similar problem and decided, in 1986, to discard the unanimity rule in order to accelerate integration. This question of decision-making is a key element of the problem of how much control states should delegate to international organisations and how much should they retain. Yogi Berra is reported to have once said that 'when you reach a crossroads, you should take it!' At the crossroads between unilateralism and collective action, the United States has hesitated, torn by advocates of each option. However, progress towards the goals identified by Wilson and FDR is not possible without unequivocal US leadership. There are threads that connect our contemporary problems to all that has gone before, but there are also new elements to our current predicaments that could not have been conceived, let alone predicted, even a few days before they occurred. We cannot escape our history, and although we seem to come close, we never quite repeat it either. The overpowering lesson of the twentieth century is that leaders can take us down a path that appeals either to mankind's basest instincts or to its highest values. Institutions and rules can make it more difficult to take the first path and easier to take the second. To paraphrase Winston Churchill, we make the institutions, and then they make us. Although international institutions and norms can constrain countries' leaders, there is no question but that national institutions provide the most potent restraints and incentives on their behaviour. Domestic and international constraints relate to each other sometimes in counterintuitive ways. It is generally believed that a country with great influence internationally will be more independent domestically, but China's recent growth suggests that these two factors might be inversely related. China's opening to the world made it more dependent, but also stronger. The fear of diminished sovereignty might simply miss the point that the traditional definition is obsolete. Germany has been more successful and influential abroad when it has accepted the constraints imposed by its neighbours than when it tried to go alone.

In this decentralised Liberal Epoch, the great powers are important not because they are trying to direct traffic but because they provide a stable and secure framework within which others can drive their ships of state. When a financial crisis occurs, as it did in the summer of 1997, or when a security or humanitarian problem emerges, great powers can lend their weight to stabilise the currency or restrain the warring factions. This does not mean they can necessarily solve the problem, but international solutions are not possible without their active involvement.

No single power has ever exercised the kind of influence in the world that the United States did at the end of the century. The source of its power is both its national assets and the international system that it helped establish. That system, that space on the canvas of the world, is the Liberal Epoch in which living standards are improved and states and other actors can define their own place. Whether it survives and succeeds will depend on several factors. First, the United States must maintain a security presence in Europe and Asia, and it must be prepared to use force at key moments on behalf of international norms, not just on behalf of its own interests. Second, the survival of the Liberal Epoch will depend on whether Russia and China make the transition to some semblance of a democratic, market economy and are prepared to approach global issues in a collaborative way with the other powers. This, in turn, requires that the other powers provide room for Russia and China to play constructive roles in addressing international issues. Third, new forms of partnerships need to be developed among the great powers. The EU should be prepared to shoulder the burden of primary responsibility in the Balkans and Eastern Europe, and Japan needs to join with the United States and China to provide a bedrock of security in East Asia. If the great powers seek good relations with each other, and if their goals and values can converge, the twenty-first century will be markedly different from the past, and the entire world would benefit.

States ruled throughout the twentieth century and will do so in the twenty-first, but their goals have changed. Their roles in the economy will evolve as they seek ways to integrate with others without losing full national control. Their primacy in the area of foreign policy will remain unchallenged. The great powers will lead but not dominate the institutions that will set the rules for the twenty-first century. If they can sustain the Liberal Epoch, the scope for world conflict will narrow and the perimeter of a global civilisation can be extended.

Notes

1. The gross product of all European governments in 1900 has been estimated by Paul Bairoch at $188 billion (in US dollars); see P. Bairoch, 'Europe's

Gross National Product: 1800–1975', *Journal of European Economic History*, 5 (July 1976) 281. General Motors had revenues of $185 billion in 2000; see www.gm.com/company/investor_information/1997

2. The term state is often used interchangeably with 'nation' and 'country.' They are related but distinct. A state is a political unit, the principal one in the international system. It includes a people, a territory, and a set of governing institutions. A 'nation' is a group of people with a shared language, culture, and history. A 'country' is the territorial component of the state. The Soviet Union was a state and country composed of many nations. For a brief discussion of these terms, see L. W. Barrington, '"Nation" and "Nationalism": The Misuse of Key Concepts in Political Science,' *PS: Political Science and Politics* (December 1997), pp. 712–716.

3. K. Ohmae, *The End of the Nation State: How Capital, Corporations, and Communications Are Reshaping Global Markets* (New York: Free Press, 1995), viii.

4. S. P. Huntington, *The Clash of Civilizations and the Remaking of the World Order* (New York: Simon and Schuster, 1996). At one point Huntington refers to seven or eight major civilisations (21), but his map (26–27) shows nine. This in itself should suggest that the dividing lines may not be as clear as one would expect of the most significant world divisions.

5. For President George Bush's description of this new world order, see his addresses to Joint Sessions of Congress before and after the Gulf War. The first, on September 11, 1990, was reprinted in *Foreign Policy Bulletin*, November–December 1990; the second was reprinted in the *New York Times*, March 7, 1991.

6. For an instructive essay on the growing 'incongruence' between the state system and global activities and on ideas for ways to respond, see S. Brown, *New Forces, Old Forces, and the Future of World Politics* (New York: HarperCollins, 1995).

7. The literature on this thesis is vast, but the reader could begin with the following: M. W. Doyle, 'Liberalism and World Politics,' *American Political Science Review*, 80, No. 4 (December 1986) 1151–1169; B. Russett, *Grasping the Democratic Peace: Principles for a Post-Cold War World* (Princeton University Press, 1993); J. L. Ray, *Democracy and International Conflict: An Evaluation of the Democratic Peace Proposition* (Columbia: University of South Carolina Press, 1995).

8. R. A. Pastor, *Toward a North American Community: Lessons from the Old World for the New* (Washington, DC: Institute for International Economics, 2001), Chapter 2, p. 21.

9. Organisation for Economic Cooperation and Development, *The World in 2020: Towards a New Global Age* (Paris: OECD, 1997) 29. World exports as a percentage of world product increased from about seven percent in 1950 to 21 percent in 1995. World Bank, *World Development Report, 1998/1999* (Washington, DC: Oxford University Press, 1999), p. 23.

10. R. Vernon, *In the Hurricane's Eye: The Troubled Prospects of Multinational Enterprises* (Cambridge, Mass.: Harvard University Press, 1998).

11. For the most insightful exploration of the many-sided effects of globalisation, see T. J. Friedman, *The Lexus and the Olive Branch: Understanding Globalization* (New York: Farrar, Straus, Giroux, 1999).

12. R. Vernon, *Sovereignty at Bay: The Multinational Spread of U.S. Enterprises* (New York: Basic Books, 1971), p. 249.
13. World Bank, *World Development Report, 1997: The State in a Changing World* (New York: Oxford University Press, 1997), pp. 2, 22–23.
14. Vernon, *In the Hurricane's Eye*.
15. See B. R. Barber, *Jihad Versus McWorld: How Globalization and Tribalism Are Reshaping the World* (New York: Ballantine Books, 1996). To see how these forces interact within North America, see R. A. Pastor and R. F. de Castro (eds), *The Controversial Pivot: U.S. Congress and North America* (Washington, DC: Brookings Institution Press, 1998), chapters 1, 9.
16. The data on peace-keeping missions is from www.un.org, January 2003.
17. B. Crosette, 'The World Expected Peace. It Found a New Brutality', *New York Times*, IV (24 January 1999), 1.
18. E. D. Mansfield and J. Snyder, 'Democratization and the Danger of War', *International Security*, 20 No. 1 (Summer 1995) 5–38. This article is reprinted, together with 13 others, in M. E. Brown, S. M. Lynn-Jones, and S. Miller (eds), *Debating the Democratic Peace* (Cambridge: MIT Press, 1996).
19. S. R. Weart, *Never at War: Why Democracies Will Not Fight One Another* (New Haven: Yale University Press, 1998).
20. B. Russett, J. R. Oneal, and D. R. Davis, 'The Third Leg of the Kantian Tripod for Peace: International Organizations and Militarized Disputes, 1950–85', *International Organization*, 52, No. 3 (Summer 1998) 441–467.
21. See R. A. Pastor, 'The Centrality of Elections: A Global Review', *New Perspectives Quarterly*, 13, No. 4 (Fall 1996). Freedom House in its annual survey. See www.freedomhouse.org
22. Huntington, *The Clash of Civilizations*, 21.
23. T. L. Friedman, 'A Manifesto for the Fast World', *New York Times Magazine* (28 March 1999) 61.
24. World Bank, *World Development Indicators, 1998* (Washington, DC: World Bank, 1998) pp. 188–203, 326–329.
25. See M. Finnemore, *National Interests in International Society* (Ithaca: Cornell University Press, 1996).
26. R. O. Keohane and J. S. Nye Jr., 'Power and Interdependence in the Information Age', *Foreign Affairs*, 77, No. 5 (September-October 1998) 82.
27. J. S. Nye Jr., *Bound to Lead: The Changing Nature of American Power* (New York: Basic Books, 1990) 25.
28. P. Kennedy, *The Rise and Fall of the Great Powers: Economic Change and Military Conflict from 1500 to 2000* (New York: Vintage Books, 1989).
29. A. Gore, 'Information Technology for the Twenty-First Century,' White House press release (24 January 1999), p. 1.
30. R. Rosecrance, 'The Rise of the Virtual State', *Foreign Affairs*, 75, No. 4 (July–August 1996) 45–61. See also Keohane and Nye, 'Power and Interdependence in the Information Age.'
31. Hans Morgenthau's definition of power was comprehensive, including geography, natural resources, industrial capacity, military preparedness, population, national character, national morale, the quality of diplomacy, and the quality of government; see H. J. Morgenthau, *Politics Among Nations* (New York: Knopf, 1978) pp. 117–154.
32. R. A. Dahl, *Who Governs? Democracy and Power in an American City* (New Haven: Yale University Press, 1961).

Robert A. Pastor 173

33. Morgenthau, *Politics Among Nations*, 5–6. He writes, 'It is futile because motives are the most illusive of psychological data, distorted...by the interests and emotions of actor and observer alike. Do we really know what our own motives are?'
34. Nye, *Bound to Lead*, 30. Nye's book is a superb analysis of the subjective and relative qualities of power and informs this section of my chapter.
35. Quoted in H. A. Kissinger, *Diplomacy* (New York: Simon and Schuster, 1994), p. 632.
36. In a conference on the Cuban Missile Crisis, Fidel Castro said that one of the reasons that he allied with the Soviet Union and accepted missiles was that he believed the Communist world was ahead of the west and that John F. Kennedy's declared concern about the 'missile gap' during the 1960 presidential campaign confirmed his view. Robert McNamara, Kennedy's Secretary of Defense, informed Castro of his press conference in early 1961 when he acknowledged that there was a missile gap, but it favoured the United States, by a ratio of nearly 20:1. Castro admitted he was not aware of that press conference. See J. G. Blight, B. J. Allyn, and D. A. Welch, *Cuba on the Brink: Castro, The Missile Crisis, and The Soviet Collapse* (NY: Pantheon Books, 1993), pp. 135–137, 198–203, 257–258.
37. For tables and data on the rankings of the great powers, see R. A. Pastor (ed.), *A Century's Journey: How the Great Powers Shape the World* (NY: Basic Books, 1999), Chapter 1.
38. The data on population are from A. S. Banks, *Cross-National Times Series, 1815–1997*; World Bank, *World Development Indicators, 1998* (Washington, DC: World Bank, 1997).
39. The data on GNP-rank and share are from Banks, *Cross-National Times Series, 1815–1997*; World Bank, *World Development Indicators, 1998*.
40. The data on research and development spending is from *OECD in Figures* (1997), cited in *The Public Perspective* (February–March 1998), 80; the data on patent applications is from World Bank, *World Development Indicators, 1998*, 298–300.
41. See their chapters in Pastor (ed.), *A Century's Journey*.
42. J. Joffe, 'The Foreign Policy of the Federal Republic of Germany', in R. C. Macridis (ed.), *Foreign Policy in World Politics*, 8th edition (Englewood Cliffs, New Jersey: Prentice Hall, 1992) p. 100.
43. J. T. Matthews, 'Power Shift', *Foreign Affairs*, 76, No. 1 (January–February 1997) 50. Lester Salamon also sees a historic transformation toward 'a global "associational revolution"'. 'The Rise of the Non-Profit Sector', *Foreign Affairs*, 73, No. 4 (July–August 1994) 109.
44. S. Strange, *The Retreat of the State: The Diffusion of Power in the World Economy* (Cambridge: Cambridge University Press, 1996). For a brief summary of her thesis, see her article 'The Erosion of the State', *Current History* (November 1997).
45. D. Yergin and J. Stanislaw, *Commanding Heights* (New York: Simon and Schuster, 1998) p. 373.
46. The data is compiled from several sources, including J. D. Singer and M. Small, *National Material Capabilities Data, 1816–1993* (Ann Arbor, Michigan: ICPSR, 1996), computer file; International Institute for Strategic Studies, *The Military Balance, 1997/98* (Oxford: Oxford University Press, 1997); A. S. Banks, *Cross-National Times Series, 1815–1997* (Binghamton,

New York: Computer Solutions Unlimited, 1998); and World Bank, *World Development Indicators, 1997* (Washington, DC: World Bank, 1998).
47. N. D. Kristoff with D. Sanger, 'How U.S. Wooed Asia To Let Cash Flow In', *New York Times* (16 February 1999), pp. 1, 10–11. Also N. D. Kristoff and E. Wyatt, 'Who Sank, or Swam, in Choppy Currents of a World Cash Ocean', *New York Times*, A1 (15 February 1999) 10–11.
48. For a fascinating essay on this theme, see A. Perlmutter, *Making the World Safe for Democracy* (Chapel Hill: University of North Carolina Press, 1997).
49. Quoted in N. D. Kristoff, 'Changing Fortunes: Hubris and Humility as U.S. Waves and Asia Wanes', *New York Times* (22 March 1998) 12; P. Kennedy, *The Rise and Fall of the Great Powers: Economic Change and Military Conflict from 1500–2000* (New York: Vintage Books, 1989).
50. US Arms Control and Disarmament Agency, *World Military Expenditures and Arms Transfers, 1995* (Washington, DC: ACDA, 1997).
51. P. Wallensteen and M. Sollenberg, 'The End of International War: Armed Conflict, 1989–1994', *Journal of Peace Research*, 33, 3 (August 1995) 353–370.
52. President B. Clinton, 'Interview with Tom Brokaw of MSNBC's "InterNight"' (15 July 1996), in *Public Papers of the Presidents of the United States: William J. Clinton, 1996* (Washington, DC: GPO, 1997), p. 1246.
53. J. E. Reilly (ed.), *American Public Opinion and U.S. Foreign Policy, 1999* (Chicago: Chicago Council on Foreign Relations, 1999). Sixty-one percent of the public and 96 percent of the leaders believe the US should 'take an active part in world affairs,' and 72 percent of the public and 48 percent of the leaders believe the US should not act alone (pp. 4–5).
54. S. P. Huntington, 'The Lonely Superpower', *Foreign Affairs*, 78, No. 2 (March–April 1999) 36.
55. Quoted in *New York Times* (12 January 1984) 2.
56. K. A. Annan, 'Walking the International Tightrope', *New York Times* (19 January 1999) A23.
57. Z. Brzezinski, *The Grand Chessboard* (New York: Basic Books, 1997).
58. E. Adler and M. Barnett (eds), *Security Communities* (Cambridge, United Kingdom: Cambridge University Press, 1998).
59. See Pastor, *Toward a North American Community: Lessons from the Old World for the New.*

Selected References

Barber, B. R. *Jihad Versus McWorld* (New York: Ballantine Books, 1996).
Brzezinski, Z. *The Grand Chessboard* (New York: Basic Books, 1997).
Doyle, M. W. 'Liberalism and World Politics,' *American Political Science Review*, 80, No. 4 (December 1986) 1151–1169.
Huntington, S. P. *The Clash of Civilizations and the Remaking of the World Order* (New York: Simon and Schuster, 1996).
Nye Jr., J. S. *Bound to Lead: The Changing Nature of American Power* (New York: Basic Books, 1990).
Pastor, R. A. (ed.), *A Century's Journey: How the Great Powers Shape the World* (NY: Basic Books, 1999).
Russett, B. *Grasping the Democratic Peace* (Princeton University Press, 1993).
Strange, S. *The Retreat of the State: The Diffusion of Power in the World Economy* (Cambridge: Cambridge University Press, 1996).

Part III
Policy Challenges

7
Human Security, Globalisation, and Global Governance

Fen Osler Hampson

Recent years have witnessed an important normative change in international relations.[1] This change is reflected in a growing body of international law and international conventions and treaties on human rights; in various international campaigns to ban anti-personnel landmines, light arms, and nuclear weapons; in efforts to establish international criminal tribunals, and an International Criminal Court (ICC) that will prosecute those accused of war crimes and other massive human rights violations; in initiatives to protect civilians and especially vulnerable groups, like women and children in armed conflict; and in efforts to pay greater attention to social and economic reconstruction efforts once the fighting has stopped. Underlying these different initiatives is a shared desire to advance and promote human rights and to ensure that individuals, especially those who are in the greatest danger of having their physical security and well being trampled upon, are placed out of harm's way.[2] Many of these human security initiatives are also the product (or ongoing focus) of international negotiations directed at fostering new international treaties and conventions that oblige states (and occasionally non-state actors) to change their existing behaviours and practices.

This chapter explores three inter-related questions or themes. First, what does human security mean and is there any conceptual coherence to the several different definitions of human security that inform current policy and scholarly thinking? Second, what is the relationship between human security and globalisation and how have the forces of globalisation shaped our understanding of what constitutes 'human security'? And, third, what are the implications of human security for global governance and the kinds of governance arrangements that may be required to promote or advance human security?

The meaning of human security

In a fundamental sense, the concept of 'human security' can be defined, negatively, as the absence of threat to various core human values, including the most basic human value, the physical safety of the individual. Because there are potentially a large number of human values that go beyond the safety of the individual from physical harm, this can lead to an enormous number of types of security. It is therefore useful to aggregate some of these values under the term human security, recognising, of course, that the problems or threats to human security are diverse and that the instruments to handle them are potentially quite varied.

Although the individual's physical security and protection of basic liberties lie at the core of evolving conceptions of human security, these are obviously minimal conditions for human welfare and survival. If individuals are to prosper and develop, their economic needs and interests will also have to be met and therefore attention also has to be paid to the broader social and economic environment – domestic and international – and how it impacts on the welfare and livelihood of the individual. There are arguably three different conceptions of human security that inform current debates and thinking about the subject. The first is what might be termed the natural rights/rule of law conception of human security, which is anchored in the fundamental liberal assumption that individuals have a basic right to 'life, liberty, and the pursuit of happiness' and that the international community has an obligation to protect and promote these rights.[3] A second view of human security is humanitarian. It is this view of human security that, for example, informs international efforts to deepen and strengthen international law, particularly regarding genocide and war crimes, and to abolish weapons of warfare that are especially harmful to civilians and non-combatants.[4] This view arguably also lies at the heart of humanitarian interventions directed at improving the basic living conditions of refugees and those who have been uprooted from their homes and communities as a result of war. On those rare occasions when military force has been used ostensibly to avert genocide and ethnic cleansing, it has also been justified usually on rather narrow humanitarian grounds such as the need to restore basic human rights and dignity.

These two views of human security, which focus on basic human rights and their privation, stand in sharp contrast to a broader view which suggests that the conception of human security should be broadly constructed to include economic, environmental, social, and other forms of privation that adversely affect the overall livelihood and well-being of individuals. There is a strong, social justice component in the broader conception of human security as well as a wider consideration of the array of threats in the international environment that may adversely affect the survival and health of individuals (or have the potential to do so). According to this third view, which is arguably the most controversial of the three conceptions of human security, the state of the global economy, the forces of 'globalisation,' and the health of the environment, including the world's atmosphere and the oceans, are all legitimate subjects of concern in terms of how they impact on the 'security' of the individual.[5]

In reality, many human security initiatives, such as the international campaign to ban international trafficking in small and light weapons, generally tend to fall somewhere in between the narrower and the broader, more encompassing definitions of human security. But, there is a lively debate among scholars and practitioners as to what legitimately should be the scope of efforts to promote and advance human security at the international level, and whether we should define human security in a more restrictive or broader terms.[6]

What these various perspectives share together is a common understanding that human security is critical to international security and that international order cannot rest solely on the sovereignty and viability of states – it depends on individuals and their own sense of security too. This is clearly a departure from traditional liberal internationalism which sees international order as resting on institutional arrangements which, in varying degrees, help secure the viability and integrity of the liberal, democratic state by attenuating threats in the state's external environment. To the extent that individual interests are served, they are of secondary importance to those of the liberal democratic state itself. In the human security 'paradigm' this order of priority is reversed: individuals and communities of individuals rather than governments or 'states' are the primary point of reference. Using the individual as the key point of reference, the human security paradigm also assumes that the safety of the individual is the key to global security; by implication, when the safety of individuals is threatened so too in a fundamental sense is international security.

If the safety and security of the individuals is one of the keys to international security, then, accordingly, the key criterion for assessing policies is their impact on people as opposed to, for example, the national interest or various conceptions of national security. Under the human security paradigm, global challenges have to be assessed in terms of the ways they affect the safety of peoples and not just states. Proponents of the enlarged or maximalist conception of human security also argue that these threats arise not just from military sources, but also non-military ones, such as worsening environmental conditions and economic inequalities that can, in some instances, exacerbate conflict processes.[7]

Although human security takes precedent over 'national' security in the human security frame of reference or paradigm, the state is still viewed as one of the principal instruments for securing the rights and physical security of the individual. Due process of law, for example, depends upon a judicial system that is both accountable and transparent. When individuals are physically threatened, it is the state that is supposed to come to their defence because it enjoys a monopoly on violence and the instruments of coercion. A liberal, democratic state in which due process and political accountability are guaranteed is ultimately the best defence against threats to the life, liberty, and property of the individual.

The other key to human security, however, is a healthy and vibrant civil society. Much of the recent work by political scientists and students of democracy underscores the proposition that a healthy and vibrant democracy depends, in turn, on a vibrant and politically active civil society through which citizens are able to participate in the political process outside of elections. Democracy is not simply about casting votes in a formal election, it is also about participating in the day-to-day decision-making process of government at all levels from the local to the national. In a fundamental sense, democracy depends upon what Gabriel Almond and Sidney Verba almost 40 years ago called a 'civic culture'.[8] As Robert Putnam argues, among the key indicators of a healthy civic culture is a society in which individuals have affiliations and memberships in a wide variety of voluntary organisations ranging from the community bowling league to the local branch of a political party.[9] These organisations not only help to inform and engage the populace, but they serve as key instruments of interest articulation and aggregation, conveying and transmitting the needs and interests of constituents to their political leaders. In societies where such organisations are lacking or where membership is limited or weak, democracy tends to suffer because citizens are not engaged in the decisions of government and political accountability is weakened.

In the human security frame of reference, civil society has a critical role to play not just in strengthening and promoting democracy within the nation-state, but also in the various tasks associated with social and economic reconstruction in war-torn societies. Because war-torn societies often lack viable state institutions and administrative structures, many of the traditional functions of the state, including the provision of basic services, have to be carried out by other actors such as nongovernmental organisations (NGOs) or various community groups and associations. These actors and institutions effectively serve as substitutes or surrogates for the various functions normally carried out by national or local governmental authorities. Their sources of funding and financial support also typically come from the outside state, that is, from external donors and international relief agencies. As international efforts shift from emergency assistance and short-term humanitarian relief to the tasks of long-term social and economic reconstruction, NGOs and civil society actors tend to play a vital role not only in providing key services and functions that are necessary for social and economic development, but also in projecting human security values and ensuring that a civic culture takes root.[10]

Human security and globalisation

Although the concept of human security is not new, there are a number of factors that help to explain the growing salience of human security concerns in international politics. Many of these factors, in fact, represent the globalisation of human security concerns and it is perhaps appropriate to view human security as both the cause and consequence of social, economic, and political change that are lumped together under the term 'globalisation.'

First, an international regime of legal norms, principles, and precedents that aims to bolster and strengthen the protection of human rights across a wide spectrum ranging from the most basic rights to include wider social, economic, and political rights has developed and been strengthened by recent initiatives such as the successful conclusion of negotiations to establish an ICC.[11] This emerging human rights regime has developed at two levels: the global and the regional. Although the regime is stronger in some corners of the globe than in others, there is some evidence of a growing convergence in the basic norms, principles, and values that inform different human rights regimes not only at the global level but also across different regions.[12]

Second, it is unquestionably true that the end of the Cold War has seen the widespread growth of democracy as the preferred system of government in the world. Not only has the absolute number of democracies in the world increased markedly with the collapse of the Soviet Union and its empire in Eastern Europe, but the democratic model has been transplanted to societies where the international community has been actively involved in implementing negotiated peace agreements which ended violent conflict such as in El Salvador, Guatemala, Namibia, Mozambique, and Cambodia.[13] Although the overall success of these efforts at broad-scale social and political engineering is a matter of continued debate, there can be no question that these efforts to promote democracy have been paralleled by growing efforts to promote human rights and to strengthen judicial and legal systems in countries where human rights have traditionally been flaunted. Human security concerns are at the forefront of these attempts to consolidate democracy because it is generally recognised that democracy depends upon the protection of human rights and the advancement of the rule of law.[14]

A third factor is the growing impact of NGOs, particularly those working in the humanitarian and development fields, which have raised the profile of the human security concerns by stressing the need to address the plight of refugees and particularly vulnerable groups, such as women and children, who are often the most seriously affected victims of armed conflict.[15] Transnational social and political movements have also developed in support of new arms control initiatives that are directed at mitigating the adverse impact of weapons of warfare that indiscriminately kill civilians and threaten the prospects of economic development once the fighting has stopped. The most notable of these in recent years has been the international campaign to ban antipersonnel landmines – a campaign that was ultimately successful in securing a new antipersonnel landmines treaty.[16] NGOs were at the forefront of this campaign and similar campaigns have developed in support of efforts to control the supply and distribution of light arms and to ban weapons of mass destruction.

A fourth factor is the media – what is sometimes dubbed the 'CNN effect.' Television brought the Vietnam War into the living rooms of citizens living around the globe. Since then, with the advent of 24-hour news channels, like CNN, and the spread of satellite and cable networks, the world has truly come to resemble a 'global village' – to coin Marshall McLuhan.[17] When conflict erupts in some far-off land, television has the capacity to create a sense of immediacy and urgency, especially when there are thousands of refugees who are starving and dying and whose story is told night after night on the evening news.[18] But it is not just television that has created a moral affinity between the viewer and the victims of war and natural disasters; the spread of the Internet is helping to shape public perceptions as well. Citizens no longer depend upon news organisations to filter the news by bringing pictures and stories of suffering and disaster into their living rooms, they can log on to the Internet and communicate with the victims directly. During the Kosovo crisis, for example, Albanian Kosovar teenagers were able to tell the story of their suffering to the world and with a much greater sense of immediacy and potency than any journalist could because it was told in the first person.

A fifth factor is the changing nature of international politics and the emergence of a new tier of 'middle powers' who are committed to advancing the conception of human security of international politics and to strengthening the normative foundations of international institutions from a human security standpoint.[19] History suggests that middle powers have regularly made important contributions to international order and international politics in the late twentieth and early twenty-first century is no exception. During the Cold War, middle powers tended to be frozen out of international politics because of the domination of the US-Soviet rivalry and its impact on world affairs. As the Cold War ended and the Soviet empire collapsed, the world was left with one superpower, the United States. However, the United States has found itself constrained by its own internal politics and longstanding, historical ambivalence about playing a global leadership role in world affairs. Middle powers, like the Lilliputians in Jonathan Swift's *Gulliver's Travels*, have tried to fill the leadership gap by trying to erect a new global order that is attentive to the needs and concerns of the world's most vulnerable citizens. They have worked closely with NGOs to fashion this new order, but the enterprise is not without controversy, and, they, like the Lilliputians, recognise that they must somehow engage the world's Gulliver if they are to succeed.

Sixth, it must be recognised that the forces of economic globalisation are transforming international politics and recasting relationships between states and peoples with important implications for human security. Globalisation is not only intensifying trade and economic connections, but the pace or velocity at which economic and social change is occurring is also speeding up. Further, it is not just goods and capital that are being exchanged across borders, but also ideas, information, and people as well. In the ongoing debate about the causes and consequences of globalisation, considerable concern has been expressed by some about the impact of globalisation on the world's poor and needy. On the one hand, the enthusiasts of globalisation argue that the breakdown of national barriers to trade and the spread of global financial and capital markets are processes that are helping to raise world incomes and contribute to the spread of wealth. Although there are clear 'winners' and 'losers' in the world economy, the old divisions between the advanced 'northern' economies and 'peripheral' southern economies are breaking down and being replaced by an increasingly complex architecture of economic power.[20] On the other hand, critics of globalisation argue that although some countries in the south have benefited from globalisation, many have not and inequalities of income between the world's richest and poorest countries are growing. They suggest that trade and investment flows are intensifying between those countries that can compete in the global economy while leaving those that cannot behind. As income gaps and deep-rooted social and economic inequalities widen, so the argument runs, so too do the prospects for violence and civil strife. According to the critics, globalisation raises a new set of challenges for human security as patterns of world trade, production, and finance take on new dimensions which, if left unregulated and uncontrolled, will further impoverish the world's poor with dire social and political consequences.[21]

A seventh factor is the changing nature of international conflict itself coupled with a new understanding about the different factors that can fuel conflict and lead to violence.[22] During the Cold War, the superpower rivalry contributed to the progress and escalation of 'proxy wars,' that is to say wars that were fought between local belligerents with the direct support and aid of the United States, the Soviet Union and sometimes China. Many of these conflicts had their origins in nationalism, intercommunal or ethnic strife, socio-economic factors, or disputes resulting from decolonisation and the drawing/redrawing of state boundaries, but they tended to be cast in ideological terms as a result of the projection of superpower influence into the far corners of the world.[23] As the Cold War ended and a new spirit of détente and co-operation set in, the superpowers worked together to disengage from these conflicts by cutting their dependents loose and forging political settlements.

However, in other regions new conflicts erupted which neither the superpowers nor regional actors seemed able or willing to control. Many of these conflicts were the result of state failure: in Asia, the Middle East, Africa, and Central and South America internally divided states (often lacking political legitimacy) found themselves unable to provide basic services and security to their citizenry, let alone adhere to democratic principles and the rule of law.[24] As these weak states fragmented, the potential for local conflict increased as different ethnic and social groups became involved in conflicts over resources and land. Some even fell prey to their more powerful neighbours seeking to expand their influence and power in the region. The growing importance of the politics of identity along with the end of communist ideology and rule in countries, like the former Yugoslavia, has also weakened social and political cohesion and undermined the artificial unity of the old social order. Even so, some armed conflicts are propelled less by the politics of identity than by the efforts of different groups to control economic resources such as diamonds, drugs, timber concessions, oil, and even so-called renewable resources like water.[25]

Human security and global governance

In the human security approach to international relations, although international order is a desirable global public good, 'order' will not be achieved until basic human security needs are met and largely fulfilled. In this respect, the content of international order does matter and as long as the world is filled with 'failed' or 'failing' states where public institutions, governance, and the physical, political, and economic security of citizens are at risk or directly threatened, there is no real prospect for 'order' in the international system. The absence of inter-state conflict is in the international system – a condition that would presumably satisfy traditional realists and/or liberals and be considered a sign of health and stability in international politics – is not sufficient for advocates of human security. It may simply mask deeper problems at the intrastate or subsystemic levels. Genuine order will only be achieved when the majority of the world's human security needs are met. This underscores the point that well-founded 'order' can contribute to human security and there are reciprocal effects of meeting the human security needs of peoples and providing for a 'just' international order.

However, if human security in all of its various dimensions represents a kind of underprovided 'public good' then what kinds of governance arrangements – and which international institutions, mechanisms, and/or actors, in particular – are best equipped to provide for human security in all of its various dimensions and guises? Among the proponents of human security, there is arguably no consensus about which institutions and governance mechanisms are best able to provide for human security. Some argue that states are ultimately the most efficient and capable providers of human security; in other words, in spite of globalisation, which may be challenging the very existence of the nation-state, the state still has its uses as far as human security is concerned. Others argue that human security is best promoted and advanced through international institutions. Still others argue that non-state actors, that is, NGOs and various elements of civil society, are the new providers of human security not simply on grounds of efficiency but also on grounds of equity and social and political accountability. For the purposes of simplification, and to isolate core assumptions and beliefs, the different positions in the ongoing debate about which actors and/or institutions are best able to promote human security the debate may be characterised in terms of four, different, competing schools of thoughts: the cosmopolitan, the institutionalist, the minilateralist, and middle power multilateralist.

Cosmopolitans

The cosmopolitan school of thought argues that civil society, especially NGOs, and broad-based social movements that have been in a real sense empowered by modern communications technologies and which transgress national boundaries are the new champions of human security and providers of it. According to the cosmopolitan viewpoint, non-state actors are playing a key role in setting the international agenda by effectively using a wide range of media (television, radio, the internet) and lobbying and persuading governments to adopt new courses of action. They are also playing a key role as well in educating citizenry and facilitating social learning and, most importantly, the promulgation of new human security norms through their various methods of information exchange and communication.[26]

These 'communities' of activists and policymakers have, in a real way, been transformed and empowered by the forces of globalisation.[27] As James Rosenau writes, 'The mushrooming of *social movements* in recent years offers still another instance of micro-macro interactions induced by globalising dynamics'.[28] Furthermore, '[w]hether it be the environmental, feminist, peace, or Islamic movement ... the symbols, membership, modes of interaction, and hierarchical arrangements are, at best, variable, and informal. Such movements tend to improvise from issue, sometimes circumventing national governments and sometimes working with them, but at all times eschewing efforts to develop and intrude formal structures into their deliberations and activities'.[29]

NGOs and social movements are seen by cosmopolitans as the inventors and providers of new social and political norms that are the building blocks of new forms of social and political discourse and, ultimately, political behaviours and institutions (national and international).[30] Although their presence is felt most acutely in the areas of human rights and environmental issues,[31] it is expanding into other issues-areas such as trade and investment policy.[32]

But it is not just in the areas of agenda-setting and norm creation that these civil society actors are providing international public goods. They are also directly involved in providing for basic human needs (food, health, education, security, and economic development) and fulfilling those functions normally provided by the state itself or by international organisations. As Mary Anderson explains, 'Churches, civic groups, labor unions, private foundations, and millions of individuals have established organisations that usually operate as tax-free entities to support some group or some cause. While many of these operate within their own borders, a very large number of NGOs have defined their mission as working with people in other countries.' They provide assistance in four different mandates: 1) provision of humanitarian relief to people in emergencies; 2) promotion of long-term social and economic development; 3) promulgation and basic monitoring of basic human rights; and 4) pursuit of peace, including the promotion of the philosophy and techniques of negotiation, conflict resolution, and non-violence.[33]

According to the cosmopolitans, civil society is not just a poor substitute for the state when it comes to human security, it is in the vanguard of human security provision. NGOs and various non-state actors are also not only more efficient than states or international organisations, but they are also more attentive to considerations of equity and social justice in meeting human security needs.[34] This is not to say that NGOs are necessarily problem free when it comes to providing these public goods,[35] cosmopolitans merely argue that these non-state actors are better able to provide these goods because of their small size, organisational flexibility, and knowledge and experience with local conditions.

Institutionalists

Human security institutionalists tend to side with traditional liberals in championing the virtues (or comparative advantage) of formal international organisations and institutions in the provision and maintenance of public goods, including human security, for many of the same reasons traditional liberals do. They believe that international organisations enjoy a much higher degree of political legitimacy and accountability than NGOs and non-state actors. This is because they tend to have universal or near-universal membership and also because they are state-based, that is, inter-governmental. The inter-governmental nature and capacity of formal international organisations also means that they can mobilise resources and the requisite political will on a vastly larger scale than can most NGOs when it comes to defending human security values. Institutionalists also argue that formal international organisations have been remarkably successful in changing the expectations and behaviours of states through the promulgation of new norms, particularly in the context of human rights and the environment.[36] Institutionalists believe that when it comes to using force in the defence and protection of human security, international institutions typically enjoy a much higher degree of *collective* political legitimacy than states. When international organisations give their blessing to the use of force in the defence of human security values it is harder to challenge and criticise such interventions as being mere extensions of state power and selfish national interests.

Even so, few institutionalists of the human security persuasion believe that all is well with existing international organisations and the machinery of interstate co-operation. Foremost among the advocates for reform is the Secretary-General of the United Nations (UN), Kofi Annan, who believes the UN has a unique role to play in halting human rights abuses around the globe and promoting human security values more generally. The Secretary-General questions those who assert that 'the Charter itself – with its roots in the aftermath of global inter-State war – is ill-suited to guide us in a world of ethnic wars and intra-State violence.' Instead, he argues that 'The Charter is a living document, whose high principles still define the aspirations of peoples everywhere for lives of peace, dignity, and development' and that '[n]othing in the Charter precludes a recognition that there are rights beyond borders'.[37] Specifically, the Secretary-General calls upon permanent members of the Security Council to have a wider conception of their national interests and to 'find far greater unity in the pursuit of such basic Charter values as democracy, human rights, and the rule of law'.[38]

The Secretary-General's view is also echoed in a wide range of reports and studies that argue for specific institutional reforms not just of the UN, but also regional and subregional organisations, in order that they can more effectively promote human security.

There are also those who believe that a more radical set of reforms is required to ensure international organisations promote human security values. For example, Richard Shell asserts that the assumptions underlying the structure of the General Agreement on Tariffs and Trade (GATT)/World Trade Organisation (WTO) system and its current organisational structure are flawed when it comes to promoting equity and social justice in international relations and that new institutional structures are required to give standing to non-state actors.[39] These new institutions should see their mission not just in terms of promoting free-trade but also providing forums where issues of fairness and social justice can be properly discussed. Similar kinds of arguments have also been advanced in the context of global environmental change where many argue that if a genuine moral discourse is to occur that is sensitive to human security concerns 'new participatory structures are needed to give voice to hitherto un-represented or underrepresented groups in society,' particularly within international organisations.[40]

Minilateralists

Human security 'minilateralists' believe that the main principles of UN Charter (and other international organisations) are on a collision course with the human security agenda. As Michael Glennon writes, 'it is not only that the UN Charter prohibits intervention where enlightened states now believe it to be just – its problems run even deeper. For the charter is grounded on a premise that is simply no longer valid – the assumption that the core threat to international security still comes from interstate violence'.[41] According to minilateralists, although there are dangers from states acting independently to secure human security values when they are threatened because such interventions will necessarily be ad hoc and 'justice formed on the fly,' the alternative – to do nothing – is worse and morally unacceptable. Because '[t]he failings of the old system were so disastrous…little will be lost in the attempt to forge a new one'.[42]

To deal with the problems of genocide, ethnic cleansing, and other egregious human rights abuses, minilateralists believe that the United States and other democracies must act using military power if necessary to defend these values. Furthermore, to prevent intrastate wars from spilling across their borders with adverse consequences for international peace and security, the minilateralists sanction *early* intervention because the subsequent humanitarian costs are likely to be even higher the initial costs of intervention.[43]

Minilateralists, however, eschew unilateral intervention by great powers because even with the best of intentions such actions will be misinterpreted as self-serving. As a safety measure, human security interventions should be multilateral in appearance, recognising that most of the 'heavy lifting' in these situations will have to be done by the great powers than by their coalition partners. Thus, the 'hope is that building a multinational coalition will filter out the worst forms of national self-interest and keep them from playing a leading role in international intervention'.[44]

Even so, minilateralism is no substitute for genuine multilateralism and interventions that have their basis and can be legitimised through the rule of law. Under this approach *just* interventions will pave the way eventually to a new set of precedents for international law and a restructuring of international institutions: formal organisations and the system of rules and law upon which they are based will eventually catch up. As Glennon explains, '[a]chieving justice is the hard part; revising international law to reflect it can come afterward. If power is used to do justice, law will follow'.[45] Thus, minilateralism is the half-way house to a new normative order – a stepping stone but not a stopping place.

What is to be noted about this viewpoint is that like traditional realism human security minilateralists believe that traditional power is the key ingredient in international politics and that hegemonic involvement (in this case by the United States) is the key to establishing a new and more just international order. But whereas realists have traditionally argued that military power should only be used in defence of broader – and usually somewhat ill-defined – goals based on the national interest, human security minilateralists believe that power can and indeed should be used in the defence of human security values – a contention that most realists would dispute. Furthermore, political appearances, that is, political legitimacy, do matter, hence the importance of assembling the 'sheriff's posse' – that is, using the veneer of multilateralism – when force has to be used to protect or promote those values.

Middle power multilateralists

Unlike minilateralists, middle power multilateralists believe that 'coalitions of the like-minded' (middle and small powers) are best positioned to promote human security in today's world. It is generally recognised that coalitions of middle powers can invent new solutions and identify new institutional options in bargaining situations where the major actors are deadlocked and unable to arrive at a cooperative agreement, particularly within negotiations that occur within formalised institutionalised settings. These actors provide a 'middle way' between major protagonists, not by 'difference splitting' but providing 'a genuine alternative middle ground upon which the major actors [can] meet'.[46] Typically bridging solutions are offered by coalitions of smaller states or middle powers who do not have structural power, that is, are not capable of providing a collective good on their own, but can compensate for a lack of structural power through the exercise of bargaining and negotiating skills directed at bringing competing interests together.[47]

Some argue that middle powers can project their influence outside of formal international institutions by tapping into the cosmopolitan sector and forming strategic alliances with NGOs and various transnational actors in civil society. Under this formulation, 'soft power' – defined as 'the art of disseminating information in such a way that desirable outcomes are achieved through persuasion rather than coercion'[48] – is the key instrument of diplomacy and the means by which an alliance of middle power state and non-state actors can promote human security values.

New information technologies like the Internet are also considered by middle power multilateralists to be key instruments for exchanging information and strengthening activities such as 'addressing human rights abuses or international crimes, areas where the rapid exchange of information across borders is essential.' These strategies are also seen as being essential 'in helping to establish free media and counter hate propaganda, and so bolster democracy and reduce the likelihood of conflict in troubled regions'.[49]

The difference between traditional, middle power multilateralism and the new multilateralism of human security is that traditionalists emphasise the importance of working through formal international institutions and organisations whereas the 'new' multilateralists seek to work outside of established institutional structures and to create new institutional forums, when necessary, to promote and advance human security interests. Middle power multilateralists also tend to be somewhat ambivalent about the utility of formal international organisations, like the UN, in promoting human security values because they recognise that entrenched state interests may be opposed to this agenda. They therefore seek to work more closely with civil society organisations because they believe that NGOs and the business sector (at least potentially) can be 'extremely effective partners in advocating the security of people'.[50] But whereas cosmopolitans argue that transnational civil society can provide human security without the direct involvement of states, middle power multilateralists generally believe that states (that is, middle powers) have a constructive role to play in advancing human security. This is because middle powers can usefully promote human security values and norms to bring about much-needed reforms in those international organisations where they are formal members. Middle power multilateralists also tend to be somewhat sceptical about the use of force in international politics because they believe that hard (that is, military or coercive) power is of declining utility in post-Cold War world where power 'is increasingly diffuse and malleable'.[51]

Because they view human security as trumping state sovereignty, human security advocates believe that sovereignty should not be allowed to stand in the way of human security and its advancement. But as with any public good, the key question is how costly is it to procure the good, who is willing (or able) to pay for the fixed costs of public goods provision, and do the perceived benefits (local, national, and global) and the declining marginal costs of extending these benefits outweigh the up-front, fixed costs and risks. To the extent that values other than efficiency are involved in public goods provision (for example, legitimacy, accountability, and distribution), there are also differing viewpoints about how to address value tradeoffs. Theories may be universal but policy is about setting priorities, confronting difficult tradeoffs, and making tough choices.

Cosmopolitans are inclined to argue on balance that it is preferable that human security be provided on a voluntary basis and through the voluntary sector. They believe that not only is this most efficient, but it also lends greater accountability and legitimacy to decision-making because NGOs are more attentive to local needs and considerations. Further, to the extent that sovereignty stands in the way of the delivery of human security, NGOs working with their counterparts in other societies are best able to circumvent and work around state actors. While recognising that international organisations are financially incapable in their current, cash-strapped state of meeting the vast array of human security needs and challenges, institutionalists nonetheless believe that international organisations are best positioned to make use of the resources that are available. International organisations also enjoy greater political legitimacy because of their mandates and membership – especially in the case of the global institutions like the UN and its various affiliated agencies. With more resources, institutionalists believe that the barriers to meeting human security needs that international organisations currently confront would be significantly lowered. Minilateralists, in contrast, believe that only great powers are in a position to assume the costs of providing human security (especially when the use of force is involved), but they recognise that the political will to mobilise these resources (financial, economic, and military) is sorely lacking and that there are profound domestic obstacles to doing so. On the other hand, middle power multilateralists tend to believe that resources per se are not the real problem, especially if one can bring about normative change that changes political behaviours and advances human security norms and values in the process. In other words, middle power multilateralists believe that many – if not most – human security goals can be secured 'on the cheap.'

Conclusion

There is obviously a continuing tension between these different conceptions of human security. On the one hand, exponents of the broader conception of human security, namely, sustainable human development focus on the need to develop correctives (institutional and otherwise) to the forces set in motion by globalisation and the world's changing political economy. On the other hand, those who couch the human security challenge in terms of the strengthening and promoting human rights and the rule of law while simultaneously addressing the needs of peoples in conflict situations (that is, enhancing the safety of peoples) typically stress the importance of promoting (exporting) democracy and the rule of law and strengthening international institutions (governmental and nongovernmental) that can provide for human security.

To the extent that there is any consensus at the international level about which conception of human security should prevail, it is one that appears to endorse the narrower conception of human security with its corresponding emphasis on promoting human rights, the rule of law, and the safety of peoples. This is reflected in the sorts of undertakings that have come to characterise the human security 'enterprise', for example, the landmines campaign and treaty, the creation of the ICC, efforts to control small arms, and so on. In some respects, the human security enterprise as it has evolved in recent years is a rather traditional liberal undertaking. It is an enterprise that for the most part has tended to focus on reforming states, not markets. But unlike traditional liberalism it is highly interventionist when it comes to reforming failed or failing states.

But it is also the case that even to the extent there is an emerging consensus that human rights/rule of law and safety of peoples are legitimate human security concerns, this consensus is not universally shared. There continue to be important differences in the way states view particular human security initiatives and the implications of these initiatives for national security and state sovereignty. Negotiations leading to the treaty to ban antipersonnel landmines were marked by the defection of the United States from the Ottawa Process as well as opposition from a number of other key countries such as Russia and China. The same is true of the ICC where the United States, a key supporter of the idea in early years, balked about signing onto the treaty that emerged from the negotiations in Rome. Although President Clinton did eventually sign the treaty as one of his last acts in office, most observers give it little chance of being ratified by the Senate of the United States any time soon. Much of the opposition to these two initiatives, in the United States has come from the Pentagon, which is reluctant to endorse the creation of new international institutions that will compromise its missions and purported US national security interests. The campaign to ban small arms is also notable for the lack of consensus, even among supporters of the idea to control international trade in light weapons because of continuing differences about the modalities and scope of a control regime.

On the matter whether force should be used in support of human security objectives, the recent history of military interventions in Kosovo, East Timor, Sierra Leone, and elsewhere also shows that the consensus is weak: Western liberal democratic states have found themselves at odds not just with developing countries, but also great powers like Russia and China, about whether international institutions should sanction the use of force in 'humanitarian' interventions.[52] Human security values have therefore tended to sit somewhat uneasily alongside more traditional international norms like sovereignty and the principle of nonintervention in the internal affairs of states. Though it would be wrong to suggest that sovereignty and nonintervention are hard and fast norms in international politics – there is simply too much evidence that sovereignty is conditional and borders are not sacrosanct[53] – it would also be wrong to argue that human security values have somehow replaced these traditional Westphalian norms in international politics. What we do see is an uneasy coexistence between these two normative systems where conflicting interpretations as to which norms should guide international behaviour and state practice have all too often polarised the international community. The norms, values, and assumptions that inform the human security 'paradigm' are in a state of flux and tension – a tension that is reflected not just among the different meanings of human security, but also between the concept of human security and other norms, values, and principles that have traditionally informed and shaped state behaviour and served as guide to action (or inaction). However, the qualified success of a number of human security initiatives and undertakings, such as the anti-personnel landmines treaty and the successful conclusion of negotiations for the ICC, suggests that a new set of norms and principles are taking root and slowly reshaping the international landscape. These gestures are not just theoretical exercises in norm creation, but are concrete undertakings directed at improving the security situation and welfare of ordinary people around the globe.

As is also argued in this paper, there are four different schools of thought about human security and the kinds of governance arrangements that may be required to promote and advance it. Minilateralists stress the importance of great powers, or what is sometimes referred to as the sheriff's posse, in defending and promoting human security values, especially when the use of force is involved. Institutionalists, on the other hand, stress the importance of formal international organisations, like the UN, in providing for human security because these institutions possess the critical ingredient – global legitimacy – which comes from their near-universal membership that miniature coalitions, when they choose to act on their own, typically lack.

Cosmopolitans consider civil society and the vast network of NGOs that span the globe as the real movers and shakers behind the human security agenda. Cosmopolitans believe that not only do civil society actors have the potential to mobilise public opinion and thus change the preferences of state (that is, governmental) actors in ways that foster co-operative solutions to human security problems, but they also have a real comparative advantage in mobilising resources (through public fund raising campaigns). Part of this advantage comes from their presence on the ground in many conflict regions and their long-standing involvement in and commitment to human development and assistance. Cosmopolitans also favour the creation of new, international governance structures that not only confer greater legitimacy to their efforts, but give them a greater voice and role in the provision of human security than they now have within existing international institutions and organisational arrangements.

Middle power multilateralists argue that middle powers, when allied with NGOs and elements of civil society, can mobilise international coalitions to promote human security. The middle power multilateralist position is that formal international organisations are too often hamstrung or paralysed by the veto power exercised by great powers (especially the United Nations Security Council) and that it is sometimes necessary to create new institutions and negotiating forums that bypass or circumvent the logjam within existing institutions. The legitimacy of these efforts is also enhanced and strengthened by supportive elements in civil society who can work with middle powers to promote the creation of new international institutions. New communications technologies, such as the Internet, are critical to the projection of influence and the mobilisation of public opinion around human security concerns.

Although we have tried to suggest that there is a degree of intellectual coherence and consistency to the meaning and concept of human security, we have also argued that human security means different things in different institutional contexts. The obvious tensions between the narrower and broader definitions of human security are all too evident and ultimately are based on rather different understandings about the sorts of problems and threats that are responsible for the human security deficit in today's world. It would clearly be a mistake to suggest that there is greater coherence and logical consistency to the ideas of human security than there is in practice. The potentially large number of diverse elements that fall within the definition of human security also poses a challenge for our understanding of global governance and the kinds of collective undertakings that may be required to promote human security.

Notes

1. This paper is based, in part, on the author's new book: F. O. Hampson with J. Daudelin, J. B. Hay, T. Martin and H. Reid, *Madness in the Multitude: Human Security and World Disorder* (Toronto and New York: Oxford University Press, 2002).
2. L. Axworthy, 'Canada and Human Security: The Need for Leadership', *International Journal*, LII, 2 (1997) 183–196; L. Axworthy and S. Taylor, 'A Ban for All Seasons', *International Journal*, LIII, 2 (1998) 189–204; United Nations Development Programme (UNDP), *Human Development Report* (New York: Oxford University Press, 1994); F. O. Hampson with J. Daudelin, J. B. Hay, T. Martin and H. Reid, *Madness in the Multitude: Human Security and World Disorder* (Toronto and New York: Oxford University Press, 2002); R. McRae and D. Hubert (eds), *Human Security and the New Diplomacy: Protecting People, Promoting Peace* (Montreal and Kingston: McGill-Queen's University Press, 2001).

3. See J. Morsink, *The Universal Declaration of Human Rights: Origins, Drafting and Intent* (University Park: University of Pennsylvania Press, 1998); P. Alston (ed.), *The United Nations and Human Rights: A Critical Appraisal* (Oxford: Oxford University Press, 1992); P. G. Lauren, *The Evolution of International Human Rights: Visions Seen* (Philadelphia: University of Philadelphia Press, 1998).

4. See B. Boutros-Ghali, *Agenda for Peace*, Report of the UN Secretary General (New York, 1992); J. Moore, *The UN and Complex Emergencies: Rehabilitation in Third World Transitions* (Geneva: UNRISD, 1996); B. Boutros-Ghali, *Supplement to an Agenda for Peace: Position Paper of the Secretary-General on the Occasion of the Fiftieth Anniversary of the United Nations*. UN GAOR/SCOR, 50th Sess., at 55, UN Docs. A/50/60 & S/1995/1.; United Nations Press Office (UN), 'Secretary-General Presents His Annual Report to the General Assembly', Press Release SG/SM/7136/GA/9596, Annex 1 (New York: United Nations, 20 September 1999). Available at: http://www.un.org/News/Press/docs/1999/19990920.sgsm7136.html; United Nations Development Programme (UNDP), *Human Development Report* (New York: Oxford University Press, 1997).

5. See United Nations Development Programme (UNDP), *Human Development Report* (New York: Oxford University Press, 1994); J. Nef, *Human Security and Mutual Vulnerability: An Exploration into the Global Political Economy of Development and Underdevelopment* (Ottawa: International Development Research Centre, 1995).

6. F. O. Hampson with J. Daudelin, J. B. Hay, T. Martin and H. Reid, *Madness in the Multitude: Human Security and World Disorder* (Toronto and New York: Oxford University Press, 2002); R. Pares, 'Human Security: Paradigm Shift or Hot Air?', *International Security*, XXVI, 2 (2001) 87–102; Y. F. Khong, 'Human Security: A Shotgun Approach to Alleviating Human Misery?', *Global Governance: A Review of Multilateralism and International Organizations*, VII, 3 (2001) 231–236.

7. United Nations Development Programme (UNDP), *Human Development Report* (New York: Oxford University Press, 1994); J. Nef, *Human Security and Mutual Vulnerability: An Exploration into the Global Political Economy of Development and Underdevelopment* (Ottawa: International Development Research Centre, 1995); R. Pares, 'Human Security: Paradigm Shift or Hot Air?', *International Security*, XXVI, 2 (2001) 87–102.

8. G. A. Almond and S. Verba, *The Civic Culture: Political Attitudes and Democracy in Five Nations* (Princeton: Princeton University Press, 1963).

9. R. D. Putnam, *Making Democracy Work: Civic Traditions in Modern Italy* (Princeton: Princeton University Press, 1993).

10. M. B. Anderson, 'Humanitarian NGOs in Conflict Intervention', in C. A. Crocker, F. O. Hampson and P. Aall (eds), *Managing Global Chaos: Sources of and Responses to International Conflict* (Washington, DC: United States Institute of Peace Press, 1996), pp. 343–354.

11. M. C. Bassiouni, *Crimes Against Humanity in International Law* (Dordrecht: Martinus Nijhoff Publishers, 1992); M. C. Bassiouni, 'From Versailles to Rwanda in Seventy-Five Years: The Need to Establish a Permanent International Criminal Court', *Harvard Human Rights Law Journal*, X (1997) 11–62; M. C. Bassiouni and C. L. Blakesley, 'The Need for an International

Criminal Court in the New International World Order', *Vanderbilt Journal of Trans-national Law*, XXV, 9 (1992) 151–82; G. J. Bass, *Stay the Hand of Vengeance: The Politics of War Crimes Tribunals* (Princeton: Princeton University Press, 2000).

12. A. Moravcik, 'Explaining International Human Rights Regimes: Liberal Theory and Western Europe', *European Journal of International Affairs*, I, 1 (June 1995) 157–89.

13. F. O Hampson, *Nurturing Peace: Why Peace Settlements Succeed or Fail* (Washington, DC: United States Institute of Peace Press, 1996).

14. J. Morsink, *The Universal Declaration of Human Rights: Origins, Drafting and Intent* (University Park: University of Pennsylvania Press, 1998); P. G. Lauren, *The Evolution of International Human Rights: Visions Seen* (Philadelphia: University of Philadelphia Press, 1998).

15. J. Moore, *The UN and Complex Emergencies: Rehabilitation in Third World Transitions* (Geneva: UNRISD, 1996); W. Korey, *NGOs and the Universal Declaration of Human Rights* (New York: St. Martin's, 1998).

16. See M. A. Cameron, R. J. Lawson and B. W. Tomlin (eds), *To Walk Without Fear: The Global Movement to Ban Landmines* (Toronto: Oxford University Press, 1998).

17. For a contrary view see C. Moisy, 'Myths of the Global Information Village', *Foreign Policy*, CVII (1997) 78–87.

18. W. P. Strobel, *Late-Breaking Foreign Policy: The News Media's Influence on Peace Operations* (Washington, DC: United States Institute of Peace Press, 1997).

19. R. McRae and D. Hubert (eds), *Human Security and the New Diplomacy: Protecting People, Promoting Peace* (Montreal and Kingston: McGill-Queen's University Press, 2001).

20. D. Held, A. McGrew, D. Goldblatt and J. Perraton, *Global Transformations: Politics, Economics, and Culture* (Stanford: Stanford University Press, 1999), p. 4.

21. For various views on this debate see R. O. Keohane and J. S. Nye, Jr. 'Globalisation: What's New What's Not (And So What?)', *Foreign Policy*, CXVII (2000) 104–119; D. Roderick, 'Sense and Nonsense in the Globalisation Debate', *Foreign Policy*, CVII (1997) 19–37.

22. M. Sollenberg, P. Wallensteen and A. Jato, 'Major Armed Conflicts', in *SIPRI Yearbook 1999: Armaments, Disarmament, and International Security* (Oxford: Oxford University Press, 1999), pp. 15–33.

23. C. A. Crocker, F. O. Hampson and P. Aall (eds), *Managing Global Chaos: Sources of and Responses to International Conflict* (Washington, DC: United States Institute of Peace Press, 1996).

24. M. Ayoob, 'State Making, State Breaking, and State Failure', in Crocker, Hampson and Aall 1996, pp. 37–52.

25. See T. R. Gurr, *Peoples versus States: Minorities at Risk in the New Century* (Washington, DC: United States Institute of Peace Press, 2000); M. Berdal and D. M. Malone (eds), *Greed and Grievance: Economic Agendas in Civil Wars* (Boulder and Ottawa: Lynne Rienner and International Development Research Centre, 2000).

26. See M. Hewson and T. J. Sinclair (eds), *Approaches to Global Governance Theory* (Albany: State University Press of New York, 1999); R. A. Falk, *On*

Humane Governance (University Park: Pennsylvania State Press, 1995); T. G. Weiss and L. Gordenker (eds), *NGOs, the UN, and Global Governance* (Boulder: Lynne Rienner, 1996).

27. See J. N. Rosenau, *Turbulence in World Politics: A Theory of Change and Continuity* (Princeton: Princeton University Press, 1990).

28. J. N. Rosenau, 'The Person, the Household, the Community, and the Globe: Notes for a Theory of Multilateralism in a Turbulent World', in Robert W. Cox (ed.), *The New Realism: Perspectives on Multilateralism and World Order* (Tokyo: United Nations Press, 1997), p. 73.

29. Rosenau 1997, p. 68.

30. See E-O. Czempiel and J. N. Rosenau, *Governance without Government: Order and Change in World Politics* (Cambridge: Cambridge University Press, 1992); R. D. Lipschutz, 'Reconstructing World Politics: The Emergence of Global Civil Society', *Millennium: Journal of International Studies*, XXI, 3 (1992); R. D. Lipschutz and J. Mayer, *Global Civil Society and Global Economic Governance: The Politics of Nature from Place to Planet* (Albany: State University of New York Press, 1996); J. N. Rosenau, *Turbulence in World Politics: A Theory of Change and Continuity* (Princeton: Princeton University Press, 1990); M. Shaw, 'Civil Society and Global Politics: Beyond Social Movements Approach', *Millennium: Journal of International Relations*, XXI, 3 (1994).

31. R. A. Falk, *On Humane Governance* (University Park: Pennsylvania State Press, 1995); P. Haas, 'Do Regimes Matter? Epistemic Communities and Mediterranean Pollution Control', *International Organization*, XLIII, 3 (1989) 377–404.

32. W. A. Dymond, 'The MAI: A Sad and Melancholy Tale', in F. O. Hampson, M. Hart, and M. Rudner (eds), *Canada Among Nations 1999: A Big League Player?* (Toronto: Oxford University Press, 1999); M. A. Hart, 'The Role of Dispute Settlement in Managing Canada-US Trade and Investment Relations', in M. A. Molat and F. O. Hampson (eds), *Canada Among Nations 2000: Vanishing Borders* (Toronto: Oxford University Press, 2000).

33. M. B. Anderson, 'Humanitarian NGOs in Conflict Intervention', in C. A. Crocker, F. O. Hampson and P. Aall (eds), *Managing Global Chaos: Sources of and Responses to International Conflict* (Washington, DC: United States Institute of Peace Press, 1996), p. 344.

34. M. B. Anderson and P. J. Woodrow, *Rising From the Ashes: Development Strategies in Times of Disaster* (Boulder and Paris: Westview and UNESCO Presses, 1989); M. Simai, *The Future of Global Governance: Managing Risk and Change in the International System* (Washington, DC: United States Institute of Peace Press, 1995).

35. M. B. Anderson, 'Humanitarian NGOs in Conflict Intervention', in C. A. Crocker, F. O. Hampson and P. Aall (eds), *Managing Global Chaos: Sources of and Responses to International Conflict* (Washington, DC: United States Institute of Peace Press, 1996), pp. 343–354.

36. O. R. Young, *Governance in World Affairs* (Ithaca: Cornell University Press, 1999).

37. United Nations Press Office (UN), 'Secretary-General Presents His Annual Report to the General Assembly', Press Release SG/SM/7136/GA/9596, Annex 1 (New York: United Nations, 20 September 1999). Available at: http://www.un.org/News/Press/docs/1999/19990920.sgsm7136.html

200   *Global Governance in the Twenty-first Century*

38. United Nations Press Office, 20 September 1999.
39. G. R. Shell, 'The Trade Stakeholders Model and Participation by Nonstate Parties in the World Trade Organization', *University of Pennsylvania Journal of International Economic Law*, XVII (1996) 359.
40. F. O. Hampson and J. V. Reppy, *Earthly Goods: Environmental Change and Social Justice* (Ithaca: Cornell University Press, 1996), p. 251.
41. M. J. Glennon, 'The New Interventionism', *Foreign Affairs*, LXXVIII, 3 (1999) 3.
42. Glennon 1999, p. 3.
43. M. S. Lund, *Preventing Violent Conflict* (Washington, DC: United States Institute of Peace Press, 1996).
44. M. J. Glennon, 1999, 5.
45. Glennon 1999, 7.
46. R. A. Higgott and A. F. Cooper, 'Middle Power Leadership and Coalition Building: Australia, the Cairns Group, and the Uruguay Round of Trade Negotiation', *International Organization*, XLV, 3 (1990) 628.
47. F. O. Hampson, *Multilateral Negotiations: Lessons From Arms Control, Trade, and the Environment* (Baltimore: The Johns Hopkins University Press, 1995).
48. L. Axworthy, 'Canada and Human Security: The Need for Leadership', *International Journal*, LII, 2 (1997) p. 192.
49. Axworthy 1997, p. 194.
50. Department of Foreign Affairs and International Trade (DFAIT), Canada, *Human Security: Safety for People in a Changing World* (Ottawa: Department of Foreign Affairs and International Trade, April 1999), p. 9.
51. DFAIT April 1999, p. 193.
52. F. O. Hampson with J. Daudelin, J. B. Hay, T. Martin and H. Reid, *Madness in the Multitude: Human Security and World Disorder* (Toronto and New York: Oxford University Press, 2002).
53. S. Krasner, *Sovereignty: Organized Hypocrisy* (Princeton: Princeton University Press, 1999).

References

Almond, G. A. and S. Verba, *The Civic Culture: Political Attitudes and Democracy in Five Nations* (Princeton: Princeton University Press, 1963).
Alston, P. (ed.), *The United Nations and Human Rights: A Critical Appraisal* (Oxford: Oxford University Press, 1992).
Anderson, M. B. 'Humanitarian NGOs in Conflict Intervention', in C. A. Crocker, F. O. Hampson and P. Aall (eds), *Managing Global Chaos: Sources of and Responses to International Conflict* (Washington, DC: United States Institute of Peace Press, 1996), pp. 343–354.
Anderson, M. B. and P. J. Woodrow, *Rising From the Ashes: Development Strategies in Times of Disaster* (Boulder and Paris: Westview and UNESCO Presses, 1989).
Axworthy, L. and S. Taylor, 'A Ban for All Seasons', *International Journal*, LIII, 2 (1998) 189–204.
Axworthy, L. 'Canada and Human Security: The Need for Leadership', *International Journal*, LII, 2 (1997) 183–196.
Ayoob, M. 'State Making, State Breaking, and State Failure' in C. A. Crocker, F. O. Hampson and P. Aall (eds), *Managing Global Chaos: Sources of and Responses to International Conflict* (Washington, DC: United States Institute of Peace Press, 1996), pp. 37–52.

Bass, G. J. *Stay the Hand of Vengeance: The Politics of War Crimes Tribunals* (Princeton: Princeton University Press, 2000).

Bassiouni, M. C. and C. L. Blakesley, 'The Need for an International Criminal Court in the New International World Order', *Vanderbilt Journal of Transnational Law*, XXV, 9 (1992) 151–82.

Bassiouni, M. C. *Crimes against Humanity in International Law* (Dordrecht: Martinus Nijhoff Publishers, 1992).

——, 'From Versailles to Rwanda in Seventy-Five Years: The Need to Establish a Permanent International Criminal Court', *Harvard Human Rights Law Journal*, X (1997) 11–62.

Berdal, M. and D. M. Malone (eds), *Greed and Grievance: Economic Agendas in Civil Wars* (Boulder and Ottawa: Lynne Rienner and International Development Research Centre, 2000).

Betts, R. K. 'The Delusion of Impartial Intervention', in *Managing Global Chaos: Sources of and Responses to International Conflict* (Washington, DC: United States Institute of Peace Press, 1996), pp. 333–342.

Cameron, M. A., R. J. Lawson and B. W. Tomlin (eds), *To Walk Without Fear: The Global Movement to Ban Landmines* (Toronto: Oxford University Press, 1998).

Crocker, C. A., F. O. Hampson and P. Aall (eds), *Managing Global Chaos: Sources of and Responses to International Conflict* (Washington, DC: United States Institute of Peace Press, 1996).

Curtis, J. and R. Wolfe, 'The WTO in the Aftermyth of the Battles of Seattle', in M. A. Molot and F. O. Hampson (eds), *Vanishing Borders: Canada among Nations 2000* (Toronto: Oxford University Press, 2000), pp. 321–41.

Czempiel, E-O. and J. N. Rosenau, *Governance without Government: Order and Change in World Politics* (Cambridge: Cambridge University Press, 1992).

Department of Foreign Affairs and International Trade, Canada, *Human Security: Safety for People in a Changing World* (Ottawa: Department of Foreign Affairs and International Trade, April 1999).

Donnelly, J. *International Human Rights* (Boulder: Westview Press, 1993).

Dymond, W. A. 'The MAI: A Sad and Melancholy Tale' in F. O. Hampson, M. Hart and M. Rudner (eds), *A Big League Player? Canada among Nations 1999* (Toronto: Oxford University Press, 1999), pp. 25–54.

Falk, R. A. *On Humane Governance* (University Park: Pennsylvania State Press, 1995).

Forsythe, D. P. *Human Rights and Peace: International and National Dimensions* (Lincoln: University of Nebraska Press, 1993).

Gilbert, A. *Must Global Politics Constrain Democracy? Great-Power Realism, Democratic Peace, and Democratic Internationalism* (Princeton: Princeton University Press, 1999).

Glennon, M. J. 'The New Interventionism', *Foreign Affairs*, LXXVIII, 3 (1999) 2–7.

Gurr, T. R. *Peoples versus States: Minorities at Risk in the New Century* (Washington, DC: United States Institute of Peace Press, 2000).

Haas, P. 'Do Regimes Matter? Epistemic Communities and Mediterranean Pollution Control', *International Organization*, XLIII, 3 (1989) 377–404.

Hampson, F. O. and J. V. Reppy, *Earthly Goods: Environmental Change and Social Justice* (Ithaca: Cornell University Press, 1996).

Hampson, F. O. *Multilateral Negotiations: Lessons from Arms Control, Trade, and the Environment* (Baltimore: The Johns Hopkins University Press, 1995).

——, *Nurturing Peace: Why Peace Settlements Succeed or Fail* (Washington, DC: United States Institute of Peace Press, 1996).

—— with J. Daudelin, J. B. Hay, T. Martin and H. Reid, *Madness in the Multitude: Human Security and World Disorder* (Toronto and New York: Oxford University Press, 2002).

Held, D., A. McGrew, D. Goldblatt and J. Perraton, *Global Transformations: Politics, Economics, and Culture* (Stanford: Stanford University Press, 1999).

Hewson, M. and T. J. Sinclair (eds), *Approaches to Global Governance Theory* (Albany: State University Press of New York, 1999).

Higgott, R. A. and A. F. Cooper, 'Middle Power Leadership and Coalition Building: Australia, the Cairns Group, and the Uruguay Round of Trade Negotiation', *International Organization*, XLV, 3 (1990).

Hoffmann, S. *World Disorders: Troubled Peace in the Post-Cold War Era* (Lanham: Rowman and Littlefield Publishers, 1998).

Kaplan, R. D. *The Coming Anarchy: Shattering the Dreams of the Post-Cold War World* (New York: Random House, 2000).

—— 'Peace in Our Time? Not Likely', *The Globe and Mail* (11 March 2000) D8–9.

Keohane, R. O. and J. S. Nye Jr. 'Globalisation: What's New What's Not (And So What?)', *Foreign Policy*, CXVII (2000) 104–119.

Khong, Y. F. 'Human Security: A Shotgun Approach to Alleviating Human Misery?', *Global Governance: A Review of Multilateralism and International Organizations*, VII, 3 (2001) 231–236.

Korey, W. *NGOs and the Universal Declaration of Human Rights* (New York: St. Martin's, 1998).

Krasner, S. *Sovereignty: Organized Hypocrisy* (Princeton: Princeton University Press, 1999).

Lipschutz, R. D. 'Reconstructing World Politics: The Emergence of Global Civil Society', *Millennium: Journal of International Studies*, XXI, 3 (1992).

—— Lipschutz, R. D. and J. Mayer, *Global Civil Society and Global Economic Governance: The Politics of Nature from Place to Planet* (Albany: State University of New York Press, 1996).

Lund, M. S. *Preventing Violent Conflict* (Washington, DC: United States Institute of Peace Press, 1996).

McRae, R. and D. Hubert (eds), *Human Security and the New Diplomacy: Protecting People, Promoting Peace* (Montreal and Kingston: McGill-Queen's University Press, 2001).

Moisy, C. 'Myths of the Global Information Village', *Foreign Policy*, CVII (1997) 78–87.

Moore, J. *The UN and Complex Emergencies: Rehabilitation in Third World Transitions* (Geneva: UNRISD, 1996).

Moravcik, A. 'Explaining International Human Rights Regimes: Liberal Theory and Western Europe', *European Journal of International Affairs*, I, 1 (June 1995) 157–89.

Morsink, J. *The Universal Declaration of Human Rights: Origins, Drafting and Intent* (University Park: University of Pennsylvania Press, 1998).

Nef, J. *Human Security and Mutual Vulnerability: An Exploration into the Global Political Economy of Development and Underdevelopment* (Ottawa: International Development Research Centre, 1995).

Pares, R. 'Human Security: Paradigm Shift or Hot Air?', *International Security*, XXVI, 2 (2001) 87–102.

Putnam, R. D. *Making Democracy Work: Civic Traditions in Modern Italy* (Princeton: Princeton University Press, 1993).

Roderick, D. 'Sense and Nonsense in the Globalisation Debate', *Foreign Policy*, CVII (1997) 19–37.

Rosenau, J. N. *Turbulence in World Politics: A Theory of Change and Continuity* (Princeton: Princeton University Press, 1990).

——, 'The Person, the Household, the Community, and the Globe: Notes for a Theory of Multilateralism in a Turbulent World', in Robert W. Cox (ed.), *The New Realism: Perspectives on Multilateralism and World Order* (Tokyo: United Nations Press, 1997), pp. 57–82.

Shaw, M. 'Civil Society and Global Politics: Beyond Social Movements Approach', *Millennium: Journal of International Relations*, XXI, 3 (1994).

Shell, G. R. 'The Trade Stakeholders Model and Participation by Nonstate Parties in the World Trade Organization', *University of Pennsylvania Journal of International Economic Law*, XVII (1996) 359.

Simai, M. *The Future of Global Governance: Managing Risk and Change in the International System* (Washington, DC: United States Institute of Peace Press, 1995).

Sollenberg, M., P. Wallensteen and A. Jato, 'Major Armed Conflicts', in *SIPRI Yearbook 1999: Armaments, Disarmament, and International Security* (Oxford: Oxford University Press, 1999), pp. 15–33.

Strobel, W. P. *Late-Breaking Foreign Policy: The News Media's Influence on Peace Operations* (Washington, DC: United States Institute of Peace Press, 1997).

United Nations Development Programme (UNDP), *Human Development Report* (New York: Oxford University Press, 1994).

——, *Human Development Report* (New York: Oxford University Press, 1995).

——, *Human Development Report* (New York: Oxford University Press, 1997).

United Nations Press Office (UN), 'Secretary-General Presents His Annual Report to the General Assembly', Press Release SG/SM/7136/GA/9596, Annex 1 (New York: United Nations, 20 September 1999). Available at: http://www.un.org/News/Press/docs/1999/19990920.sgsm7136.html

Weiss, T. G. and L. Gordenker (eds), *NGOs, the UN, and Global Governance* (Boulder: Lynne Rienner, 1996).

Young, O. R. *Governance in World Affairs* (Ithaca: Cornell University Press, 1999).

8
Globalisation and Global Governance in the Twenty-first Century: The Environment and Global Governance[1]

Ronnie D. Lipschutz

Introduction

It has become conventional wisdom that the state of the global environment matters. It matters for a number of reasons, not the least of which are the potential consequences for the long-term survival of human civilisation as well as the welfare of both nature and people today. And, while much of this wisdom is of relatively recent provenance, environmental change has been, and will be, a continuous process, whatever human beings might or might not do. What, then, *has* changed? As Clarke and Edwards argue in the introduction to this book, globalisation is key. To be sure, the concept of globalisation is an essentially-contested one,[2] but few observers deny that the pace of technological, economic, and social change has increased drastically over the past generation. Linked to this, wide-ranging environmental changes that once took centuries, mostly as a result of variability in geological and physical systems, now happen on a timescale of decades or less, as a result of human practices. Social responses to such changes, which once took centuries, are now compressed into much shorter periods of time, sometimes as little as weeks or days.

As I will argue below, the key element of globalisation that is generally ignored by most observers is precisely this last one: its impact on social organisation.[3] Without falling into the error of functionalism, I argue in this chapter that societies are organised primarily in response to their material conditions and, only secondarily, by their social ones. This is not to say that substructure is everything or that historical materialism explains all; far from it. But inasmuch as the environment

– nature, landscape, resources, and so on – is undeniably a central part of the material base of all human societies and industrial civilisation, changes in the environment are bound to have a major impact on societies and civilisation, and the social organisation of both.

In this chapter, I address four aspects of global environmental change (GEC) arising from globalisation. First, I examine *geological, biological*, and *physical* impacts, which arise from the expansion of human activities over the past couple of centuries so as to encompass the entire planetary environment and the resulting context, which is said by some to be leading to significant changes in the conditions under which contemporary civilisation has developed. Second, I discuss the effects of the reorganisation of production on the environment that have taken place during the past 50 years as a result of a *globalisation*, specifically the transition from Fordism to a post-Fordist information-based economy.[4] Third, I consider the impacts of *cultural* globalisation on the environment as individuals have changed their patterns of consumption and behaviour. Finally, I examine these changes within the frameworks of *global governance* and *governmentality*,[5] that is, in terms of the ways in which people and institutions seek to respond to or to manage these changes by regulating the practices contributing to those changes.

Several initial notes: throughout this chapter, I use the term *globalisation* to denote a material, an ideological, and a cognitive process.[6] Globalisation is *material* in the sense that it involves the movement of capital, technology, goods and, to a limited degree, labour to areas with high returns on investment, without regard to the social or political impacts on either the communities and people to which it moves or on those left behind. Globalisation is *ideological* in the sense that such movement is rationalised in the name of 'efficiency, competition and profit.' And, globalisation is *cognitive* in the sense that it fosters social innovation and reorganisation in existing institutions, composed of real, live people, without regard to the consequences for them. In all three regards, although globalisation opens numerous political opportunities for social movements and other forms of political organisation and action, a not uncommon result is disruption to existing forms of beliefs, values and behaviours.

Changing planet, changing world, changing politics?

Over the past 50 years or so, the impacts of human activities on the global environment have become increasingly evident.[7] That humans have played a major role in the modification of nature has been obvious for millennia, and such impacts certainly date back to the beginning of the Agricultural Revolution some 10,000 years ago or even earlier. But effects at a *global* scale have only begun to appear over the last half-century, and these have become apparent only as a result of careful study and measurement with equipment and methods developed mostly for other purposes.[8] Thus, although industrialisation based on the burning of coal began to add to the atmosphere's stock of greenhouse gases prior to 1800, it was not until scientists began to measure the concentration of carbon dioxide in the air above Manua Loa in 1957 that there emerged the first clear evidence of human modification of the atmosphere's composition.[9]

Today, there is little question that the scale of human activity has the potential to seriously alter the biogeophysical state of Planet Earth. While the conclusions of scientists regarding the quantitative aspects of these changes are relatively firm (although always subject to change), a number of claims remain the subject of rather fierce political contestation within countries and among them, a point to which I will return later in this chapter. A brief review of the relevant issues will serve to illustrate the changes underway.

Population: In mid-October, 1999, the number of human beings on Earth passed the six billion mark and, by January 1, 2004, it exceeded 6.3 billion. The first date was marked by both celebration and mourning, especially as some noted that the world's population had almost tripled since 1950. What was and is less clear, perhaps, are the social consequences of such numbers. The conventional (environmentalist) view has it that, sooner or later, we will meet the 'limits to growth' of the material world, which will be followed by rapid ecological collapse and descent into a true 'state of nature'.[10] A more optimistic assessment, propounded most loudly by the late Julian Simon,[11] proposes that people are the 'ultimate resource' and that the environment is, in every way, in better shape today than it was 100 years ago,[12] when there were many fewer people on the planet. Who is correct? The key variable is likely to be the combination of distribution of people and social organisation, and not the absolute numbers on Earth or in any specific place. Where social institutions are strong and legitimate, high population densities can be accommodated; where they are not, crowding and numbers may be correlated with hunger, poverty, and social upheaval.[13]

Resources: Thirty years ago, the publication of *Limits to Growth*,[14] in concert with tightening supplies of commodities in international markets, raised fears that humanity would, sooner or later, run out of material resources. The Arab oil embargo and rising gasoline prices in the United States appeared to bear out the predictions of the MIT group that wrote the book. Today, however, the world seems awash in commodities and oil has rarely been less expensive. Many economists, such as Simon, are fond of pointing out that, based on prices, raw materials are in greater supply than ever. Moreover, goes the standard argument, if and when supplies of particular materials begin to run short, as indicated by rising prices, substitutes will be developed as inventors and entrepreneurs seek to profit from market opportunities.[15] Trends are not destiny, of course, and there must certainly be a point at which supplies of specific material resources are no longer adequate to meet demand (substitution notwithstanding). Again, however, distribution is key: those who are wealthy are unlikely to ever suffer from absolute scarcity; those who are poor already find it difficult or impossible to purchase basic necessities.

A more important, near-term resource problem has to do with renewable resources, such as water, biomass, solar and wind energy, and so on. For some decades, environmentalists argued that it would be better to exploit these resources, since their supply was, in effect, unlimited. What was less noted was that, first, flows of renewable resources may not always be adequate to provide the quantities demanded[16] and, second, that those renewable resources which are destroyed cannot be restored.[17] In a global economy that continues to grow and make unprecedented demands on the renewable resource base – even where people are poor – demand frequently exceeds supply, with predictable consequences for nature. But, once again, these impacts tend to hit hardest those who are poor, who have lost access to those resources needed for subsistence production, and who are unable to participate fully in the market.[18]

One global environmental arena in which the limits to renewable resources appear to be quite pressing is the Earth's climate. There is broad agreement among scientists studying climate that emission of so-called anthropogenic greenhouse gases into the Earth's atmosphere is changing the global climate system in an unpredictable fashion, possibly in ways that will be environmentally and socially disruptive.[19] The key concern here is not so much the possibility of global climate change, or its magnitude, as the disruptive effects that may follow and their distribution. These effects range from the disappearance of low-lying islands and flooding of coastal regions to major geographic changes in agricultural productivity, destruction of habitat, and extinction of species. Some argue, too, that massive population displacements and threats to security are inevitable, as coastal zones in Asia and Africa are gradually inundated.[20] For national and corporate leaders, it seems, the important questions continues to be 'Do we win or lose if we do nothing?' and 'How much do we have to pay if we do something?' Again, those who can pay for adaptation are most likely to fair well as the climate changes; those who are too poor to pay will suffer most.

Wealth and poverty: What these, and other, changes suggest is that, as both cause and effect, globalisation's impacts on the Earth's environment are mediated largely through the global economic system. Impacts have become globally-significant as a result of human production and reproduction for both basic subsistence and luxury consumption.[21] Although total numbers of people must have some relevance in terms of negative effects, it is what and how much we consume and where we consume it that is most critical. The richest 20 percent of the planet's people consumes some 80 percent of the world's gross product.[22] In other words, each individual in the top income quintile (1.2 billion) consumes on average about as much as five people in the other four-fifths (and more than 20 times as much as someone in the lowest quintile).

But the actual picture is even more lopsided: the average per capita income of an individual in a 'high income country' ($26,440) is more than 13 times as much as that in a 'middle income country' ($1,980) and more than 62 times larger than in a 'low income country' ($425; this category includes both India and China).[23] Indeed, more than one billion people live on less than one dollar a day, and 2.8 billion on less than two dollars a day.[24] At the same time, these numbers don't fully reflect the distribution of environmental impacts resulting from contemporary patterns of consumption. How, for example, should one allocate the damages resulting from the production of bananas in Central America for sale to North American consumers, a phenomenon sometimes called an 'ecological footprint'? This is a point to which I return, below.

Global environmental change and the global economy

Given these effects and related statistics, we begin to see that a major source of contemporary environmental change arises from the system of production, trade and sale, and consumption associated with globalisation. In historical terms, the present cycle of capitalist expansion is only the latest in a centuries-old process of international economic integration[25] but, in combination with the rapid growth of international trade and consumption, this phase is having, by far, the broadest and deepest impacts yet seen. Earlier periods of international integration were characterised, first, by the extraction and export of raw materials and commodities from the colonial periphery to Europe and, later, by their transformation into semi-processed materials and finished goods and resale in both core and periphery states.[26] The scale of extraction, production, and consumption not only was much smaller, but so were markets and demand. Environmental impacts were, for the most part, localised.

Under contemporary globalisation, production has become much more complex, with raw materials, commodities, semi-processed materials, parts and finished goods moving among locales in different countries according to both the traditional and intrafirm logics of comparative advantage. The form of these processes is determined less by the absolute cost of factors of production, as we would expect from the classical theory of comparative advantage, and more by the logic of cost factors internal to the production chain, the relative costs of capital, both financial and human, the burden of social costs imposed in a specific location and the size of local subsidies, if any.[27]

What is not especially clear, as a consequence, is the distribution of environmental externalities that arise from these shifts. It has long been argued that capital will seek to produce goods in locations where environmental and other social standards are lowest, since this will minimise variable costs.[28] While there is considerable evidence that this occurs in some places, and for some producers, as seems to be the case in the *maquila* zone along the US-Mexico border,[29] there are contrasting findings that suggest that environmental regulations play a minimal role in capital's choice of production location.[30] Nevertheless, it is the case that there is little consistency in environmental regulation, monitoring and enforcement among countries, and a general worsening of environmental quality in a number of countries where production for export has been a driving force behind rapid economic growth.[31]

An example of this phenomenon can be found in the forest industries of the North American Pacific Coast. Although counted among the industrialised countries, Canada's economy remains heavily dependent on resource production, especially in its Western provinces. For years, lumber and raw logs from British Columbia, produced with government subsidies, were shipped in volume to Japan, where they commanded premium prices. Despite high levels of environmental regulation, the rules governing lumbering actually fostered rapid deforestation. When the Japanese economy collapsed during the 1990s, exports to Japan declined significantly, and timber producers in British Columbia turned to the United States. American producers, unable to compete with Canada's low lumber prices, put pressure on the US government to impose tariffs on timber imports. The result was the first Softwood Lumber Agreement (SLA) in 1996, which imposed escalating tariffs on all Canadian lumber imports above 14.7 billion board feet per year into the United States.

The results were both unexpected and perverse. During the 1990s, the demand for lumber in the United States increased as a result of the economic boom. A flood of Canadian imports put downward pressure on American lumber prices, leading to unemployment in the US timber industry as well as increased cutting in some places to make up for revenue declines. The tariffs did make Canadian lumber prices higher than they would have been otherwise, and caused unemployment in Canada, but barely put a dent in US imports. Then, Canadian companies began to export raw logs, which were not covered by the Agreement, southward, and the Canadian Maritime Provinces, excluded from the SLA, increased their exports, too. Deforestation across Canada proceeded at an ever faster rate, threatening biodiversity, rivers, and lands. Low lumber prices are good for developers and homeowners, but bad for the environment.[32]

In another apparent paradox, as environmental standards have risen around the world, the international transport and disposal of wastes and toxic materials from production and consumption have become a significant problem. In the United States, for example, the cost of disposing of a ton of toxic wastes domestically has risen from $5–25 in the early 1970s to more than $1,000 today, whereas it is still possible to export such wastes for disposal in some locations abroad for a few hundred dollars or less per ton. Recent international efforts to regulate global trade in toxics has met with some measure of success in controlling such activities, but there remain significant loopholes through which large volumes continue to pass.[33]

The international effort to protect the ozone layer has also had its share of successes and failures. On the one hand, the Montreal Protocol and associated agreements have managed to reduce production of ozone-damaging chemicals within many of the signatory countries. Because, however, some of the signatories are being permitted to continue production of these substances for some years to come, a thriving transnational black market has developed in chlorofluoro-carbons. In the United States, it now costs upward of $100 for the legal Freon required to recharge an automobile's air conditioning compressor and, so, the chemical is being smuggled across the border from Mexico, where it is much less expensive. The size of this black market is uncertain, although it may comprise from 10 to 20 percent of the remaining global production of some 200,000 metric tons per year.[34]

Climate change, too, is strongly affected by globalisation. Despite the possible ratification of the Kyoto Protocol to the UN Framework Convention on Climate Change[35] sometime in the near future, global fossil fuel consumption and greenhouse gas emissions are projected to continue increasing well into the twenty-first century. The growth in emissions is driven by two factors, one social, the other political. The growth in automobile usage around the world will be fuelled primarily by petroleum, while industrial expansion in developing countries will depend heavily on natural gas and coal. Compared to other energy sources, fossil fuels remain remarkably inexpensive, even in countries where they are heavily taxed. As a result, incentives to drive a technological shift to more environmentally-friendly energy sources are quite weak.

At the same time, a near-term international convention to stabilise and reduce greenhouse gas emissions in a deliberate and systematic way seems highly unlikely. The US President, George W. Bush, declared that the United States will never ratify the Kyoto Protocol, thereby pulling the world's largest consumer of fossil fuels out of the agreement. Instead, the United States will opt for adaptation to climate change and voluntary reductions by industrial polluters. Moreover, the final statement by the Conference of the Parties to the Framework Convention meeting in New Delhi in 2002 omitted any mention of Kyoto, arguing instead that adaptation would be the best strategy for responding to climate change. The Bush Administration, it would seem, has determined that unrestricted growth in the global economy and emissions, whatever the consequences, is to be preferred to limits on the activities of US consumers.[36]

Another area in which globalisation has major environmental impacts is in food production. With technological changes in farming, refrigeration and shipping, a growing demand in industrialised countries for fruits and vegetables year-round, and the expansion of international markets in grains (partly abetted by the Green Revolution), massive shifts have taken place in world agriculture over the past half-century from subsistence farming to cash-cropping. For those countries with limited raw materials or human capital, the export of cash crops has become a favoured generator of hard currency.[37] Specialisation in production has also been fostered by trade barriers to some kinds of agricultural exports from South to North, as well as consumer expectations. Thus, during the Northern winter, it is possible to purchase virtually all kinds of foods, imported from the Southern hemisphere, that were simply not available 20 years ago.

There are several general consequences that result from these changing patterns of agricultural production. First, most cash cropping is capital, rather than labour, intensive. Production for export relies on chemicals for uniformity, machinery for volume, and high-quality land for yield, and these requirements tend to favour richer farmers and corporations who are considered more credit-worthy.[38] Labour inputs into export agriculture are almost always less than required for subsistence farming, and this greatly disadvantages the poor and landless, who find themselves working for inadequate wages, shifted to lower-quality, often hilly land or forced to migrate to urban areas. In the former instance, serious land degradation may follow while, in the latter, large increases in the numbers of residents outstrip the capacity of urban infrastructures to cope with them.[39]

There is a further twist on the growing complexity of commodity chains and the environmental damages that result from them. To a growing degree, the chains include not only the production of goods but also of bodies and identities, fuelling excess consumption and the waste that accompanies it (see the next section). Goods are being marketed not only for their end uses but also as ways for individuals to differentiate themselves as unique from others. If 'you are what you consume,' it requires a great deal of time, effort, and money to make sure that others do not buy the same things and that appearances differ. Automobiles, clothing, health, adornments, makeup, pharmaceuticals, even food are sold with promises that they can create a 'new' individual, as often as might be desired. The consumer thus becomes, somewhat unwittingly, an integral part of the globalised commodity chain, generating wastes for reasons of vanity.

These are only a few of the consequences of globalisation and, it might be added, none of them are new; many were already observed two centuries ago.[40] What has changed is scale. The increase in transnational flows of capital has facilitated investment in 'emerging economies.' Increasingly, free-trade, combined with high labour and social costs in industrialised countries has facilitated offshore movement of production, along with environmental impacts. The shift from

Fordism to post-Fordism has facilitated complexity in production systems, thereby diffusing environmental impacts. Finally, the growth in global trade has made it easier to 'export' environmental bads to countries less able to afford strict regulation and less willing to impose it.[41]

Consumers 'R Us

The transition from Fordism to post-Fordism entails more than just changes in modes and patterns of production; it also affects modes of consumption. The latest phase of capitalism rests as much on the 'commodification and consumption of everything,' and the associated 'production of identities,' as it does on post-industrialism, with important impacts on social relations. The global economy has expanded from less than five trillion dollars in 1950 to more than $35 trillion today (in 1990 dollars), while world exports have grown from about $300 billion in 1950 to about $6 trillion today (in 1990 dollars), this even as the population has increased only by about 250 percent.[42] In recent years, much of this economic growth has come through expansion of the service, information and 'intellectual capital' sectors, which are generally assumed to have minimal environmental impacts. Yet, the accompanying increases in individual incomes around the world, especially in North America, Europe and Japan, have also fostered growing demand for goods and services whose environmental impacts may not be so benign.[43] Such consumer demand is fuelled by the globalisation of largely-American cultural norms and practices through media – films, televisions, advertising, magazines – communications networks, international travel, free trade, and higher education.

Indeed, the post-World War Two 'miracle' of the West rested largely on the success of consumer capitalism. In a world economy whose prosperity was driven by production of raw materials, industrial machinery, and heavy consumer goods (cars, appliances, and so on), as was largely the case during the 1920s, even a small downturn in economic growth could lead quickly to surplus capacity, as happened during the Great Depression.[44] The post-World War Two expansion did not really take off until forced by military-based Keynesian economics during the Korean War, but the boom of the 1950s and 1960s rested on the spread of American-style consumer demand to other industrialised countries. Even this model proved susceptible to recession, inasmuch as most 'white goods' were built to last 10 to 20 years (or more). The saturation of white goods in North American households led to the search for new markets in Europe and elsewhere but, once again, demand in these regions was not perpetually-expandable (especially with the slowdown in birthrates in industrialised countries). Automobiles were the one major exception to this trend, and the US auto industry long relied for its prosperity on a replacement cycle of about three years, driven by consumer tastes. Today, this cycle is much longer, but a major fraction of automaker profits comes from large, expensive, trucklike vehicles.

With the collapse of the dot-com sector during 2001, it is clear that the Information Age is not immune from the business cycle and cannot really provide 'growth without waste.' The latest mode of consumer capitalism therefore relies heavily on the consumption of goods with limited lifetimes, and their limited recycling as raw materials. In the area of material goods, this includes electronic devices such as computers, media players and even appliances, which are rendered obsolescent in a matter of months, for the first two, or quickly malfunction as a result of shoddy construction, in the case of the latter. As successive generations of Intel- and Mac-based microprocessors render computers ever-faster, they turn older models into prematurely-obsolescent junk for which there is little demand, either at home or abroad. Software written for older and slower chips and operating systems disappears from the market, and newer software cannot be run on older computers because of its prodigious Random-Access Memory (RAM) and hard drive memory requirements. Disposal of the growing numbers of discarded computers, laced with toxic metals, is no easy proposition, and is creating a serious hazardous waste problem abroad. Finally, there is little point in fixing a two year-old malfunctioning $150 microwave oven or Video Cassette Recorder (VCR) when repairs start at $75 just to take the screws off the back.

In the area of services and information, consumers are motivated to take advantage of all kinds of opportunities that may reduce some environmental impacts while increasing others. A rather trivial example might be found in the global proliferation of automatic teller (ATM) and cash machines. One once went to the bank once a week, withdrawing sufficient cash to last until the next trip; today, it is a simple matter to drive to the nearest ATM at any time of day or night. The ease and availability of long-distance travel for business and pleasure, facilitated by growing incomes, increased leisure, and media exposure have had their effects on the atmosphere and oceans, too, not to mention on the places to which relatively-wealthy travellers take their high-consumption habits.

The globalisation of the information and intellectual capital industries – which include all of those activities associated with finance capital as well as culture and education – have, somewhat paradoxically, begun to have environmental consequences, too. First, expanding reliance on the Internet, an advertisement-saturated medium, not only fosters consumer temptation but also helps to 'spread the wealth' through diversified forms of information processing and production. Second, as drivers of the economic prosperity of the 1990s, these industries have fostered the growth of a relatively-wealthy global middle and upper class, one of whose most visible features is conspicuous consumption. Third, the worldwide dissemination of cultural norms and practices, as noted earlier, sets examples for consumers in other societies, who emulate many of them. And, fourth, growing levels of education – primary, secondary, higher – are all associated with increased incomes and cultural awareness, again a facilitator of higher levels of consumption.

Finally, the commodification, enclosure, and privatisation of knowledge and information, evidenced in the intellectual property rights 'gold rush,' is having several perverse and tragic effects not unlike those that followed from the more traditional 'enclosure of the commons'[45] While Garrett Hardin's 'Tragedy of the Commons'[46] remains a dominant metaphor for environmental degradation – that there are too many people using too few resources, and that resources publicly-owned are resources likely to be abused – the actual experience of historical commons users is that joint possession, with appropriate rules, can conserve resources.[47] The globalisation of intellectual property rights represents the effort by capital to enclose what were formerly considered 'public commons,' so that profits may be made from resale of products to those who previously had unrestricted access to the resource.

For example, the Biodiversity Convention, intended to protect species and their habitats, has been framed largely in terms of access to 'genetic resources' and the rights of host countries to share in the economic benefits that might accrue from their development as marketable products. Genetically-engineered seeds are now patented in such a way that farmers are forbidden from saving seed stock for future planting (indeed, such seeds would probably not germinate or breed true, were they to be sown).[48] Increasingly, food products are being produced – especially in North America – using bioengineered fruits and vegetables, without a clear idea as to their long-term impacts on either environmental or consumer health.[49] And pharmaceutical companies have been especially zealous in protecting patents for high-cost drugs, including those derived from indigenous knowledge.[50] Ultimately, while it is difficult to quantify the environmental impacts of the service, information, and intellectual industries, there is no gainsaying the longer-term environmental consequences of the spread of consumer capitalism. The global automobile fleet is expected to rise from its current 500 million to over a billion in the next decade or so. The world's automotive industry is already in a state of surplus capacity, even as a number of developing countries are planning to launch their own car companies, with hopes of exporting low-cost vehicles to other markets. There is a strong likelihood, as well, that prices on lower-end models will be subsidised so that consumers in the emerging economies can afford to buy them. The global environment is unlikely to benefit even if national economies and transnational corporations do.

None of this is meant to claim flatly that globalisation is inevitably inimical to environmental quality. Germany, for example, has instituted a rigorous program of recycling that is being adopted throughout the European Union (EU). Consumers pay for the costs of recycling their cars and computers, and something like a 'steady-state' system of production and consumption might be achieved in some areas.[51] Some research has suggested that, at levels of per capita income above about $5,000, environments become cleaner,[52] although the existence of such an 'environmental Kuznets curve' is widely disputed.[53] Nonetheless, there is a clear relationship between growing global numbers of consumers and consequent environmental degradation. This is not, I should note, an argument about population growth, per se, although there is clear evidence that poverty is also implicated in environmental damage,[54] and that globalisation may well be contributing to an increase in the number of the world's poor ($1,000 pc or less) relative to the number of the world's rich ($10,000 pc or more).[55]

Global environmental change, global governance, and global governmentality

According to those who study it, GEC differs from more 'ordinary' intrastate environmental problems – toxics disposal, air and water pollution, soil erosion, habitat destruction – by virtue of its being *transboundary* and *interstate*.[56] This is correct, of course, but it is a social 'truth' rather than a natural one,[57] and tends to simplify what is a much more complex reality. The 'globalisation' of environmental impacts is, therefore, not automatic; it takes place in two ways. First, it happens through complex coupling with local or regional biogeo-physical systems and linkages with the hydrologic cycle, terrestrial and marine ecosystems, and climate that, in turn, interact with other, more distant ones. Second, it takes place via socio-economic systems of transnational extent through a complex network of exploitation, trans-action, and exchange that can have impacts as near as next door and as far away as the other side of the world. In addition, local physical changes can be linked to each other and aggregated through these socio-economic networks, both in terms of causes (for example, global market pressures) and consequences (for example, global food productivity and distribution).

Nevertheless, for reasons having to do with the division of the world's surface into states or countries, we tend to speak of the process of aggregation of environmental impacts in ways that are constructed around and constrained by the spatial characteristics of those very units. The implications of this view are several-fold. First, environmental damage across borders is addressed in capitals often located far from the affected locale. Second, these loci of political power may have very different political institutions and cultures both between them and within them. And, third, practical solutions may be held hostage to poor relations between governments.

Consequently, co-operation between governments is framed as the starting point for addressing GEC and, to date, co-operation through interstate negotiation has been the approach adopted by those con-cerned about the causes and consequences of GEC. This concern is reflected in the various agreements protecting the ozone layer, in the conventions signed at the UN Conference on Environment and Development in Rio de Janeiro in June 1992, in the ongoing efforts to craft a climate agreement that will, it is hoped, control global warming, and in many others.[58] While international diplomacy has much to re-commend it, its application is more the result of historical practice than efficiency or effectiveness. States have conducted diplomatic relations along similar lines for much of the past 500 years and such negotiations are fairly predictable, if not always successful. There is no reason to think that such practices will change at any time in the foreseeable future.

At the same time, however, globalisation is gradually undermining the ability of states, individually and collectively, to address GEC. The reasons are complicated, but they have much to do with the impacts of globalisation on state sovereignty and authority.[59] Thus, in the interests of economic competitiveness and growth, states have begun to yield a substantial amount of their domestic regulatory authority to transnational regimes and organisations,[60] such as the International Monetary Fund (IMF) and the World Trade Organisation (WTO), certain trade-based environmental regimes, and private corporate initiatives such as 'Responsible Care' and ISO 14000.[61] These arrangements are intended to accomplish two goals, both of which exclude popular participation or representation and downplay or ignore social and environmental matters.

First, international public and transnational private regulation is meant to 'eliminate politics' from potentially-conflictual issue areas, thereby eliminating the problem of 'double-edged diplomacy',[62] by shifting regulatory authority from the domestic sphere to the international one, where representative national and sub-national institutions lack power and influence. Second, they are meant to reduce the transaction costs associated with a plethora of national regulations. From the perspective of international investors, it is preferable to deal with single sets of rules that apply to *all* countries, as is supposed to be the case within the EU or among the members of international regimes,[63] than to observe 190 individual sets of laws.

In many cases, however, national governments pay little heed to either international conventions or their own rules, especially where social and environmental matters are concerned.[64] In response to such lacunae, there are a growing number of proposals and campaigns to extend international regulation to include social and environmental issues; this was the objective of the protests that took place in Seattle, Washington, during the November 1999 meeting of the WTO, and the demonstrations at various international conclaves since then. As was seen in response to environmentalist demands and President Clinton's suggestions, such regulation is strongly opposed by government authorities, corporate officials and numerous academics, who appear to consider supra-national regulation to be admissible if it involves barter, banking, budget deficits or borrowing, but unacceptable if environmental protection, human rights, labour standards or distributive justice are involved.[65]

The truth of the matter is that existing international regulatory law does not eliminate politics from contentious issue areas as much as it privileges the political desires and goals of transnational capital and corporations. By limiting debates and decisions to small groups of national policymakers and representatives of capital, and 'letting the free market do it,' most international regulatory regimes have deliberately been made both opaque and non-democratic as well as quite limited in scope. And, with a few exceptions, where transnational social regulations have been promulgated, the direction of harmonisation has been more in the direction of the 'lowest common denominator'.[66]

What, then, is to be done? In the past, those who contemplated such trends looked to the eventual establishment of a world government or federation that could rule a globalised welfare state and impose equal and equitable regulation on all countries and peoples. Today, a world state looks rather improbable and, in any case, there are good reasons for thinking that a centralised global government would not be either very democratic or accountable to the world's peoples. The fact is, nevertheless, that international regulation has become quite common and additional rules are being promulgated constantly. While 'deregulation' is the mantra repeated endlessly in virtually all national capitals and by all international capitalists, it is *domestic* deregulation that they desire, not the wholesale elimination of *all* rules.[67] Selective deregulation at home may create a lower-cost environment in which to produce, but deregulation everywhere creates uncertainty and economic instability. Hence, international regulation and governance are becoming increasingly important in keeping globalised capitalism together and working. But this globalised system resembles *governmentality* more than it does governance.

Governmentality, a concept developed by Michel Foucault, 'has as its purpose not the action of government itself, but the welfare of the population, the improvement of its condition, the increase of its wealth, longevity, health, etc.'.[68] It is, in other words, about *management*, about ensuring and maintaining the 'right disposition of things.' That which challenges this disposition is to be absorbed; that which disrupts it is to be eliminated. Foucault's notion of governmentality is associated with the practice of *bio-politics* which, according to Mitchell Dean, 'is concerned with matters of life and death, with birth and propagation, with health and illness, both physical and mental, and with the processes that sustain or retard the optimisation of the life of a population.'[69]

> Bio-politics must then also concern the social, cultural, environmental, economic and geographic conditions under which humans live, procreate, become ill, maintain health or become healthy, and die. From this perspective bio-politics is concerned with the family, with housing, living and working conditions, with what we call 'lifestyle,' with public health issues, patterns of migration, levels of economic growth and the standards of living. It is concerned with the bio-sphere in which humans dwell.[70]

One consequence of global governmentality is that, although the state remains the most visible actor in *international relations*, the *sovereign authority* monopolised by states during the past century or so in international affairs has spread throughout a multi-level and, for the moment, very diffuse system of globalising governance. What is striking, especially in terms of relationships between social actors and institutionalised mechanisms of government, as well as capital and international regimes, is the growth of institutions of governmentality at and across *all* levels of analysis.[71]

What this seems to suggest is that, even though there is no world government as such, governmentality extends from the local to the global. Subsumed within this system are both institutionalised regulatory arrangements, such as international regimes, and less formalised norms, rules and procedures that pattern behaviour without the presence of written constitutions or material power. Within this system, 'local' management and regulation become as important to coordination within and among local, national, and global economic and political 'hierarchies,' institutions, regions and countries as the international management manifested in traditional regimes and international organisations. Regulatory authority is distributed among many foci of political action, organised to address specific issue-areas rather than to exercise a generalised rule over a specific territory (in the national context, Foucault described this as a shift from sovereignty to governmentality).[72]

There is nothing especially remarkable about this trend. International regulation has a long history and it has not always been so public.[73] Historically, major activities within society were governed by laws contracted between individuals and groups, often but not always with the approval of the state. For example, the medieval guilds formulated strict rules governing membership and practice;[74] this form of self-regulation has been carried over into the present in the medical and legal professions (which, nevertheless, do so only with the explicit authorisation of state and national governments). Private maritime law regimes, date back centuries, while customary law governing relations among traders of different nationalities are even older.[75] As well, there is a considerable body of 'private international law' to which varying numbers of countries adhere, applying to various kinds of relations among individuals or corporations in different countries, overseen by inter-governmental organisations such as the 'Hague Conference on Private International Law' (http://www.hcch.net/e/) and the 'International Institute for the Unification of Private Law' (http://www.

unidroit.org/default.htm). But, whereas private law was, historically, constituted by contract among the signing parties, and is now backed up through ratification by states, the private regulation about which I write here rests more on the hope of a kind of 'social contract' between producers and consumers. This, as I shall argue, is a weak reed on which to base the Earth's environmental future.

The tendency toward public interstate regulation was, as documented by Craig Murphy, a consequence of the growing marketisation and industrialisation of society during the nineteenth century.[76] With bonds of social trust dissolved in the acids of economic exchange, *caveat emptor* was no longer a sufficient guide against fraud and dangerous practices. In any event, after World War II, most such regulation remained national, although there were certain sectors in which international public regulation was deemed necessary, as in the control of the spread of nuclear weapons, the allocation of radio and television frequencies and geosynchronous satellite slots, and so on. Some national regulatory systems have been 'internationalised,' as well. For example, the safety rules of the United States Federal Aviation Administration (USFAA) and/or the EU have been generally adopted by all national aviation authorities,[77] although they are not always rigorously adhered to. Finally, the tradition of semi-private (for example, International Red Cross) and private voluntary organisations (for example, CARE) providing assistance internationally is one that never disappeared completely, even during World War II.

What kinds of actors are involved in contemporary global regulatory activity (or, governmentality)? We find that they run the gamut from wholly-public to wholly private, from more conventional interstate organisations that have begun to 'bring in' non-state actors, to corporate associations and social movement service providers that have little or nothing to do with duly-constituted political authorities. There are several identifiable trends in terms of global regulation. These can be categorised along two dimensions, corresponding roughly to 'politics' and 'markets' along one axis, and 'public' and 'private' along the other, as seen in Table 1.

While the 'real world' is not, of course, quite as simple as suggested by this matrix, it is possible to identify four basic categories of actors involved in global regulation and governmentality:

1. **Public-political**: Primarily interstate and inter-governmental regimes or organisations that seek harmonisation of international standards (Climate change regime and Kyoto Protocol). The resulting

Table 1 Forms of global regulatory activity

	Politics	Markets
Public	1. Interstate regimes (Climate change regime)	3. Municipal foreign policies (Country & company boycotts; sanctions)
Private	2. Global civil society (Land mine ban movement; 'Blood Diamonds')	4. Consumer/producer behaviour (ISO 14000; Forest Stewardship Council; corporate codes)

regulations are expected to be legislated domestically, where they will apply to both public and private actors.

2. **Private-political**: Mixed or private organisations charged with authorised semi-public functions (Mine ban movement). Membership may involve representatives of both public authorities and private actors.

3. **Public-market**: Organisations and movements that seek public pressure on government purchasing authorities to impose sanctions on violators (Burma boycott).

4. **Private-market**: NGOs or groups composed of mixed NGO, social and corporate representatives (Forest Stewardship Council) or corporate associations (International Organisation for Standardisation) or individual companies. Regulations tend to be voluntary and to apply to corporate activities, in either public or private realms, but are not subject to state vetting or rejection.

One issue area in which the governmentalisation of environmental regulation is particularly visible is in sustainable forestry.[78] Regulatory instruments, institutions, and actors addressing forestry include: provisions in the Kyoto Protocol; the still-born but possibly soon to be revived international forestry convention; organisations providing scientific information to regulators (Center for International Forestry Research); private certification bodies (International Organization for Standardisation); timber associations (Canadian Paper and Pulp Association); and non-governmental organisations (Forest Stewardship Council).[79] Each of these are, more or less, in competition with all others, offering a veritable marketplace of alternatives while seeking to acquire a monopoly in setting standards. As might be expected, however, specific standards and practices vary widely from one regulator to the next, so that there is no way for an informed consumer to compare competing standards. The lack of a single standard is of considerable frustration to many environmentalists and corporations, yet this is exactly one of the characteristic features of, in this case, environmental governmentality.

This process of global regulatory privatisation and free-lancing has been accompanied, too, by a growing reliance on markets and market-based strategies as mechanisms to foster observance. This is especially evident in the environmental issue area. Historically, regulation of economic activities and regulation to protect the environment were treated as distinct categories (although economic considerations often entered into the latter). Figure 1 illustrates in a very simple fashion the traditional relationship between economic practices and environmental externalities. I use the term 'economic activities' to include all behaviours involved in the production, transportation, sale, consumption and disposal of material goods. There are clearly-stipulated international regulations that apply to such economic activities, primarily in the areas of transportation, trade, and sale but, also, increasingly, to production, consumption and disposal. For the sake of brevity, I call these 'economic regulations,' inasmuch as they are meant primarily to deal with transaction costs and 'unfair' advantages in international exchange.

I use the term 'environmental effects' to include all of the undesirable transnational and transborder material externalities of these economic activities, including air and water pollution, toxics production, health impacts, and so on; things that 'ignore borders,' in other words. Such effects have, for the most part, been addressed through 'environmental regulations' that take the form of state-sanctioned limits on offending activities originating within one country and affecting another. Until quite recently, most environmental regimes have not

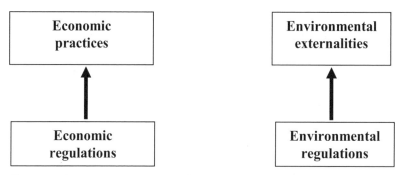

Figure 1   The conventional relationship between function and regulation

attempted to construct or manage markets as a means of controlling environmental effects, relying instead on what are commonly called 'command and control' regulations.[80]

Over the past decade or so, for ideological reasons as well as those involving governmentality, this pattern has begun to change, as shown in Figure 2. Market-based mechanisms, such as tradable pollution permits and independent certification, are being utilised in an effort not so much to reduce externalities, per se, as to redistribute the costs and benefits of regulation.[81] This approach has the supposed virtue of increasing the efficiency with which financial resources are used, but it also grants to the rich the possibility of purchasing rights to pollute from the poor, which will result in a transfer of financial resources from the former to the latter. There could be undesirable consequences from this approach because, if market-based auctions and sales operate as suggested by neo-classical economics, wealthier states and polluters may be able to outbid poorer ones, pricing the latter completely out of the market to pollute.[82]

What is interesting is that, parallel to the *marketisation of environmental regulations*, there has developed a trend toward *environmental regulation of economic activities*. In this case, producers absorb the costs (or pass them on to consumers) of internalising environmental externalities by adhering or subscribing to a set of regulated behaviours and practices that, when vetted by the appropriate authority, certify them as environmentally friendly. These regulations are expected to appeal to consumers who, looking for the appropriate certifying mark, will prefer environmentally-friendly goods to unfriendly ones. While the change in behaviour is motivated by economic concerns, the form of the regulations is not market-based; rather, they are

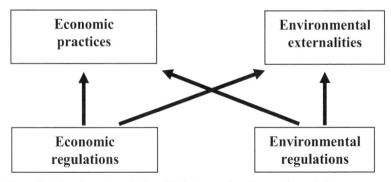

Figure 2   The changing relationship between function and regulation

somewhat akin to a moral code that fosters an environmental 'civic virtue.'

This shift toward private market-based approaches to global regulation is also driven by the relative ease with which such schemes, and their authority, can be established, in the 'marketplace of ideas.' More traditional forms of regulation were legitimised through their promulgation via sovereign authority, either by states or among them. Under globalisation, state authority has been undermined,[83] and authority has come to be centred in the market,[84] which legitimates practices by virtue of the size of their consumer base. As a result, there sometimes develops a fierce competition among different campaigns and schemes to establish a global standard. In the sustainable forestry sector, for example, there are at least a dozen different certification processes from which to choose.[85] So far, the consumers of these processes have not yet settled on a winner.

There appears to be a growing demand for such regulation (although the size of the market is quite uncertain), a demand that is driven in no small part by globalisation and the consumerism that it fosters. Corporations engaged in the production of material goods have no inherent interest in environmental protection, with two exceptions.[86] First, a failure to reduce externalities may increase variable costs from fines and lost business; second, a 'green' reputation could increase profits.[87] Purchasing rights to pollute, as opposed to reducing pollution, may be efficient in aggregate but, in an open-bid market setting, there is no theoretical ceiling to the cost of such permits, and there is little favourable publicity to be gained from admitting that one continues to pollute. A producer who voluntarily controls externalities, and engages in virtuous behaviour, can advertise such practices and, with luck, grab a little extra market share. It might even be possible to charge a premium for green certification, for which high-income consumers will gladly pay. So, there is available here both a moral and a market opportunity. Corporations can do well by doing good, while certifiers can do good by doing well.

Can action through the market provide the incentives for the maintenance and enforcement of the kind of private, self-regulation described here? Producers will only be attracted to such approaches if environmentally-conscious consumers choose environmentally-friendly certified products in preference to those that lack the label. But setting the premium for such products at the 'correct' level is no easy task. Moreover, it is one thing to tack a 10 percent green surcharge on a piece of furniture that may cost between $100 and $1,000; it is quite another to charge an extra 10 percent on a $20,000 remodelling job or a $300,000 house. Over the past 50 years, industrial societies have been built on the premise that lower prices enhance purchasing power which maximises individual satisfaction; it will not be so easy to convince people that they will be better off if they exercise virtue in the marketplace. The success and adequacy of such approaches can only be demonstrated through empirical evidence that is, so far, in short supply. More broadly, however, the *demand* for regulation might be seen in terms of Karl Polanyi's[88] 'double movement' and best understood as a social self-protective mechanism: if globalisation proceeds unfettered and unregulated, the resulting disruption might well destroy not only the economic system but the biogeophysical system on which life depends, as well. If these emerging patterns of global governmentality, both environmental and social, prove not to be up to the task of maintaining systems of both production and reproduction, the resulting crisis could prove a major setback to twenty-first century civilisation.

Conclusion

In this chapter, I have put forth four arguments about globalisation and its impacts on environmental protection and governance. First, I summarised the effects of a growing and globe-girdling civilisation on the Earth's physical and biological bases, both of which appear to be deteriorating. Second, I discussed the ways in which the shifting patterns of industrial and intellectual production associated with globalisation have also resulted in the relocation of environmental externalities from one country to another. Third, I proposed that the 'commodification of everything' inherent in post-Fordism has also changed more traditional patterns of pollution and waste production in unforeseen ways. Finally, I suggested that in response to domestic deregulation and interstate reregulation, there is a growing demand for social and environmental regulation that put limits on the worst depredations of unregulated global markets.

To put the argument presented here another way, the global environment should not be seen as an arena somehow separated from other social realms. Its role as the material base of human society is special, to be sure, but the ways in which that base is used and abused are fully social. Physical 'facts' alone will not change social 'facts' and, at the end of the day, global governance and governmentality, whether environmental or not, will depend on changing the latter. Whether activist campaigns and corporate codes of conduct can play a central role in changing these social facts remains to be seen. That such social facts *must* be changed is hardly to be questioned.

Notes

1. In the preparation of this chapter, I am especially appreciative of the research and editing help of Angela McCracken.
2. See, for example, P. Hirst and G. Thompson, *Globalization in Question: The International Economy and the Possibilities of Governance*, 2nd edn (Cambridge: Polity Press, 1999); J. A. Scholte, *Globalization – A Critical Introduction* (New York: St. Martin's, 2000).
3. K. Polanyi, *The Great Transformation*, 2nd edn (Boston: Beacon, 2001).
4. M. Rupert, *Producing Hegemony: The Politics of Mass Production and American Global Power* (Cambridge: Cambridge University Press, 1995); M. Hardt and A. Negri, *Empire* (Cambridge: Harvard University Press, 2000).
5. M. Foucault, 'Governmentality', in G. Burchell, C. Gordon, and P. Miller (eds), *The Foucault Effect: Studies in Governmentality* (Chicago: University of Chicago Press, 1991), pp. 87–104; M. Dean, *Governmentality – Power and Rule in Modern Society* (London: Sage, 1999).
6. R. D. Lipschutz, *After Authority – War, Peace, and Global Politics in the 21st Century* (Albany: State University of New York Press, 2000), ch. 2.
7. A. Goudie, *The Human Impact on the Natural Environment* (Cambridge: MIT Press, 2000).
8. Such as surveillance satellites; K. Litfin, 'Satellites and Sovereign Knowledge: Remote Sensing of the Global Environment', in K. D. Litfin (ed.), *The Greening of Sovereignty in World Politics* (Cambridge: MIT Press, 1998), pp. 193–222.
9. G. E. Christianson, *Greenhouse – The 200-Year Story of Global Warming* (New York: Penguin, 1999).
10. W. Ophuls and A. S. Boyan, Jr. *Ecology and the Politics of Scarcity Revisited: The Unravelling of the American Dream* (New York: W. H. Freeman, 1992).
11. J. Simon, *The Ultimate Resource 2* (Princeton: Princeton University Press, 1996).
12. B. Lomborg, *The Skeptical Environmentalist: Measuring the Real State of the World* (Cambridge: Cambridge University Press, 2001).
13. A. Sen, *Development as Freedom* (New York: Knopf, 1999).
14. D. Meadows, *et al. The Limits to Growth* (New York: University Books, 1972).
15. See, for example, O. Tahvonen, 'Economic Sustainability and Scarcity of Natural Resources: A Brief Historical Review' (Washington, DC: Resources for the Future, 2000), online: http://www.rff.org/issue_briefs/PDF_files/tahvonen_naturalres.pdf (accessed on 2 February 2003).
16. As in the case of water; A. Goudie, *The Human Impact on the Natural Environment* (Cambridge: MIT Press, 2000), ch. 5.
17. Such as old-growth forests, species; Goudie 2000, ch. 2.
18. A. Sen, *Development as Freedom* (New York: Knopf, 1999).
19. Intergovernmental Panel on Climate Change (IPCC), *Climate Change 2001: The Scientific Basis,* A Report of Working Group I of the Intergovernmental Panel on Climate Change (2001a), online: http://www.grida.no/climate/

ipcc_tar/wg1/index.htm (accessed 2 February 2003). There is a relatively small group that believes that accumulated data show no such tendencies and that computer models of climatic processes are simply wrong; see, for example, R. S. Lindzen, Testimony of Richard S. Lindzen before the Senate Environment and Public Works Committee on 2 May 2001, online: http://www.senate.gov/~epw/107th/lin_0502.htm (accessed 2 February 2003).

20. Intergovernmental Panel on Climate Change, *Climate Change 2001: Impacts, Adaptation, and Vulnerability*, A Report of Working Group II of the Intergovernmental Panel on Climate Change (2001b), ch. 4–7, online: http://www.grida.no/climate/ipcc_tar/wg2/index.htm (accessed 2 February 2003).

21. P. Stern, T. Dietz, V. Ruttan, R. Socolow and J. Sweeny, *Environmentally Significant Consumption – Research Directions* (Washington, DC: National Academy Press, 1997).

22. Of course there are enormous variations even within this 20 percent: 2000 per capita income was about $11,000 in Portugal and about $32,000 in the United States; World Bank, 'GNP per capita, 2000: Atlas Method and PPP' (2001a), online: www.worldbank.org/data/databytopic/GNPPC.pdf (accessed on 2 February 2003).

23. World Bank, 'Size of the Economy' (2001b), online: www.worldbank.org/data/wdi2001/pdfs/tab1_1.pdf (accessed on 2 February 2003).

24. World Bank, 'Facts and Figures from the *World Development Indicators 2001*' (2001c) at http://www.worldbank.org/data/databytopic/bullets.pdf (accessed on 2 February 2003). Strictly speaking, these numbers are not entirely commensurate. A dollar's equivalent in Chinese currency has a purchasing power parity (PPP) equal to about $5.20; for India, the corresponding number is $4.15. The $11,000 per capital GDP for Portugal has a PPP equal to almost $17,000. Finally, the PPP for middle income countries is $5,200 and for low income countries, $1,870 (see World Bank, 'GNP per capita, 2000: Atlas Method and PPP' (2001a), online: www.worldbank.org/data/databytopic/GNPPC.pdf (accessed on 2 February 2003) and World Bank, 'Size of the Economy' (2001b), online: www.worldbank.org/data/wdi2001/pdfs/tab1_1.pdf (accessed on 2 February 2003).

25. P. Hirst and G. Thompson, *Globalization in Question: The International Economy and the Possibilities of Governance,* 2nd edn (Cambridge: Polity Press, 1999).

26. For example, R. H. Grove, *Green Imperialism* (Cambridge: Cambridge University Press, 1995).

27. G. Gereffi and M. Korzeniewicz (eds), *Commodity Chains and Global Capitalism* (Westport: Praeger, 1994).

28. M. Mani and D. Wheeler, 'In Search of Pollution Havens? Dirty Industries in the World Economy, 1960–1995' (PRDEI, The World Bank, April 1997), online: http://www.worldbank.org/research/peg/wps16/index.htm (accessed on 2 February 2003).

29. J. DiMento and P. Doughman, 'Soft Teeth in the Back of the Mouth: The NAFTA Environmental Side Agreement Implemented', *The Georgetown International Environmental Law Review*, X, 3 (Spring 1998) 651–752.

30. M. Mani, S. Pargal and M. Huq, 'Is There an Environmental "Race to the Bottom"? Evidence on the Role of Environmental Regulation in Plant

Location Decisions in India' (The World Bank, January 1997), online: http://www.worldbank.org/research/peg/wps15/index.htm (accessed on 2 February 2003).

31. As in Southeast Asia; see UN Environment Programme (UNEP), 'Chapter Two: The State of the Environment – Asia and the Pacific, Social and Economic Background', *Global Environmental Outlook 2000* (Nairobi, Kenya: UNEP/Earthscan, 1999), online: http://www.unep.org/geo2000/english/0063.htm (accessed on 2 February 2003).

32. B. Cashore, 'What Should Canada Do When the Softwood Lumber Agreement Expires?', *Policy.ca* (20 April 2001) online: http://www.policy.ca/PDF/20010205.pdf (accessed on 23 February 2003).

33. J. Clapp, *Toxic Exports: The Transfer of Hazardous Wastes from Rich to Poor Countries* (Ithaca: Cornell University Press, 2001).

34. J. Clapp, 'The Illegal CFC Trade: An Unexpected Wrinkle in the Ozone Protection Regime', *International Environmental Affairs* (1997) 259–273.

35. UN Framework Convention on Climate Change, online: http://unfccc.int/ (accessed 2 February 2003).

36. D. Bodansky, 'US Climate Policy after Kyoto: Elements for Success', Carnegie Endowment for International Peace, *Policy Brief 15* (April, 2002), online: http://www.ceip.org/files/pdf/Policybrief15.pdf (accessed 2 February 2003).

37. K. Hoggart, 'Global Economic Structures and Agricultural Change', in K. Hoggart (ed.), *Agricultural Change, Environment and Economy* (London: Mansell, 1992), pp. 1–24.

38. M. Altieri, 'Poor Farmers Won't Reap the Benefits', *Foreign Policy* (Summer 2000) 123.

39. J. C. H. Chai and B. K. Chai, 'China's Floating Population and its Implications', *International Journal of Social Economics*, XXIV, 7–9 (1997) 1038–52.

40. See, for example, K. Polanyi, *The Great Transformation*, 2nd edn (Boston: Beacon, 2001).

41. K. Conca, 'Consumption and Environment in a Global Economy', *Global Environmental Politics*, I, 3 (August 2001) 53–71.

42. A. Maddison, *The World Economy – A Millennial Perspective* (Paris: Development Centre of the Organisation for Economic Co-operation and Development, 2001), pp. 173, 362, 175.

43. T. Princen, M. Maniates and K. Conca, *Confronting Consumption* (Cambridge: MIT Press, 2002).

44. C. P. Kindleberger, *The World in Depression, 1929–1939*, 2nd edn (Berkeley: University of California, 1986).

45. K. Polanyi, *The Great Transformation*, 2nd edn (Boston: Beacon, 2001); M. A. L. Miller, 'Tragedy for the Commons: The Enclosure and Commodification of Knowledge', in D. Stevis and V. J. Assetto (eds), *The International Political Economy of the Environment* (Boulder: Lynne Rienner, 2001), pp. 111–134.

46. G. Hardin, 'The Tragedy of the Commons', *Science*, CLXII (13 December 1967) 1243–48.

47. D. W. Bromley *et al.*, *Making the Commons Work – Theory, Practice, and Policy* (San Francisco: Institute for Contemporary Studies, 1992).

48. M. Kaufmann, 'Farmer Loses Fight Against Monsanto', *San Francisco Chronicle* (30 March 2001), online: http://www.sfgate.com/cgi-bin/article.cgi?file=/chronicle/archive/2001/03/30/BU136969.DTL (accessed 2 February 2003).
49. D. Ferber, 'Risks and Benefits: GM Crops in the Cross Hairs', *Science*, CCLXXXVI (26 November 1999), 1662–66 online: http://www.aces.uiuc.edu/~asap/expanded/gmo/ sci_main.html (accessed on 2 February 2003); M. Perelman, 'The Costs of Capitalist Agriculture: A Challenge to Radical Political Economy', *Review of Radical Political Economics*, XXXII, 2 (2000) 317–30.
50. M. A. L. Miller, 'Tragedy for the Commons: The Enclosure and Commodification of Knowledge', in D. Stevis and V. J. Assetto (eds), *The International Political Economy of the Environment* (Boulder: Lynne Rienner, 2001), pp. 122–28.
51. Duales System Deutschland AG, 'Der greuner punkt', no date, online: http://www.gruener-punkt.de/en/home.php3 (accessed on 2 February 2003).
52. N. Bailey, 'Foreign Direct Investment and Environmental Protection in the Third World', in D. Zaelke, P. Orbuch, and R. F. Houseman (eds), *Trade and the Environment – Law, Economics, and Policy* (Washington, DC: Island Press), pp. 133–43; P. Ekins, 'The Kuznets Curve for the Environment and Economic Growth: Examining the Evidence', *Environment and Planning*, XXIX, 5 (1997) 805–830.
53. W. Harbaugh, A. Levinson and D. Wilson, 'Reexamining the Empirical Evidence for an Environmental Kuznets Curve', NBER Working Paper No. w7711 (May 2000), online: http://papers.nber.org/papers/w7711.pdf (accessed on 2 February 2003).
54. European Commission, 'Environment and Poverty', *Social, Human and Cultural Development, Briefing Paper 21* (May 2000), online: http://europa.eu.int/comm/development/briefing/briefing21_en.pdf (accessed on 2 February 2003).
55. B. Milanovic, 'True World Income Distribution, 1988 and 1993: First Calculation Based on Household Surveys Alone', World Bank, Development Research Group (1999), online: http://econ.worldbank.org/files/978_wps2244.pdf (accessed on 2 February 2003).
56. P. C. Stern, O. R. Young and D. Druckman (eds), *Global Environmental Change: Understanding the Human Dimensions* (Washington, DC: National Academy Press, 1992).
57. M. Redclift and T. Benton, *Social Theory and the Global Environment* (London: Routledge, 1994).
58. See, for example, P. M. Haas, R. O. Keohane and M. A. Levy (eds), *Institutions for the Earth: Sources of Effective International Environmental Protection* (Cambridge: MIT Press, 1993); V. P. Nanda, *International Environmental Law and Policy* (Irvington-on-Hudson: Transnational Publishers, 1995); Keohane, R. O. and M. A. Levy (eds), *Institutions for Environmental Aid: Pitfalls and Promise* (Cambridge: MIT Press, 1996).
59. R. D. Lipschutz, *After Authority – War, Peace, and Global Politics in the 21st Century* (Albany: State University of New York Press, 2000).
60. R. Mishra, *Globalization and the Welfare State* (Cheltenham: Edward Elgar, 1999).

61. R. Garcia-Johnson, *Exporting Environmentalism – US Multinational Chemical Corporations in Brazil and Mexico* (Cambridge: MIT Press, 2000); J. Clapp, *Toxic Exports: The Transfer of Hazardous Wastes from Rich to Poor Countries* (Ithaca: Cornell University Press, 2001).
62. P. B. Evans, H. Jacobson and R. Putnam (eds), *Double-Edged Diplomacy: International Bargaining and Domestic Politics* (Berkeley: University of California Press, 1993).
63. D. Vogel, *Trading Up – Consumer and Environmental Regulation in a Global Economy* (Cambridge: Harvard University Press, 1995); J. Braithwaite and P. Drahos, *Global Business Regulation* (Cambridge: Cambridge University Press, 2000).
64. R. D. Lipschutz, 'Doing Well by Doing Good? Transnational Regulatory Campaigns, Social Activism, and Impacts on State Sovereignty', in J. Montgomery and N. Glazer (eds), *Challenges to Sovereignty: How Governments Respond* (New Brunswick, NJ: Transaction, 2002), pp. 291–320.
65. See D. Zaelke, P. Orbuch and R. F. Houseman (eds), *Trade and the Environment – Law, Economics, and Policy* (Washington, DC: Island Press, 1993), especially J. Bhagwati, 'Trade and the Environment: The False Conflict?', in D. Zaelke, P. Orbuch and R. F. Houseman (eds), 1993, pp. 159–90; J. Bhagwati, *Free Trade Today* (Princeton, N.J.: Princeton University Press, 2002).
66. S. Charnovitz, 'Environmental Harmonization and Trade Policy', in D. Zaelke, P. Orbuch and R. F. Houseman (eds), *Trade and the Environment – Law, Economics, and Policy* (Washington, DC: Island Press, 1993), pp. 267–86.
67. E. M. Graham, *Global Corporations and National Governments* (Washington, DC: Institute for International Economics, 1996); S. K. Vogel, *Freer Markets, More Rules – Regulatory Reform in Advanced Industrial Countries* (Ithaca: Cornell University Press, 1996); J. Braithwaite and P. Drahos, *Global Business Regulation* (Cambridge: Cambridge University Press, 2000).
68. M. Foucault, 'Governmentality', in G. Burchell, C. Gordon, and P. Miller (eds), *The Foucault Effect: Studies in Governmentality* (Chicago: University of Chicago Press, 1991), p. 100; see also M. Dean, *Governmentality – Power and Rule in Modern Society* (London: Sage, 1999), ch. 1.
69. Dean 1999, p. 99.
70. Dean 1999, p. 99.
71. See below; also see J. Smith, C. Chatfield, and R. Pagnucco (eds), *Transnational Social Movements and Global Politics: Solidarity Beyond the State* (Syracuse: Syracuse University Press, 1997); J. Smith and H. Johnston (eds), *Globalization and Resistance – Transnational Dimensions of Social Movements* (Lanham, Md.: Rowman and Littlefield, 2002).
72. See M. Foucault, 'Governmentality', in G. Burchell, C. Gordon, and P. Miller (eds), *The Foucault Effect: Studies in Governmentality* (Chicago: University of Chicago Press, 1991), pp. 87–104; and M. Dean, *Governmentality – Power and Rule in Modern Society* (London: Sage, 1999).
73. A. C. Cutler, V. Haufler and T. Porters (eds), *Private Authority and International Affairs* (Albany: State University of New York Press, 1998).
74. J. Braithwaite and P. Drahos, *Global Business Regulation* (Cambridge: Cambridge University Press, 2000).
75. A. C. Cutler, V. Haufler and T. Porters (eds), *Private Authority and International Affairs* (Albany: State University of New York Press, 1998).

232 *Global Governance in the Twenty-first Century*

76. C. Murphy, *International Organization and Industrial Change: Global Governance since 1850* (New York: Oxford University Press, 1994).
77. US Federal Aviation Administration, 'Introduction to the Model Civil Aviation Safety Act and Model Regulations', *Model Aviation Regulatory Document*, no date, online: http://www.faa.gov/avr/iasa/INTRO.doc (accessed 2 February 2003).
78. R. D. Lipschutz, 'Why Is There No International Forestry Law? An Examination of International Forestry Regulation, both Public and Private', *UCLA Journal of Environmental Law & Policy*, XIX, 1 (2001) 155–82.
79. Lipschutz, 2001.
80. D. Pearce and K. Turner, *Economics of Natural Resources and the Environment* (Baltimore: Johns Hopkins University Press, 1990).
81. Note that a permit system does not eliminate entirely command and control rules. Some cap must be set on pollution, either as a total for each individual consumer of permits or as a total for the system as a whole, in which individual consumers can then buy and sell permits.
82. The long-term prospects of the UN Framework Convention on Climate Change may rest on this point. If and when developing countries do make commitments to control emissions, and if they need to purchase emission credits, they may very well discover that the rich countries have bid permit prices to levels that poorer ones cannot afford to pay.
83. R. D. Lipschutz, *After Authority – War, Peace, and Global Politics in the 21ˢᵗ Century* (Albany: State University of New York Press, 2000).
84. Lipschutz, 2000, ch. 2.
85. R. D. Lipschutz, 'Why Is There No International Forestry Law? An Examination of International Forestry Regulation, both Public and Private', *UCLA Journal of Environmental Law & Policy*, XIX, 1 (2001) 155–82.
86. Of course, some corporations and executives may be motivated by ethical concerns and environmentalist beliefs. It is no easy task to disentangle motivations, given that shareholder pressure on company managers often drives them to behave in ways that are not environmentally-friendly.
87. At least, this is the hope; see B. Milani, *Designing the Green Economy* (Lanham: Rowman & Littlefield, 2000).
88. K. Polanyi, *The Great Transformation* 2ⁿᵈ edn (Boston: Beacon, 2001); see also R. D. Lipschutz, 'Doing Well by Doing Good? Transnational Regulatory Campaigns, Social Activism, and Impacts on State Sovereignty', in J. Montgomery and N. Glazer (eds), *Challenges to Sovereignty: How Governments Respond* (New Brunswick, NJ: Transaction, 2002), pp. 291–320.

References

Altieri, M. 'Poor Farmers Won't Reap the Benefits', *Foreign Policy* (Summer 2000) 123.
Bailey, N. 'Foreign Direct Investment and Environmental Protection in the Third World', in D. Zaelke, P. Orbuch, and R. F. Houseman (eds), *Trade and the Environment – Law, Economics, and Policy* (Washington, DC: Island Press), pp. 133–43.
Bhagwati, J. *Free Trade Today* (Princeton, N.J.: Princeton University Press, 2002).

——, 'Trade and the Environment: The False Conflict?', in D. Zaelke, P. Orbuch and R. F. Houseman (eds), *Trade and the Environment – Law, Economics, and Policy* (Washington, DC: Island Press, 1993), pp. 159–90.

Bodansky, D. 'US Climate Policy after Kyoto: Elements for Success', Carnegie Endowment for International Peace, *Policy Brief 15* (April, 2002), online: http://www.ceip.org/files/pdf/Policybrief15.pdf (accessed 2 February 2003).

Braithwaite, J. and P. Drahos, *Global Business Regulation* (Cambridge: Cambridge University Press, 2000).

Bromley, D. W. *et al.*, *Making the Commons Work – Theory, Practice, and Policy* (San Francisco: Institute for Contemporary Studies, 1992).

Cashore, B. 'What Should Canada Do When the Softwood Lumber Agreement Expires?', *Policy.ca* (20 April 2001) online: http://www.policy.ca/PDF/20010205.pdf (accessed on 23 February 2003).

Chai, J. C. H. and B. K. Chai, 'China's Floating Population and its Implications', *International Journal of Social Economics* XXIV, 7–9 (1997) 1038–52.

Charnovitz, S. 'Environmental Harmonization and Trade Policy', in D. Zaelke, P. Orbuch and R. F. Houseman (eds), *Trade and the Environment* (Washington, DC: Island Press, 1993), pp. 267–86.

Christianson, G. E. *Greenhouse – The 200-Year Story of Global Warming* (New York: Penguin, 1999).

Clapp, J. *Toxic Exports: The Transfer of Hazardous Wastes from Rich to Poor Countries* (Ithaca: Cornell University Press, 2001).

——, 'The Illegal CFC Trade: An Unexpected Wrinkle in the Ozone Protection Regime', *International Environmental Affairs* (1997) 259–273.

Conca, K. 'Consumption and Environment in a Global Economy', *Global Environmental Politics* I, 3 (August 2001) 53–71.

Cutler, A. C., V. Haufler and T. Porters (eds), *Private Authority and International Affairs* (Albany: State University of New York Press, 1998).

Duales System Deutschland AG, 'Der greuner punkt', no date, online: http://www.gruener-punkt.de/en/home.php3 (accessed on 2 February 2003).

Dean, M. *Governmentality – Power and Rule in Modern Society* (London: Sage, 1999).

DiMento, J. and P. Doughman, 'Soft Teeth in the Back of the Mouth: The NAFTA Environmental Side Agreement Implemented', *The Georgetown International Environmental Law Review* X, 3 (Spring 1998) 651–752.

Ekins, P. 'The Kuznets Curve for the Environment and Economic Growth: Examining the Evidence', *Environment and Planning* XXIX, 5 (1997) 805–830.

European Commission, 'Environment and Poverty', Social, Human and Cultural Development, Briefing Paper 21 (May 2000), online: http://europa.eu.int/comm/development/briefing/briefing21_en.pdf (accessed on 2 February 2003).

Evans, P. B., H. Jacobson and R. Putnam (eds), *Double-Edged Diplomacy: International Bargaining and Domestic Politics* (Berkeley: University of California Press, 1993).

Ferber, D. 'Risks and Benefits: GM Crops in the Cross Hairs', *Science* CCLXXXVI (26 November 1999) 1662–66, online: http://www.aces.uiuc.edu/~asap/expanded/gmo/ sci_main.html (accessed on 2 February 2003).

Foucault, M. 'Governmentality', in G. Burchell, C. Gordon, and P. Miller (eds), *The Foucault Effect: Studies in Governmentality* (Chicago: University of Chicago Press, 1991), pp. 87–104.

Garcia-Johnson, R. *Exporting Environmentalism – US Multinational Chemical Corporations in Brazil and Mexico* (Cambridge: MIT Press, 2000).

Gereffi, G. and M. Korzeniewicz (eds), *Commodity Chains and Global Capitalism* (Westport: Praeger, 1994).

Goudie, A. *The Human Impact on the Natural Environment* (Cambridge: MIT Press, 2000).

Graham, E. M. *Global Corporations and National Governments* (Washington, DC: Institute for International Economics, 1996).

Grove, R. H. *Green Imperialism* (Cambridge: Cambridge University Press, 1995).

Hoggart, K. 'Global Economic Structures and Agricultural Change', in K. Hoggart (ed.), *Agricultural Change, Environment and Economy* (London: Mansell, 1992), pp. 1–24.

Haas, P. M., R. O. Keohane and M. A. Levy (eds), *Institutions for the Earth: Sources of Effective International Environmental Protection* (Cambridge: MIT Press, 1993).

Harbaugh, W., A. Levinson and D. Wilson, 'Reexamining the Empirical Evidence for an Environmental Kuznets Curve', NBER Working Paper No. w7711 (May 2000), online: http://papers.nber.org/papers/w7711.pdf (accessed on 2 February 2003).

Hardin, G. 'The Tragedy of the Commons', *Science* CLXII (13 December 1967) 1243–48.

Hardt, M. and A. Negri, *Empire* (Cambridge: Harvard University Press, 2000).

Hirst, P. and G. Thompson, *Globalization in Question: The International Economy and the Possibilities of Governance* 2nd edn (Cambridge: Polity Press, 1999).

Intergovernmental Panel on Climate Change (IPCC), *Climate Change 2001: The Scientific Basis* A Report of Working Group I of the Intergovernmental Panel on Climate Change (2001a), online: http://www.grida.no/climate/ipcc_tar/wg1/index.htm (accessed 2 February 2003).

——, *Climate Change 2001: Impacts, Adaptation, and Vulnerability, A Report of Working Group II of the Intergovernmental Panel on Climate Change* (2001b), online: http://www.grida.no/climate/ipcc_tar/wg2/index.htm (accessed 2 February 2003).

Kaufmann, M. 'Farmer Loses Fight Against Monsanto', *San Francisco Chronicle* (30 March 2001), online: http://www.sfgate.com/cgi-bin/article.cgi?file=/chronicle/archive/2001/03/30/BU136969.DTL (accessed 2 February 2003).

Keohane, R. O. and M. A. Levy (eds), *Institutions for Environmental Aid: Pitfalls and Promise* (Cambridge: MIT Press, 1996).

Kindleberger, C. P. *The World in Depression, 1929–1939* 2nd edn (Berkeley: University of California, 1986).

Lindzen, R. S. Testimony of Richard S. Lindzen before the Senate Environment and Public Works Committee on 2 May 2001, online: http://www.senate.gov/~epw/107th/lin_0502.htm (accessed 2 February 2003).

Lipschutz, R. D. 'Doing Well by Doing Good? Transnational Regulatory Campaigns, Social Activism, and Impacts on State Sovereignty', in J. Montgomery and N. Glazer (eds), *Challenges to Sovereignty: How Governments Respond* (New Brunswick, NJ: Transaction, 2002), pp. 291–320.

——, 'Why Is There No International Forestry Law? An Examination of International Forestry Regulation, both Public and Private', *UCLA Journal of Environmental Law & Policy* XIX, 1 (2001) 155–82.

——, *After Authority – War, Peace, and Global Politics in the 21st Century* (Albany: State University of New York Press, 2000).

Litfin, K. 'Satellites and Sovereign Knowledge: Remote Sensing of the Global Environment', in K. D. Litfin (ed.), *The Greening of Sovereignty in World Politics* (Cambridge: MIT Press, 1998), pp. 193–222.

Lomborg, B. *The Skeptical Environmentalist: Measuring the Real State of the World* (Cambridge: Cambridge University Press, 2001).

Maddison, A. *The World Economy – A Millennial Perspective* (Paris: Development Centre of the Organisation for Economic Co-operation and Development, 2001).

Mani, M. and D. Wheeler, 'In Search of Pollution Havens? Dirty Industries in the World Economy, 1960–1995' (PRDEI, The World Bank, April 1997), online: http://www.worldbank.org/research/peg/wps16/index.htm (accessed on 2 February 2003).

Mani, M., S. Pargal and M. Huq, 'Is There an Environmental 'Race to the Bottom'? Evidence on the Role of Environmental Regulation in Plant Location Decisions in India' (The World Bank, January 1997), online: http://www.worldbank.org/research/peg/wps15/index.htm (accessed 2 February 2003).

Meadows, D. *et al.*, *The Limits to Growth* (New York: University Books, 1972).

Milani, B. *Designing the Green Economy* (Lanham: Rowman & Littlefield, 2000).

Milanovic, B. 'True World Income Distribution, 1988 and 1993: First Calculation Based on Household Surveys Alone', World Bank, Development Research Group (1999), online: http://econ.worldbank.org/files/978_wps2244.pdf (accessed on 2 February 2003).

Miller, M. A. L. 'Tragedy for the Commons: The Enclosure and Commodification of Knowledge', in D. Stevis and V. J. Assetto (eds), *The International Political Economy of the Environment* (Boulder: Lynne Rienner, 2001), pp. 111–134.

Mishra, R. *Globalization and the Welfare State* (Cheltenham: Edward Elgar, 1999).

Murphy, C. *International Organization and Industrial Change: Global Governance since 1850* (New York: Oxford University Press, 1994).

Nanda, V. P. *International Environmental Law and Policy* (Irvington-on-Hudson: Transnational Publishers, 1995).

Ophuls, W. and A. S. Boyan Jr. *Ecology and the Politics of Scarcity Revisited: The Unraveling of the American Dream* (New York: W. H. Freeman, 1992).

Pearce D. and K. Turner. *Economics of Natural Resources and the Environment* (Baltimore: Johns Hopkins University Press, 1990).

Perelman, M. 'The Costs of Capitalist Agriculture: A Challenge to Radical Political Economy', *Review of Radical Political Economics* XXXII, 2 (2000) 317–30.

Polanyi, K. *The Great Transformation* 2nd edn (Boston: Beacon, 2001).

Princen, T., M. Maniates and K. Conca, *Confronting Consumption* (Cambridge: MIT Press, 2002).

Redclift, M. and T. Benton, *Social Theory and the Global Environment* (London: Routledge, 1994).

Rupert, M. *Producing Hegemony: The Politics of Mass Production and American Global Power* (Cambridge: Cambridge University Press, 1995).

Scholte, J. A. *Globalization – A Critical Introduction* (New York: St. Martin's, 2000).

Sen, A. *Development as Freedom* (New York: Knopf, 1999).

Simon, J. *The Ultimate Resource 2* (Princeton: Princeton University Press, 1996).

Smith, J., C. Chatfield, and R. Pagnucco (eds), *Transnational Social Movements and Global Politics: Solidarity Beyond the State* (Syracuse: Syracuse University Press, 1997).

Smith, J. and H. Johnston (eds), *Globalization and Resistance – Transnational Dimensions of Social Movements* (Lanham, Md.: Rowman and Littlefield, 2002).

Stern, P., T. Dietz, V. Ruttan, R. Socolow and J. Sweeny, *Environmentally Significant Consumption – Research Directions* (Washington, DC: National Academy Press, 1997).

Stern, P. C., O. R. Young and D. Druckman (eds), *Global Environmental Change: Understanding the Human Dimensions* (Washington, DC: National Academy Press, 1992).

Tahvonen, O. 'Economic Sustainability and Scarcity of Natural Resources: A Brief Historical Review' (Washington, DC: Resources for the Future, 2000), online: http://www.rff.org/issue_briefs/PDF_files/tahvonen_naturalres.pdf (accessed on 2 February 2003).

UN Environment Programme, 'Chapter Two: The State of the Environment – Asia and the Pacific, Social and Economic Background', *Global Environmental Outlook 2000* (Nairobi, Kenya: UNEP/Earthscan, 1999), online: http://www. unep.org/geo2000/english/0063.htm (accessed on 2 February 2003).

UN Framework Convention on Climate Change, no date, online: http:// unfccc.int/ (accessed 2 February 2003).

US Federal Aviation Administration, 'Introduction to the Model Civil Aviation Safety Act and Model Regulations', *Model Aviation Regulatory Document*, no date, online: http://www.faa.gov/avr/iasa/INTRO.doc (accessed 2 February 2003).

Vogel, D. *Trading Up – Consumer and Environmental Regulation in a Global Economy* (Cambridge: Harvard University Press, 1995).

Vogel, S. K. *Freer Markets, More Rules – Regulatory Reform in Advanced Industrial Countries* (Ithaca: Cornell University Press, 1996).

World Bank, 'GNP per capita, 2000: Atlas Method and PPP' (2001a), online: www.worldbank.org/data/databytopic/GNPPC.pdf (accessed on 2 February 2003).

——, 'Size of the Economy' (2001b), online: www.worldbank.org/data/wdi2001/ pdfs/tab1_1.pdf (accessed on 2 February 2003).

——, 'Facts and Figures from the *World Development Indicators 2001*' (2001c), online: http://www.worldbank.org/data/databytopic/bullets.pdf (accessed on 2 February 2003).

Zaelke, D., P. Orbuch and R. F. Houseman (eds), *Trade and the Environment – Law, Economics, and Policy* (Washington, DC: Island Press, 1993).

9
A More Perfect Union? The Liberal Peace and the Challenge of Globalisation

Michael W. Doyle

Global democratisation rose to the international agenda in the past year as the three peak global economic associations all came under attack.[1] In Seattle, at the meeting of the new World Trade Organization (WTO), and in Washington at the meetings of the World Bank and the International Monetary Fund (IMF), a diverse collection of labour unions and environmentalists from the industrial North and trade and finance ministers from the developing countries of the South each launched sharply critical barbs. The critics successfully disrupted the WTO meeting that had been designed to launch (and celebrate) a 'Millennium Round' of further reductions of barriers to global trade. The aims of the critics were very different, but together they derailed the entire proceedings and exposed important differences in priority among the developed states, and particularly the US and Europe. Charlene Barshefsky, the US Trade Representative and the meeting's chair, later conceded, 'We needed a process which had a greater degree of internal transparency and inclusion to accommodate a larger and more diverse membership'.[2] This highly-regarded trade-o-crat had come to recognise that the eminently oligarchic WTO needed some democratisation (as yet undefined).

Joe Stiglitz, until recently the chief economist of the World Bank, offered a still broader criticism of the Bank's sister institution, the IMF. The IMF was designed to rescue countries in temporary balance of payments difficulties. It actually operates, Stiglitz charges, more like a bureaucratic cabal than an international rescue team.

The IMF likes to go about its business without outsiders asking too many questions. In theory, the fund supports democratic institutions in the nations it assists. In practice, it undermines the democratic process by imposing policies. Officially, of course, the IMF doesn't 'impose' anything. It 'negotiates' the conditions for receiving aid. But all the power in the negotiations is on one side – the IMF's – and the fund rarely allows sufficient time for broad consensus-building or even widespread consultations with either parliaments or civil society. Sometimes the IMF dispenses with the pretence of openness altogether and negotiates secret covenants.[3]

Two themes resonate through the denunciations: global governance and global (or international) democratisation. The key question is how they relate to each other. Three issues connect them. The first is the broad ethical question of how could and should the world be organised politically?[4] I present the claims for the leading organisational political framework today, one designed to bring world order while recognising the reality of sovereign independence, which is the Kantian idea of a pacific union of free republics, or the liberal democratic peace. More controversially, I then argue that however good the Kantian peace has been and could be, it has significant limitations that have been exposed by increasing globalisation. Globalisation both sustains elements of the Kantian peace and also undermines it, making it less sustainable and indeed vitiating some of the democracy on which it is founded. And third, I discuss a range of possible responses to the challenges that globalisation poses for the existing international order, and conclude with a comment on why global democratic sovereignty is not yet viable while global norms – more democratically derived – seem needed to promote a more perfect a union of order and democracy.

Global political theory

How could and should the world be politically organised? That is, how should one assess various forms of political organisation of world politics with respect to their ability to fulfil a set of human values that would be very widely shared – even if not exactly in the same way – around the world? Take, for example, these values: peace; prosperity; national independence, cultural identity or pluralism (so that people can express their identities in some public form); and individual human rights (including democracy, participation, equality and self-determination).

How well do various schemes of international order fulfil these basic human values at the global scale? Political philosophers have told us that the international system is a mix of hard choices among values. The political theorist Michael Walzer has reformulated those choices well in an essay that explores the range of values from little to much international governance, that is from national autonomy (and international anarchy) to a global, hierarchical, centralised government over all individuals.[5] There is no single arrangement that obtains everything – one that procures international peace, domestic peace, liberty, democracy, prosperity, and pluralistic identity. Instead, while the virtues of the nation state are domestic peace and perhaps national identity and national democracy, those same virtues are the foundations of international anarchy, geopolitical insecurity and international economic rivalry. Global government can be a foundation for global peace and a single efficient world market, and maybe even a global democratic polity, but it could also be the institution that represses national particularity, the global 'soul-less despotism' against which the eighteenth century German philosopher, Immanuel Kant, eloquently warned the liberals of his day. In between global authority and national independence, one can imagine confederal arrangements that allowed room for a diversity of civil societies, but again only at the cost of both national autonomy and international insecurity. The message of Michael Walzer's spectrum of global governance is hard choices: there is no perfect equilibrium.

Although there is no perfect solution to the problem of implementing human values on a global scale, the Kantian liberal peace lays claim to being the optimal combination, the one that gets us the most peace and global prosperity at the least cost in liberty, independence, and the least trampling on national identities. Immanuel Kant's essay, *Perpetual Peace*, published in 1795, was a direct response and alternative to both the autarkic nation state and a sovereign world government.

The key to the liberal argument is the claim that by establishing domestic liberty, political participation, and market exchange one can have the international payoff of peace as well.[6] Kant described a decentralised, self-enforcing peace achieved without the world government that the global governance claim posits as necessary. This is a claim that has resonated in the modern literature on the 'democratic peace'. It draws on the ideas of American presidents as diverse as Woodrow Wilson, Ronald Reagan and Bill Clinton and British prime ministers from Gladstone to Blair. Promoting freedom and 'enlarging' the zone of democratic rule were the doctrinal centrepieces of their foreign policies. Advocates of the 'democratic peace' have claimed that over time, country by democratising country, a peace would spread to cover the entire world, building one world order – democratic, free, prosperous, and peaceful.

Kant's argument was much more complicated, presented in three necessary conditions, each an 'article' in a hypothetical peace 'treaty' he asks sovereigns to sign. First, states should adopt a liberal constitutional, representative, republican form of government which would constrain the state such that the sovereign would, on average, usually follow the interest of most of the people, or the majority. Second, the citizens of this liberal, constitutional, representative republic must affirm a commitment to human rights, one holding that all human beings are morally equal. Then states that represent liberal democratic majorities in their own countries will regard with respect other states that also represent free and equal citizens. Tolerance for various national liberal cultures and trust emerges, as does nonaggression and peace among fellow liberal republics. Third, given trust, states then lower the barriers that would have been raised to protect the state from invasion or exploitation in the competition of the balance of power. Trade, tourism and other forms of transnational contact grow which lead to prosperity, reinforcing mutual understanding with many opportunities for profitable exchange, and producing contacts that offset in their multiplicity the occasional sources of conflict.

For many, this seems the optimal equilibrium given both the world as it is and a commitment to the values of peace, liberty, prosperity, national identity and democratic participation. Does that mean that there are no tradeoffs? No. There is no such thing as a perfect political equilibrium. There are two major limitations. One is that this peace is limited only to other liberal republics. International respect is only extended to other, similarly republican liberal states. The very same principle of trust that operates among liberal republics tends to corrode attempts at co-operation between liberal republics and autocratic states, whether modern dictatorships or traditional monarchies. The liberal warns: 'If the autocrat is so ruthless that he is unwilling to trust his own citizens to participate in the polity and control his behaviour, just think what he will do to us'. Liberals then raise trade and other barriers, ensuring that conflicts are not dampened. The prejudice may be true. Many dictators – think of Napoleon or Hitler – have been aggressive. Many dictators, however, are also quite shy and cautious. They like the benefits of being absolute ruler and may fear overburdening the quiescence of their subjects with costly foreign adventures. The distrust and hostility are probably thus a joint product. The autocrats do like to gain the profits and glory of expansion and the citizens – cannon fodder and taxpayers – have no constitutional right to stop them. At the same time, the liberals are prejudiced against the autocratic regime and do not extend to those regimes the normal trust in international exchanges or negotiations and may, indeed, launch 'freedom fighters' against them. Although the record of wars between liberals and non-liberals and the history of liberal imperialism testify to the depth of this tension, it can be overcome by autocratic prudence and liberal statesmanship.

The second limitation is associated with the assumption of minimal interdependence. In order for liberal republics to remain effectively sovereign and self-determining, allowing free citizens to govern themselves, material ties to other liberal republics would need to be limited. Kant assumed that those ties were limited to nonaggression, collective security and hospitality (free trade and mutual transit privileges). This is 'light' interdependence[7] – some mutual sensitivity, some limited vulnerability, but not enough to challenge the liberal republic's ability to govern itself in the face of social and economic forces outside itself. Kantianism presumes marginal trade, marginal investment, marginal tourism; not extensive interdependence. This second limitation is increasingly unrealistic today.

Does modern interdependence challenge the Kantian liberal peace? Can the liberal peace sustain extensive, 'heavy' interdependence? That is the question to which I turn next.

Challenges of globalisation

The first challenge of global interdependence is to the sustainability of the liberal peace. Can it operate in a much more intensive environment of social and economic exchange? And the second is to the legitimacy of the liberal democratic system. Can the people truly govern themselves when much of their social and economic interaction is with other societies outside their borders and outside the reach of their representative government? Two major challenges, indeed.

Globalisation I

The first challenge to liberal sustainability was articulated in one of the great books of the twentieth century, Karl Polanyi's *The Great Transformation*.[8] His book is a profound study of the effects of the market economy both domestically and internationally. Polanyi's argument, in summary, holds that marketisation makes peace unsustainable. Kantian liberals hoped that over time, with some ups and downs, international markets would tend to liberalise non-liberal societies leading to more and more liberal republics, which would eventually cover the whole world and thus create global peace. Polanyi says it cannot work that way: there are built-in sources of corrosion produced by economic interdependence that make liberal politics and the liberal peace unsustainable.

He acknowledges that, indeed, the combination of the domestic market economy, political representation, the gold standard and the international balance of power did create a sustaining circle of mutually reinforcing economic contacts that helped produce the peace of the nineteenth century – the Long Peace of 1815 to 1914. But, he warns us, contrary to Immanuel Kant, trade is not just an exchange of commodities at arms length or at the border. Trade is a revolutionary form of exchange. Exchanging commodities changes the value in relative and absolute terms of the factors that go into producing the commodities that are exchanged. As was later elaborated in a set of theorems concerning factor price equalisation, trade in commodities has potentially revolutionary effects in changing the returns to various factors – land, labour, and capital – that go into the production of these commodities. Countries tend to export commodities that intensively use the factors with which they are most endowed and import commodities that embody scarce domestic factors. Trade thus increases demand and price, and eventually factor return for relatively abundant factors as it shrinks demand, price and return for scarce domestic factors. Together this tends toward global 'factor price equalisation' (in theory, with many assumptions, and thus real-world qualifications).[9] In 1795, however, Kant seemed to assume that trade was arms length commodity exchange. He neglected the potential effects of commodity trade on the factors that go into the production of the commodities exchanged (land, labour, and capital).

Why is this important? Trade, whether national or international, destabilises the social relations among land, labour, and capital, disrupting relations that had become embedded in social hierarchies and in political power. Treating land, labour and capital as commodities dislocates established communities, village life, regional life, the relations among classes, industries and sectors and eventually changes the international balance of power. Trade therefore produces a reaction. Farmers do not like to have the prices of their farm products drop to the prices set by more competitive rivals. Consumers might prefer the lower prices, but the usually better organised producers resist. Labourers and manufacturers do not want to compete with labour that makes one tenth of their income or with firms that have costs a fraction of their own, whether in a newly integrated national or international market. When peoples livelihoods are marginalised, they tend to react.

Polanyi recounts that, at the end of the nineteenth century, the reaction to the market took the form of either social democracy on the left or fascism on the right. National economies attempted to protect themselves from the swings of the global economy by raising tariffs in order to protect national consumption or by launching imperial conquests to expand national resources. The resulting rivalry produced, Polanyi continues, World War I, the Great Depression and its competitive devaluations, and eventually World War II. Liberal peace, prosperity, democracy collapsed under the weight of heavy interdependence.

Globalisation II

Following World War II, the allied leaders successfully rebuilt liberal interdependence, constructing a new way to mix together democracy and social stability. They developed a series of safety nets that would make people less vulnerable to the vagaries of the market both domestically and internationally. Rather than adjusting to an autarkic world of intense national competition (as in the 1930s) or letting trade and finance flow freely in response to market incentives (the nineteenth century); the capitalist democracies in the post-war period constructed the IMF, the General Agreement on Tariffs and Trade (GATT), and the World Bank to help regulate and consciously politically manage the shape of the world market economy. Trade was opened on a regulated basis, currencies were made convertible when economies could sustain the convertibility and cushioned with financing to help maintain parities. Long term financing, a form of global Keynesianism, was provided first to Europe and then (in lesser amounts) to the developing countries in order to spread opportunity and reduce the conflicts between haves and have nots that had wracked the interwar period. All this helped promote stability, co-operation, and solidarity in the Cold War struggle against the Soviet Union. Thus with a set of political-economic policies that have been called 'embedded liberalism', the post-war leaders of the West found a way to manage the tensions that Polanyi had described, the dangers of marketisation.[10]

It was good while it lasted, but by the 1980s, frustration with over-regulation, falling productivity and the oil shock, together with a demand for ever more profit and cheap goods produced a move back to marketisation, the Thatcher–Reagan 'magic of the marketplace'. Reacting to the welfare state's restrictions on consumption and profit and seeking a more dynamic spur to industrial reallocation and profits,

244 Global Governance in the Twenty-first Century

many of the protections embedded in the post-war political economy were relaxed. Increasing trade, floating exchange rates, and opening financial markets became the 'Washington Consensus', the watchword of international economic orthodoxy and the standard prescription of the IMF.

As the barriers to global marketisation fell, the forces that propelled ever closer interdependence accelerated. One force accelerating the effects of global marketisation was advances in communication and transportation technology. The costs of transportation and communication began to fall radically in the post-war period. In 1930, the cost of a telephone call between New York and London was (in 1990 dollars) $245 for three minutes. By 1998, the same call cost 35¢: a vast reduction in the cost of communications. That and the related explosion of the Internet are what makes much of global banking and all of global academia possible. If we were still paying $245 for three minutes across the Atlantic, there would be less that we could afford to say.

The second force was trade. There has been a near revolution in the amount of trade tying the countries of the world together. Let me inflict a few figures on you. Even the US, which because of its continental scale is one of the less interdependent economies, has experienced a large change in the impact of trade. In 1910 (that is, during Globalisation I), 11 percent of US gross domestic product (GDP) was in trade (exports and imports). By 1950, this fell to nine percent. That is what the Globalisation I crisis – the Great Depression and the two world wars – was all about. But by 1995, trade had risen to 24 percent. This is more than double the extent of interdependence in the previous era of globalisation. In the Germany of 1910, 38 percent of its GDP was in trade exports and imports. By 1950, this fell to 27 percent; by 1995, up to 46 percent. The UK, the leader of the first wave of globalisation and the most globalised economy at the time, in 1910 had 44 percent of its GDP in trade. In 1950, this dropped to 30 percent. By 1995, 57 percent was in exchangeables. Among the highly developed industrial economies, only Japan is less dependent upon trade and investment income than it was in 1910. It is the only major industrialised economy that is less globalised now than it was in 1910.

And if you think trade is globalising the world, you should examine foreign direct investment (FDI) and portfolio flows of finance. Between 1980 and 1994, trade doubled; but in that same period, FDI grew six times, and portfolio flows of finance grew by nine times.

As in the earlier age of globalisation, these flows of trade and finance are beginning to change the operation of the world's political economy

– altering what is profitable, what is politically sustainable, and what is not. Perhaps most strikingly from an economic point of view, the world now increasingly appears as one large market, a single division of labour. From the standpoint of the multinational company, production strategies are genuinely global, as parts of the production process are allocated to subsidiaries and contractors in countries or regions around the world where they are most cost-effective, forming a global process of production and marketing that is a highly interdependent whole at the global level. In the old global interdependence, cars and shoes were traded among many countries or even made in many countries by one company; now one company makes cars or shoes globally with component factories spread around the world.[11]

Challenges to liberal democratic peace

The new market interdependence poses three challenges to the liberal scheme of global democratic peace.

Commodification

The WTO meeting, and demonstrations in Seattle against it, demonstrate the first trade-off, the trade-off between globally regulated market prosperity and democracy. The tradeoffs are becoming more politically costly as interdependence increases. Politically, the democratic challenge was well put recently by Ed Mortimer (then *Financial Times* foreign editor) when he said that too much democracy kills the market (that's Polanyi's account of national and social democracy in reaction to Globalisation I) and, on the other hand, too much market kills democracy (this is the threat some see posed by Globalisation II). Commodities seem to rule citizens.

US environmentalists struggled for years in order to lobby for a US Endangered Species Act that protects turtles inadvertently caught in the course of the fishing for shrimp. It requires that shrimp nets be designed in a way that permits turtles to escape. The environmentalists struggled long and hard in order to pass the Bill, but they forgot that a new arena of interdependence had engendered a new arena of regulation. When the US government attempted to reduce the impact of the Bill on favoured allies, the WTO not surprisingly declared the effort discriminatory, and therefore illegal under international trade law.

In the European Union (EU), many of its consumer advocates struggled for a campaign to protect European consumers from genetically engineered food – so called 'Frankenfood'. The WTO has yet to rule on this issue that pits American corporations against European food activists. Signs of more sympathy toward health regulation are recently in evidence in WTO decisions. But the WTO earlier ruled that bans against hormone treated food were a form of trade discrimination and illegal under international trade law.[12]

In a wider challenge, the developing countries have insisted upon the right not to be bound by the standards of labour safety, child labour prohibitions, and the minimum wages that hold within the industrialised world. They believe that it is only by taking advantage of their large supplies of talented, hard-working inexpensive labour that they will be able to develop their countries. But the US, responding to pressure from labour unions and human rights advocates, argued at Seattle that the US-level standards on labour rights and environmental protection be applied to all traded goods. This the developing countries see as a denial of their ability to choose their own development path. At the WTO in Seattle, moreover, the developing countries were outraged with the prevalence of so-called 'green room' procedures under which the wealthy industrial countries caucus and decide how to manage the WTO. The developing country majority of the membership want much broader participation in order to avoid having rules imposed upon them that favour the industrialised market economies. National policymakers in the developing world thank the World Bank and IMF for the doors to development they open and for not as yet succumbing to the demands for increased global regulation made by the environmentalist protesters at Seattle and Washington.[13]

In each of these cases, globally regulated norms of non-discrimination – however efficient and fair from a global point of view – are eroding democratic, or at least national, accountability.

Inequality

The second challenge to democratisation concerns both intra-national and international equality. Globalisation allows for those who are most efficient to earn the most. That is what markets usually do. And as the barriers fall to global sales, production, and investment, inequality also tends to rise.

Let me give you some figures. Domestically in the US, beginning about 1975, the economic fates of the top five percent and bottom 20 percent of the US population substantially diverged. By 1995, the real family income of the top five percent stood at 130 percent of the 1973 level, but over the same period, the real family income of the bottom 20 percent stayed at the 1973 level.[14] Internationally, let us compare the Organisation for Economic Co-operation and Development (OECD) (the rich industrial economies) to the rest of the world and compare the 1970s to 1995. In 1970, the OECD enjoyed 66 percent of global GDP. By 1978, its share was up to 68 percent; in 1989, to 71 percent; and in 1995, to 78 percent. The rest of the entire world lived on the complement to that: their figures go from 34 percent in 1970, sinking to 22 percent in 1995. Increasing global inequality is associated with global marketisation. The most productive are winning, accumulating wealth in their own hands. The consequences of globalisation appear to be relatively depriving some in favour of others – the rising tide is not lifting all the boats at the same rate. Not surprisingly, demands for accountable control rise.

Security

The third challenge is security. Kantian liberalism produces security and peace (among the liberal republics). But globalisation challenges the stability of liberal geopolitics in two ways. On the one hand, what Americans call *globalisation* is what many others call *Americanisation*. That is, the US leading role within the world economy, which to Americans appears as an economic issue of dollars and cents, is to other countries a power issue, one fraught with control and guns. The other hand is that global rules for trade and investment have allowed China to benefit from its high savings rate and labour productivity, becoming one of the fastest growing economies in the world. If you add rapid growth to a large population (and if the World Bank projections are correct and if China continues to grow at recent past rates) then by the year 2020, China will have a GDP that is not only larger than that of the United States or Europe, but as big as them both together. From an economic point of view, the prospect of many more Chinese consumers and producers should make everyone content. But from a geopolitical point of view, China's growth entails a massive shift of world political power eastward. That makes the statesmen of the US and Europe nervous, especially if, referring again to the Kantian liberal argument, China has not democratised.

Responses

Those are some of the challenges. There have been a variety of responses of widely varying purpose and consequence. The key question that faces us today is whether and how the liberal equilibrium can be renovated, reincorporating a combined prospect of peace, prosperity and self-government.

Protectionism

Polanyi called this the 'Crustacean' strategy – one that reinforced the hard shell of the nation state. It focuses on each nation protecting itself from globalisation. This is familiar to us. In the US, Ross Perot and Pat Buchanan made these kind of arguments; in France, Jose Bove (the anti-McDonald impresario); in Austria, Jorg Haider. Their themes are simple: 'globalisation is a threat to the cultural integrity and prosperity of many of us who are vulnerable, it is a threat to democracy, to our way of life. Let us build a thick shell'.

In a much more sophisticated version, this is the heart of claims made by the organisers at Seattle. Lori Wallach, the chief organiser of the wide coalition that disrupted the WTO meeting, described her alternative to current globalisation in this way: 'There would be a global regime of rules that more than anything create the political space for the kinds of value decisions that mechanisms like the WTO now make, at a level where people living with the results can hold decision makers accountable'.[15] Interdependence would then be made subject to the reach of democratic accountability at the local level. This could lead to effective global rules for interdependence, but it is more likely to build national 'shells'. Apart from national non-discrimination (national treatment) provisions, each country would make its own rules for environmental standards, intellectual property, child labour, wages and have a right to bar any import that did not reflect those standards.

These movements may create democratic control and they may be good for national solidarity, but they could be very bad for overall national prosperity, as nation retaliates against nation for each restriction it finds unjustifiable. A recent study by a group of economists who are associated with the EU estimates the possible benefits from the next Millennium Round of the WTO at $400 billion per year.[16] For many, whether rich or poor, that is too much extra world income to forego. If they are correct, there is a great deal to be lost if global trade suddenly starts closing down, or global investments start being drawn back.

National champions

A second strategy is also attractive to some. If protectionism is a 'crustacean' strategy, we can extend Polanyi's aquatic metaphor, bringing into view 'sea slug' strategies. The sea slug, a voracious and nondiscriminating eater, consumes anything that is smaller than itself. This is the strategy of *national champions*. The nation-state supports its own firms in order to compete to win more global sales and seeks to lure foreign firms, increasing shares of inward FDI for the national economy. The Clinton administration was very successful in persuading Saudi Arabia to buy just American aircraft, built by McDonnell/ Boeing, headquartered in Seattle. The large sale included both F-15s and passenger airliners. It was very popular in the American Northwest. Not so popular in France (which also engages in the same practice) where Airbus was seen to be just as good a plane. Why did the Europeans not get the sale to Saudi Arabia? Many speculate that the US security relationship with the Gulf, and particularly the protection offered against the ambitions of Saddam Hussein, had much to do with the business deal. But, that does not make the French or other Europeans happy. Nor were Americans pleased when Quaddafi gave the contract to build the Mediterranean pipeline from Libya solely to a European consortium.

To the extent that states try to foster national champions or subsidise inward FDI to attract capital and jobs, they produce similar behaviour by other countries. This may benefit international consumers. It may also lead to a 'race to the bottom' with fewer and fewer environmental and labour standards, or increased international conflicts, as short-term prosperity is again pitted against long-run democratic autonomy.

Democratic solidarity

Let us turn to a third strategy, 'democratic solidarity'. Here statesmen seek to extend the liberal *political* peace into an economic arrangement. Forget about the rest of the world, let us build a stronger WTO for the democracies, a democratic WTO. (Bill Antholis, recently of the National Security Council's economic staff, is writing a fascinating book on this topic.) Why not have a *democratic* WTO where we will solve our problems more easily than we would in a *global* WTO? If you look at the recent US trade bill extending 'most favoured nation' status to China and exempting it from annual reviews, one of the things that made it more difficult for the Administration to mobilise a Congressional majority is that China is regularly vulnerable to charges that it is threatening Taiwan with invasion and abusing its own nationals' human rights. If democracies limited their most extensive trade privileges to the area of fellow democracies, they would find progress toward further integration easier, or at least free from the baggage of political strife over human rights and security concerns. The problem, of course, is that such a 'democratic WTO' leaves China and other rapidly developing countries out. Excluding the potentially biggest, fastest growing economy in the world is not good for prosperity or for global co-operation on other issues. If you will pardon me for paraphrasing President Lyndon Johnson's apt reference to the higher logic of co-operating with an opponent, recall his words: 'Do you want him inside the tent pissing out, or outside the tent pissing in?' That is the China problem. If China is not part of the WTO, it is very likely to cause an immense amount of strife in the world political economy and be absent from important efforts to curb pollution or stabilise East Asian rivalry.

Disaggregated cooperation

The fourth response is the most pragmatic of the hopeful responses. It is 'disaggregated cooperation'. Proponents urge us to break down the problem. Let's let the multinational corporations (MNCs) deal with other MNCs and markets solve as many of the problems as they can. State bureaucracies will scramble to keep up, doing less than may be ideal but enough to avoid catastrophe. Genetically engineered food may be sold with less controversy if the United States labels organic food and then lets consumers buy it or not as they wish. US organic food exports, having been certified, could be sold in Europe. Consumers, not governments, will decide; hopefully, depoliticising the issue. Furthermore, courts will deal with courts, bureaucrats with bureaucrats, experts with experts. Take it out of politics and solve the problems pragmatically.[17]

Unfortunately, there are some problems that just are not pragmatic. For the environmental organisation that worked so hard to reform the Endangered Species Act in order to protect turtles, a turtle was not a technical question that they were willing to see negotiated away. It became a part of their own sense of identity, their own sense of moral worth, their sense of responsibility to the globe – not something that they would let the bureaucrats decide. And second, when things get tougher, that is when the world economy moves into the next recession, it will be more difficult to delegate to careful bureaucrats and their allegedly objective global criteria.

Global democratisation

Responding to the concerns noted above, some have begun to wonder, 'Don't we need some increased accountability, increased legitimacy, to contain and govern the practical negotiations among the experts? Don't we need to have norms that are more broadly shared, or even decisions that are legitimate because people across borders have participated in outlining their direction?'[18] We want expert pilots to fly the planes we ride in, but do we want them to choose our destinations?[19] We are thus concerned about the dangers of increasingly non-democratic control of key financial decisions.[20] For some it is now time for a global parliament or civic assembly, structured on the model of the European parliament in Strasbourg. That pillar of the burgeoning EU represents voters across Europe and operates through cross-national parties, not national delegations. Others hoped that the recent Millennium Assembly of the United Nations which provided a forum for non-governmental organisations (NGOs) from around the world, would take a first step in this direction.

Realistically, however, no strong version of global democracy is viable at the present time. We will not soon see global legislation deciding new regulatory standards for the global economy. Why not? Because global democracy is not about being willing to *win* democratically, it is about being willing to *lose* democratically. None of the popular advocates of increased democratisation, whether in Seattle or Strasbourg or New Delhi, are willing to lose an issue and accept it because it went through a democratic process. The world is simply too unequal and too diverse. To give an example, the top one-fifth of the countries have 74 times the income of the bottom one-fifth of the countries, and it is getting worse. That is more than double the greatest degree of inequality within the most unequal domestic economy, the Brazilian economy, where the ratio between the top fifth and the bottom fifth is 32 to 1. More than double the Brazilian ratio, and yet Brazil itself has found its democratic processes repeatedly subject to extra-constitutional pressures.

With respect to culture, moreover, the globe falls far short of the pre-conditions of ordinary democracy. India, the largest and one of the most linguistically diverse democracies, has 81 percent of its population describing itself as Hindu and an elite all of whom are fluent in English. That is a huge core of common identity that helps sustain the Indian democracy despite all of its diversity and internal dissension. There is no such core identity in the globe today. There is no single such identity (other than the thin identity of basic human dignity) to which 81 percent of the world will subscribe.

Our primitive political global condition is reflected in disputes about the very meaning of global democracy. Is the world more democratic when the majority of nations decide, when the most populous nations decide, when only democratic nations participate, or when the majority of the world's people decide? Unfortunately, there is as yet no agreed meaning of 'global democratisation'. Therefore, I suggest that we must be more moderate in our democratising ambitions. The role of global democratisation should be limited to helping to develop norms. Not legislation, but deliberation over norms will make the process of co-operation among the bureaucrats easier, more readily achievable, more legitimate, less contested. We must be very modest because norms do not do that much work, usually. What they do, however, is make it easier for national politicians and international bureaucrats to cut pragmatic deals. Therefore, global democratisation should be limited to endorsing measures such as those advocated in the Carlsson-Ramphal Commission, the *Global Neighbourhood* report.[21] In addition to sending diplomats to the annual meetings of the United Nations General Assembly, we should also send legislators. Every country can put five members in the General Assembly. At least two of them should be elected from the legislatures of their home countries. Bringing in the other branches of government, those somewhat more tied to the people, may help to begin to create a transmission belt between home and globe, fostering a more legitimate articulation of global standards at the international level. The hope is that these elected legislators will take the role seriously and participate actively in the annual general debate in the fall of each year and interject a sense of democratic legitimacy and accountability.

The second way to enhance global normative articulation is to bring in civil society. In 1955 there were fewer than 2,000 international NGOs; today there are more than 20,000.[22] None of them are genuinely democratic; their virtue is that they are voluntary and broad-based. But it is worth establishing an annual global forum that brings together representatives of global civil society, meeting the week before the General Assembly meets each year. NGOs would be invited from all over the world to discuss and issue recommendations about global standards for the environment, humanitarian intervention, international economic assistance and reforms of international institutions such as the IMF or the World Bank, or the United Nations itself.

Conclusion

These recommendations constitute far from a cure-all. Electing legislators from non-democratic legislatures to the UN does not enhance global democracy strikingly. Others will ask who elected the NGOs, for whom there is no internal process of democratic accountability to their members or to those whom their policies affect. But, merely that act of debating in a global forum about who is there legitimately and who is not – all in the same room, talking about global problems – will itself be a process which helps build global norms and gives more voice to those who will bear the consequences of globalisation. This is far short of democratic legitimation. In terms of democratic evolution, this represents much less than a modern equivalent of the meeting of the English barons at Runnymede in 1215, a cautious consultation far short of accountability. There will be mounting tension among prosperity, stability and accountability. Global interdependence will subject the liberal peace to increasing stress. But it can be the preliminary to increasingly responsible deliberation. And that may well be the best we can do in the world as it is today.

Notes

1. This chapter was originally published as:'A More Perfect Union? The Liberal Peace and the Challenge of Globalisation', *Review of International Studies*, 26(5) (2000) 81–94. A version of that article was delivered as 'The 2000 Welling Lecture' at George Washington University, on 9 March, 2000. I thank Monique Ramgoolie and Daniel H. Else for assistance. I am grateful for comments and discussion at a Millennium Seminar of GWU on 10 March, organised by Harry Harding, and for comments from William Antholis and Sophie Meunier.
2. Quoted from M. Khor, 'Take Care, the WTO Majority is Tired of Being Manipulated', *International Herald Tribune* (21 December 1999).
3. J. Hayward (ed.), *The Crisis of Representation in Europe* (Ilford: Frank Cass, 1995).
4. A similar debate engages the European Union. See, for example, W. Sandholtz and A. Stone (eds), *European Integration and Supranational Governance* (Oxford: Oxford University Press, 1998); J. Hayward (ed.), *The Crisis of Representation in Europe* (Ilford: Frank Cass, 1995); and R. Keohane and S. Hoffmann (eds), *The New European Community* (Boulder: Westview, 1991).
5. M. Walzer, 'Governing the Globe', *Dissent* (Fall 2000).
6. I contributed a two-part essay to the elaboration of Kant's proposition ('Kant, Liberal Legacies and Foreign Affairs'), *Philosophy and Public Affairs* (Summer and Fall 1983). The extensive debate is well presented in M. E. Brown *et al.* (ed.), *Debating the Democratic Peace* (Cambridge: MIT Press, 1996).
7. For a discussion of the features of interdependence see R. Keohane and J. Nye, *Power and Interdependence* (Boston: Little, Brown, 1977).
8. K. Polanyi, *The Great Transformation: The Political and Economic Origins of Our Time* (New York: Beacon Press, 1980), originally published in 1944.
9. The key theoretical contributions were made by Heckscher, Ohlin, Rybczynski, Stolper and Samuleson. For a non-technical survey, see J. Williamson, *The Open Economy and the World Economy* (New York: Basic Books, 1983), ch. 3.

10. See J. Ruggie, 'International Regimes, Transactions and Change: Embedded Liberalism in the Postwar Economic Order', *International Organization*, XXXVI (Spring 1982) 379–415.
11. P. Drucker, 'The Global Economy and the Nation State', *Foreign Affairs* (September/October 1997) 168 calls this 'transnational strategy'. M. Whitman, *New World, New Rules: The Changing Role of the American Corporation* (Cambridge: Harvard Business School, 1999) explores how American companies that were once stable, lumbering, globe-striding giants with paternalistic ties to their home communities have become lean, mean and footloose.
12. S. Meunier, 'Globalization and the French Exception', *Foreign Affairs*, LXXIX, 4 (July/August 2000).
13. Ambassador F. Aguirre-Sacassa, 'A Debt of Thanks to the World Bank', *Financial Times* (4 May 2000).
14. R. Gilpin, *The Challenge of Global Capitalism* (Princeton: Princeton University Press, 2000), p. 307. For global GDP comparisons, see T. Beg, 'Globalization, Development and Debt-Management', *The Balance* (Spring 2000), table 2, http://balanceddevelopment.org/articles/globalization.html
15. Foreign Policy (FP) Interview, 'Lori's War', *Foreign Policy*, CXIIX (Spring 2000) 34.
16. http://www.europa.eu.int/commm/trade/2000_round/ecowtomr.htm
17. See W. Reinicke, *Global Public Policy: Governing Without Government* (Washington, DC: Brookings, 1998) and A-M. Slaughter, 'The Real New World Order', *Foreign Affairs*, LXXVI, 5 (September/October 1997) 183–97.
18. A good introduction to this issue is in D. Archibugi and D. Held, *Cosmopolitan Democracy* (Cambridge: Polity, 1995). For further discussion of cosmopolitan individual rights and democratic governance, see T. Pogge, 'Creating Supra-National Institutions Democratically', *Journal of Political Philosophy*, V, 2 (June 1997) 163–82, and D. Thompson, 'Democratic Theory and Global Society', *Journal of Political Philosophy*, VII, 2 (June 1999) 1–15.
19. R. Dahl, *Democracy and Its Critics* (New Haven: Yale University Press, 1989), ch. 5.
20. S. Berman and K. McNamara, 'Bank on Democracy', *Foreign Affairs*, LXXVIII, 2 (March/April 1999) 2–8.
21. I. Carlsson and S. Ramphal, *Our Global Neighborhood: The Report of the Commission on Global Governance* (Geneva: The Commission on Global Governance, 1995), as seen online: http://www.cgg.ch/contents.htm
22. K. Annan, *We the Peoples: The Role of the United Nations in the 21st Century* (New York: UN, 2000), Figure 13, p. 70.

References

Aguirre-Sacassa, Ambassador F. 'A Debt of Thanks to the World Bank', *Financial Times* (4 May 2000).
Annan, K. *We the Peoples: The Role of the United Nations in the 21st Century* (New York: UN, 2000), Figure 13.
Archibugi, D. and D. Held, *Cosmopolitan Democracy* (Cambridge: Polity, 1995).
Beg, T. 'Globalization, Development and Debt-Management', *The Balance* (Spring 2000), table 2, online: http://balanceddevelopment.org/articles/globalization.html

Berman, S. and K. McNamara, 'Bank on Democracy', *Foreign Affairs*, LXXVIII, 2 (March/April 1999).

Brown, M. E. *et al.* (ed.), *Debating the Democratic Peace* (Cambridge: MIT Press, 1996).

Carlsson, I. and S. Ramphal, *Our Global Neighborhood: The Report of the Commission on Global Governance* (Geneva: The Commission on Global Governance, 1995), as seen at online: http://www.cgg.ch/contents.htm

Dahl, R. *Democracy and Its Critics* (New Haven: Yale University Press, 1989), ch. 5.

Doyle, M. 'Kant, Liberal Legacies and Foreign Affairs', *Philosophy and Public Affairs* (Summer and Fall, 1983).

Drucker, P. 'The Global Economy and the Nation State', *Foreign Affairs* (September/October 1997).

Foreign Policy (FP) Interview, 'Lori's War', *Foreign Policy* (CXIIX, Spring 2000).

Gilpin, R. *The Challenge of Global Capitalism* (Princeton: Princeton University Press, 2000).

Hayward, J. (ed.), *The Crisis of Representation in Europe* (Ilford: Frank Cass, 1995).

Keohane, R. and S. Hoffmann (eds), *The New European Community* (Boulder: Westview, 1991).

Keohane, R. and J. Nye, *Power and Interdependence* (Boston: Little, Brown, 1977).

Khor, M. 'Take Care, the WTO Majority is Tired of Being Manipulated', *International Herald Tribune* (21 December 1999).

Meunier, S. 'Globalization and the French Exception', *Foreign Affairs*, LXXIX, 4 (July/August 2000).

Pogge, T. 'Creating Supra-National Institutions Democratically', *Journal of Political Philosophy* (V, 2, June 1997).

Polanyi, K. *The Great Transformation: The Political and Economic Origins of Our Time* (New York: Beacon Press, 1980).

Reinicke, W. *Global Public Policy: Governing Without Government* (Washington, DC: Brookings, 1998).

Ruggie, J. 'International Regimes, Transactions and Change: Embedded Liberalism in the Postwar Economic Order', *International Organization* (XXXVI, Spring 1982).

Sandholtz, W. and A. Stone (eds), *European Integration and Supranational Governance* (Oxford: Oxford University Press, 1998).

Slaughter, A-M. 'The Real New World Order', *Foreign Affairs*, LXXVI, 5 (September/October 1997).

Thompson, D. 'Democratic Theory and Global Society', *Journal of Political Philosophy*, VII, 2 (June 1999).

Walzer, M. 'Governing the Globe', *Dissent* (Fall 2000).

Whitman, M. *New World, New Rules: The Changing Role of the American Corporation* (Cambridge: Harvard Business School, 1999).

Williamson, J. *The Open Economy and the World Economy* (New York: Basic Books, 1983).

Conclusion: Dimensions and Processes of Global Governance

John N. Clarke

Background

The various processes of globalisation are often treated as if inevitable, determined by technological change and capable of intentions and purpose independent of human control.[1] Our understanding of the nature of globalisation unavoidably informs our assessment of how it can be shaped, if at all. Nonetheless, today, many of the key challenges of globalisation are so diffuse that they are seemingly beyond the control of any one state. But as Frost and other contributors make clear, whether in terms of 'governmentality' as Lipschutz suggests, or governance, the key concern is management. Globalisation is clearly an empirical process, but one which a number of contributors recognise is accompanied by an ideological substructure described, for example, by Ward as 'globalism'. Others highlight the fact that states are neither weak nor endangered, but rather, deeply involved in the delegation of authority to supra-national institutions. As such, many emerging norms and institutions are increasingly constraining state decision making capacity. This, in turn, highlights a fundamental problem of accountability, that is, the disjunction between the increasing number of decisions that are of necessity taken at an international level and what remain primarily national systems of political accountability. The central premise of this volume is that globalisation can and must be shaped through the development of more effective global governance.

Two inter-related issues are examined in this concluding chapter. First, three separate dimensions of global governance, that is, normative, technical (scientific and social) and institutional are examined. Normative governance helps us define the type of international society we want to create, technical governance helps us realise that vision in practical terms and institutional governance helps ensure adequate means of implementing policy prescriptions. The second issue examined is the process through which governance evolves, becomes routinised/ institutionalised and, in an increasing number of cases, becomes legalised and legitimised. The aim, therefore, is to clarify several discrete processes of governance and to provide a preliminary conceptualisation which advances our understanding of the processes of governance, which can be tested empirically and developed further. While global governance clearly already exists in discrete areas, innovations in each of the three dimensions of governance will be needed to meet the ever increasing demands of globalisation. Taken together, these innovations could ultimately represent more than the sum of their individual parts and, writ large, may well come to resemble a social fabric through which the global system is governed.

Historically, the state has been forced to adapt to systemic dynamics of which globalisation is only the most recent, though undeniably the most complex.[2] Though globalisation's many challenges transcend Cold War decision making paradigms and state centric approaches to policy, states retain a central role, as aggregators of domestic political will, as authoritative decision-making entities internationally and in helping to maintain international order. They also remain primary ethical and social communities secured against outside interference by the principles of sovereignty and non-intervention.[3] As John Agnew points out in his chapter in this volume, there is a tension between states as the primary political and spatial organisations, and the increasingly variegated world of global policy challenges, that governments are ill-suited to manage and represent. A re-envisioning of how states might govern more effectively both, domestically and internationally is therefore required if the international system is to keep pace with the ever increasing demands of globalisation described in the introduction to this volume. Inevitably, this will require a closing of the growing disjunction between governments and citizens, and more inclusive policy-making processes that draw in the increasing number of non-state actors.

Since September 2001, policy makers have, unsurprisingly, focussed on the security dimensions of the aftermath of the attack on the World Trade Center. The horrific events of September 11th made it clear that the means of violence are now diffuse and accessible as never before.[4] This concluding chapter, however, does not deal directly with the terrorist issue. Instead, it focuses upon the array of transnational challenges such as the environment, that remain as, or perhaps more pressing than they were prior to September 11ᵗʰ 2001.

Three dimensions of governance

Though specific to their contexts and purposes, three inter-related dimensions of governance are examined below: normative, technical (scientific and social) and institutional.

Normative governance

Normative debate helps us understand what sort of international system we wish to create. This is a critical first step in clarifying the technical governance mechanisms which serve that vision, as well as creating or refining the institutions needed to implement these mechanisms. Normative governance consists of the assessment of that which 'ought' to be the case and the extent to which these norms (whether legalised or other) shape behaviour. In recent years, new norms have emerged and been strengthened in a manner that many would have thought inconceivable even a decade ago.[5] Human rights rhetoric and practice have a growing influence in international affairs, while the concept of human security has provided a growing focus for international policy initiatives as Hampson demonstrates in his contribution to this volume.[6]

The ability to define norms is an increasingly important means of influencing and shaping the international system. Not surprisingly, then, normative change is not simply an evolutionary reality, but an objective of policy-makers; for example, *The Responsibility to Protect: Report of The International Commission on Intervention and State Sovereignty* established by the Canadian government in September 2000 represents an attempt to reconfigure the international norms of sovereignty and intervention. The report emphasises the responsibilities that accrue to states as part of the more traditional norms of state sovereignty and non-intervention.[7] As Pastor recognises – a firm foundation of shared norms can contribute to stability in the system. As several examples discussed below suggest, the speed with which ideas are translated from purely normative principles into rules, policies and institutions embodying these norms is increasing. This is a theme examined in greater detail in Section III of this conclusion.

Technical governance (scientific and social)

Technical governance consists of arrangements at a bilateral, regional and global level. It is designed to solve practical policy challenges which have scientific and social dimensions; the former consist of managing the natural and man-made challenges of the physical world, the latter, deal with the means by which human beings create, regulate and institutionalise their relationships with each other. In both cases, the production of innovative ideas that bridge the gap between what we know and what we need to know, is central. Thomas Homer Dixon refers to this as closing the 'ingenuity gap', in order to provide necessary scientific innovation and systems for the effective management of social systems.[8] In many cases, social governance mechanisms represent a means of institutionalising and entrenching the gains realised through scientific research.

Scientific

As the pace of globalisation increases so too does the need for enhanced scientific innovation to deal with natural and man-made hazards. The transnational nature of many of these challenges means individual states are incapable of solving them unilaterally, for example, the various environmental stresses that accompany urbanisation, wasteful consumption, the build-up of greenhouse gases, the decline of marine fisheries, declining stocks of freshwater and deforestation, among others.[9] Institutions are already making efforts to deal with some of these challenges. For example, the United Nations Development Programme (UNDP) provided support to a variety of organisations engaged in research to develop new rice varieties. The result is 'NERICA' a grain that produces larger crop yields without fertiliser and which resists pests and encroachment by weeds.[10]

States continue to play a central role in addressing these challenges, albeit one which they increasingly share with a variety of non-state actors, including multinational enterprises and Non Governmental Organisations (NGOs).[11] *Médecins sans Frontières* (MSF), for example, is developing drugs for neglected diseases which 'do not constitute a valuable enough "market" to stimulate adequate R&D for new medicines by traditional drug developers.'[12] The initiative has led to a trisectoral partnership between NGOs, industry and governments.[13] Such partnerships are an increasingly influential means of mobilising expertise and generating momentum behind specific initiatives. Since the capacity for scientific innovation is unevenly distributed, ensuring the transfer of knowledge to those who most need it, will be critical and will require improved networking between scientists, institutions and governments.

Social

Social governance is the realm within which state and non-state actors order their relations at bilateral, regional and global levels. Examples include electoral assistance programs, the transplantation of legal principles and institutions,[14] ensuring security, combating corruption and various forms of development assistance. The European Union (EU), for example, funds an NGO that provides legal advice to a number of Missions to the United Nations (UN), via their Judicial Assistance Programme, which helps states with a nascent legal capacity participate more effectively in multilateral processes.[15] The inter-governmental organisation International Institute for Democracy and Electoral Assistance seeks to nurture and support sustainable democracy. It does so through a variety of programming, including, building the capacity to develop and strengthen democratic institutions, providing a forum for expert dialogue (academics, policy-makers and democracy practitioners), synthesising research and field experience and finally, developing practical policy tools.[16] In some cases, the regular functions of government have been assumed by international organisations, NGOs and in other cases, corporations, which support the construction of schools and hospitals. For example, in the late 1990s, the UN increasingly engaged in social governance activities, when the Security Council vested complete legislative and executive authority over the territories and peoples concerned, in the UN Missions, United Nations Transitional Administration for East Timor (UNTAET) and United Nations Interim Administration Mission in Kosovo (UNMIK) respectively. In turn, the Centre for Humanitarian Dialogue, an independent impartial organisation, works towards the resolution and mitigation of conflict by facilitating dialogue between belligerents.[17] Other NGOs have played a prominent role in shaping and enforcing policy initiatives.[18]

While these examples cited above are primarily social in nature, social mechanisms can also play a role in the implementation of scientific innovation. Take, for example, the Montreal Protocol on CFC emissions which sets the 'elimination' of ozone depleting substances as its final objective.[19] Industry had vital input into negotiations on ozone depletion which produced the Montreal Protocol through both the activities of individual chemical companies such as Du Pont and industry groups. Such chemical companies possessed financial and technical expertise that enabled them to develop the alternative chemicals that made progress in phasing out chlorofluorocarbons (CFCs) possible.[20] In this sense, scientific progress which reduced the cost incurred by states in meeting their targets made a social arrangement at a multilateral level possible. Similarly, the World Commission on Dams provides a good model for tri-sectoral partnerships which bridge the social and scientific elements of governance, and could be replicated in dealing with other similarly contentious issues. Its report demonstrates the need for a holistic approach which merges scientific analysis with social, environmental, cultural and political factors.[21] Finally, as Lipschutz argues in this volume, the Kyoto agreement seeks to regulate environmental damage through the creation of a market for the exchange of permits to pollute. Science is therefore 'less an independent input to global governance than an integral part of it: a human institution deeply engaged in the practice of ordering social and political worlds.'[22]

Global public policy networks such as these are playing an increasingly important role in developing both scientific and social governance.[23] However, the ideas generated still require viable, politically legitimate implementing institutions – whether in international fora or within states which retain a primary role in ensuring the legitimacy of the decision. But if globalisation continues at its current pace, an even greater focus on the resulting scientific and social governance challenges will be needed. This is a trend with budgetary and structural consequences at all levels and for a range of actors and institutions, including civil society, states and international organisations. The following section discusses the central role of institutions in delivering global governance.

Institutional governance

Institutions and policy innovation

The institutions which currently shape the global system still reflect the policy pre-occupations and political realities of the Cold War.[24] Effective governance therefore requires the transformation of existing institutions and where necessary, the development of new institutions that incorporate a diverse array of stakeholders.

As UN Secretary General Kofi Annan recognised:

'many challenges that we confront today are beyond the reach of any state to meet on its own. At the national level we must govern better, and at the international level we must learn to govern better together. Effective states are essential for both tasks, and their capacity for both needs strengthening. We must also adapt international institutions, through which states govern together, to the realities of the new era. We must form coalitions for change, often with partners well beyond the precincts of officialdom.'[25]

We have moved rapidly from a world dominated exclusively by states to a more complex system in which a variety of actors (states, citizens, international organisations, corporations and NGOs among others) interact in a multi-layered system shaped by a variety of norms and institutional arrangements. For example, the Ottawa process to ban anti-personnel landmines was built by a coalition of global NGOs, with political and institutional support from several states. This model was remarkable for its inclusive nature and for the leading role which small and medium sized states, particularly Canada played.

Multilateral institutions have already made efforts to make their activities more open and inclusive. The Security Council now consults on a more routine basis with civil society. For example, the International Committee of the Red Cross/Red Crescent addressed formal sessions of the Security Council for the first time ever – during the February 1999 and April 2000 debates on the Protection of Civilians in Armed Conflict.[26] The Security Council has also mobilised outside expertise in support of its work, commissioning expert reports on a variety of issues,[27] while 'think tanks' are also being engaged more systematically and more regularly.[28] In many cases, policy issues are now dealt with increasingly through global policy networks[29] – inclusive 'communities' which are particularly well suited to developing innovations in technical governance. These networks have three advantages: first, they involve experts in managing knowledge; second, they help overcome market and inter-governmental co-ordination failures; and thirdly, they broaden participation, lending wider credibility to the resulting policy prescriptions.[30] The Drugs for Neglected Diseases initiative (referred to above) attempts to mobilise and co-ordinate existing researchers, institutions and drug companies in a manner that maximises their output, while minimising the formal structure required for their co-operation.[31] Delivering effective global governance will therefore require a mutually supportive relationship between traditional institutions and global public policy networks which can help 'integrate incomplete knowledge with experimental action into programs of adaptive management and social learning.'[32] The results can then be translated into practical policy prescriptions.

Institutions and political processes

Institutions also serve as arenas for bargaining between interested parties/governments, reflecting the power realities in their structure and often, in the decisions they reach. Arguably, the most important of these is the Security Council, a body which serves as a fulcrum, enabling the powerful to build support for their preferred policy while also serving as a means through which the less powerful gain some, albeit limited, measure of influence over the powerful. Without the participation of the powerful in global institutions, or in the case of thematically oriented institutions, the key stakeholders, they become marginalised; without broad participation and multilateral sanction, the policy preferences of the powerful lose legitimacy.[33] Multilateral sanction can also enable governments to legitimise preferred outcomes in the eyes of domestic constituencies and legislatures. Great powers can place issues on the agenda of institutions, though they are often unable to dictate outcomes unilaterally. However, in helping create the institutional order following World War II, Ikenberry asserts that the US entered into an 'institutional bargain' through which it:

> spun a web of institutions that connected other states to an emerging American-dominated economic and security order. But in doing so, these institutions also bound the United States to other states and reduced – at least to some extent – Washington's ability to engage in the arbitrary and indiscriminate exercise of power. Call it an institutional bargain. The price for the United States was a reduction in Washington's policy autonomy, in that institutional rules and joint decision-making reduced U.S. unilateralist capacities. But what Washington got in return was worth the price. America's partners also had their autonomy constrained, but in return were able to operate in a world where U.S. power was more restrained and reliable.[34]

Institutions can serve as a means of entrenching international order. Power is therefore embedded in institutions that are often neither apolitical nor neutral in their development or operation. As such, it is perhaps not surprising that for some, globalisation and the institutions that shape it are viewed as tantamount to westernisation, marketisation and even Americanisation. Their purpose, in this view, is simply to create and entrench an international order that disproportionately benefits wealthy, developed countries.[35] Already, developing states are lobbying for enhanced representation on the Security Council.[36] As noted earlier, a key question is 'whether the council can meet the unprecedented current and future challenges while structured essentially as it was 50 years ago and following procedures that, aside from increased reliance on informal consultations have remained remarkably unchanged.'[37] There is, in short, pressure for greater inclusion and representation within political and policy-making bodies.

Though the growing disparity in wealth between states is undeniable, an exclusively economic reading of globalisation inevitably underplays many other areas where globalisation is having positive and negative effects. It is, however, undeniable that a democratic deficit exists in terms of both the participation and influence of many developing countries in international policy-making processes (see Michael Doyle's chapter in this volume). The following section examines this growing sense of disenfranchisement.

Globalisation and disenfranchisement

The challenges of globalisation make it increasingly important that the rules and institutions developed to ensure adequate governance must be and as importantly, must be seen to be fair and legitimate. International co-operation will be of central importance in, for example, curbing fundraising for terrorist organisations. Combating the arguably growing sense of disenfranchisement will be critical to enhancing the international co-operation that will be necessary to deal effectively with new challenges. There is, first, a need to involve less powerful states (some of which feel that they have lost their ability to shape the international system) and second, to enhance civil society participation in the processes of global governance. The following sections examine these two inter-related issues.

Enhancing state participation

Though political interests and processes will inevitably come into play, the mechanisms for governance must, to the greatest extent possible, be perceived as legitimate by a geographically diverse group of states. Smaller states and middle powers have successfully cooperated in coalitions to develop shared policies through new channels of influence. An example is the joint Canadian/Norwegian initiative to create a human security network – a coalition of willing states focussed on the human security agenda.[38]

Members of the G-77, however, increasingly see themselves as norm takers, not norm shapers, a trend which has and will likely continue to compromise global governance.[39] This has led to a certain degree of reluctance on the part of some members of the G-77 to 'undermine' state sovereignty and non-intervention.[40] The effective inclusion of this group in policy-making processes is not only an ethical requirement, if a more democratic process of governance is sought, but it is also a practical requirement as the transnational nature of many policy challenges places a premium on broad participation in legal and other regimes. In recent years, they have sometimes contributed to the collapse of multilateral processes where they have seen their concerns as not being adequately met. This need for global participation provides many less powerful states with enhanced bargaining power if and when they strengthen their position through collective action. Coalitions of less powerful countries could increasingly shape certain global policy-making processes.

Given the complexity and ramifications of these multilateral processes, states unable to participate effectively in international fora must be given the means to do so and also to ensure the implementation of international agreements to which they accede.[41] The increasing interdependence between domestic and international spheres requires that the gap between international and domestic decision making processes be closed. Effective governance therefore depends on improving collaboration between departments and agencies that have previously operated in relative isolation from each other. Foreign ministries, for example, cannot deal effectively with the spread of infectious disease unless the ministry responsible for health is directly involved in international policy-making processes.[42] Global policy-making must therefore be reflexive – from the intra-national to the inter-national spheres and vice versa.

Enhancing civil society participation

The impact of globalisation within states underscores the need to improve levels of domestic participation in the policy-making process. Globalisation '... exposes the limits of the democratic structures which are most familiar, namely the structures of parliamentary democracy. We need to further democratise institutions, and to do so in ways that respond to the demands of the global age.'[43] As Michael Doyle argues in this volume, one remedy for the democratic deficit at the international level is involving civil society more directly in decision-making and involving legislators more directly in the United Nations General Assembly. The Organisation of American States (OAS), for example, involves parliamentarians directly in policy development through the Inter-Parliamentary Forum of the Americas,[44] while globally, the Inter-Parliamentary Union already provides a forum for interaction among national parliaments.[45]

Though international co-operation remains primarily an inter-governmental process, the examples of the International Campaign to

266 Global Governance in the Twenty-first Century

Ban Landmines (ICBL) and the International Criminal Court (ICC) underscore the increasingly prominent role that civil society is already playing in decision making and policy development. Involving civil society can help sharpen the analysis of problems within traditional fora, provide a clear sense of the real world effect of decisions taken and hold institutions and states publicly accountable when their actions are inconsistent with their rhetorical position. For some, a greater inclusiveness at the intra-national level, and a greater openness in terms of information sources and participation at the policy formulation stage has been considered vital. Others, though, go so far as to suggest 'incorporating NGOs on official delegations, giving them access to negotiation fora as participants, and accrediting them not as individual NGOs but as international coalitions.'[46]

The inclusion of civil society representatives in interstate decision-making processes might well prove to be a necessity if decisions are to be perceived as legitimate and a popular political disengagement in Western Societies is to be slowed if not halted. Tri-sectoral partnerships between civil society, governments and businesses are increasingly common. A further expansion of this trend seems likely, though the process and results achieved may not in future be as startling as those of the ICBL or the ICC. Ethically and practically, there is a need to enhance inclusive policy processes which enjoy the widest legitimacy possible. The question is therefore how to harness the potential contribution of civil society most effectively.

Reconciling the three dimensions of global governance

In summary, the international community must work to develop and clarify normative principles and in certain cases, codify them in law. These principles define the environment within which political bargaining takes place and therefore, the types and levels of technical and social governance that are possible. An increasingly diverse array of actors have become involved in policy research and development that is translated into realistic social and scientific governance measures. Political will underpins the commitment to ideas and institutions that will respond to the diverse policy challenges of global governance. Institutions are central to this process as the conduits for both domestic and international political legitimacy and as mechanisms for the implementation of normative principles and technical policy. For example, the issue of international migration has a normative component in so far as people, whether asylum seekers or economic migrants suffer from sometimes repressive political or economic practices; protocols, systems and social governance innovations are necessary to develop practices in the shared interests of states and finally, consideration should be given to developing an institutional architecture that will deal with the challenge.[47] As this example illustrates, and as Fen Hampson argues, any of these policy issues pose direct challenges to traditional Westphalian norms such as sovereignty and non-intervention.

How, then, do norms and mechanisms become part of the social fabric that defines the international system? One of the most important forms of institutional governance is legalisation – a process that is linked to recent normative and political trends.

Evolution and legalisation of governance

Governance mechanisms are often created and entrenched through legal principles and regimes. The following section presents two key issues in matrix form: the level and type of codification of a governance arrangement and the nature of the codification, that is, moral covenants and interest based contracts.[48] This matrix is then modified to incorporate two elements that recur in both this volume and elsewhere: first, a normative level of pre-legal development and second the inclusion of principles that are in the shared interests of states, as an intervening level between covenants and contracts. The result is a three by three matrix on which the various types of governance arrangements can be located. Specific agreements and arrangements are then added in order to illustrate how they might fit.

Legal arrangements can be defined according to three criteria: obligation, precision and delegation, each of which can be assessed from low to high levels, enabling categorisation along a continuum from soft to hard codification.[49] High **obligation** means states are legally bound by rules or commitments and therefore subject to the general rules and procedures of international law. High **precision** means that the rules are definite, unambiguously defining the conduct they require, authorise or proscribe. Finally, a high level of **delegation** is characterised by the granting of authority to third parties for the implementation of rules including their interpretation and application, dispute settlement, and possibly further rule making. Though these are independent, and each remains a matter of degree, these three criteria represent the means of assessing the 'hardness' of codification. Hard law consists of binding obligations that are precise, or can be made so, through adjudication or the issuance of detailed regulations that delegate authority for interpreting and implementing the law, thereby restricting actors' behaviour and sovereignty. In turn, soft legal arrangements are weaker than hard law in either their level of obligation, precision or delegation.[50]

Legal agreements are also described according to the extent to which they embody ethical principles (covenants) or self-interest (contracts). Covenants and contracts are not mutually exclusive, but rather legal principles often contain elements of each in varying degrees.[51] For example, the principles of state sovereignty and non-intervention protect states from outside interference (in principle, maintaining the possible flourishing of plural conceptions of the good), help order international relations and also serve the interests of individual governments. It is possible to show these two axes on a two by two matrix (Table 1). Moving from left to right on the horizontal axis, legal arrangements harden (as measured through obligation, precision and delegation). On the vertical axis, legal arrangements embody an increasing level of interests. While the use of a matrix suggests rigid categorisation, it is more useful to think of each axis as a continuum.[52]

Table 2 adds two additional elements to this matrix – agreements that are in the shared interests of states (in some cases, termed Global Public Goods) and purely normative principles, already examined in section II of this concluding chapter.[53] Normative principles are added in the first column, representing pre-legal, non-codified principles while shared interests are added in the middle row of the matrix.[54] Given the transnational scope of globalisation, many pressing problems will increasingly fall into this category, for example, the protection of the environment.

Table 1   The process of legalisation

		Increasing 'hardness' →	
Increasing level of interests ↓		Soft (measured in terms of the three dimensions)	Hard (measured in terms of the three dimensions)
	Covenant (ethically based)		
	Contract (interest based)		

Table 2 Development and legalisation of governance with illustrative examples

→ Increasing 'hardness' →

Increasing level of interests ↓

Category	Normative	Soft	Hard
Ethical (Covenant when legalised)	International Campaign to Ban Landmines Corporate social responsibility	Ottawa Convention ICC Sovereignty (plural conceptions of the good, self-determination) Optional protocol on war-affected children	Ottawa Convention (once hardened) European Convention for the Protection of Human Rights and Fundamental Freedoms[62] Universal Declaration on Human Rights
Shared interest (global public good)	Multi-lateral evaluation mechanism (Organisation of American States)	Kyoto protocol Kimberley process of certification Non-Proliferation Treaty[63]	Convention on the Suppression of Terrorist Fundraising Principles of Sovereignty/ Non-intervention
Interest based (Contract when legalised)	Balance of power	World Bank Guidelines[64]	Investment Treaties and Agreements World Trade Organisation

In many cases, norms derive their force from informal sanction and/or shared understanding, a process that is logically prior to codification in legal form, but which shapes behaviour nonetheless. As legal scholar Philip Allott has argued elsewhere, law is the fundamental institution for transmitting theory into regularised behaviour.[55] Legalisation helps mediate and codify interests in areas where predictability is important and advantageous, but it also introduces normative principles into law, albeit 'soft' law, in many cases. Soft law can, however, serve as an intermediary step towards harder codification, creating influential mechanisms and an acceptable middle ground in cases where actors are unwilling or unable to commit to harder codification.

Purely normative arrangements include informal understandings between actors: for example, the ICBL before it was codified in first soft and increasingly hard form (Table 2).[56] Even where normative principles are not codified they can influence the behaviour of actors: for example, realist international relations theory has influenced international decision-making and behaviour in profound ways.

The first row of Table 2 includes pure covenants, or agreements that are primarily of an ethical nature. The second row of shared interests represents a combination of areas which both embody ethical principles but which also serve the interests of states, particularly where unilateral action would fail to achieve a desired outcome. This category encompasses what have often been described as global public goods embodying elements of both pure covenants and pure contracts.[57] Finally, the category 'contracts', which embody purely self-interested arrangements are shown in the third row. As in Table 1, the hardness of codification increases as one reads from left to right on the horizontal axis, while on the vertical axis, the level to which the codification is based on interests increases as one reads down the vertical axis.[58] Each box provides illustrations of the form of agreement only and does not make reference to the specific issues being codified explicitly.

Table 2 adds specific examples to the matrix. Disagreements as to where a particular treaty, principle or instrument should be located are inevitable. Indeed, this matrix does not aim for rigid categorisation, but rather, represents a working depiction for further testing and research. The categories outlined here are far from rigid. Human rights, for example, are seen by many as a universal moral principle (suggesting legal instruments are covenants), but they can also be viewed as an integral part of the post-Cold War order which privileges the position of the United States.[59] These very different views suggest competing conceptions of human rights as moral principle and/or self-interested principles. To provide a number of additional illustrative examples:

- the Non-Proliferation Treaty represents both a shared interest in that it reduces the possibility of conflict, but it is also in the interests of states that already possess nuclear weapons as it 'freezes' their superiority in that key strategic area;
- the Kyoto Protocol[60] is viewed by some as denying the means of industrial progress to 'have not' states;
- some argue that the World Trade Organisation (WTO) is in fact a vehicle for a new form of neo-colonial repression and finally,
- sovereignty has both a normative and an interest based dimension to it.

In short, interpretation as to where these agreements and issues sit on this matrix is a matter of substantive debate; the point, however, is that even these diverse interpretations can be located on this matrix.[61]

The concept of delegation denotes the extent to which a legal measure assigns responsibility (formal terms of the text and the rule it embodies) to third parties – it is a reflection of the way in which the legal instrument is constructed. In contrast, enforcement relates not to the legal delegation of authority, but rather, the extent to which a rule is **actually** enforced when violated. It is, for example, possible to have agreements 'on the books' with a high level of delegation for which there is little or no political will to enforce its provisions.

The increasingly rapid codification of normative principles

Non-binding, soft legal instruments can have a substantial international and domestic impact. For example, though the Universal Declaration is explicitly aspirational in its description of human rights, it is generally thought to have 'ripened over the past five decades into customary international law binding upon all states.'[65] Human rights norms have also been institutionalised, for example, in the Commission on Human Rights and strengthened through, for example, the creation of the European Court of Human Rights (ECHR). In this manner, the normative principles of human rights have hardened and now play an increasingly important role in international relations.[66]

Over the past decade, the transition from purely normative arrangements to soft and in some cases, hard codification has become increasingly rapid. As noted earlier, the landmines ban, for example, began as an ethically driven campaign, and moved rapidly to codification in the Ottawa Treaty and subsequent ratifications. With each additional signature and ratification, the norms it codifies harden further (Table 2). Three illustrative examples are examined briefly below: conflict diamonds, sanctions and the Kimberley process, the development of the ICC and the ICBL.

Conflict diamonds, sanctions and the Kimberley process

Civil conflict is correlated with the presence of natural resources, suggesting that the possible wealth, which accrues from extraction, can motivate belligerents to seize control of resource rich areas by force. In addition, natural resources can provide a ready source of funding for sustaining conflict. Whether fuelled by greed or grievance, resources provide a viable means of financing conflict, and amassing individual wealth.[67] Diamonds, for example, can be easily transported and have fuelled conflict in both Sierra Leone and Angola among other countries and have proven particularly difficult to control. The UN has responded in a number of specific cases – for example, in 1998 the Security Council imposed sanctions prohibiting the import of rough diamonds from Angola, Sierra Leone, and Liberia (a transhipment point for diamonds from Sierra Leone).

For Kim Richard Nossal, this response demonstrates 'the importance of the ability to transform norms as a feature of innovation and leadership in global governance.'[68] One of the keys to the success of Angolan sanctions was the ability of Canadian Ambassador Bob Fowler and his allies in other governments and the NGO community (particularly Global Witness) to transform the legitimacy of the global diamond trade. In the first instance, this involved tainting diamonds from conflict areas. 'This reconstruction of diamonds as a product with a possible negative taint had a powerful impact on the global diamond market, creating fears that diamonds could go the way of fur and tobacco as products increasingly reviled in the market-place. This prompted key players in the global diamond industry to alter their attitudes towards diamonds from conflict areas, and change much of their market behaviour.'[69]

The international community has since developed a more holistic approach through the Kimberley Process which creates a 'chain of warranties' intended to provide an audit trail linking each diamond to its mine of origin. Chaired by South Africa, it includes 44 countries that produce, process, import and export rough diamonds (accounting for 98 percent of the global trade in and production of rough diamonds).[70]

International Criminal Court

From 1995–1998, a like minded group of approximately 60 countries pushed for progress towards the creation of an International Criminal Court (ICC), with a core group developing a draft treaty. At its heart, this agenda was developed by traditional middle powers, including the Nordic countries, Australia, New Zealand and Canada, countries that provided the driving force behind the Rome statute of 17 July 1998, which has given birth to the first permanent international enforcement mechanism in the evolution of the humanitarian law regime. The ICC provides a venue for addressing violations of the most significant international crimes: genocide, crimes against humanity and war crimes. It therefore has the potential to make these into instrumental norms, 'that is, norms that not only reflect social expectations (intrinsic norms) but also encourage compliance through repeated and consistent application.'[71] Some have gone so far as to suggest that '…the very basis of the prevailing global normative order has been modified by the content of the statute and by some of the diplomatic practices that gave birth to it.'[72] Though some might argue that this overstates the case, it is clear that the ICC has the potential to change the normative order and moreover provide a means for compelling adherence to international criminal law, thereby entrenching it.

International campaign to ban landmines

In some measure, the widespread appeal and perhaps even success of the landmines campaign to ensure a rapid shift from the normative level to codification resulted from the fact that the issues codified involved (at some level) simple moral/political questions around which the public could coalesce in a shared conviction that their own governments need to take responsibility for change.[73]

As with both the ICC and the issue of conflict diamonds, the campaign both sought a normative shift and built upon it: 'By reframing the terms of the debate on AP [anti-personnel] mines from an arms control to a humanitarian issue, the ban advocates shifted the focus from military security to human security. The public was encouraged to think of AP mines not in terms of disarmament but as an obstacle to development, a hindrance to humanitarian relief, a form of pollution, and, above all, a source of widespread human suffering.'[74] NGOs were able to recast the problem in human terms, create evocative symbols and messages that were conveniently adapted to media and communications technology, and build the climate of public opinion that made policy change both possible and politically attractive to governments.[75] The attempt to create a norm was central to Canada's efforts in this area: 'when Lloyd Axworthy announced his challenge in October 1996, the principle concern was not *how many* states would sign the treaty in the initial stage but rather, the need to establish a *clear, new norm*. The Ottawa Process was based on the premise that universality would not be the enemy of the good. The force of public opinion would be the engine to move the landmine norm towards universal adherence.'[76]

As such, a combination of likeminded small and middle sized states and mine-affected states from the South worked in partnership with transnational social movements and NGOs in particular. Indeed, the 'combination of forces created a larger normative environment which non-signatories and the non-compliant could not ignore.'[77] The pace of progress was unparalleled – the Ottawa treaty represents the fastest multilateral disarmament treaty ever to enter into force.

It is, as yet, too early to determine whether the processes and results which characterised these three initiatives – the ICC, the Kimberley Process and the ICBL – will continue as a fundamental trend in international policy making processes. Still nascent normative issues which could in future be susceptible to a similar process include the small arms trade and the development of corporate codes of conduct.

Conclusion

Existing mechanisms and approaches have proven inadequate in dealing with many of globalisation's most pressing challenges. At the moment, global governance emerges in a somewhat haphazard form in discrete issue areas. What is needed is a renewed normative vision of how governance should operate, institutions that reflect and foster this vision and a greater emphasis on the technical 'knowledge' in areas where it is most likely to mitigate against the downside of globalisation.

In its most ambitious and forward looking form, global governance seeks to create an international social fabric, albeit decentralised, ill woven and uneven, driven on an issue by issue basis, but cumulatively amounting to more than the sum of its parts. It is not exclusively a moral fabric as much of the existing international system has and will continue to codify norms, because they are in the interests of states in various groupings and in particular, the powerful. It has a legal basis, in that international law codifies many of the norms that evolved between states. However, it is also an arena of proactive norm creation in which single issue campaigns, the land mines campaign, the ICC and attempts to deal with blood diamonds have shifted rapidly from a purely normative level to soft and increasingly hard codification.

Notes

1. The comments and opinions expressed in this chapter are those of the author and not the United Nations.
2. As Martin Van Creveld argues, states are 'merely one of the forms which, historically speaking the organisation of government has assumed, and which, accordingly need not be considered eternal and self-evident any more than were previous ones.' M. Van Creveld, *The Rise and Decline of the State* (Cambridge: Cambridge University Press, 1999), p. 415.
3. G. Jusdanis, *The Necessary Nation* (Princeton: Princeton University Press, 2001), p. 13.
4. 'The clearest conclusion to emerge from the events of September 11 is that the geographical position and the military power of the US are no longer sufficient to ensure its security.' J. L. Gaddis, 'And Now This: Lessons from the Old Era for the New one', in S. Talbott and N. Chanda (eds), *The Age of Terror* (New York: Basic Books, 2001), p. 6.
5. For a recent study of how ethical arguments influence policy, see N. C. Crawford, *Argument and Change in World Politics: Ethics, Decolonisation and Humanitarian Intervention* (Cambridge: CUP, 2002).
6. As Ken Booth has previously argued: 'the major task for the post-Cold War era is preeminently that of developing ideas about global governance that will recapture a sense of the future and of a concept of progress in the interests of human needs, world community and environmental sustainability.' (K. Booth, 'Conclusion: security within global transformation?', *Statecraft and Security: the Cold War and Beyond* (Cambridge: CUP, 1998), p. 345).
7. The report not only emphasises the responsibility of states to protect their own citizens but outlines a set of 'core' principles, including conditions under which military intervention is justified. After examining the various legal, moral, operational and political questions related to this debate the Commission focused on the central theme of the 'responsibility to protect', the view that sovereign states have a responsibility to protect their own citizens, but that when they are either unable or unwilling to do so, this responsibility is then borne by the broader community of states. *The Responsibility to Protect: Report of the International Commission on Intervention and State Sovereignty* (Ottawa, Canada: IDRC, December 2001), p. viii.
8. See: T. Homer-Dixon, 'The Ingenuity Gap: Can Poor Countries Adapt to Resource Scarcity?', *Population and Development Review,* 21, No. 3 (1995), 587–612. For a discussion of international technical cooperation in a development context, see: A. P. Bravo and I. Sierra, *Contemporary Trends in International Technical Cooperation* (Mexico: Mexican Institute for International Cooperation, 1999). In particular, see Chapter 6, 'Relevant Documents on

International Development Cooperation' wherein the following documents are reprinted: 'Shaping the 21st Century: The Contribution of Development Cooperation' (approved by the Development Assistance Committee (DAC) of the Organization for Economical Development and Cooperation (OECD)); 'Buenos Aires Plan of Action for Promoting and Implementing Technical Co-operation among Developing Countries' (United Nations Conference on Technical Co-operation among Developing Countries) and, 'OAS: Strategic Plan for Partnership for Development 1997–2001'.

9. For a survey of a range of these and other similar stresses, see the volume prepared by the US National Research Council, *Our Common Journey: a Transition Toward Sustainability*, which seeks to 'reinvigorate the essential strategic connections between scientific research, technological development, and societies' efforts to achieve environmentally sustainable improvements in human well-being.' (National Research Council, *Our Common Journey: a Transition Toward Sustainability* (Washington, DC: National Academy Press, 1999), p. 2). The report stresses the short term horizon for dealing with questions of sustainability: '... over the next two generations ... serious progress in a transition toward sustainability will need to take place if interactions between the earth's human population and life support systems are not to significantly damage both.' (p. 3). A variety of other efforts in this vein exist. The growing importance of the scientific challenges to global governance have witnessed responses, such as through the Club of Rome, an interdisciplinary group of scientists, which issues reports on a variety of subjects, including economic, social and environmental challenges. Similarly, the 1987 World Commission on Environment and Development (the Bruntland Commission) emphasised the political, economic, social and ecological conditions for sustainable development. As societies become more complex, these technical elements will increase in importance, creating an additional source of competition, but also a new locus of political leverage.

10. United Nations Development Programme, *2002 Annual Report* (New York: Communications Office, Office of the Administrator, 2003), p. 13.

11. In 1955 there were fewer than 2,000 international non-governmental organisations; today there are more than 20,000 (K. Annan, *We the Peoples: The Role of the United Nations in the 21st Century* (New York: UN, 2000), Figure 13, p. 70).

12. The DNDi Task Force, 'Towards a New Paradigm: The Drugs for Neglected Diseases Initiative (DNDi)', Concept and preliminary proposal (February 2002). Available at: http://www.neglecteddiseases.org/thedndwg.shtml, p. 228.

13. This is particularly noteworthy as until recently, NGOs were depicted as demagogic, industry was vilified, and governments were thought inactive – a characterisation provided by Michel de Rosen (from the biotech company, ViroPharma). See: K. Nelson, 'Stimulating Research in the Most Neglected Diseases', *The Lancet* (23 March 2002).

14. For a discussion of this idea and a series of hypotheses to be tested, see: F. Schauer, 'The Politics and Incentives of Legal Transplantation', in J. S. Nye and J. D. Donahue (eds), *Governance in a Globalising World* (Washington: Brookings Institution Press, 2000), pp. 253–268.

15. This program initially seconded legal advisors to government delegations that required expert assistance during the International Criminal Court Preparatory Commission sessions and more recently, directly to Government Missions to the United Nations. In some cases lawyers are seconded to work in capitals, drafting implementing legislation for the ICC and other issues related to international human rights law. In providing advisors to government delegations, the aim is to even out the playing field between delegations with a great deal of expertise and those that could only afford to send a few people to the Rome conference. No Peace Without Justice can be found at: http://www.npwj.org/index.php and receives contributions from the European Union (http://europa.eu.int) and the Open Society Institute (http://www.soros.org/osi).

16. IDEA currently has 21 member states and four associate members (International Press Institute, Parliamentarians for Global Action, the Inter-American Institute for Human Rights and Transparency International (http://www.idea.int/). IDEA is currently working in Guatemala, Burkina Faso, Nigeria, Bosnia and Herzegovina, Slovakia, Burma/Myanmar, Indonesia and Nepal, among others.

17. The Centre has been supported at various times by the governments of Denmark, the Netherlands, Norway, Sweden, Switzerland, the United Kingdom and the United States of America. See: http://www.hdcentre.org

18. 'Non-governmental organizations (NGOs), in particular, have emerged as important allies in efforts to render the sanctions effective. Global Witness and Human Rights Watch were among the NGOs that have provided vital and very valuable assistance.' See: R. Fowler and D. Angell, 'Angola Sanctions', in R. McRae and D. Hubert (eds), *Human Security and the New Diplomacy* (Montreal & Kingston: McGill-Queen's University Press, 2001), p. 192.

19. The protocol was agreed upon on 16 September 1987 and entered into force on 1 January 1989, when 29 countries and the EEC (representing approximately 82 percent of world consumption) ratified it.

20. B. Hocking and D. Kelly, 'Doing the Business? The International Chamber of Commerce, the United Nations and the Global Compact', in A. F. Cooper, J. English, and R. Thakur (eds), *Enhancing Global Governance: Towards a New Diplomacy?* (Tokyo: United Nations University Press, 2002), p. 208.

21. *Human Development Report 2002: Deepening democracy in a fragmented world* (New York: Oxford University Press, 2002), Box 5.3, p. 109.

22. C. A. Miller and P. N. Edwards, *Changing the Atmosphere: Expert Knowledge and Environmental Governance* (Cambridge, Massachussetts: MIT Press, 2001), p. 5.

23. 'Surveys by the World Bank in 1999 identified some 50 different global public policy networks, ranging in focus from crime to fisheries and public health. From the World Commission on Dams to the Roll Back Malaria initiative, these mostly new groupings thrive in a borderless environment and capitalise on technological innovation, the very conditions that hamper policy-makers in traditional institutions. Perhaps most importantly, global public policy networks give once ignored groups from civil society a greater voice, thus narrowing the participatory gap and 'democratic deficit' for which international decision-making is often criticised. Although their

objectives and budgets are still relatively modest, their record of success holds the promise not only of untangling a knot of global problems, but of improving the principles and methods of global governance. See: W. H. Reinicke, 'The Other World Wide Web: Global Public Policy Networks', *Foreign Policy*, No. 117 (Winter 1999–2000) pp. 44–45. See also, D. Stone (ed.), *Banking on Knowledge: The Genesis of the Global Development Network* (London: Routledge, 2000) and D. Stone, *Capturing the Political Imagination: Think Tanks and the Policy Process* (London: Frank Cass, 1996).

24. A lively debate exists, for example, on the related questions of expanding the Security Council's membership and also the elimination of the veto. Pressure to make the Security Council more accountable and transparent has also increased, particularly as a result of pressure from Australia, Canada and Sweden (*Human Development Report 2002: Deepening democracy in a fragmented world* (New York: Oxford University Press, 2002), Box 5.6, p. 120).

25. K. Annan, *We the Peoples: The role of the United Nations in the 21st Century* (New York: United Nations, 2000), pp. 6–7.

26. E. Golberg and D. Hubert, 'The Security Council and the Protection of Civilians', in McRae and Hubert (eds), *Human Security and the New Diplomacy*, p. 229.

27. Expert input into the policy-making process is sometimes even more direct. The Security Council has made increasing use of expert studies, for example, Security Council Resolutions 1229 (26 February 1999) and 1237 (7 May 1999) resulted in the creation of an expert panel on sanctions on Angola. A similar report has also recently been released on the DRC, while Canada commissioned a study on sanctions, which it issued during its presidency of the Security Council. Its findings can be found in: D. Cortright and G. A. Lopez, *The Sanctions Decade: Assessing UN Strategies in the 1990s* (Boulder, Colorado: Lynne Rienner Publishers Inc., 2000).

28. For example, the International Peace Academy (see: http://www.ipacademy.org/) and the Conflict Prevention and Peace Forum (see: http://www.ssrc.org/programs/conflictprev/) work with both member states and the UN bureaucracy.

29. As the Secretary General has noted, global policy networks 'or coalitions for change – bring together international institutions, civil society and private sector organizations, and national governments, in pursuit of common goals.' (Kofi Annan, *We the Peoples*, p. 70).

30. W. H. Reinicke, 'The Other World Wide Web: Global Public Policy Networks', p. 47.

31. D. Butler, 'MSF Plans Public Sector Drug Development Initiative for Neglected Diseases', *Nature*, 416 (14 April 2002), p. 465.

32. National Research Council, *Our Common Journey: a Transition Toward Sustainability* (Washington, DC: National Academy Press, 1999), p. 10.

33. The same argument applies to issue specific institutions/arrangements which are all but useless without the participation of key stakeholders.

34. G. J. Ikenberry, 'Getting Hegemony Right', *The National Interest*, Number 63 (Spring 2001) p. 22.

35. See J. A. Scholte, *Globalization: A Critical Introduction* (New York: Palgrave, 2000). For a collection of diverse views critical of globalisation, see:

'Globalisation: a focus', *World Affairs: The Journal of International Issues*, Vol. 6, No. 2 (April–June 2002).
36. W. A. Knight, 'The Future of the UN Security Council: Questions of legitimacy and representation in multilateral governance', in Cooper *et al.*, *Enhancing Global Governance*, p. 25.
37. B. Russett, B. O'Neil and J. Sutterlin, 'Breaking the Security Council Logjam', *Global Governance*, 2, No. 1 (January–April 1996) p. 67 as cited in W. A. Knight, 'The future of the UN Security Council: Questions of legitimacy and representation in multilateral governance', in Cooper *et al.*, *Enhancing Global Governance*, p. 30.
38. The network had its genesis in the close relationship that developed between Canada and Norway during the negotiation of the Ottawa Convention. The network also provides a venue through which states can 'tap into' transnational NGO expertise (See: M. Small, 'The Human Security Network' in McRae and Hubert (eds), *Human Security and the New Diplomacy*, p. 235).
39. S. Tharoor and S. Daws, 'Humanitarian Intervention', *World Policy Journal*, Volume XVIII, No. 2 (Summer 2001) 25.
40. For a version of this argument in the context of the norms of humanitarian intervention, please see: J. N. Clarke, 'Revisiting the New Interventionism', *Peace Review*, Vol. 14, No. 1 (March 2002) 93–100.
41. This is already underway in some areas, for example, in the Judicial Assistance Program discussed above, as well as a range of technical assistance mechanisms intended to ensure ratification of the Rome Statute.
42. Domestic bureaucratic processes whereby departments work together to arrive at common positions must also be refined and, to reverse the chain, to implement international agreements as efficiently as possible. Departments with a domestic focus must therefore be brought into international policy making processes. Indeed, national bureaucracies influence the relationship between governments and Inter-governmental organisations in a range of ways. First, national bureaucracies are responsible for the implementation of international agreements; as such, a lack of coordination at a national level can undermine the ability to ratify multilateral agreements. Clearly, however, under certain circumstances, the disjunction, between international signing of agreements and domestic implementation is a political strategy, not a function of poor coordination.
43. A. Giddens, *Runaway World* (New York: Routledge, 2000), 23.
44. IPFA was founded, 'pursuant to Resolutions adopted by the OAS General Assembly in June 1998 and again in June 1999, which called for the facilitation of dialogue amongst the national congresses or parliaments of the 34 OAS member states in order to promote the hemispheric agenda.' (Canadian section of the Inter-Parliamentary Forum of the Americas (FIPA), http://www.parl.gc.ca/information/InterParl/Associations/Forum_Interparle mentair/Prin-e.htm).
45. The IPU serves a range of different roles, including: 1) fostering contact, co-ordination, and the exchange of experience among parliaments and parliamentarians of all countries; 2) considering questions of international interest and concern and expressing its views on such issues in order to bring about action by parliaments and parliamentarians; 3) contributing to the defence and promotion of human rights, an essential factor of parliamentary

democracy and development; 4) contributing to better knowledge of the
working of representative institutions and to the strengthening and development of their means of action (see: http://www.ipu.org/english/whatipu.htm
or for its statutes, see: http://www.ipu.org/strct-e/statutes.htm).
46. M. A. Cameron, 'Global civil society and the Ottawa process: Lessons from
the movement to ban anti-personnel mines', in Cooper *et al.*, *Enhancing
Global Governance*, p. 83. 'By including NGOs in the negotiation process as
delegates in meetings and as equals with states in certain negotiation fora,
the Ottawa process guaranteed that the reasons provided by diplomats for
the policies of their governments were made in public and exposed to criticism by groups from civil society and other governments.' (Cameron,
Enhancing Global Governance, p. 87).
47. J. Bhagwati, 'Borders Beyond Control', *Foreign Affairs*, Vol. 82, No. 1
(January/February 2003) 98–104. Bhagwati suggests that this last function
could be served through the creation of a World Migration Organisation.
48. This section reviews and expands upon an argument developed in the
Summer 2000 issue of *International Organisation*. J. Goldstein, M. Kahler,
R. O. Keohane, and A. M. Slaughter, 'Introduction: Legalization and World
Politics', in J. Goldstein, M. Kahler, R. O. Keohane, and A. M. Slaughter
(eds), *International Organisation: Legalisation and World Politics*, 54, 3
(Summer 2000) 385–399.
49. K. W. Abbott, R. O. Keohane, A. Moravcsik, A. M. Slaughter and D. Snidal,
'The Concept of Legalisation', in Goldstein *et al.*, *International Organisation*,
401–419.
50. Soft law is often criticised by realist IR scholars as unenforceable and in many
cases a negligible influence on international relations; commonly when contrasted with domestic forms of law where clear enforcement mechanisms
exist. For a discussion of hard and soft law, see: K. W. Abbott and D. Snidal,
'Hard and Soft Law in International Governance', in Goldstein *et al.*,
International Organisation, 421–456. The authors analyse the spectrum of international legalisation from soft informal agreements to intermediate blends of
soft obligation, precision and delegation to hard legal instruments.
51. *Ibid.*, 424–425.
52. A more detailed representation of the level of 'hardness' is shown in Table 1
(p. 406) in K. W. Abbott, R. O. Keohane, A. Moravcsik, A. M. Slaughter, and
D. Snidal, 'The Concept of Legalisation', in Goldstein *et al.*, *International
Organization*, 401–419.
53. For a discussion of global public goods, see: I. Kaul, I. Grunberg and
M. A. Stern, *Global Public Goods: International Cooperation in the 21st Century*
(New York: Oxford University Press, 1999).
54. The conclusion to the volume synthesises a number of points raised,
regarding the relationship between norms and legalisation. See especially
pp. 677–680: Miles Kahler, 'Conclusion: The Causes and Consequences of
Legalisation', in Goldstein *et al.*, *International Organisation*, 661–683.
55. See: P. Allott, 'The future of the human past', in K. Booth, 'Conclusion:
security within global transformation?', *Statecraft and Security: the Cold War
and Beyond* (Cambridge: Cambridge University Press, 1998), pp. 323–337
and P. Allott, *Eunomia – New Order for a New World* (Oxford: Oxford
University Press, 1990).

56. The example of the ICC is more complicated, as in many ways, the court embodies and strengthens pre-existing humanitarian and human rights norms which have emerged over the last 50 years. In this sense, the court had a longer genesis than this statement implies. The emerging corporate social responsibility agenda represents another area in which a similar transformation could conceivably take place.

57. In their ideal form, they are **non-excludable** – that is, no one can be barred from consuming them and non-rival as they can be consumed by many without depletion. They are often a pre-requisite of private goods which are secured through the third category on the vertical axis, contracts. Ultimately, however, global public goods are only one form that these principles take – shared interests, those that contain both ethical and self-interest of states are manifest in other forms as discussed below (See I. Kaul, I. Grunberg and M. A. Stern, *Global Public Goods: International Cooperation in the 21st Century* (New York: Oxford University Press, 1999)).

58. Interpretation will differ depending on the actor assessing the regime. For example, a given instrument may serve the interests of one set of actors, while undermining the interests of another. Similarly, the principle of state sovereignty is seen in very different lights, by some as a last defence of powerless states against the powerful and by others, as the major impediment to a just international order.

59. I. Clark, *The Post-Cold War Order: The Spoils of Peace* (Oxford: Oxford University Press, 2001).

60. The idea behind the Kyoto protocol is that a number of pollution permits will be issued and companies will then be able to buy and sell them. Those who can reduce emissions cheaply will then be able to sell their unused permits to others, creating a profit incentive to reduce pollution.

61. Much, however, is excluded from this matrix, including the level of ambitiousness of the measure depicted and the level of difficulty in implementing a measure within a state. An additional assessment of the level of implementation and who adheres to the principle will be necessary. There is also a question of whether the lack of adherence results from the absence of will to implement or the absence of a capacity to implement agreements states have signed on to internationally. El Salvador, for example, arguably lacks the capacity to implement, whereas in the United States Congress might refuse to ratify that which has been signed internationally. This, in turn, begs the question as to what type of principle is being codified and its ultimate effectiveness. While it is problematic to rank different arrangements, it is clear that these arrangements differ in their focus and in the types of behaviour they are intended to shape. It is, nevertheless, possible to evaluate these diverse conventions in terms of the extent to which they fulfil their objectives and shape behaviour in the manner that was intended. Shaping codification and shaping behaviour are two very different things.

62. This according to many is widely accepted as the most advanced and effective international regime for formally enforcing human rights in existence. See: A. Moravcsik, 'The Origin of Human Rights Regimes: Democratic Delegation in Postwar Europe', *International Organisation*, 54, 2 (Spring

2000) 217–252. His argument is problematic for this table as he suggests that one of the main reasons states accede to such treaties is to 'lock in' domestic principles in the interests of governing parties. Governments turn to international enforcement when an international commitment effectively enforces the policy preferences of a particular government at a particular point in time against future domestic political alternatives. This tactic is employed when the benefits of reducing future political uncertainty outweigh the 'sovereignty costs of membership.'

63. The Non-Proliferation Treaty serves the interests of nuclear states as it freezes the current position, privileging those already in possession of nuclear capacity. However, it is in the interests of all in some sense as nuclear proliferation has consequences for the stability of all countries.

64. J. Goldstein, M. Kahler, R. O. Keohane, and A. M. Slaughter, 'Introduction: Legalization and World Politics', in Goldstein *et al.*, *International Organisation: Legalisation and World Politics*, 390.

65. A. D. Edgar, 'Peace, justice and politics: The International Criminal Court, "new diplomacy" and the UN system', in Cooper *et al.*, *Enhancing Global Governance*, p. 138.

66. The table contains both principles of customary international law, such as sovereignty/non-intervention and human rights instruments such as the Universal Declaration on Human Rights. It also includes treaties which can 'harden' in status over time.

67. M. Berdal and D. Malone, *Greed and Grievance: Economic Agendas in Civil Wars* (Boulder, Co: Lynne Rienner Publishers, 2000); K. Ballentine and J. Sherman (eds), *The Political Economy of Armed Conflict: Beyond Greed and Grievance* (Boulder, Co: Lynne Rienner Publishers, 2003).

68. K. R. Nossal, 'Smarter, sharper, stronger? UN sanctions and conflict diamonds in Angola', in Cooper *et al.*, *Enhancing Global Governance*, p. 249.

69. *Ibid.*

70. On 28 January 2003, the Security Council passed a resolution offering its strong support for the Kimberly Process Certification Scheme (S/Res/1459 (2003)). This issue has also been taken up in the UN General Assembly. In December 2000 and March 2002, the General Assembly adopted resolutions calling for the development of a certification scheme for rough diamonds in order to prevent conflict diamonds from entering legitimate markets. As much of the traffic in diamonds is via unofficial channels, it is far from clear that such a regime will eliminate the trade in diamonds. Representatives of 70 countries have since met again to assess the first months of the Kimberley Process reached in November. While the pact has been hailed by governments of diamond importing and exporting countries, human rights groups have criticised it as lacking mechanisms to deal with violators as well as the fact that it deals only with uncut diamonds. The official website of the Kimberley Process is: http://www.kimberleyprocess.com/default.asp or alternatively see http://mmsd1.mms.nrcan.gc.ca/kimberleyprocess/intro_e.asp.

71. P. Nel, 'Between counter-hegemony and post-hegemony: the Rome Statute and normative innovation in world politics', in Cooper *et al.*, *Enhancing Global Governance*, p. 152.

72. *ibid.*, p. 153.

73. M. A. Cameron, 'Global Civil society and the Ottawa process: Lessons from the movement to ban anti-personnel mines', in Cooper *et al.*, *Enhancing Global Governance*, p. 71.
74. *Ibid.*
75. *Ibid.*, p. 86.
76. M. Gwozdecky and J. Sinclair, 'Landmines and Human Security', in McRae and Hubert (eds), *Human Security and the New Diplomacy*, p 37.
77. A. F. Cooper, 'Like-minded nations, NGOs, and the changing pattern of diplomacy within the UN system: An introductory perspective', in Cooper *et al.*, *Enhancing Global Governance*, p. 9.

References

Allott, P. *Eunomia – New Order for a New World* (Oxford: Oxford University Press, 1990).

Annan, K. *We the Peoples: The Role of the United Nations in the 21st Century* (New York: UN, 2000).

Ballentine, K. and J. Sherman (eds), *The Political Economy of Armed Conflict: Beyond Greed and Grievance* (Boulder, Co: Lynne Rienner Publishers, 2003).

Berdal, M. and D. Malone, *Greed and Grievance: Economic Agendas in Civil Wars* (Boulder, Co: Lynne Rienner Publishers, 2000).

Bhagwati, J. 'Borders Beyond Control', *Foreign Affairs*, Vol. 82, No. 1 (January/February 2003) 98–104.

Booth, K. (ed.), *Statecraft and Security: the Cold War and Beyond* (Cambridge: Cambridge University Press, 1998).

Bravo, P. and I. Sierra, *Contemporary Trends in International Technical Cooperation* (Mexico: Mexican Institute for International Cooperation, 1999).

Butler, D. 'MSF Plans Public Sector Drug Development Initiative for Neglected Diseases', *Nature*, 416 (14 April 2002).

Clark, I. *The Post-Cold War Order: The Spoils of Peace* (Oxford: Oxford University Press, 2001).

Clarke, J. N. 'Revisiting the New Interventionism', *Peace Review*, Vol. 14, No. 1 (March 2002) 93–100.

——, 'Ethics and Humanitarian Intervention', *Global Society: Journal of Interdisciplinary International Relations* (Volume 13, No. 4, October 1999), 489–510.

Cooper, A. F., J. English, and R. Thakur (eds), *Enhancing Global Governance: Towards a New Diplomacy?* (Tokyo: United Nations University Press, 2002).

Cortright, D. and G. A. Lopez, *The Sanctions Decade: Assessing UN Strategies in the 1990s* (Boulder, Colorado: Lynne Rienner Publishers Inc., 2000).

Crawford, N. C. *Argument and Change in World Politics: Ethics, Decolonisation and Humanitarian Intervention* (Cambridge: Cambridge University Press, 2002).

Gaddis, J. L. 'And Now This: Lessons from the Old Era for the New one', in S. Talbott and N. Chanda (eds), *The Age of Terror* (New York: Basic Books, 2001).

Giddens, A. *Runaway World* (New York: Routledge, 2000).

Goldstein, J., M. Kahler, R. O. Keohane, and A. M. Slaughter (eds), *International Organisation: Legalisation and World Politics* (*Special Issue*), 54, 3 (Boston: MIT Press, Summer 2000).

Homer-Dixon, T. 'The Ingenuity Gap: Can Poor Countries Adapt to Resource Scarcity?', *Population and Development Review*, 21, No. 3 (1995), 587–612.

Human Development Report 2002: Deepening democracy in a fragmented world (New York: Oxford University Press, 2002).

Ikenberry, G. J. 'Getting Hegemony Right', *The National Interest*, Number 63 (Spring 2001).

Jusdanis, G. *The Necessary Nation* (Princeton: Princeton University Press, 2001).

Kaul, I., I. Grunberg and M. A. Stern, *Global Public Goods: International Cooperation in the 21st Century* (New York: Oxford University Press, 1999).

McRae, R. and D. Hubert (eds), *Human Security and the New Diplomacy* (Montreal & Kingston: McGill-Queen's University Press, 2001).

Miller, C. A. and P. N. Edwards, *Changing the Atmosphere: Expert Knowledge and Environmental Governance* (Cambridge, Massachussetts: MIT Press, 2001).

Moravcsik, A. 'The Origin of Human Rights Regimes: Democratic Delegation in Postwar Europe', *International Organisation*, 54, 2 (Spring 2000) 217–252.

National Research Council (US), *Our Common Journey: a Transition Toward Sustainability* (Washington, DC: National Academy Press, 1999).

Nelson, K. 'Stimulating Research in the Most Neglected Diseases', *The Lancet* (23 March 2002).

Nye, J. S. and J. D. Donahue (eds), *Governance in a Globalising World* (Washington: Brookings Institution Press, 2000).

Reinicke, W. H. 'The Other World Wide Web: Global Public Policy Networks', *Foreign Policy*, No. 117 (Winter 1999–2000).

Russett, B., B. O'Neil and J. Sutterlin, 'Breaking the Security Council Logjam', *Global Governance*, 2, No. 1 (January–April 1996).

Scholte, J. A. *Globalization: A Critical Introduction* (New York: Palgrave, 2000).

Security Council Resolution 1229 (26 February 1999).

Security Council Resolution 1237 (7 May 1999).

Stone, D. (ed.), Banking on Knowledge: The Genesis of the Global Development Network (London: Routledge, 2000).

—— *Capturing the Political Imagination: Think Tanks and the Policy Process* (London: Frank Cass, 1996).

Tharoor, S. and S. Daws, 'Humanitarian Intervention', *World Policy Journal*, Volume XVIII, No. 2 (Summer 2001).

The DNDi Task Force, 'Towards a New Paradigm: The Drugs for Neglected Diseases Initiative (DNDi)', Concept and preliminary proposal (February 2002). Available at: http://www.neglecteddiseases.org/thedndwg.shtml

The Responsibility to Protect: Report of the International Commission on Intervention and State Sovereignty (Ottawa, Canada: IDRC, December 2001).

United Nations Development Programme, *2002 Annual Report* (New York: Communications Office, Office of the Administrator, 2003).

Van Creveld, M. *The Rise and Decline of the State* (Cambridge: Cambridge University Press, 1999).

Index